HUGH JOHNSON'S

POCKET ENCYCLOPEDIA

OF WINE

1993

A Fireside Book
Published by Simon & Schuster Inc.
New York London Toronto
Sydney Tokyo Singapore

Key to Symbols

r	red
p	rosé
w	white
br	brown
(r)	denotes less important wine
sw	sweet
s/sw	semi-sweet
dr	dry
sp	sparkling
*	plain, everyday quality
**	above average
***	well known, highly reputed
****	grand, prestigious, expensive
▓	usually particularly good value in its class
90 91 etc	recommended years which may be currently available
87' etc	vintage regarded as particularly successful for the property in question
85 etc	Years in **bold** should be ready for drinking (the others should be kept). Where both reds and whites are indicated the red is intended unless otherwise stated.
	NB German vintages are codified by a different system. See note on page 104.
(89)	provisional rating
DYA	drink the youngest available
NV	Vintage not normally shown on label. In Champagne, means a blend of several vintages for continuity.
SMALL CAPS	properties, areas or terms cross-referred within the section.

See page 5 for extra explanation.
A quick-reference vintage chart for France and Germany appears on page 208.

© Mitchell Beazley International Ltd 1977-1992
Text © Hugh Johnson 1977-1992
Maps © Mitchell Beazley International Ltd 1977-1992
First edition published 1977
Revised editions published 1978, 1979, 1980, 1981, 1982, 1983, 1984, 1985, 1986, 1987, 1988, 1989, 1990, 1991, 1992

Fireside
Simon & Schuster building
Rockefeller Center
1230 Avenue of the Americas
New York, New York 10020

ISBN 0 671 78515 X
Library of Congress Cataloging Data Number 87-640762

FIRESIDE and colophon are registered trademarks of Simon & Schuster Inc.

The author and publishers will be grateful for any information which will assist them in keeping future editions up to date. Although all reasonable care has been taken in the preparation of this book, neither the publishers nor the author can accept any liability for any consequences arising from the use thereof, or from the information contained herein.

Executive Editor Anne Ryland
Editors Susan Keevil, Kirsty Seymour-Ure
Art Director Tim Foster
Production Sarah Schuman
Film by Tradespools Ltd, Frome, Somerset
Map origination by Mandarin Offset, Hong Kong
Produced by Mandarin Offset
Printed in Hong Kong

Contents

Introduction

Research for this new edition of my little annual has convinced me more than ever of the way the world's wine industry is heading. It is aspiring towards higher quality as never before in its millennia of existence. The number of worthwhile, interesting (though often tiny) producers that it would be a shame to leave out just keeps on growing.

This rush for the high ground is caused by two things. The first is that worldwide demand for wine as a simple commodity – the old *vin ordinaire*, jug wine, call it what you will – is contracting rapidly in the countries that were always its biggest drinkers: France and Italy. The second is the volume of technical knowledge that puts good, clean, characterful wine within reach of every halfway-intelligent producer.

There is much talk of the anti-alcohol movement, and even more, in 1992, of recession. These two factors put further pressure on wine producers to excel. Nature, on the whole, has been exceptionally friendly over the last few years. The world's cellars have never been so full of good wines in such dazzling variety. Nor have there ever been so many people who realize their value in enhancing their own lives.

And that is to speak nothing of the benefits of good wine to health and morale, the unique complex of sensual, aesthetic and intellectual rewards that only wine, of all products, can offer: it is a perfect expression of modern civilization at its best. There is simply nothing that so perfectly encapsulates physical pleasure, social well-being and aesthetic exploration at the same time.

My aim in this book, as ever, is to squeeze the essence of all this richness, the facts that you need to help you choose, into as narrow a compass as possible.

To new readers I must explain that my information is gathered from many sources through innumerable visits and tastings and a perpetual state of correspondence. The process of revision never stops, whether it involves a change of emphasis or fact, or new vintages, or a new entry. There is a constant pressure for inclusion from new producers. Newness itself, however, is not a qualification for entry. Old producers also do newsworthy things.

The book is designed to take the panic out of buying; the panic that comes when you are faced with a long restaurant wine list or shelf upon mind-numbing shelf of bottles in a store. Your mind goes blank. You fumble for your little book. All you need to establish is what country a wine comes from. Look up the principal words on the label in that country's section. You will find enough potted information to let you judge whether this is the wine you want.

Specifically, you will find information on the type and colour of wine, its status or prestige, whether it is usually good value for money, which vintages are recommendable and which are ready to drink – and often considerably more, about the quantity made, grapes used, ownership and the rest. Thousands of cross-references help you delve further. I find I can browse for hours...

How to Read an Entry

The top line of most entries consists of the following information.

1　Which part of the country in question the wine comes from.

2　Whether it is red, rosé or white (or brown/amber), dry, sweet or sparkling, or several of these (and which is most important).

3　Its general standing as to quality: a necessarily rough and ready guide based on its current reputation as reflected in its prices.

　　* plain, everyday quality

　　** above average

　　*** well known, highly reputed

　　**** grand, prestigious, expensive

So much is more or less objective. Additionally there is a subjective rating: shading around the stars of any wine which in my experience is usually particularly good within its price range. There are good everyday wines as well as good luxury wines. The shading system helps you find them.

4　Vintage information: which of the recent vintages that *may* still be available can be recommended; of these, which are ready to drink this year, and which will probably improve with keeping. Your first choice for current drinking should be one of the vintage years printed in **bold** type. Buy light-type years for further maturing.

The German vintage information works on a different principle: *see* the note on page 104.

Acknowledgements

This store of detailed recommendations comes partly from my own notes and partly from those of a great number of kind friends. Without the generous help and cooperation of the many winemakers, merchants and critics I have approached, I could not attempt it. I particularly want to thank the following for help with research or in the areas of their special knowledge.

Burton Anderson	Christian Moueix
Jean-Claude Berrouet	Douglas Murray
Vicky Bishop	Nobuko Nishioka
Bernhard Breuer	Jordanis Petridis
Michael Broadbent MW	Stuart S Piggott
Len Evans	John Platter
Dereck Foster	Carlos Read
Rosemary George MW	Jan and Maite Read
Howard Goldberg	Belle Rhodes
Garry Grosvenor	Dr Bernard Rhodes
Marlies Grosvenor	James Ross
James Halliday	Anne Ryland
Russell Hone	Serena Scott
Ian Jamieson	Peter A Sichel
Matt Kramer	Stephen Skelton
Gabriel Lachmann	Stephen Spurrier
Tony Laithwaite	Sue Style
David Lake MW	Charles Sydney
Miles Lambert-Gócs	Bob Thompson
Christopher Lindlar	Peter Vinding-Diers
Giles MacDonogh	Manfred Völpel
Maggie McNie	Rebecca Wassermann-Hone
Andreas März	Dr Kurt Weibel
Vladimir Moskvan	David Wolfe

Grape Varieties

As more and more wine is being sold under its grape-variety name, especially in regions and countries with no 'classic' traditions, a knowledge of the flavours and qualities of the most-planted (or rather most-sold) varieties becomes a vital part of the wine buyer's armoury. Centuries of selection have resulted in each of Europe's traditional wine areas having its favourite variety, or group of varieties. Red burgundy is made of one grape, the Pinot Noir; red Bordeaux of three or four (the proportions at the discretion of the grower). The laws say which grapes must be used, so the labels do not mention them.

But in newer regions the choice of grapes is the growers' most crucial decision. Where they are proud of it, and intend the wine to have the flavour of a particular grape, its variety is the first thing they put on the label. Hence the originally Californian term 'varietal wine' – meaning, in principle, one grape variety.

At least seven varieties – Cabernet, Pinot Noir, Riesling, Sauvignon Blanc, Chardonnay, Gewürztraminer and Muscat – have memorable tastes and smells distinct enough to form international categories of wine. To these you might add Merlot, Syrah, Sémillon, Chenin Blanc, Pinots Blanc and Gris, Sylvaner, Nebbiolo, Sangiovese, Tempranillo...

Further notes on grapes will be found in the sections on Germany, Italy, Central and Southeast Europe, California, etc. The following are the best and/or commonest wine grapes (with abbreviations used in the text in square brackets).

Grapes for white wine

Albariño The Spanish name for N Portugal's Alvarinho, newly emerging as excellently fresh and fragrant wine in Galicia.

Aligoté Burgundy's second-rank white grape. Crisp (often sharp) wine, needs drinking in 1–3 years. Perfect for mixing with cassis (black-currant liqueur) to make a 'Kir'. Also used in E Europe.

Blanc Fumé Another name for SAUV BL, referring to the reputedly 'smoky' smell of the wine, particularly on the upper Loire (Sancerre and Pouilly). In California the name is often reversed to 'Fumé Blanc'.

Bual Makes top quality sweet madeira wines.

Chardonnay [Chard] The white burgundy grape, one of the grapes of Champagne, and the best white grape of the New World, partly because it is one of the easiest and most forgiving to grow and vinify. All regions are now trying it, mostly aged (or fermented) in oak to reproduce the flavours of burgundy. Australia, California and South Africa make classics. Those of Italy, Spain, New Zealand, New York State, Bulgaria, and the Midi are all worth trying.

Chasselas A prolific early-ripening grape with little aroma, also grown for eating. Best known as Fendant in Switzerland (where it is supreme), Gutedel in Germany.

Chenin Blanc [Chenin Bl] The great white grape of the middle Loire (Vouvray, Layon etc). Wine can be dry or sweet (or very sweet), but always retains plenty of acidity – hence its popularity in California, where it can make fine wine, but is rarely so used. *See also* Steen.

Clairette A dull, neutral grape formerly widely used in the S of France.

Colombard Slightly fruity, nicely sharp grape, now hugely popular in California, gaining ground in SW France, South Africa etc.

Fendant *See* Chasselas.

Folle Blanche High acid/little flavour make this ideal for brandy. Called Gros Plant in Brittany, Picpoul in Armagnac. Respectable in California.

Fumé Blanc [Fumé Bl] *See* Blanc Fumé.

Furmint A grape of great character: the trademark of Hungary both as the principal grape in Tokay and as vivid, vigorous table wine with an appley flavour. Called Sipon in Slovenia. Some grown in Austria.

Grechetto or Greco Ancient grape of central and S Italy with vitality and style.

Gewürztraminer (alias Traminer) [Gewürz] One of the most pungent grapes, distinctively spicy to smell and taste, with aromas often identified as being like rose petals and grapefruit. Wines are often rich and soft, even when fully dry. Best in Alsace; also good in Germany, E Europe, Australia, California, New Zealand.

Grauburgunder *See* Pinot Gris.

Grüner Veltliner Austria's favourite. Around Vienna and in the Wachau and Weinviertel (also in Moravia) it can be delicious: light but dry and lively. Drink young.

Italian Riesling Grown in N Italy and all over central E Europe. Much inferior to Rhine RIES, with lower acidity. Alias Welschriesling, Olaszrizling (but no longer legally labelled simply 'Riesling').

Kerner The most successful of a score of recent German varieties, largely made by crossing RIES X SYLVANER (but in this case RIES X [red] Trollinger). Early-ripening, flowery (but often too blatant) wine with good acidity. Popular in Rheinpfalz, Rheinhessen etc.

Macabeo The workhorse white grape of N Spain, widespread in Rioja (alias Viura) and in Catalan *cava* country.

Malvasia Known as Malmsey in Madeira, Malvasia in Italy, Malvoisie in France. Alias Vermentino (esp in Corsica). Also grown in Greece, Spain, W Australia, E Europe. Makes rich, brown wines or soft whites, ageing magnificently with superb potential not often realized.

Marsanne Principal white grape (with Roussanne) of the N Rhône (eg St-Joseph, St-Péray, Crozes-Hermitage). Also used to effect in Victoria and (as Ermitage Blanc) in the Valais. Soft, full wines.

Müller-Thurgau [Müller-T] Dominant variety in Germany's Rheinhessen and Rheinpfalz; a cross between RIES and SYLVANER. Ripens early to make soft, flowery wines for drinking young. Makes good sweet wines but usually dull, often coarse, dry ones.

Muscadet (alias Melon de Bourgogne) Makes light, very dry wines with a seaside tang round Nantes in Brittany. They should not be sharp, but faintly salty and very refreshing. (Californian 'Pinot Bl' is this grape.)

Muscat (Many varieties; the best is Muscat Blanc à Petits Grains.) Universally grown, easily recognized, pungent grapes, mostly made into perfumed sweet wines, often fortified (as in France's *vins doux naturels*). Muscat d'Alsace is unusual in being dry.

Palomino (alias Listan) Makes all the best sherry but poor table wine.

Pedro Ximénez (PX) Makes very strong wine in Montilla and Málaga. Used in blending sweet sherries. Also grown in Argentina, the Canaries, Australia, California, South Africa.

Pinot Blanc [Pinot Bl] A cousin of PINOT N; not related to CHARD, but with a similar but milder character; light, fresh, neutral: good for eg Italian *spumante*. Grown in Champagne, Alsace (increasingly), N Italy, S Germany, E Europe. Called Weissburgunder in Germany. *See also* Muscadet.

Pinot Gris [Pinot G] At best makes rather heavy, even 'thick', full-bodied whites with a certain spicy style. Known as Tokay in Alsace, Ruländer, or Grauburgunder, in Germany, Tocai in NE Italy and Slovenia (but much thinner wine). Traditional but almost extinct in Burgundy and Champagne.

Pinot Noir [Pinot N] Superlative black grape (*see* Grapes for red wine) used in Champagne and occasionally elsewhere (eg California) for making white wine, or a very pale pink '*vin gris*'.

Riesling [Ries] Germany's finest grape, and at the moment the world's most underrated. Wine of brilliant sweet/acid balance, flowery in youth but maturing to subtle oily scents and flavours. Successful in Alsace, Austria, parts of E Europe, Australia (where it is widely grown), California, South Africa. Often called White, Johannisberg or Rhine Riesling. Subject to 'noble rot'. Due for a major revival, since (unlike CHARD) it does not need high alcohol for character.

Ruländer German name for PINOT GRIS.

Sauvignon Blanc [Sauv Bl] Makes very distinctive, aromatic, grassy and sometimes smoky-scented wine; can be austere (on the upper Loire) or buxom (in Sauternes, where it is combined with SÉM, and parts of California). Recently a brilliant success in New Zealand. Also called Fumé Blanc or vice versa.

Scheurebe Spicy-flavoured German RIES X SYLVANER, very successful in Rheinpfalz, esp for *Auslesen*. Can be weedy in dry wines.

Sémillon [Sém] The grape contributing the lusciousness to great Sauternes; subject to 'noble rot' in the right conditions but increasingly important for Graves and dry white Bordeaux too. Makes soft dry wine of great potential. Traditionally called 'Riesling' in parts of Australia. Old Hunter Valley Sém can be great wine.

Sercial Makes the driest madeira; (where legend says it is really RIES!).

Seyval Blanc [Seyval Bl] French-made hybrid between French and American vines. Very hardy and attractively fruity. Popular and reasonably successful in the eastern States and England.

Steen South Africa's most popular white grape: good, lively, fruity wine. Said to be the CHENIN BL of the Loire.

Sylvaner (Silvaner) Germany's former workhorse grape: wine rarely better than pleasant except in Franconia where it is savoury and ages admirably, and in Rheinhessen, where it is enjoying a renaissance. Good in the Italian Tyrol and useful in Alsace. Very good (and powerful) as Johannisberg in the Valais, Switzerland.

Tokay See Pinot Gris. Also a table grape in California and a supposedly Hungarian grape in Australia. The wine 'tokay' is made of FURMINT.

Traminer See Gewürztraminer.

Trebbiano Important but mediocre grape of central Italy, used in Orvieto, Chianti, Soave, etc. Also grown in S France as Ugni Bl, and Cognac as St-Emilion. Thin, neutral wine; really needs blending.

Ugni Blanc [Ugni Bl] See Trebbiano.

Verdejo The grape of Rueda in Castile, potentially fine and long-lived.

Verdelho Madeira grape making excellent medium-sweet wine.

Verdicchio Gives its name to good, dry wine in central-eastern Italy.

Vermentino See Malvasia.

Vernaccia Grape grown in central and S Italy and Sardinia for strong, smooth, lively wine, sometimes inclining towards sherry.

Viognier Rare grape of the Rhône valley, grown at Condrieu to make very fine, fragrant wine. Much in vogue in the Midi, California, etc, but still only a trickle.

Viura See Macabeo.

Weissburgunder See Pinot Blanc.

Grapes for red wine

Aleatico Dark Muscat variety, alias Aglianico, used the length of W Italy for fragrant sweet wines.

Barbera Most popular of several productive grapes of N Italy, esp Piedmont, giving dark, fruity, often sharp wine. Useful in blends in California.

Brunello S Tuscan form of SANGIOVESE, splendid at Montalcino.

Cabernet Franc (alias Bouchet) [Cab F] The lesser of two sorts of Cab grown in Bordeaux but dominant (as 'Bouchet') in St-Emilion. The Cab of the Loire making Chinon, etc, and rosé.

Cabernet Sauvignon [Cab S] Grape of great character: spicy, herby and tannic, with a characteristic 'blackcurrant' aroma. The first grape of the Médoc, also makes most of the best Californian, Australian, S American and E European reds. Its red wine always needs ageing and usually benefits from blending with eg MERLOT, CAB F or SYRAH. Makes very aromatic rosé.

Carignan By far the commonest grape of France, covering hundreds of thousands of acres. Prolific with dull but harmless wine. Best from old vines in Corbières. Also common in N Africa, Spain, California.

Cinsaut Common bulk-producing grape of S France; in S Africa crossed with PINOT N to make Pinotage.

Dolcetto Source of soft, seductive, dry, daily red in Piedmont.

Gamay The Beaujolais grape: light, very fragrant wines, at their best young. Makes even lighter wine on the Loire and in Switzerland and Savoie. Known as 'Napa Gamay' in California.

Gamay Beaujolais Not GAMAY but a (poor) variety of PINOT N grown in California.

Grenache (alias Garnacha, Alicante, Cannonau) Useful grape for strong and fruity but pale wine: good rosé and *vin doux naturel*. Grown in S France, Spain, California. Usually blended.

Grignolino Makes one of the good, cheap table wines of Piedmont.

Lambrusco Productive grape of the lower Po valley, giving quintessentially Italian, cheerful sweet and fizzy red.

Malbec (alias Cot) Minor in Bordeaux, major in Cahors and Argentina. Dark, dense and tannic wine capable of real quality.

Merlot Adaptable grape making the great fragrant and rich wines of Pomerol and (with CAB F) St-Emilion, an important element in Médoc reds, soft and strong in California and Australia, lighter but often good in N Italy, Italian Switzerland, Slovenia, Argentina, etc.

Montepulciano Confusingly, a major central-eastern Italian grape of good quality, as well as a town.

Mourvèdre (alias Mataro) Excellent, dark, aromatic, tannic grape used for blending in Provence (especially in Bandol) and the Midi.

Nebbiolo (alias Spanna and Chiavennasca) One of Italy's best red grapes, the grape of Barolo, Barbaresco, Gattinara and Valtellina. Intense, nobly fruity and perfumed wine but very tannic, taking years to mature.

Petit Verdot Excellent but awkward Médoc grape now largely superseded by CAB S.

Pinot Noir [Pinot N] The glory of Burgundy's Côte d'Or, with scent, flavour, and texture unmatched anywhere. Less happy elsewhere; makes light wines rarely of much distinction in Germany, Switzerland, Austria, Hungary. The great challenge to California and Australia (and recently S Africa). Shows real promise in Oregon and the Yarra Valley, Australia.

Pinotage Singular S African grape (PINOT N X CINSAUT). Can be very fruity and age interestingly, but often jammy.

Sangiovese The main red grape of Chianti and much of central Italy. BRUNELLO is the Sangiovese Grosso.

Spätburgunder German for PINOT N, but a very pale shadow of burgundy.

Syrah (alias Shiraz) The best Rhône red grape, with tannic, purple wine, which can mature superbly. Very important as Shiraz in Australia, increasingly so in the Midi and California.

Tempranillo The pale, aromatic, fine, Rioja grape, called Ull de Lebre in Catalonia, Cencibel in La Mancha. Early ripening.

Zinfandel [Zin] Fruity, adaptable grape peculiar to California with blackberry-like, and sometimes metallic, flavour. Also makes 'blush' white wine.

Wine & Food

Attitudes to matching wine and food range from the slapdash to the near-neurotic. Oddly, it is a subject that has attracted relatively little ink until very recently: it is fertile ground for experiment. Few combinations can be dismissed outright as 'wrong', but generations of experience have produced certain working conventions that certainly do no harm. The following is a list of ideas intended to help you make quick decisions. Any of the groups of recommended wines could be extended almost indefinitely. In general I have stuck to the wines that are widely available, at the same time trying to ring the changes so that the same wines don't come up time and time again – as they tend to do in real life. Remember that in a restaurant that is truly regional (Provençal, Basque, Tuscan, Catalan, Austrian...) there is a ready-made answer – the wine of the country.

References to these wines will be found in national A-Z sections. The stars refer to the rating system used throughout the book.

Before the meal – aperitifs

The conventional aperitif wines are either sparkling (epitomized by champagne) or fortified (epitomized by sherry). They are still the best, but avoid peanuts, which destroy wine flavours. Olives are also too piquant for most wines; they need sherry or a martini. Eat almonds or walnuts, crisps or cheese straws instead. A glass of white or rosé table wine before eating is presently in vogue. It calls for something light and stimulating, fairly dry but not acid, with a degree of character, such as:

In France:
Alsace Pinot Blanc, Sylvaner or Riesling; Chablis or a good Aligoté; Muscadet; Sauvignon de Touraine; Graves Blanc; Mâcon Blanc; Crépy; Bugey; Haut-Poitou; Côtes de Gascogne; St Pourçain-sur-Sioule. In Bordeaux the fashion is for a glass of sweet Sauternes.

In Germany:
Any *Kabinett* wine or QbA. Choose a *halbtrocken* – nearly dry. Or open a mature *Spätlese* (5–12 yrs old). A great old (eg 76) *Auslese* can make the finest aperitif of all.

In Italy:
Pinot Bianco; Soave; Orvieto Secco; Frascati; Gavi; Montecarlo; Greco di Tufo; Vernaccia; Tocai; Lugana; Albana di Romagna; Marsala.

In Spain:
Fino or *manzanilla* sherry, or Montilla (with *tapas*).

In Portugal:
Any *vinho verde* or, better, Alvarinho; Bucelas.

In Eastern Europe:
Grüner Veltliner; Welschriesling; Riesling; Leanyka; Müller-Thurgau. Tokay Szamarodni is Hungary's especially tasty contribution.

In the USA:
(California:) 'Chablis'; Riesling; Chenin Blanc; Colombard; Fumé Blanc; Gewürztraminer; or a good 'house blend'. (New York, Oregon:) Riesling. (Washington:) Sémillon. *Not* Chardonnay.

In Australia:
Barossa, Clare or Coonawarra Riesling; Houghton's 'White Burgundy'; or a Marsanne from Victoria.

In South Africa:
Steen is ideal (the KWV labels it Chenin Blanc).
In England:
Almost any English wine makes a good talking point as an aperitif, especially in the garden in summer.

First courses

Aïoli A thirst-quencher is needed for its garlic heat. *→*** Rhône, or Provence rosé, or Frascati, or Verdicchio, and *marc,* for courage.

Antipasto in Italy ** dry or medium white, Italian (Soave, Pinot Grigio, Greco di Tufo), or light red (Dolcetto, young ** Chianti).

Artichoke vinaigrette * young red: Bordeaux, Côtes du Rhône; or acidic white: Sauvignon de Touraine.
hollandaise * or ** full-bodied dry or medium white: Mâcon Blanc, Rheinpfalz, or a California 'house blend'.

Asparagus A difficult flavour for wine, so the wine needs plenty of its own. **→*** white burgundy or Chardonnay, or Jurançon Sec.

Avocado with prawns, crab, etc **→*** dry to medium or slightly sharp white: Rheingau or Rheinpfalz *Kabinett,* Sancerre, Pinot Bianco; California or Australian Chardonnay or Sauvignon, Cape Steen, or dry rosé.
vinaigrette * light red, or *manzanilla* sherry.

Bisques ** dry white with plenty of body: Pinot Gris, Chardonnay. *Fino* or dry *amontillado* sherry, or Montilla.

Boudin (blood sausage) Aligoté.

Bouillabaisse *→*** very dry white: Muscadet, Alsace Sylvaner, Entre-Deux-Mers, Pouilly-Fumé, Cassis, Grechetto, Verdicchio, California Blanc Fumé.

Carpaccio beef Seems to work well with the flavour of most wines, including *** reds. Top Tuscan *vino da tavola* is appropriate.
salmon **→*** Chardonnay, or champagne.

Caviar *** champagne or iced vodka (or indeed both).

Ceviche ** California or Australian Chardonnay, NZ Sauvignon Blanc.

Cheese fondue ** dry white: Fendant or Johannisberg du Valais, Grüner Veltliner, Alsace Riesling, NZ Sauvignon Blanc.

Clams and chowders ** big-scale white, not necessarily bone dry: Pinot Gris, dry Sauternes, Napa Chardonnay, Rhine *Spätlese*. Or *fino* sherry.

Crostini Rustic Tuscan red, Montepulciano d'Abruzzo, Corsican rosé.

Consommé **→*** medium-dry sherry, dry madeira, Marsala Vergine.

Crudités *→*** light red or rosé: Côtes du Rhône, Beaujolais, Minervois, Chianti, Zinfandel; or *fino* sherry.

Eggs (*See also* Soufflés) These present difficulties: they clash with most wines and spoil good ones. So *→*** of whatever is going. As a last resort I can bring myself to drink champagne with scrambled eggs.

Escargots White Mâcon-Villages, **→*** California Chardonnay or Beaujolais-Villages; or ** red Rhône.

Fish terrine Rheingau Riesling *Spätlese trocken,* Chablis, Washington or Australian Sémillon, Sonoma Chardonnay; or *fino* sherry.

Foie gras ***→**** white. In Bordeaux they drink Sauternes. Others prefer vintage champagne or a late-harvest Gewürztraminer. Old dry *amontillado* can be sublime.

Gazpacho A glass of *fino* before and after.

Goat's cheese, grilled (warm salad) Chilled Chinon or Saumur, Champigny, Provence rosé.

Grapefruit If you must start a meal with grapefruit try port, madeira or sweet sherry with (or in) it.

Gravlax Akvavit, or Grand Cru Chablis, or *** Californian or Australian Chardonnay. Or vintage champagne.

Guacamole ** California Chardonnay or Mexican beer.

Haddock, smoked, mousse of A wonderful dish for showing off any stylish full-bodied white, incl Grand Cru Chablis.

Hangtown Fry (oysters, bacon and eggs) NV champagne.

Ham, raw or cured (*See also* Prosciutto) Lively young Spanish or Italian red.

Herrings, raw or pickled Dutch gin (young, not aged) or Scandinavian akvavit, and cold beer.

Hors d'oeuvres (*See also* Antipasto) *→** clean, fruity, sharp white: Sancerre or any Sauvignon, Alsace Silvaner, Muscadet, Cape Steen; or young, light, red Bordeaux, Rhône or equivalent. Or *fino* sherry.

Mackerel, smoked An oily wine-destroyer. *Manzanilla* sherry, or schnapps.

Mayonnaise Adds richness that calls for a contrasting bite in the wine. Côte Chalonnaise whites (eg Rully) are good. Try NZ Sauvignon Blanc, Yugoslavian Zilavka, Verdicchio or a *Spätlese trocken*.

Melon Needs a strong sweet wine (if any): ** port, Bual madeira, Muscat, *oloroso* sherry or *vin doux naturel*.

Minestrone * red: Grignolino, Chianti, Zinfandel, Shiraz, etc. Or *fino*.

Mushrooms à la Grecque Greek Verdea or Mantinia, or any hefty dry white, or fresh young red.

Omelettes *See* Eggs.

Pasta *→** red or white according to the sauce or trimmings:
>   **cream sauce** Orvieto, Frascati, Italian Chardonnay.
>   **meat sauce** Chianti, Montepulciano d'Abruzzo, Montefalco d'Arquata.
>   **pesto (basil) sauce** Barbera, NZ Sauvignon Blanc.
>   **seafood sauce (vongole, etc)** Verdicchio, Soave, Pomino, Sauvignon Blanc.
>   **tomato sauce** Barbera, Sicilian or Yugoslav red, Zinfandel.

Pâté According to constituents and quality: chicken livers call for pungent white, a smooth red like a light Pomerol, or even *amontillado* sherry. With simple pâté choose a ** dry white: Mâcon-Villages, Graves, Fumé Blanc. For duck: Chianti Classico.

Pizza Any ** dry Italian red or ** Rioja, Australian Shiraz or California Zinfandel. Or Corbières or Roussillon.

Prawns or shrimps **→*** dry white: burgundy, Bordeaux, Chardonnay, Riesling. ('Cocktail sauce' kills any wine, and I suspect, in time, any human being.)

Prosciutto with melon **→*** full-bodied dry or medium white: Orvieto, Frascati, Pomino, Fendant, Grüner Veltliner, Alsace or California Gewürztraminer, Australian Riesling, Jurançon Sec.

Quiches *→** dry white with body (Alsace, Graves, Sauvignon, Rheingau dry) or young red (Beaujolais-Villages), according to the ingredients. Never a fine-wine dish. (A friend suggests sake.)

Salade niçoise ** very dry, not too light or flowery white or rosé: Rhône or Corsican; Catalan white; Dão; California Sauvignon Blanc.

Salads As a first course, especially with blue cheese dressing, any dry and appetizing white wine. After a main course: no wine.
NB Vinegar in salad dressings destroys the flavour of wine. If you want salad at a meal with fine wine, dress the salad with wine or a little lemon juice instead of vinegar.

Seafood salad Chablis or unoaked Chardonnay.

Salami *→** very tasty red or rosé: Barbera, young Zinfandel, Tavel or Ajaccio rosé, young Bordeaux, Toro, or Chilean Cabernet.

Salmon, smoked A dry but pungent white: *fino* sherry, Alsace Pinot Gris, Chablis Grand Cru, Rheinpfalz Riesling *Spätlese*, vintage champagne.

Soufflés As show dishes these deserve **→*** wines.
>   **fish** Dry white: burgundy, Bordeaux, Alsace, Chardonnay, etc.
>   **cheese** Red burgundy or Bordeaux, Cabernet Sauvignon, etc.
>   **spinach** Mâcon-Villages, St-Véran.

Taramasalata Calls for a rustic southern white of strong personality; not necessarily the Greek Retsina. *Fino* sherry works well. Try Australian Chardonnay.

Terrine As for pâté, or the equivalent red: Mercurey, Beaujolais-Villages, fairly young ** St-Emilion, California Cabernet or Zinfandel, Bulgarian or Chilean Cabernet.

Tomato sauce (on anything) The acidity of tomato sauce is no friend to fine wines. ** red will do. Try Chianti or a German wine with some sweetness.

Trout, smoked Sancerre, Pouilly-Fumé, California or NZ Fumé Blanc. Or Rully.

Vegetable terrine Not a great help to fine wine, but California and Australian Chardonnays make a fashionable marriage.

Fish

Abalone **→*** dry or medium white: Sauvignon Blanc, Chardonnay, Pinot Grigio, Muscadet sur Lie.

Bass, striped or sea As for sole.

Beurre blanc, fish with Muscadet sur Lie.

Carpaccio of salmon or tuna Puligny-Montrachet or top-notch Australian Chardonnay. (*See also* First courses.)

Cod A good neutral background for fine dry or medium whites: **→*** Chablis, Meursault, *cru classé* Graves, German *Kabinett,* or dry *Spätlesen* and their equivalents.

Coquilles St Jacques *See* Scallops.

Crab, cioppino Sauvignon Blanc; but West Coast friends say Zinfandel.
   cold, with salad Rheinpfalz Riesling *Kabinett* or *Spätlese,* dry California or Australian Riesling, or Viognier from Condrieu.
   softshell *** Chardonnay or top quality German Riesling.

Eel, jellied NV champagne or a nice cup of tea.
   smoked Either strong or sharp wine: *fino* sherry, Bourgogne Aligoté. Or schnapps.

Fish and chips, fritto misto (or tempura) * Chablis, * white Bordeaux, Sauvignon Blanc, Alsace Riesling, Torres, Waltraud, Montilla, Koshu, tea...

Fish pie (with creamy sauce) Napa Chardonnay, Pinot Gris d'Alsace.

Haddock **→*** dry white with a certain richness: Meursault, California or Australian Chardonnay.

Halibut As for Turbot.

Hake Sauvignon Blanc or any freshly fruity white.

Herrings Need a white with some acidity to cut their richness. Bourgogne Aligoté, Gros Plant from Brittany, dry Sauvignon Blanc.

Kippers A good cup of tea, preferably Ceylon (milk, no sugar). Scotch?

Lamproie à la Bordelaise **→*** 5-yr-old red Bordeaux, St-Emilion, or Fronsac.

Lobster, richly sauced Vintage champagne, fine white burgundy, *cru classé* Graves, California or Australian Chardonnay, Rheinpfalz *Spätlese,* Hermitage Blanc.
   salad **→**** white: NV champagne, Alsace Riesling, Chablis Premier Cru, Condrieu, Mosel *Spätlese.*

Mackerel ** hard or sharp white: Sauvignon Blanc from Bergerac or Touraine, Gros Plant, *vinho verde*, white Rioja. Or Guinness.

Mullet, red A chameleon, adaptable to good whites or reds.

Mussels *→*** Gros Plant, Muscadet, California 'Chablis'.
   stuffed, with garlic *See* Escargots.

Oysters **→*** white: NV champagne, Chablis or (better) Chablis Premier Cru, Muscadet, white Graves, Sancerre. Or Guinness.

Oyster stew California or Australian Chardonnay.

Perch, sandre An exquisite fish for finest wines: Puligny-Montrachet

Premiers Crus or noble Mosels.

Salmon, fresh ★★★ fine white burgundy (Puligny- or Chassagne-Montrachet, Meursault, Corton-Charlemagne, Chablis Grand Cru), Condrieu, California, Idaho or Australian Chardonnay, Rheingau *Kabinett/Spätlese*, California Riesling or equivalent. Young Pinot Noir can be perfect.

Sardines, fresh grilled ★→★★ very dry white: *vinho verde*, Dão, Muscadet.

Sashimi If you are prepared to forego the wasabi, sparkling wines, incl Californian; or California or Australian Chardonnay, Chablis Grand Cru, Rheingau Riesling *Halbtrocken*. Otherwise, sake or beer.

Scallops An inherently slightly sweet dish, best with medium-dry whites.

   in cream sauces ★★★ German *Spätlese* or a Montrachet.

   grilled or fried Hermitage Blanc, Gewürztraminer, California Chenin Blanc, Riesling or champagne.

Shad ★★→★★★ white Graves or Meursault or Hunter Sémillon.

Shellfish Dry white with plain boiled shellfish, richer wines with richer sauces.

Shrimps, potted *Fino* sherry, Chablis, Gavi or New York Chardonnay.

Skate with black butter ★★ white with some pungency (Alsace Pinot Gris) or a clean straightforward one like Muscadet or Entre-Deux-Mers.

Snapper Serious Sauvignon Blanc country.

Sole, plaice, etc, plain, grilled or fried An ideal accompaniment for fine wines: ★★★→★★★★ white burgundy, or its equivalent.

   with sauce Depending on the ingredients: sharp, dry wine for tomato sauce, fairly rich for sole véronique, etc.

Sushi Hot wasabi is usually hidden in every piece. German QbA *trocken* wines or simple Chablis are good enough. Or of course sake.

Swordfish ★★ dry white of whatever country you are in.

Trout Delicate white wine, eg ★★★ Mosel (esp from the Saar).

   smoked A full-flavoured ★★→★★★ white: Gewürztraminer, Alsace Pinot Gris, Rhine *Spätlese*, Pinot Blanc from Italy or Australian Hunter white.

Tuna, grilled ★★ white or red (or rosé) of fairly fruity character. NZ Sauvignon Blanc or a top Côtes du Rhône would be fine.

Turbot Fine rich dry white: ★★★ Meursault or its California, Australian or NZ equivalent. Condrieu. Mature Rheingau, Mosel or Nahe *Spätlese* or *Auslese* (not *trocken*).

Meat, poultry, etc

Barbecues ★★ red with a slight rasp, therefore young: Shiraz, Chianti, Zinfandel, Turkish Buzbag. Bandol for a treat.

Beef, boiled ★★ red: Bordeaux (Bourg or Fronsac), Roussillon, Australian Shiraz. Or good Mâcon-Villages white.

   roast An ideal partner for fine red wine. ★★→★★★★ red of any kind.

Beef stew ★★→★★★ sturdy red: Pomerol or St-Emilion, Hermitage, Cornas, Barbera, Shiraz, California/Oregon Pinot Noir, Torres Sangre de Toro.

Beef Stroganoff ★★→★★★ suitably dramatic red: Barolo, Brunello, Valpolicella, Amarone, Hermitage, late-harvest Zinfandel – or even Georgian Saperavi.

Cabbage, stuffed Hungarian Cabernet Franc/Kadarka, Bulgarian Cabernet.

Cajun food Côtes de Brouilly. With gumbo: *amontillado* sherry or Mexican beer.

Cassoulet ★★ red from SW France (Madiran, Cahors, Corbières), or Barbera or Zinfandel or Shiraz.

Chicken casserole Lirac, St-Joseph, Crozes-Hermitage.

   Kiev Alsace Riesling, Bergerac Rouge.

Chicken/turkey/guinea fowl, roast Virtually any wine, incl very best bottles of dry/medium white and finest old reds (esp burgundy). The meat of fowl can be adapted with sauces to match almost any fine wine (eg coq au vin: red burgundy). Avoid tomato sauces for any good bottles.

Chilli con carne ★→★★ young red: Chianti, Barbera, Beaujolais, Navarra, Zinfandel.

Chinese food: Canton or Peking style **→*** dry to medium-dry white –
Sauvignon Blanc or (better) Riesling – can be good throughout a
Chinese banquet. Dry sparkling (esp *cava*) is good for cutting the oil.
Eschew sweet/sour dishes but try an 86/88 St-Emilion ** or St-
Estèphe *cru bourgeois*, or Châteauneuf-du-Pape with duck. I often
serve both white and red concurrently with Chinese meals.
    Szechuan style Very cold beer.

Cold meats Generally taste better with full-flavoured white wine than red.
Mosel *Spätlesen*, Hochheimer are very good.

Confit d'oie **→*** Young, tannic, red Bordeaux Cru Bourgeois helps to
cut the richness. Alsace Tokay or Gewürztraminer matches it.

Coq au vin **→**** red burgundy. In an ideal world one bottle of
Chambertin in the dish, two on the table.

Corned beef hash ** Zinfandel, Chianti, Côtes du Rhône red.

Curry *→** medium-sweet white, very cold: Orvieto *abboccato*, California
Chenin Blanc, Yugoslav Traminer, Indian 'champagne'. Or emphasize
the heat with a tannic Barolo or Barbaresco, or deep-flavoured reds
such as St-Emilion, Cornas, Shiraz, Shiraz-Cabernet blends,
Valpolicella Amarone.

Duck or goose *** rather rich white (Rheinpfalz *Spätlese* or Alsace
réserve exceptionelle); or *** Bordeaux or burgundy. With oranges or
peaches, the Sauternais propose Sauternes, others a Loire red.
    Peking *See* Chinese food.
    wild duck *** big-scale red: Hermitage, Châteauneuf-du-Pape,
Cornas, Bandol, California or S African Cabernet, Australian Shiraz,
Torres Gran Coronas.

Frankfurters *→*** German, Australian white; Beaujolais. Or Budweiser.

Game birds Young birds plain-roasted and not too well hung deserve the
best red wine you can afford. With older birds in casseroles **→***
red (Gevrey-Chambertin, Pommard, Grand Cru St-Emilion, Napa
Cabernet). With well-hung game, Hermitage, Châteauneuf-du-Pape,
Vega Sicilia.

Game pie (Hot) *** red wine. **(Cold)** Equivalent white.

Goulash ** strong young red: Zinfandel, Bulgarian Cabernet, Hungarian
Kadarka, Australian Shiraz.

Grouse *See* Game birds – but push the boat right out.

Ham **→*** fairly fresh red burgundy (Volnay, Savigny, Beaune, or red
Loire); slightly sweet German white (Rhine *Spätlese*); Czech Müller-
Thurgau; Tuscan red; lightish Cabernet (eg Chilean).

Hamburger *→** young red: Beaujolais, Corbières or Minervois, Chianti,
Zinfandel, Kadarka from Hungary.

Hare Jugged hare calls for **→*** red with plenty of flavour: not-too-old
burgundy or Bordeaux, or Rhône (eg Gigondas), or Bandol, or a fine
Rioja *reserva*. The same for saddle. Australia's Grange Hermitage
would be an experience.

Kebabs ** vigorous red: Greek Demestica, Turkish Buzbag, Bulgarian or
Chilean Cabernet, Zinfandel.

Kidneys **→*** red: Pomerol or St-Emilion, Rhône, Barbaresco, Rioja,
California, Spanish or Australian Cabernet, Portuguese Bairrada.

Lamb, cutlets or chops As for roast lamb, but a little less grand.
    roast One of the traditional and best partners for very good red
Bordeaux – or its Cabernet equivalents from the New World. In
Castile, the partner of the finest old Rioja *reservas*.

Liver **→*** young red: Beaujolais-Villages, St-Joseph, Médoc, Italian
Merlot, Zinfandel, Oregon Pinot Noir.

Meatballs **→*** red: Mercurey, Crozes-Hermitage, Madiran, Rubesco,
Dão, Bairrada, Zinfandel or Cabernet.

Mixed grill A fairly light, easily swallowable red: ** Bordeaux from Bourg,
Fronsac or Premières Côtes; Chianti; Bourgogne Passe-Tout-Grains;
Chilean Cabernet; or a Cru Beaujolais such as Juliénas.

Moussaka *→** red or rosé: Naoussa from Greece, Chianti, Corbières, Côtes de Provence, Ajaccio or Patrimonio, California 'burgundy'.

Oxtail or osso bucco **→*** rather rich red: St-Emilion or Pomerol, Nuits-St-Georges, Barolo or Chianti Classico, Rioja *reserva*, California or Coonawarra Cabernet, or a dry Riesling *Spätlese*.

Paella ** Young Spanish red, dry white or rosé: Penedès or Rioja.

Partridge, pheasant *See* Game birds.

Pigeons or squab **→**** red Bordeaux, Chianti Classico, California or Australian Cabernet. Silvaner *Spätlese* from Franconia.

Pork, roast A good, rich, neutral background to a fairly light red or rich white. It deserves *** treatment. Portugal's famous sucking pig is eaten with Bairrada *garrafeira*.

Quail As for pigeon.

Rabbit *→*** young red, Italian for preference. Or Rhône rosé.

Ris de veau *See* Sweetbreads.

Risotto Pinot Grigio from Friuli, Gavi, youngish Sémillon, Dolcetto, or Barbera d'Alba.

Satay Australian Cabernet-Shiraz or Alsace Pinot Gris or Gewürztraminer.

Sauerkraut Lager.

Sausages The British banger requires a 2½-yr-old NE Italian Merlot (or a red wine, anyway). *See also* Frankfurters, Salami.

Shepherd's Pie *→*** rough and ready red seems most appropriate, but no harm would come to a good one.

Spare Ribs Gigondas or St-Joseph, or Australian Shiraz, or Zinfandel.

Steak and kidney pie or pudding Red Rioja *reserva* or mature **→*** Bordeaux.

Steak, au poivre A fairly young *** Rhône red or Cabernet.

    tartare ** light young red: Beaujolais, Bergerac, Valpolicella.

    filet or tournedos *** any red (but not old wines with Béarnaise sauce).

    T-bone **→*** reds of similar bone structure: Barolo, Hermitage, Australian Cabernet or Shiraz.

    fiorentina (bistecca) Chianti Classico Riserva or Brunello.

Stews and casseroles A lusty full-flavoured red: young Côtes du Rhône, Corbières, Barbera, Shiraz, Zinfandel, etc.

Sweetbreads These tend to be a grand dish, suggesting a grand wine: *** Rhine Riesling or Franken Silvaner *Spätlese*, or well-matured Bordeaux or burgundy, depending on the sauce.

Tandoori chicken Sauvignon Blanc, or young ** red Bordeaux.

Thai food Ginger and lemon grass call for Gewürztraminer; coconut curries, Hunter Valley Chardonnay. Alsace Pinot Blanc for refreshment.

Tongue Ideal for favourite bottles of any red or white of abundant character, esp Italian.

Tripe *→*** red (eg Corbières, Mâcon Rouge), or rather sweet white (eg Liebfraumilch). Better: W Australian'white burgundy'.

Veal, roast A good neutral background dish for any fine old red which may have faded with age (eg a Rioja *reserva*) or a *** German white.

Venison *** big-scale red (Rhône, Bordeaux of a grand vintage) or rather rich white (Rheinpfalz *Spätlese* or Tokay d'Alsace).

Vitello tonnato Light red (Valpolicella, Beaujolais) served cool.

Wiener Schnitzel **→*** light red from the Italian Tyrol (Alto Adige) or the Médoc; Austrian Riesling, Grüner Veltliner or Gumpoldskirchener. Or Czech Veltlinski.

Vegetarian dishes

Bean salad Red Rioja *reserva*.

Bean stew Bairrada from Portugal, Toro from Spain.

Choucroute (*See also* Sauerkraut) Alsace Pinot Gris or Sylvaner.

Couscous Young red with a bite: Shiraz, Corbières, Minervois, etc.

Fennel-based dishes Pouilly-Fumé, Beaujolais.

'Meaty' aubergine, lentil or mushroom bakes Corbières, Côtes du Ventoux.

Onion/leek tart *→*** fruity, concentrated dry white: Alsace Pinot Gris or Gewürztraminer. Mâcon-Villages of a good vintage, Jurançon, California or Australian Riesling. Or Beaujolais or Loire red.

Peppers or aubergines (eggplant), stuffed ** vigorous red: Chianti, Dolcetto, Zinfandel, Bandol, Vacqueyras.

Ratatouille ** vigorous young red: Chianti, Zinfandel, Bulgarian, young red Bordeaux or young Côtes du Rhône.

Spinach/pasta bakes Chianti Classico, Crozes-Hermitage, Shiraz.

Cheese

Very strong cheese completely masks the flavour of wine. Only serve fine wine with mild cheeses in peak condition.

Bleu de Bresse, Dolcelatte, Gorgonzola, Stilton, other English blue Need emphatic accompaniment: young ** red wine (Barbera, Dolcetto, Moulin-à-Vent, etc) or Sauternes – or port.

Cream cheeses: Brie, Camembert, Bel Paese, Edam, etc In their mild state marry with any good wine, red or white.

Hard English (Scottish, Welsh, Irish) cheeses Can be either mild or strong and acidic. The latter need sweet or strong wine.

Cheddar, Cheshire, Wensleydale, Gloucester, etc If mild: fine burgundy or claret. If mature: good ruby, or vintage character (not vintage) port, old dry *oloroso* sherry, or a very big red (Hermitage, Châteauneuf-du-Pape, Barolo, Barbaresco, etc).

Goat's cheeses **→*** white wine of marked character, either dry (Sancerre) or sweet (Monbazillac, Sauternes).

Hard Cheese, Parmesan, Gruyère, Emmenthal, old Gouda, Jarlsberg Full-bodied dry whites: Tokay d'Alsace or Vernaccia, or *fino* or *amontillado* sherry. But it is worth experimenting with any fine wine: old Gouda ('Mimolette') and Jarlsberg have a sweetness that encourages fine old reds.

Roquefort, Danish Blue So strong-flavoured that only the youngest, biggest or sweetest wines stand a chance. Sauternes is traditional with Roquefort. Old dry *amontillado* or *oloroso* sherries have the necessary horse-power for Danish Blue.

Desserts

Apple pie or strudel **→*** sweet German, Austrian, Hungarian white.

Apples, Cox's Orange Pippins Vintage port (55, 60, 63, 66, 70, 75, 82).

Bread and butter pudding 10-yr-old Barsac from a good château.

Cakes Bual or Malmsey madeira, *oloroso* or cream sherry.

Cheesecake **→*** sweet white from Vouvray or Anjou.

Chocolate cake, mousse, soufflés Bual madeira, Huxelrebe *Auslese*, California orange Muscat, Beaumes de Venise.

Christmas pudding, mince pies Tawny port, cream sherry, Asti Spumante.

Creams, custards and fools **→*** Sauternes, Loupiac, Ste-Croix-du-Mont, or Monbazillac.

Crème brûlée The most luxurious dish, demanding ***→**** Sauternes or Rhine *Beerenauslese*, or the best madeira or tokay.

Crêpes Suzette Sweet champagne or Asti Spumante.

Fruit, fresh Sweet Coteaux du Layon light sweet or liqueur Muscat.

    stewed, ie apricots, pears, etc Sweet Muscatel: Muscat de Beaumes de Venise, Moscato di Pantelleria or from Tarragona.

Fruit flans (ie peach, raspberry) *** Sauternes, Monbazillac or sweet Vouvray or Anjou.

Fruit salads, orange salad A fine sweet sherry.

Nuts *Oloroso* sherry, Bual madeira, vintage or tawny port, Vin Santo.

Oranges, caramelized Experiment with old Sauternes.

Pears in red wine A pause before the port.

Raspberries (no cream, little sugar) Excellent with fine reds.

Rhubarb Only rhubarb wine.

Rice Pudding Liqueur Muscat, Moscatel de Valencia, or Loupiac.

Sorbets, ice-creams Asti Spumante, or (better) Moscato d'Asti Naturale. Or Cointreau.

Strawberries and cream ∗∗∗ Sauternes or similar sweet Bordeaux, or Vouvray Moelleux.

Strawberries, wild (no cream) Serve with ∗∗∗ red Bordeaux poured over them and in your glass.

Summer pudding Fairly young Sauternes of good vintage (82, 83, 85, 86).

Sweet soufflés Sauternes, sweet Vouvray or Coteaux du Layon. Sweet champagne.

Treacle tart Too sweet for any wine but a treacly Malmsey madeira.

Trifle Should be sufficiently vibrant with sherry.

Walnuts Nature's match for finest port, madeira, *oloroso* sherry.

Zabaglione Light gold Marsala.

The Right Temperature

No single aspect of serving wine makes or mars it so easily as getting the temperature right. White wines almost invariably taste dull and insipid served warm and red wines have disappointingly little scent or flavour served cold. The chart below gives an indication of what is generally found to be the most satisfactory temperature for serving each class of wine.

		°F ● °C	
		68 ● 20	
Room		66 ● 19	
temperature		64 ● 18	
		63 ● 17	Best red wines especially Bordeaux
	Red burgundy	61 ● 16	
		59 ● 15	Chianti, Zinfandel Côtes du Rhône
	Best white burgundy		
	Port, madeira	57 ● 14	
		55 ● 13	*Ordinaires*
		54 ● 12	Lighter red wines eg Beaujolais
Ideal	Sherry	52 ● 11	
cellar	*Fino* sherry	50 ● 10	Rosés Lambrusco
	Most dry white wines	48 ● 9	
	Champagne	46 ● 8	
Domestic		45 ● 7	
fridge		43 ● 6	Most sweet white wines
		41 ● 5	Sparkling wines
		39 ● 4	
		37 ● 3	
		35 ● 2	
		33 ● 1	
		32 ● 0	

A Little Learning. . .

The jargon of laboratory analysis is increasingly seen on the back-labels of New World wines. It is creeping menacingly into newspapers and magazines. What does it mean? This hard-edged wine-talk is very briefly explained below.

The most frequent technical references are to the ripeness of grapes at picking; the resultant alcohol and sugar content of the wine; various measures of its acidity; the amount of sulphur dioxide used as a preservative; and occasionally the amount of 'dry extract' – the sum of all the things that give wines their character.

The **sugar** in wine is mainly glucose and fructose, with traces of arabinose, xylose and other sugars that are not fermentable by yeast, but can be attacked by bacteria. Each country has its own system for measuring the sugar content or ripeness of grapes, known in English as the '**must weight**'. The chart below relates the three principal ones (German, French and American) to each other, to specific gravity, and to the potential alcohol of the wine if all the sugar is fermented.

Sugar to alcohol: potential strength

Specific Gravity	°Oechsle	Baumé	Brix	% Potential Alcohol v/v
1.065	65	8.8	15.8	8.1
1.070	70	9.4	17.0	8.8
1.075	75	10.1	18.1	9.4
1.080	80	10.7	19.3	10.0
1.085	85	11.3	20.4	10.6
1.090	90	11.9	21.5	11.3
1.095	95	12.5	22.5	11.9
1.100	100	13.1	23.7	12.5
1.105	105	13.7	24.8	13.1
1.110	110	14.3	25.8	13.8
1.115	115	14.9	26.9	14.4
1.120	120	15.5	28.0	15.0

Residual sugar is the sugar left after fermentation has finished or been artificially stopped, measured in grams per litre.

Alcohol content (mainly ethyl alcohol) is expressed in percent by volume of the total liquid. (Also known as 'degrees'.)

Acidity is both fixed and volatile. **Fixed acidity** consists principally of tartaric, malic and citric acids which are all found in the grape, and lactic and succinic acids which are produced during fermentation. **Volatile acidity** consists mainly of acetic acid, which is rapidly formed by bacteria in the presence of oxygen. A small amount of volatile acidity is inevitable and even attractive. With a larger amount the wine becomes 'pricked' – starts to turn to vinegar.

Total acidity is fixed and volatile acidity combined. As a rule of thumb for a well-balanced wine it should be in the region of one gram per thousand for each 10° Oechsle (*see above*).

pH is a measure of the strength of the acidity, rather than its volume. The lower the figure the more acid. Wine normally ranges in pH from 2.8 to 3.8. Winemakers in hot climates can have problems getting the pH low enough. Lower pH gives better colour, helps prevent bacterial spoilage and allows more of the SO_2 to be free and active as a preservative.

Sulphur dioxide (SO_2) is added to prevent oxidation and other accidents in winemaking. Some of it combines with sugars etc and is known as '**bound**'. Only the '**free**' SO_2 that remains in the wine is effective as a preservative. **Total SO_2** is controlled by law according to the level of residual sugar: the more sugar, the more SO_2 needed.

The 1991 Vintage

In Bordeaux and many parts of France, 1991 will easily be remembered as the year of the great April frost, which dramatically brought to an end the almost too-good-to-be-true series of successes of the late eighties climaxing in 1990. That at least was the reaction when a bitter night on April 21 killed the new shoots on perhaps two-thirds of the vines in the Gironde, as well as much of the rest of France – particularly in the west.

Whatever else the vintage might be it would be a fraction of the size Bordeaux has got used to. When was the last time such a frost had struck? In 1945: the greatest vintage so far this century.

In '91 there followed a fair summer, a record heat-wave in August, then rain just before the vintage. It was a harrowing sequence of events for growers. Some, especially in St-Emilion and Pomerol, had their little remaining Merlot almost washed away in late September. But many in the Médoc harvested a small crop of richly ripe Merlot before the rain, and fetched in some very healthy Cabernet between the later showers. These châteaux are talking, if not of another '45, at least of another high-quality vintage, though of derisory size. They also acknowledge that another big vintage, following huge ripe crops in '89 and '90, would have swamped the already glutted and recession-battered market.

Burgundy was far less affected by the frost than Bordeaux, although the potential crop was significantly reduced. The whole region enjoyed a very hot, dry summer (marred by hailstorms in the Côte de Nuits) and was on course for another excellent vintage when it started to rain. Heavy but irregular showers sadly diluted the very promising quality of the white wines. They will not be exceptional. Hard-working *vignerons* have made some excellent, concentrated reds; in the Côte de Nuits comparisons are even being made with 1985. Chablis has a useful 'honest' vintage to report, though few remarkable wines.

In the south of Burgundy the picture was quite different. Beaujolais had a splendid vintage, with rich, tannic Crus to keep for future pleasure, and there was a high level of quality among very ripe Mâcon Chardonnays.

Despite some frost, Champagne produced another huge, if not especially distinguished crop (the fifth-largest on record). The frost caught the Loire badly, and so did rain; nonetheless the depleted crop contains some good wines.

Late flowering, the long dry summer and some rain during harvest spoilt German winemakers' hopes of a fourth golden vintage. Most is average QbA quality. Some of the top estates of the Mosel-Saar-Ruwer and the Rhine made small amounts of QmP wines which they hope will be as good as the outstanding 1990s. Reverting to its reliable self after a trio of exceptional vintages Alsace produced a fair crop of sturdy wines.

The '91 northern Rhône vintage produced balanced wines for fairly early drinking. In the southern Rhône, vineyards were badly damaged by rains, and quality is compromised. Provence was affected by frost but was happy with the eventual quality. The Midi had no problems; Languedoc-Roussillon wines will be better than ever.

Italy's 1991 was again a predominantly red-wine vintage, but with quality more localized and variable than in 1990. The parched vineyards of Spain yielded another good, if contracted, crop; probably best in Penedès and Rioja. Sadly, a strike at vintage time resulted in half the sherry crop being entirely lost. Summer heat was a blessing for the port-makers of the Douro. 1991 ports are looking magnificent; tannic and intense. This will almost certainly be declared a vintage year – and a very good one.

On Madeira the government's initiatives for revitalizing the island's quality wine industry are taking effect. The vintage was good, big, and best of all – excellent for Sercial and Bual.

Australia had ideal grape-growing conditions almost everywhere. 1991 will be a famous vintage; perhaps the best for decades in the Hunter Valley and outstanding for Barossa reds in particular. Victoria was cockahoop over a vintage that will confirm its soaring reputation. New Zealand had an ideal autumn for its typical concentration of fruit flavours, especially in Sauvignon Blanc, and plenty of botrytis for the dessert wines that are its growing speciality.

1991 in California began with a winter so cold that the giant gum trees in the Napa Valley appeared to have been killed outright. It continued with a constipated summer that remained cool but rainless (the drought had already endured for almost five years without real relief). Happily the sun came out in September for a late harvest. Cool-ripened grapes picked in a warm October have made especially aromatic wines, with finesse and intensity that should give the best a long future.

France

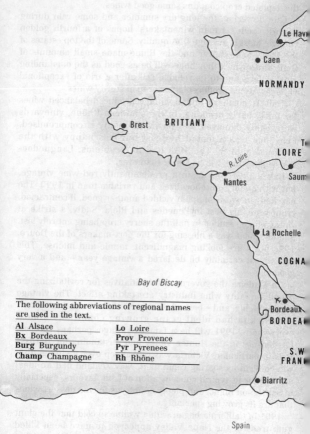

Le Hav[r]

● Caen

NORMANDY

● Brest

BRITTANY

R. Loire

● Nantes

T
LOIRE

Saum

● La Rochelle

COGNA

Bay of Biscay

The following abbreviations of regional names are used in the text.

Al Alsace	**Lo** Loire
Bx Bordeaux	**Prov** Provence
Burg Burgundy	**Pyr** Pyrenees
Champ Champagne	**Rh** Rhône

× Bordeaux
BORDEA

S.W
FRAN

● Biarritz

Spain

Every year sees fresh challenges to France's pole position in the wine world. Yet no-one has displaced her by definitively bettering even one of the many kinds of wine made; it is hard to imagine that anyone ever will. Tens of thousands of properties make wine of all complexions over a large part of her surface. This is a guide to their names, types and producers: essential information in identifying what is authentic and good of its kind.

All France's best wine regions (producing about 30% of all her wine) have *appellations contrôlées*, which may apply to a single small vineyard or to a whole large district. The system varies from region to region, with Burgundy on the whole having the smallest and most precise appellations, grouped into larger units by complicated formulae, and Bordeaux the widest and most general, within which it is the particular property ('château')

that matters. In between lies an infinity of variations.

An *appellation contrôlée* is a guarantee of origin, production method, grape varieties and quantities produced, but only partially one of quality. All AC wines are officially tasted, but many of shoddy quality get through the net. The AC therefore is the first thing to look for on a label. But the next is the name of the maker. The best makers' names are a vital ingredient of the pages that follow. Regions without the overall quality and traditions required for an appellation can be ranked as *vins délimités de qualité supérieure* (VDQS), a shrinking category. Government policy seems to be to promote remaining VDQS regions to AC status, and develop the relatively new and highly successful *vins de pays* (*see* page 55). *Vins de pays* are increasingly worth trying. They include some brilliant originals and often offer France's best value for money.

Recent vintages
of the French classics

Red Burgundy

Côte d'Or Côte de Beaune reds generally mature sooner than the bigger wines of the Côte de Nuits. Earliest drinking dates are for lighter commune wines, eg Volnay, Beaune; latest for the biggest wines of eg Chambertin, Romanée. But even the best burgundies are much more attractive young than the equivalent red Bordeaux.

1991 Very good to poor. Depends on date of harvest; before/after rain.
1990 A vintage to rival 88: perfect weather compromised only by drought on some slopes and over-production in some v'yds.
1989 A yr of great charm, not necessarily for v long maturing, but will age. 1992–2015.
1988 Exceptional quality; a great vintage. 1996–2020?
1987 Small crop with promising ripe fruit flavours esp in Côte de Beaune. Now–2010.
1986 A v mixed bag – aromatic but rather dry: generally lacks flesh. Now–2000.
1985 At best a great vintage. Concentrated wines will be splendid. Now–2010.
1984 Lacks natural ripeness; tends to be dry and/or watery. Now–96.
1983 Powerful, vigorous, tannic and attractive vintage, compromised by rot. The best are splendid, but be careful. Now–2000.
1982 Big vintage, pale but round and charming. Best in Côte de Beaune. Drink soon.
1981 A small crop, ripe but picked in rain.
1980 A wet yr, but attractive wines from best growers who avoided rot. Côte de Nuits best. Drink.
1979 Big, generally good, ripe vintage with weak spots. Drink up.
1978 A small vintage of outstanding quality. The best will live to 2000.
1977 V wet summer. Better wine than expected, but drink up.
1976 Hot summer, excellent vintage. As usual great variations, but the best (esp Côte de Beaune) tannic, rich and long lived – to 2000.
1973 Light wines, but many fruity and delicate. Most are already too old.
1972 Firm and full of character, the best are ageing v well. Drink soon.
1971 V powerful and impressive wines, not as long-lasting as they first appeared. Drink.
Older fine vintages: 69, 66, 64, 62, 61, 59 (all mature).

Beaujolais 91: small crop of vg wines, Crus excellent. 90 was a lusciously ripe vintage, wonderful *en primeur*. Top Crus will keep. 89 was outstanding both short- and long-term. 88 was v attractive with Crus to keep. 87 wines should be finished. 86s should be drunk. 85 was a wonderful vintage, but generally avoid older wines except possibly some Moulin-à-Vent.

White Burgundy

Côte de Beaune Well-made wines of good vintages with plenty of acidity as well as fruit will improve and gain depth and richness for some yrs – anything up to 10. Lesser wines from lighter yrs are ready for drinking after 2 or 3 yrs.

1991 Mostly lack substance. For early drinking.
1990 Very good, perhaps great, but with a tendency to fatness.
1989 Revealing itself as a model. At best ripe, tense, structured and long. Now–2005.
1988 Extremely good, some great wines but others rather dilute. Now–2000.
1987 Mainly disappointing, though a few exceptions are emerging. Now–98.
1986 Powerful wines; most with better acidity and balance than 85. Now–2000.
1985 V ripe; those that still have balance are ageing v well. Now–2000.
1984 Most rather lean or hollow. Drink soon.
1983 Potent wines; some exaggerated, some faulty, but the best splendid. To 95.
1982 Fat, tasty but delicate whites of low acidity. Drink up.
1981 A sadly depleted crop with great promise. But time to drink up.
1980 A weak, but not bad, vintage. Should be finished.
1979 Big vintage. Overall good and useful, not great. Drink up.
1978 Vg wines, firm and well balanced. Keep only the best.
1973 V attractive, now nutty, typical and plentiful. Drink up.
1972 High acidity, but plenty of character. All are now ready to drink.
1971 Great power and style. Top wines are now wonderful. Drink up.

The white wines of the Mâconnais (Pouilly-Fuissé, St-Véran, Mâcon-Villages) follow a similar pattern, but do not last as long. They are more appreciated for their freshness than their richness.

Alsace 90 was the third outstanding vintage in succession. 89 and 88 also both made wines of top quality (though rain spoiled some 88s). 87s should be drunk fairly soon and 86s finished. Top 85s and 83s may be drunk or kept.

24

Chablis Grand Cru Chablis of vintages with both strength and acidity can age superbly for up to 10 yrs. Premiers Crus proportionately less.

1991	Generally better than Côte d'Or. Useful wines.
1990	Grands Crus will be magnificent; other wines may lack intensity and acidity.
1989	Excellent vintage of potent character. Now–2000.
1988	Almost a model: great pleasure now in store. Now–98.
1987	Rain at harvest but balanced wines for the short term. Drink up.
1986	A splendid, big vintage. Now–95.
1985	Good but often low-acid wines. The best Grands Crus will age to 95.
1984	A small vintage. Most too feeble to last long. Drink up.
1983	Superb vintage if not over-strong. Wonderful Grands Crus now.
1982	Charming, soft wines. Not to keep.
1981	Small, concentrated and fine harvest. Drink up.
1978	Excellent wines, now passing their peak.

Red Bordeaux

Médoc/red Graves For some wines bottle-age is optional: for these it is indispensable. Minor châteaux from light vintages need only 2 or 3 yrs, but even modest wines of great yrs can improve for 15 or so, and the great châteaux of these yrs need double that time.

1991	Catastrophic frost in April halved crop and rain interrupted vintage. Choose with great care.
1990	A paradox: a drought year with a threat of over-production. Self-discipline was essential. Its results will be magnificent. To 2020.
1989	Early spring and splendid summer. The top wines will be classics of the ripe, dark kind with elegance and length. Small ch'x are uneven. To 2020.
1988	Generally excellent; ripe, balanced, for long keeping. To 2020.
1987	Much more enjoyable than seemed likely. Not for long keeping. Now–98.
1986	Another splendid, huge heatwave harvest. Superior to 85 Pauillac and St-Julien. Now–2020.
1985	Very good vintage, in a heatwave. Some great wines already accessible. Now–2010.
1984	Only fair. Little Merlot but good ripe Cabernet. Originally overpriced. To 98?
1983	A classic vintage: abundant tannin with fruit to balance it. To 2010.
1982	Made in a heatwave. Huge, rich, strong wines which promise a long life, but are developing unevenly. Most petits châteaux are now ready. Now–2010.
1981	Admirable despite rain. Not rich, but balanced and fine. Now–98.
1980	Small, late harvest, ripe but rained-on. Some delicious light wines. Drink up.
1979	Abundant harvest of above average quality. Now–2000.
1978	A miracle vintage: magnificent, long, warm autumn. Some superb wines. Now–2000.
1976	Excessively hot, dry summer; rain just before vintage. Generally vg; now ready.
1975	A v fine vintage, with deep colour, high sugar content and (sometimes excessive) tannin. For long keeping, but begin to drink: some may not improve; many have lost their fruit.
1973	A huge vintage, attractive young and still giving pleasure. Now or v soon.
1971	Small crop. Less fruity than 70 and less consistent. All are ready to drink.
1970	Big, excellent vintage with scarcely a failure. Now–2000.
1967	Never seductive, but characterful in its maturity. Drink soon.
1966	A v fine vintage with depth, fruit and tannin. Now.

Older fine vintages: 62, 61, 59, 55, 53, 52, 50, 49, 48, 47, 45, 29, 28.

St-Emilion/Pomerol

1991	A sad story. Terrible frost and little chance to recover.
1990	Another chance to make great wine or a lot of wine. 1994–2020.
1989	Large, ripe, early harvest; an overall triumph. To 2020.
1988	Generally excellent; ideal conditions. But some overproduced. Now–2000+.
1987	Some v adequate wines (esp in Pomerol) but for drinking soon.
1986	A prolific vintage; most wines need drinking soon. St-Emilions are generally better.
1985	One of the great yrs, with a long future. To 2010.
1984	A sad story. Most of the crop wiped out in spring. Avoid.
1983	Less impressive than it seemed. Drink soon.
1982	Enormously rich and concentrated wines, most excellent. Now–2000+.
1981	A vg vintage, if not as great as it first seemed. Now–95+.
1980	A poor Merlot yr; v variable quality. Choose carefully. Now.
1979	A rival to 78, but not developing as well as hoped. Now–95.
1978	Fine wines, but some lack flesh. Drink soon.
1976	V hot, dry summer, but vintage rain. Some excellent. Drink soon.
1975	Most St-Emilions good, the best superb. Pomerol made splendid wine. Now–2000.
1971	On the whole better than Médocs, but now ready.
1970	Beautiful wines with great fruit and strength. V big crop. Now.

Older fine vintages: 67, 66, 64, 61, 59, 53, 52, 49, 47, 45.

Abel-Lepitre Brut NV; Cuvée 134 Bl de Blancs 82 83 85; Réserve Crémant 83 85; Rosé 83 85   CHAMPAGNE house, also owning GOULET and St-Marceaux. Luxury Cuvée: Prince A de Bourbon-Parme.

Abymes Savoie w dr ★ DYA   Hilly little area nr Chambéry; light, mild wine from Jacquère grape.

Ackerman-Laurance CHAMPAGNE-method house of the Loire, at SAUMUR, said to be the first in the region. Fine CREMANT DE LOIRE.

Ajaccio Corsica r p w dr ★→★★ 88 89' 90 91   The capital of CORSICA. AC for some vg SCIACARELLO reds. Top grower: Peraldi.

Aligoté Second-rank burgundy white grape and its wine, should be agreeably sharp and fruity with considerable local character when young. BOUZERON (AC) makes the best, but don't hesitate to try others from good growers. NB PERNAND-VERGELESSES. Value.

Aloxe-Corton Burg r w ★★→★★★ 78 85 86 87 88' 89 90   Northernmost village of COTE DE BEAUNE famous for its two GRANDS CRUS: CORTON (red) and CORTON-CHARLEMAGNE (white). Village wines (called Aloxe-Corton) are much lighter but can be good value.

Alsace Al w (sp r) ★★→★★★ 85' 86 88 89 90' 91   Aromatic, fruity, often strong, dry white of rather Germanic character from E foothills of Vosges Mts, bordering on the R Rhine. Generally dry but increasingly made sweet (*see* Vendange tardive, Sélection des Grains Nobles). Normally sold by grape variety (Pinot Bl, Ries, Gewürz, etc). Matures well up to 5, even 10, yrs; GRAND CRU even longer. Also good quality and value CREMANT.

Alsace Grand Cru w ★★★ 83 85 86 88 89' 90 91   Appellation restricted to about 45 of the best named v'yds, and noble grapes (Riesling, Pinot G ['Tokay'], Gewürz and MUSCAT).

Ampeau, Robert Exceptional grower and specialist in MEURSAULT; also POMMARD, etc. Perhaps unique in only releasing matured bottles.

d'Angerville, Marquis Famous burgundy grower with immaculate 30-acre estate in VOLNAY. Top wines: Champans and Clos des Ducs.

Anjou Lo r p w (sw dr sp) ★→★★★ 76 78 82 83 85' 86 88 89' 90 91   Loire AC embracing wide spectrum of styles. Esp good red (Cab) ANJOU-VILLAGES, strong dry SAVENNIERES, luscious COTEAUX DU LAYON Chenin Bl whites.

Anjou-Coteaux de la Loire AC for Chenin Bl whites, incl the notable dry SAVENNIERES.

Anjou-Villages Lo r ★→★★   New AC for reds (mainly Cab F) from less limited zone than SAUMUR-CHAMPIGNY. Potentially juicy and good value.

Appellation Contrôlée ('AC' or 'AOC') Government control of origin and production of all the best French wines (*see* France Introduction).

Apremont Savoie w dr ★★ DYA   One of the best villages of SAVOIE for pale delicate whites, mainly from Jacquère grapes, recently incl Chard.

Arbin Savoie r ★★   Deep-coloured, lively red from Mondeuse grapes, rather like a good Loire Cab. Ideal après-ski wine. Drink at 1–2 yrs.

Arbois Jura r p w (dr sp) ★★   Various good and original light wines; speciality VIN JAUNE. On the whole, DYA.

l'Ardèche, Coteaux de Central France r p (w dr) ★→★★ DYA   Bargain country reds; best from Syrah, Gamay and recently Cab. Also powerful, almost burgundy-like Chard 'Grand Ardèche' from Louis LATOUR.

Armagnac Region of SW France and its often excellent brandy, a fiery spirit of rustic character. The excellent red of the area is MADIRAN.

Auxey-Duresses Burg r w ★★→★★★ 78 82 83 85 86 87 88' 89 90   Second-rank (but v pretty) COTE DE BEAUNE village: affinities with VOLNAY and MEURSAULT. Best estates: Cuvée Boillot, Diconne, HOSPICES DE BEAUNE, LEROY, Prunier. Drink whites in 4–5 years.

Auxerre Once vast, now a tiny part of N Burgundy with 400 acres of AC BOURGOGNE.

Avize Champ ★★★★   One of CHAMPAGNE's best Chard-growing villages.

Aÿ Champ ★★★★   One of the best Pinot N-growing villages of CHAMPAGNE.

Ayala NV; Château d'Aÿ 82 83 85; Grande Cuvée 82 83 85; Blanc de Blancs

82 83 Once-famous Aÿ-based old-style CHAMPAGNE concern. Deserves more notice for ripe, fresh, appley wines.

Bachelet, Denis Brilliant young grower of GEVREY-CHAMBERTIN. Top wine: CHARMES-CHAMBERTIN.

Bahuaut, Donatien Leading Loire-wine merchants based at Ch de la Cassemichère, MUSCADET.

Bandol Prov r p (w) *** 79 82 83 84 85' 86 87' 88 89 90 Little coastal region near Toulon producing Provence's best wines; vigorous, tannic reds from the Mourvèdre grape; esp Dom OTT, Dom de Pibarnon, Ch Pradeaux, Mas de la Rouvière, Dom Tempier, Ch Vannières.

Banyuls Pyr br sw ** One of the best VINS DOUX NATURELS of the S of France, made chiefly of Grenache (a Banyuls GRAND CRU is over 75% Grenache, aged for 2+ yrs). Technically a distant relation of port. Best wines are RANCIOS eg from Domaine des Hospices, Dom du Mas Blanc (***), at 10–15 yrs old. Also cheap NV wines.

Bar-sur-Aube Champ w (p) *** Important secondary CHAMPAGNE region 100 miles SE of R Marne, Epernay etc. Some good lighter wines and excellent Rosé des RICEYS.

Barancourt Brut Réserve NV; Rosé NV; Bouzy GRAND CRU Vintage 81 83; Rosé Vintage Grower at Bouzy making full-bodied CHAMPAGNE. Major reorganization and investment in '92.

Barsac Bx w sw **→**** 70 71 75 76' 78 79' 80 81 82 83' 84 85 86' 88' 89' 90' Neighbour of SAUTERNES with similar superb golden wines, generally less rich and more racy. Top ch'x: CLIMENS, COUTET, DOISY-DAENE, DOISY-VEDRINES.

Barton & Guestier BORDEAUX shipper since 18th C, now owned by Seagram.

Bâtard-Montrachet Burg w dr **** 78 79 82 83 85 86 87 88 89 90 Larger (55-acre) neighbour of MONTRACHET, the top white burgundy. Should be v long-lived and intense in flavour. Bienvenues-Bâtard-M is a separate adjacent 9-acre GRAND CRU with 15 owners; thus no substantial bottlings and v rare. Top growers incl BOUCHARD PERE, DROUHIN, Gagnard, Louis LATOUR, LEFLAIVE, Lequin-Roussot, MOREY, Niellon, RAMONET, SAUZET.

Baumard, Domaine des Leading grower of ANJOU wine, esp SAVENNIERES and COTEAUX DU LAYON (Clos Ste-Catherine).

Baur, Léon Small but vigorous ALSACE family firm at Eguisheim, easily confused with Léon BEYER. Esp for Ries: Elisabeth Stumpff.

Béarn SW France r p w dr *→** DYA Wide-spread, low-key AC of growing local (Basque country) interest, esp wines from the coop of Sallies de Béarn-Bellocq.

Beaujolais Burg r (p w) * DYA The simple AC of the v big Beaujolais region: light, short-lived, fruity red from Gamay grapes.

Confusingly, the best wines of the Beaujolais region are not identified as such on their labels by their appellations. They are known simply by the names of their 'crus': Brouilly, Côte de Brouilly, Chénas, Chiroubles, Fleurie, Juliénas, Morgon, Moulin-à-Vent, Regnié, St-Amour. See entries for each of these. Since 1984 the Confrèrie des Compagnes du Beaujolais have offered a 'Beaujolais Grumé' label to selected wines from the region with ageing potential.

Beaujolais de l'année The BEAUJOLAIS of the latest vintage, until the next.

Beaujolais Primeur (or Nouveau) Same as the above, made in a hurry (often only 4–5 days fermenting) for release at midnight on the third Wednesday in November. Is ideally soft, fruity and tempting; but is often crude, sharp and too alcoholic. BEAUJOLAIS-VILLAGES *should* be a better bet.

Beaujolais Supérieur Burg r (w) * DYA BEAUJOLAIS of 1% natural alcohol stronger than the 9% minimum. Since sugar is almost always added for strength this means little or nothing.

Beaujolais-Villages Burg r ** 90 91 Wines from better (N) half of BEAUJOLAIS; should be much tastier than plain Beaujolais. The 10 (easily) best 'villages' are the 'CRUS': FLEURIE etc (*see* note above). Of the 30 others the best lie around Beaujeu. Crus cannot be released *en primeur* before December 15th. Best kept until spring (or longer).

Beaumes de Venise Rh (r p) br *** DYA Generally France's best dessert MUSCAT, from the S CÔTES DU RHÔNE; can be high-flavoured, subtle, lingering (eg Domaine de Coyeux, Domaine Durban, JABOULET). The red and rosé from Ch Redortier and the coop are also good.

Beaune Burg r (w dr) *** 76 78' 82 83 85' 86 87 88' 89 90 Middle-rank classic burgundy. Many fine growers. *Négociants'* CLOS wines (usually PREMIER CRU) are often best eg DROUHIN's superb 'Clos des Mouches', JADOT's Clos des Ursules. Beaune du Château is a (good) BOUCHARD PÈRE brand. Best v'yds: Bressandes, Fèves, Grèves, Marconnets, Teurons.

Becker, Caves J Proud old family firm at Zellenberg, ALSACE. Classic Ries Hagenschlauf. Second label: Gaston Beck.

Bégadan Leading village of the N MÉDOC (AC Médoc). Ch'x incl GREYSAC, LAUJAC, PATACHE D'AUX, LA TOUR-DE-BY, Vieux-Ch-Landon. Often vg value. Also commendable coop (Cave St-Jean).

Bellet Prov p r w dr *** Fashionable, much above average, local wines from nr Nice. Serious producers: Ch'x de Bellet and Crémat – pricey.

Bergerac Dordogne r w sw dr ** 86 88 89 90 Lightweight, often tasty, BORDEAUX-style. Drink young, the white v young. *See also* Monbazillac, Montravel, Pécharmant. Growers incl Courts-les-Muts, JAUBERTIE, Michel de Montaigne, Ch de Panisseau, Tiregand.

Besserat de Bellefon 'B de B' NV; Cuvée Bl de Blancs; 82 85; Cuvée des Moines Brut; Rosé 82 85 Rising CHAMPAGNE house for light wines.

Beyer, Léon Ancient ALSACE family firm at Eguisheim making forceful dry wines that need ageing at least 2–3 yrs, esp Comtes d'Eguisheim.

Bichot, Maison Albert One of BEAUNE's biggest growers and merchants. V'yds (Domaine du Clos Frantin is excellent) in CHAMBERTIN, RICHEBOURG, CLOS DE VOUGEOT, etc, and Domaine Long-Depaquit in CHABLIS; also many other brand names.

Billecart-Salmon NV; 85; Rosé NV; Bl de Blancs 83 85; Grande Cuvée 82 One of the best small CHAMPAGNE houses. Fresh-flavoured wines incl a v tasty rosé.

Bize, Simon Admirable red burgundy grower with 35 acres at SAVIGNY-LES-BEAUNE. Model wines, racy and elegant; fair prices.

Blagny Burg r w dr **–*** 76 78 82 83 85 86 87 88' 89 90 Hamlet between MEURSAULT and PULIGNY-MONTRACHET: affinities with both (whites are sold under these ACs), and reds with VOLNAY (sold as AC Blagny). All need age. Growers incl AMPEAU, Jobard, LATOUR, LEFLAIVE, Matrot, G Thomas.

Blanc de Blancs Any white wine made from (only) white grapes, esp CHAMPAGNE, which is usually made of both red and white. *Not* an indication of quality.

Blanc de Noirs White (or slightly pink or 'blush') wine from red grapes.

Blanck, Marcel ALSACE grower at Kientzheim, esp for Pinot Bl.

Blanquette de Limoux Midi w dr sp ** Good bargain sparkler from nr Carcassonne, made by a version of the MÉTHODE CHAMPENOISE. V dry and clean and increasingly tasty as Chard is added to the original grapes. Normally NV.

Blaye Bx r w dr * 88 89 90 Your daily BORDEAUX from E of the Gironde. PREMIÈRES CÔTES DE BLAYE is the AC of the better wines.

Boisset, Jean Claude Dynamic burgundy merchant/grower at NUITS-ST-GEORGES, owns the houses of Bassot, Lionel Bruck, Pierre Ponnelle and VIÉNOT. High commercial standards.

Bollinger NV; 'Special Cuvée'; Grande Année 69 70 73 75 76 79 82 83 85; Rosé 81 82 83 85 Top CHAMPAGNE house, at AY. Dry, very full-flavoured style. Luxury wines: RD (73, 75, 76, 79, 82), Vieilles Vignes

Françaises (69, 70, 75, 79, 80, 81, 82, 85) from ungrafted vines.

Bommes One of the 5 villages of SAUTERNES. Best châteaux: LAFAURIE-PEYRAGUEY, LA TOUR-BLANCHE, etc.

Bonneau du Martray, Domaine The major grower (with 27 acres) of CORTON-CHARLEMAGNE of the highest quality; also red GRAND CRU CORTON. Cellars at PERNAND-VERGELESSES.

Bonnes-Mares Burg r **** 66 69 71 76 78' 79 80 82 83 85' 86 87 88' 89 90 37-acre GRAND CRU between CHAMBOLLE-MUSIGNY and MOREY-ST-DENIS. V sturdy, long-lived wines, sometimes (not often) better than CHAMBERTIN. Top growers: DUJAC, Groffier, JADOT, MUGNIER, ROUMIER, Dom des VAROILLES, DE VOGUE.

Bonnezeaux Lo w sw *** 76' 78 81 83 85 86 88 89' 90 Unusual, rich, tangy wine from Chenin Bl grapes, the best of COTEAUX DU LAYON. Esp Ch de Fesles, Domaine du Petit Val. Ages well.

Bordeaux Bx r w (p) * 88 89 90 (for châteaux *see* pages 56–76) Basic catch-all AC for low-strength Bordeaux wine. Not to be despised. There is no more satisfactory daily drink.

Bordeaux Supérieur *→** As above, with slightly more alcohol.

Borie-Manoux Admirable BORDEAUX shippers and château-owners, owned by the Castéja family. Ch'x incl BATAILLEY, BEAU-SITE, DOMAINE DE L'EGLISE, HAUT-BAGES-MONPELOU, TROTTEVIEILLE.

Bouchard Aîné Long-established burgundy shipper and grower with 62 acres in BEAUNE, MERCUREY, etc. Good, not top quality.

Bouchard Père et Fils Important burgundy shipper (est 1731) and grower with 209 acres of excellent v'yds, mainly in the COTE DE BEAUNE, and cellars at the Château de Beaune. Steady, if not quite top, quality.

Bourg Bx r (w dr) ** 82 83 85 86 88' 89 90 Un-fancy claret from E of the Gironde. For châteaux *see* Côtes de Bourg.

Bourgogne Burg r w (p) dr ** 88' 89 90' Catch-all AC for Burgundy, but with theoretically higher standards than basic BORDEAUX. Light but often good flavour, best at 2–3 yrs. Top growers make some beauties; do not despise. BEAUJOLAIS CRUS can also be labelled Bourgogne.

Bourgogne Grand Ordinaire Burg r (w) * DYA The lowest Burgundy AC for Gamay wines. Rare.

Bourgogne Passe-Tout-Grains Burg r (p) * Age 1–2 yrs Often enjoyable junior burgundy. 33% Pinot N and 67% Gamay grapes mixed in the vat. Not as 'heady' as BEAUJOLAIS.

Bourgueil Lo r *** 76' 83' 85 86 88 89' 90' Normally delicate fruity Cab red from TOURAINE. Deep-flavoured and long-lasting in good years, ageing like BORDEAUX. ST-NICOLAS-DE-BOURGUEIL is often lighter. Growers incl Audebert, Billet, Caslot, Cognard, Druet, Jamet, Lamé-Delille-Boucard, Thouet-Bosseau.

Bouvet-Ladubay Major producer of sparkling SAUMUR, controlled by TAITTINGER. Excellent CREMANT DE LOIRE. 'Saphir' is vintage wine.

Bouzeron Village of the COTE CHALONNAISE distinguished for the only single-village AC ALIGOTE. Top grower: de Vilaine.

Bouzy Rouge Champ r *** 85 86 88 89 90 Still red wine from famous red-grape CHAMPAGNE village. Like light burgundy, ageing early but sometimes lasting well.

Brédif, Marc One of the most important growers and traders of VOUVRAY, owned by LADOUCETTE.

Bricout Brut 82 85 Small CHAMPAGNE house at AVIZE making light wines.

Brouilly Burg r *** 90 91 One of the 10 best CRUS of BEAUJOLAIS: fruity, round, refreshing, and can age 3–4 yrs. Ch de la Chaize is biggest estate. Top grower: Michaud.

Brut Term for the driest wines of CHAMPAGNE.

Bugey Savoie r p w dr sp *→** DYA District with a variety of light sparkling, still or half-sparkling wines. Grapes incl Roussette (or Roussanne) and good Chard. Best from Cerdon and Montagnieu.

Buxy Burg w dr ** Village in AC MONTAGNY with good coop for Chard.

Buzet SW France, r w dr ** 85 86 88 89 90 Good BORDEAUX-style wines from just SE of Bordeaux. Good value area with well-run cooperative. Best wines are barrel-aged: Ch de Gueyze, Cuvée Napoléon and Ch de Padère. Also Ch Sauvagnères.

Cabardès Midi r (p w) *→*** 85 86 88 89 90 Newcomer VDQS region N of Carcassonne, CORBIÈRES, etc. MIDI and BORDEAUX grapes show promise at Ch Rivals, Ch Ventenac, Coops de Conques sur Orbiel and Pézenas.

Cabernet *See* Grapes for red wine (pages 8–9).

Cabernet d'Anjou Lo p *→*** DYA Delicate, grapey, often rather sweet rosé.

Cabrières Midi p (r) ** DYA COTEAUX DU LANGUEDOC vintage best for fragrant rosé from eg Domaine du Temple.

Cahors SW France r *→** 82 83 85 86 88 89 90 Historically a 'black', tannic wine from Malbec grapes, now made like BORDEAUX, but can be full-bodied and distinct. Top growers: Baldès (esp 'Prince Probus'), Ch de Caix, Ch de Chambert, Clos la Coutale, Ch St-Didier, Dom Eugénie, Clos de Gamot, Jouffreau, Ch Lagrezette, Dom de Paillas, Vigouroux (esp Ch de Haute-Serre). Lighter wines from coop, Caves d'Olt.

Cairanne Rh r p w dr ** 85 86 88 89 90 Village of COTES DU RHONE-VILLAGES. Good solid wines, esp from Dom Brusset, Dom l'Oratoire St-Martin, Domaine Rabasse-Charavin.

Calvet Famous old shippers of BORDEAUX and burgundy, now owned by Allied-Hiram Walker. Some reliable standard wines, esp from Bordeaux.

Canard-Duchêne Brut NV; 'Patinmoine' NV; Rosé; Charles VII NV; Vintage 83 Quality CHAMPAGNE house owned by VEUVE-CLICQUOT, hence the Moët-Hennessy group.

Canon-Fronsac Bx r ***→**** 78 79 81 82 83' 85 86 88 89' 90 Full-flavoured reds of increasing quality and style from small area W of POMEROL. They generally need less age than formerly (85s are excellent now). Ch'x include CANON, CANON DE BREM, CANON-MOUEIX, Coustolle, Junayme, Mazeris-Bellevue, Moulin-Pey-Labrie (esp since '88), Toumalin, La Truffière, Vraye-Canon-Boyer. *See also* Fronsac.

Cantenac Bx r *** Village of the HAUT-MEDOC entitled to the AC MARGAUX. Top châteaux include BRANE-CANTENAC, PALMER, etc.

Cap Corse Corsica w dr br **→*** CORSICA's wild N cape. Splendid Muscat; rare, soft, dry Vermentino white. *Vaut le détour*, if not *le voyage*.

Caramany Pyr r (w dr) * 88 89 90 New AC for part of COTES DU ROUSSILLON-VILLAGES.

Cassis Prov w (r p) dr ** DYA Seaside village E of Marseille known for its lively, dry white, exceptional for Provence (eg Domaine du Paternel). Not to be confused with *cassis*, a blackcurrant liqueur made in Dijon.

Castellane, de NV; Croix Rouge 86; Bl de Blancs 82; new Prestige Florens de Castellane 82 Long-established Epernay CHAMPAGNE house. Good, rather light wines incl Maxim's house champagne.

Cave Cellar, or any wine establishment.

Cave coopérative Wine-growers' cooperative winery. Coops now account for 55% of all French production. 4 out of 10 of all French growers are coop members. Almost all coops are now well run, well equipped and making some of the best value wine of their areas.

Cellier des Samsons BEAUJOLAIS/MACONNAIS coop at Quincié with 2,000 grower-members. Widely distributed.

Cépage Variety of vine, eg Chard, Merlot.

Cérons Bx w dr sw ** 81 83 85 86 88 89 90 Neighbour of SAUTERNES with some good sweet-wine ch'x, eg Ch de Cérons et de Calvimont, Grand Enclos, Ch Haura. Ch Archambeau also makes vg dry GRAVES.

Chablis Burg w dr **→**** 88 89 90 91 Distinctive, full-flavoured, dry, minerally wine. Made in N Burgundy of Chard only. Top growers incl R Dauvissat, Droin, DURUP, FEVRE, Geoffroy, LAROCHE, LONG-DEPAQUIT, Michel, PIC, Raveneau, Vocoret. Simple unqualified 'Chablis' may be thin; best is PREMIER or GRAND CRU (*see below*). The modern growers' coop, La Chablisienne, has v high standards: many different labels.

FRANCE/Buz-Cha

Chablis Grand Cru Burg w dr **** 78 83 85 86 88 89 90 Some of the greatest white burgundies, in maturity a match for almost any. Forceful but often dumb in youth, gaining almost SAUTERNES-like richness in maturity. There are 7 v'yds: Blanchots, Bougros, Clos, Grenouilles, Preuses, Valmur, Vaudésir. *See also* Moutonne.

Chablis Premier Cru Burg w dr *** 85 86 88 89 90 91 Technically second-rank but often excellent, more typical of CHABLIS than of GRANDS CRUS. Often outclasses more expensive MEURSAULT and other Chards in finesse. Best v'yds incl Côte de Lechet, Fourchaume, Mont de Milieu, Montée de Tonnerre, Montmains, Vaillons. *See* Chablis for producers.

Chai Building for storing and maturing wine, esp in BORDEAUX.

Chambertin Burg r **** 69 71 76 78 79 82 83 85 86 87 88 89 90 32-acre GRAND CRU giving the meatiest, most enduring and sometimes the best red burgundy, 15 growers, incl BOUCHARD PERE, Camus, Damoy, DROUHIN, PONSOT, ROUSSEAU, Rebourseau, Tortochot, Trapet.

Chambertin-Clos de Bèze Burg r **** 69 71 76 78 79 82 83 85 86 87 88 89 90 37-acre neighbour of CHAMBERTIN. Similarly splendid wines. May legally be sold as Chambertin. 10 growers incl Bruno CLAIR, CLAIR-DAU, Damoy, DROUHIN, Drouhin-Larose, FAIVELEY, JADOT, ROUSSEAU, Trapet.

Chambolle-Musigny Burg r (w) ***→**** 76 78 82 83 85 86 87 88' 89 90 420-acre COTE DE NUITS village with fabulously fragrant, complex, never heavy wine. Best v'yds: Les Amoureuses, part of BONNES-MARES, Les Charmes, MUSIGNY. Growers to note: Barthod, DROUHIN, FAIVELEY, Hudelot-Noëllat, JADOT, Moine-Hudelot, Mugneret, MUGNIER, RION, ROUMIER, Serveau, DE VOGUE.

Champagne Sparkling wine of Pinots N and Meunier and/or Chard from 70,000+ acres 90 miles E of Paris, made by the METHODE CHAMPENOISE. Wines from elsewhere, however good, cannot be champagne.

Champigny *See* Saumur.

Chandon de Briailles, Domaine Small burgundy estate at SAVIGNY. Makes wonderful CORTON and vg PERNAND-VERGELESSES.

Chanson Père et Fils Growers (with 110 acres) and *négociants* at BEAUNE.

Chantovent Major brand of VIN DE TABLE, largely from MINERVOIS.

Chapelle-Chambertin Burg r *** 76 78 82 83' 85 86 87 88 89 90 13-acre neighbour of CHAMBERTIN. Wine more 'nervous', not so meaty. Top producers: Drouhin-Larose, JADOT, LEROY, Trapet.

Chapoutier Long-established growers and traders of fine Rhône wines.

Charbaut, A et Fils NV; Bl de Blancs; Rosé NV; 79 82 85; Certificate 82 85; Certificate Rosé 79 82 85 Epernay CHAMPAGNE house. Clean, light wines. Good rosé.

Chardonnay *See* Grapes for white wine (pages 6–8).

Charmes-Chambertin Burg r *** 71 76 78 79 82 83 85 86 87 88 89 90 76-acre neighbour of CHAMBERTIN. Wine more 'supple', rounder. Growers incl BACHELET, Castagnier, DROUHIN, DUJAC, LEROY, ROTY, ROUSSEAU.

Chartron & Trebuchet Young company with some delicate, harmonious white burgundies, esp Domaine Chartron's PULIGNY-MONTRACHET, Clos de la Pucelle, and BATARD- and CHEVALIER-MONTRACHET. Also ALIGOTE.

Chassagne-Montrachet Burg r w dr ***→**** r (***) 78 82; w 78 83 85 86 87 88 89 90 750-acre COTE DE BEAUNE village with excellent, rich, dry whites and sterling hefty reds. The white wines rarely have the exceptional finesse of those of PULIGNY-MONTRACHET next door but can be better value. Best v'yds incl part of MONTRACHET, BATARD-MONTRACHET, Boudriottes (r w), Caillerets, CRIOTS-BATARD-MONTRACHET, Morgeot (r w), Ruchottes, CLOS ST-JEAN (r). Growers incl Bachelet-Ramonet, M Colin-Deleger, Delagrange-Bachelet, DROUHIN, J-N Gagnard, GAGNARD-DELAGRANGE, Lamy-Pillot, MAGENTA, MOREY, Niellon, RAMONET-PRUDHON.

Chasseloir, Domaine du The HQ of the firm of Chéreau-Carré, makers of several excellent domaine MUSCADETS (esp Ch du Chasseloir) which are among the AC's leaders.

31

Château An estate, big or small, good or indifferent, particularly in BORDEAUX. In Burgundy the term 'domaine' is used. For Bordeaux châteaux *see* pages 56–76.

Château-Chalon Jura w dr *** Unique, strong, dry, yellow wine, rather like a sharpish *fino* sherry. Usually ready to drink when bottled (at about 6 yrs). A curiosity.

Château Corton-Grancey Burg r *** 78 82 83 85 86 88 89 90 Famous estate at ALOXE-CORTON, the property of Louis LATOUR.

Château d'Arlay Major JURA estate; 160 acres in skilful hands with wines incl Pinot N and MACVIN.

Château de Beaucastel Rh r w dr *** 78 79 80 81 83 84 85 86 87 88 89 90 One of the biggest (173 acres), best-run CHATEAUNEUF-DU-PAPE estates. Deep-hued wines for at least 10 yrs ageing. A small amount of wonderful white to keep 5–10 yrs. Second label: Coudelet de Beaucastel. New interest: Beaucastel Estate in California's Central Coast region.

Château de la Chaize Burg r *** 89 90 91 The best-known estate of BROUILLY, with 200 acres.

Château de Meursault Burg r w *** 100-acre estate owned by PATRIARCHE with good v'yds and vg wines in BEAUNE, MEURSAULT, POMMARD, VOLNAY. Splendid cellars open to the public for tasting.

Château de Mille Prov r p w dr ** Leading property of the advancing COTES DU LUBERON. A local star.

Château de Selle Prov r p w dr ** 100-acre estate of the OTT family nr Cotignac, Var. Well-known and typical wines. Cuvée Spéciale is largely Cab S.

Château du Nozet Lo w dr *** 86 88 89 90 91 Biggest and best-known estate of POUILLY (FUME) -SUR-LOIRE. Top wine, Baron de L, can be wonderful (at a price).

Château Fortia Rh r (w dr) *** 78 81 83 84 85 86 88 89 90 First-class CHATEAUNEUF-DU-PAPE property. Traditional methods. The owner's father, Baron Le Roy, also fathered the APPELLATION CONTROLEE system in the '20s.

Château-Grillet Rh w dr **** 88 89 90 7.5-acre v'yd: one of France's smallest ACs. Intense, fragrant, wildly over-expensive. Drink young.

Châteaumeillant Lo r p w dr * DYA Tiny VDQS area nr SANCERRE. Light Gamay and Pinot N. Good pale rosé.

Châteauneuf-du-Pape Rh r (w dr) *** 78' 79 81 83 84 85 86 88 89 90 7,400 acres nr Avignon with v mixed standards, but many fine wines. Best estate ('domaine') wines are dark, strong, exceptionally long-lived. Others may be light and/or disappointing. The white can be heavy: most now made to DYA. Top growers incl châteaux DE BEAUCASTEL, Dom les Cailloux, FORTIA, La Nerthe, MONT-REDON, Clos des Papes, RAYAS, VIEUX TELEGRAPHE, etc.

Château Rayas Rh r (w dr) *** 78' 79 81 85 86 87 88 89 90 Famous old-style property of only 38 acres in CHATEAUNEUF-DU-PAPE. Concentrated wines are entirely Grenache, yet can age superbly. Pignan is second label. Also vg Ch Fonsalette, COTES DU RHONE.

Château Simone Prov r p w dr ** Age 2–6 yrs Famous old property in Palette; the only one with a name in this AC nr Aix-en-Provence. The red is best: smooth but herby and spicy. White has been catching up.

Château Vignelaure Prov r **→**** 82' 83' 85 86 87 88 89 90 135-acre Provençal estate nr Aix, making exceptional, more-or-less BORDEAUX-style wine with Cab, Syrah and Grenache grapes.

Châtillon-en-Diois Rh r p w dr * DYA Small AC E of the middle Rhône nr Die. Adequate, largely Gamay reds; white (some ALIGOTE) mostly made into CLAIRETTE DE DIE.

Chauvenet, F Substantial company in NUITS; buys grapes on contract from good estates to make a wide range of much-appreciated COTE D'OR wines, incl CORTON-CHARLEMAGNE, CHARMES-CHAMBERTIN, etc.

Chave, Gérard To many the superstar grower of HERMITAGE, red and white.

Chavignol Village of SANCERRE with famous v'yd, Les Monts Damnés. Chalky soil gives vivid wines that age 4–5 yrs. Also Fromage de Chèvre.

Chénas Burg r *** 85 88 89 90 91   The smallest BEAUJOLAIS CRU and one of the weightiest; neighbour to MOULIN-A-VENT and JULIENAS. Growers incl Benon, Champagnon, Charvet, Ch Chèvres, Robin and the coop.

Chenin Blanc *See* Grapes for white wine (pages 6–8).

Chevalier-Montrachet Burg w dr **** 78 83 85 86 87 88 89 90   17-acre neighbour of MONTRACHET producing similar luxurious wine, perhaps a little less powerful. Incl: 2.5-acre Les Demoiselles (LATOUR, JADOT), BOUCHARD PERE, CHARTRON & TREBUCHET, Deleger, LEFLAIVE, Niellon, PRIEUR.

Cheverny Lo r p w dr (sp) *→*** DYA   Loire VDQS from nr Chambord. Dry, crisp whites from Romorantin or Sauv Bl; Gamay, Pinot N or Cab reds; generally light but tasty.

Chevillon, R 21-acre estate at NUITS-ST-GEORGES; outstanding winemaking.

Chignin Savoie w dr s DYA   Light, soft white from Jacquère grapes for Alpine summers. Chignin-Bergeron is best and liveliest.

Chinon Lo r *** 82 83' 85 86 88 89' 90' 91   Juicy, variably rich Cab F from TOURAINE. Drink cool, young; treat exceptional vintages like BORDEAUX. Top growers: Baudry, Couly-Dutheil (esp Clos de l'Echo), Druet, Joguet, Raffault, Dom de Roncée.

Chiroubles Burg r *** 88 89 90 91   Good but tiny BEAUJOLAIS CRU next to FLEURIE; freshly fruity, silky wine for early drinking (1–3 yrs). Growers incl Cheysson, DUBOEUF, Fourneau, Passot, Raousset, and the coop.

Chorey-lès-Beaune Burg r ** 83 85 86 87 88 89 90   Minor AC on flat land N of BEAUNE, notable for 2 fine growers: Jacques Germain (Ch de Chorey) and TOLLOT-BEAUT.

Chusclan Rh r p w dr *→** 88 89 90   Village of COTE DU RHONE-VILLAGES. Middle-weight wines (rosé best) from the coop. Labels incl Cuvée des Monticaud, Seigneurie de Gicon.

Cissac HAUT-MEDOC village just W of PAUILLAC.

Clair, Bruno Recent little domaine at MARSANNAY. Vg wines from GEVREY-CHAMBERTIN (esp CLOS DE BEZE), FIXIN, MOREY-ST-DENIS, SAVIGNY.

Clairet Very light red wine, almost rosé.

Clairette Traditional white grape of the MIDI. Can give soft, pretty wine.

Clairette de Bellegarde Midi w dr * DYA   Nr Nîmes: plain, neutral white.

Clairette de Die Rh w dr s/sw sp ** NV   Popular dry or (better) semi-sweet, MUSCAT-flavoured, sparkling wine from E Rhône; or straight, dry CLAIRETTE white, surprisingly ageing well 3–4 yrs. Worth trying.

Clairette du Languedoc Midi w dr * DYA   Plain, neutral white from nr Montpellier, but watch for improvements.

Clape, La Midi r p w dr *→**   A name to note. Full-bodied VDQS wines from limestone hills between Narbonne and the sea. The red gains character after 2–3 yrs, the Malvasia white even longer. Vg rosé. Some experiments with Chard.

Claret Traditional English term for red BORDEAUX.

Climat Burgundian word for individual named v'yd, eg BEAUNE Grèves.

Clos A term carrying some prestige, reserved for distinct, usually walled, v'yds, often in one ownership. Frequent in Burgundy and ALSACE. Les Clos is CHABLIS' Grandest Cru.

Clos de Bèze *See* Chambertin-Clos de Bèze.

Clos de la Roche Burg r *** 71 72 76 78 82 83 85' 86 87 88' 89 90   38-acre GRAND CRU at MOREY-ST-DENIS. Powerful, complex wine like CHAMBERTIN for v long ageing. Producers incl BOUCHARD PERE, BOUREE, CASTAGNIER, DUJAC, Lignier, PONSOT, REMY, ROUSSEAU.

Clos des Lambrays Burg r *** 78 83 85 86 87 88' 89 90   15-acre GRAND CRU v'yd at MOREY-ST-DENIS. Changed hands in '79 after a shaky period. Now looking good (for a v long life).

Clos des Mouches Burg r w dr ***   Splendid PREMIER CRU BEAUNE v'yd, largely owned by DROUHIN. Drouhin's white from this v'yd is spicy, oaky, memorable.

Clos de Tart Burg r *** 76 78 79 82 83' 85' 86 87 88' 89 90 18-acre GRAND CRU at MOREY-ST-DENIS, owned by MOMMESSIN. At best wonderfully fragrant, whether young or old.

Clos de Vougeot Burg r *** 76 78 82 83 85 86 87 88 89 90 124-acre COTE DE NUITS GRAND CRU with many owners. Variable, occasionally sublime. Maturity depends on the grower's philosophy, technique and position on hill. Top growers incl CLAIR-DAU, DROUHIN, Drouhin-Laroze, ENGEL, FAIVELEY, GRIVOT, Gros, Hudelot-Noëllat, JADOT, LEROY, Chantal Lescure, MEO-CAMUZET, Mugneret, Rebourseau, ROUMIER.

Clos du Roi Burg r *** Part of GRAND CRU CORTON. Also a BEAUNE PREMIER CRU.

Clos St-Denis Burg r *** 76 78 79 82 83' 85 86 87 88 89 90 16-acre GRAND CRU at MOREY-ST-DENIS. Splendid sturdy wine growing silky with age. Growers incl DUJAC, Lignier, PONSOT.

Clos St-Jacques Burg r *** 71 76 78 79 80 82 83 84 85' 86 87 88' 89 90 17-acre PREMIER CRU of GEVREY-CHAMBERTIN. Excellent, powerful, velvety wine, often better (and dearer) than some of the CHAMBERTIN GRANDS CRUS. Main grower: ROUSSEAU.

Clos St-Jean Burg r *** 78 79 82 83' 85 86 87 88 89 90 36-acre PREMIER CRU of CHASSAGNE-MONTRACHET. Vg red, more solid than subtle, from eg Ch de la Maltroye. NB Domaine RAMONET.

Coche-Dury 16-acre MEURSAULT domaine (1+ acre CORTON-CHARLEMAGNE) with sky-high reputation for oak-perfumed wines. Also vg ALIGOTE.

Cognac Town and region of W France, and its brandy.

Collioure Pyr r ** 82 83 85 86 88 89 90 Strong, dry red from BANYULS area. Tiny production. Top growers include de Baillaury, Guy de Barlande, Dom du Mas Blanc.

Condrieu Rh w dr **** DYA Outstanding soft, fragrant white of great character (and price) from the VIOGNIER grape, planted on only 35+ acres. Top growers: DELAS, Dumazet, GUIGAL, Pinchon, Ch du Rozay, Vernay. CHATEAU-GRILLET is similar.

Corbières Midi r (p w) *—*** 88 89 90 Good, vigorous, bargain reds, steadily improving and now rewarded with AC. Rarely disappointing at their price. Best growers incl Ch'x Aiguilloux, de Cabriac, des Ollieux, de Quéribus, Dom de Villemajou; Coops de Embrès et Castelmaur, Paziols, St-Laurent-Cabrerisse, etc.

Cordier, Ets D Important BORDEAUX shipper and château-owner, including Ch'x CANTEMERLE, GRUAUD-LAROSE, LAFAURIE-PEYRAGUEY, MEYNEY, TALBOT, and also SANCERRE, Clos de la Poussie. Active in Texas, too.

Cornas Rh r ***—**** 78' 79 80 81 83' 84 85' 86 88 89 90 Expanding 400-acre district S of HERMITAGE. Typical sturdy dark Rhône Syrah wine of vg quality. Needs 5–15 yrs' ageing. Top growers incl de Barjac, Clape, DELAS, JABOULET, Verset.

Corsica (Corse) Strong wines of all colours. Better ACs incl AJACCIO, CAP CORSE, PATRIMONIO, SARTENE. Vin de Pays: ILE DE BEAUTE!

Corton Burg r **** 76' 78' 82 83 85' 86' 87 88 89 90 Only GRAND CRU red of the COTE DE BEAUNE. 200 acres in ALOXE-CORTON incl CLOS DU ROI and Les Bressandes. Rich and powerful, should age well. Many good growers.

Corton-Charlemagne Burg w dr **** 78' 79 82 83 85 86 87 88 89 90 The white section (one-third) of CORTON. Rich, spicy, lingering wine. Behaves like a red and ages magnificently. Top growers: BONNEAU DU MARTRAY, Dubreuil-Fontaine, JADOT, LATOUR, Rapet.

Costières de Nîmes Midi r p w dr *—*** DYA Large new AC of improving quality from the Rhône delta. Formerly Costières du Gard. NB Ch de Nages, Ch de la Tuilerie.

Coteaux Champenois Champ r w (p) dr *** DYA for whites The AC for non-sparkling CHAMPAGNE. Vintages (if mentioned) follow those for Champagne. Do not pay inflated prices.

Coteaux d'Aix-en-Provence Prov r p w dr *—*** AC on the move. Established CH VIGNELAURE challenged by Ch'x de Beaupré, Commanderie de la Bargemone, Fonscolombe. *See also* COTEAUX DES BAUX-EN-PROVENCE.

Coteaux d'Ancenis Lo r p w dr ★ DYA   Light Cab and Gamay reds, and rosés; sharpish whites from MUSCADET country.

Coteaux de la Loire Lo w dr sw ★★→★★★★ 79 82 85 86 88' 89 90'   Forceful and fragrant Chenin Bl whites from ANJOU. The best are in SAVENNIERES. Excellent as an aperitif.

Coteaux de l'Ardèche See l'Ardèche.

Coteaux de l'Aubance Lo p w dr/sw ★★ DYA   Light and typical minor ANJOU wines. The best are MOELLEUX from Dom Richou and Dom des Rochettes (to age, not DYA).

Coteaux de Peyriac Midi r p ★ DYA   The most-used VIN DE PAYS name of the Aude *département*. Huge quantities.

Coteaux de Pierrevert Rh r p w dr sp ✳ DYA   Minor southern VDQS nr Manosque. Well-made coop wine, mostly rosé, with fresh whites.

Coteaux de Saumur Lo w dr/sw ★★ DYA   Potentially fine, semi-sweet Chenin Bl.

Coteaux des Baux-en-Provence Prov r p w dr ★→★★★   Neighbour of COTEAUX D'AIX, also gathering speed. NB The excellent Domaine de Trévallon (Cab and Syrah) and Mas de Gourgonnier.

Coteaux du Giennois Lo r p w dr ★ DYA   Up-and-coming Loire area N of SANCERRE. Light Gamay and Pinot N, Sauvignon à la SANCERRE. Top grower: Balland-Chapuis.

Coteaux du Languedoc Midi r p w dr ★→★★   Scattered well-above-ordinary Midi areas with AC status. The best reds (eg CABRIERES, LA CLAPE, FAUGERES, St-Georges-d'Orques, Quatourze, ST-CHINIAN, St-Saturnin) age for 2–3 yrs. Now also some good whites from Chard, etc. Follow with increasing interest.

Coteaux du Layon Lo w s/sw sw ★★ 79 82 85 86 88' 89 90   The heart of ANJOU, centred on Rochefort, S of Angers, making sweet Chenin Bl with admirable acidity, ageing almost forever: excellent aperitif. Top ACs: BONNEZEAUX, C du L-Chaume. Top producer: TOUCHAIS.

Coteaux du Loir Lo r p w dr sw ★→★★ 78 82 83 85 86 88 89' 90   Small region N of Tours. Occasionally excellent wines of Chenin Bl, Gamay, Cab, etc. Best v'yd: JASNIERES. The Loir is a tributary of the Loire.

Coteaux du Lyonnais Rh r p (w dr) ✳ DYA   Junior BEAUJOLAIS, and whites in keeping. Best EN PRIMEUR.

Coteaux du Tricastin Rh r p w dr ✳ 85 86 88 89 90   Fringe COTES DU RHONE of increasing quality from S of Valence. Attractive PRIMEUR red. Domaine de Grangeneuve is best.

Coteaux du Vendômois Lo r p w dr ★ DYA   Fringe Loire from N of Blois with VDQS rank. Mainly Gamay and Pineau d'Aunis (for rosé).

Coteaux Varois Prov r p w dr ★→★★   Substantial new VDQS zone: California-style Dom de St-Jean de Villecroze makes vg red.

Côte(s) Means hillside; generally a superior v'yd to those on the plain. Many ACs are prefixed by either 'Côtes' or 'Coteaux', meaning the same thing. In ST-EMILION it distinguishes the valley slopes from the higher plateau.

Côte Chalonnaise Burg r w dr sp ★★→★★★   Lesser-known v'yd area between BEAUNE and MACON. See Givry, Mercurey, Montagny, Rully. Alias 'Région de Mercurey'.

Côte de Beaune Burg r w dr ★★→★★★★   Used geographically: the S half of the COTE D'OR. Applies as an AC only to parts of BEAUNE.

Côte de Beaune-Villages Burg r w dr ★★ 85 86 87 88 89 90   Regional AC for secondary wines of the classic area. Cannot be labelled 'Côte de Beaune' without either '-Villages' or the village name.

Côte de Brouilly Burg r ★★★ 88 89 90 91   Fruity, rich, vigorous BEAUJOLAIS CRU. One of best. Leaders: Dom de Chavanne, Ch Delachanel, Ch Thivin.

Côtes de la Malpère Midi r ✳   Recent VDQS for reds half-way in style between BORDEAUX and Midi.

Côte de Nuits Burg r (w dr) ★★→★★★★ N half of CÔTE D'OR. Mostly red wine.

Côte de Nuits-Villages Burg r (w) ★★ 85 86 87 88 89 90 A junior AC for extreme N and S ends of Côte; well worth investigating for bargains.

Côte d'Or *Département* name applied to the central and principal Burgundy v'yd slopes, consisting of the CÔTE DE BEAUNE and CÔTE DE NUITS. The name is not used on labels.

Côte Rôtie Rh r ★★★→★★★★ 78 79 80 82 83' 84 85' 86 88 89 90 Potentially the finest Rhône red, from just S of Vienne; achieves complex, almost BORDEAUX-like delicacy with age. Top growers include Champet, CHAPOUTIER, DELAS, Dervieux, Gentaz-Barge, GUIGAL, JABOULET, Jamet, Jasmin, Rostaing, VIDAL-FLEURY.

Côtes d'Auvergne Central France r p (w dr) ★ DYA Flourishing small VDQS area nr Clermont-Ferrand. Red (at best) like light BEAUJOLAIS. Chanturgues is the best known. Corent is a rosé.

Côtes de Blaye Bx w dr ★ DYA Run-of-the-mill BORDEAUX white from BLAYE. (Better reds are called PREMIÈRES CÔTES DE BLAYE.)

Côtes de Bordeaux Saint-Macaire Bx w dr/sw ★ DYA Run-of-the-mill BORDEAUX white from E of SAUTERNES.

Côtes de Bourg Bx r ★→★★★ 82 83 85 86 88 89 90 Appellation used for many of the better reds of BOURG. Ch'x incl DE BARBE, La Barde, DU BOUSQUET, Brûlesécaille, La Croix de Millorit, Falfas, Font Guilhem, Grand-Jour, de la Grave, La Grolet, Guerry, Lalibarde, Lamothe, Mendoce, Peychaud, Rousset, Tayac, de Thau.

Côtes de Castillon Bx r ★→★★★ 82 85 86 88 89 90 Flourishing region just E of ST-ÉMILION. Similar wines, though a touch lighter. Ch'x incl Beauséjour, La Clarière-Laithwaite, Ste-Colombe, Fonds-Rondes, Haut-Tuquet, Lartigue, Moulin-Rouge, PITRAY, Rocher-Bellevue.

Côtes de Duras Dordogne r w dr ★ 88 89 90 Neighbour to BERGERAC, dominated by its v competent coop. Similar light wines.

Côtes-de-Francs Bx r w dr ★★ 82 83 85 86 88' 89' 90 Fringe BORDEAUX from E of ST-ÉMILION, next door to CASTILLON. Increasingly attractive and tasty wines, esp from Ch'x de Belcier, La Claverie, de Francs, Lauriol, PUYGUERAUD, la Prade.

Côtes de Fronsac *See* Fronsac.

Côtes de Gascogne SW France w (r) dr ★ DYA VIN DE PAYS gaining a name for deliciously floral Sauv whites in bountiful supply. Top growers: Domaine de Biau, Grassa, the Coop de Plaimont.

Côtes de Montravel Dordogne w dr/sw ★ DYA Part of BERGERAC; traditionally medium-sweet wine, now often dry.

Côtes de Provence Prov r p w dr ★→★★★ The wine of Provence; still often with more alcohol than character, though standards are rapidly improving as new investors move in. Commanderie de Peyrassol, Dom Gavoty, Domaine OTT, Dom Richeaume are leaders. 60% is rosé, 30% red. *See* Coteaux d'Aix, Bandol, etc.

Côtes de St-Mont SW France r w p dr ★ Promising VDQS from the Gers, not unlike MADIRAN. The same coop as CÔTES DE GASCOGNE.

Côtes de Thongue Midi r w dr ★ DYA Above average VIN DE PAYS from the HÉRAULT.

Côtes de Toul E France p r w dr ★ DYA Very light wines from Lorraine; mainly VIN GRIS (rosé).

Côtes de Forez Central France r p ★ DYA Light Beaujolais-style Gamay red, can be good in warm yrs.

Côtes du Frontonnais SW France r p →★★ DYA Local wine of Toulouse, gaining admirers everywhere. Ch Bellevue-la-Forêt (250 acres) makes outstanding, silky red and rosé 'l'Allégresse'.

Côtes du Haut-Roussillon SW France br sw ★→★★ NV Area for VINS DOUX NATURELS N of Perpignan.

Côtes du Jura Jura r p w dr (sp) ★ DYA Various light tints and tastes. ARBOIS is theoretically better.

Côtes du Luberon Rh r p w dr sp ★→★★ Improving country wines from N

Provence. The stars are Ch de Mille and Ch Val-Joanis, with good, largely Syrah, red, and whites as well. Others incl a good coop and Ch de la Canorgue.

Côtes du Marmandais Dordogne r p w dr ✶ DYA Light wines from SE of BORDEAUX. The coop at Cocumont makes most of the best.

Côtes du Rhône Rh r p w dr ✶→✶✶✶ 88 89 90 The basic AC of the Rhône valley. Best drunk young – even as PRIMEUR. Wide variations of quality due to grape ripeness: tending to rise with alcohol %. *See* Côtes du Rhone-Villages.

Côtes du Rhône-Villages Rh r p w dr ✶→✶✶✶ 88 89 90 The wine of the 17 best villages of the S Rhône. Substantial and on the whole reliable. Sometimes delicious. *See* Beaumes de Venise, Cairanne, Chusclan, Laudun, Rasteau, etc.

Côtes du Roussillon Pyr r p w dr ✶→✶✶✶ 88 89 90 91 Country wine of E Pyrenees. The hefty CARIGNAN reds are best and can be very tasty. Some whites are sharp VINS VERTS.

Côtes du Roussillon-Villages Pyr r ✶✶ 85 86 88 89 90 91 The region's best reds; incl CARAMANY, LATOUR DE FRANCE. Best labels: Cuvée Blanes, Cazes Frères, Ch de Corneilla, Ch de Jau, Coop Les Vignerons Catalans.

Côtes du Ventoux Prov r (w dr) ✶✶ 88 89 90 Booming AC for tasty reds between the Rhône and Provence. La Vieille Ferme, owned by J-P Perrin of CH DE BEAUCASTEL, is top producer.

Côtes du Vivarais Prov r p w dr ✶ DYA Pleasant country wines from S Massif Central. Like light COTES DU RHONE: eg Domaine de Belvezet.

Côtes Roannaises Central France r ✶ DYA Minor Gamay region between Lyon and the Loire.

Coulée de Serrant Lo w dr/sw ✶✶✶ 76 78 79 81 82 83 85 86 88 89' 90' 10-acre Chenin Bl v'yd on N bank of LOIRE at SAVENNIERES, ANJOU. Intense, strong, fruity/sharp wine, good as an aperitif. Ages almost for ever.

Coussergues, Domaine de Midi r w p d ✶ DYA Large estate in notorious territory nr Beziers. Experiments with Chard etc producing bargains.

Crémant In CHAMPAGNE means 'creaming' – ie half-sparkling. Since '75 an AC for high quality, champagne-method sparkling wines from ALSACE, the Loire, BOURGOGNE and most recently LIMOUX – often a notable bargain. The term will be phased out in Champagne.

Crémant de Loire w dr sp ✶✶ NV High quality sparkling wine from ANJOU, TOURAINE and Pays Nantais.

Crépy Savoie w dr ✶✶ DYA Light, soft, Swiss-style white from S shore of Lake Geneva. 'Crépitant' has been coined for its faint fizz.

Criots-Bâtard-Montrachet Burg w ✶✶✶ 78 79 83 85 86 88 89 90 4-acre neighbour to BATARD-MONTRACHET. Similar wine without extreme pungency.

Crozes-Hermitage Rh r (w dr) ✶✶ 83 86 88 89 90 Larger less distinguished neighbour to HERMITAGE. Often robust and excellent reds, but choose carefully: eg Fayolle et Fils, Alain Graillot, Domaine de Thalabert of JABOULET, GAEC de la Syrah. Jaboulet's Mule Blanche is good white.

Cru Growth, as in first-growth – meaning v'yd. Also, in BEAUJOLAIS, one of the top 10 villages.

Cru Bourgeois General term for MEDOC châteaux below CRU CLASSE.

Cru Bourgeois Supérieur (Cru Grand Bourgeois) Official rank one better than the last. Must be aged in barrels.

Cru Classé Classed growth. One of the first five official quality classes of the MEDOC, classified in 1855. Also any classed growth of another district (eg GRAVES, ST-EMILION, SAUTERNES).

Cru Grand Bourgeois Exceptionnel Official rank above CRU BOURGEOIS SUPERIEUR, immediately below CRU CLASSE. Several fine châteaux are unofficially acknowledged as Exceptionnel, which makes them on a par with many CRUS CLASSES.

Cruse et Fils Frères Senior BORDEAUX shipper. Owned by Société des Vins de France. The Cruse family (not the company) own CH D'ISSAN.

Cussac Village just S of ST-JULIEN. Appellation HAUT-MEDOC. Top ch'x: BEAUMONT, LANESSAN.

Cuve Close Short-cut method of making sparkling wine in a tank. The sparkle dies away in the glass much quicker than with METHODE CHAMPENOISE wine.

Cuvée The quantity of wine produced in a *cuve* or vat. Also a word of many uses, incl 'blend' (as in CHAMPAGNE). In Burgundy interchangeable with 'Cru'. Often just refers to a 'lot' of wine.

Cuvée de la Commanderie Pleasant blends of MEDOC, GRAVES and (best) SAUTERNES made for the Commanderie du Bontemps, the ceremonial/promotional body of the MEDOC and GRAVES.

Degré alcoolique Degrees of alcohol, ie percent by volume.

Deiss, Marcel Fine ALSACE grower at Bergheim with 50 acres, incl splendid Ries from GRAND CRU Schoenenberg.

Delas Frères Old and worthy firm of Rhône wine specialists with v'yds at Colnas, CONDRIEU, COTE ROTIE, HERMITAGE. Top wines: Condrieu, Marquise de Tourette HERMITAGES (red and white). Owned by DEUTZ.

Delorme, André Leading COTE CHALONNAISE merchants and growers. Specialists in sparkling wine and excellent RULLY.

De Luze, A & Fils BORDEAUX shipper owned by Rémy-Martin of COGNAC. Members of the De Luze family own CH PAVEIL DE LUZE.

Demi-Sec Half-dry: in practice more than half sweet.

Depagneux, Jacques de Cie Well-regarded merchants of BEAUJOLAIS.

Deutz Brut NV; 79 81 82 85; Rosé 82 85; Bl de Blancs 81 82 85 One of the best of the smaller CHAMPAGNE houses. Full-flavoured wines. Luxury brands: Cuvée William Deutz (79, 82, 85) and Rosé.

Domaine Property, particularly in Burgundy.

Dom Pérignon 71 73 75 76 78 82 83 85 87; Rosé 78 80 83 85 Luxury brand of MOET & CHANDON, named after the legendary Abbey cellarmaster who 'invented' CHAMPAGNE. Astonishing consistent quality.

Dopff 'au Moulin' Ancient and top-class family wine house at Riquewihr, ALSACE. Best wines: GEWURZ Eichberg, Ries Schoenenbourg. Pioneers of sparkling wine in Alsace.

Dopff & Irion Another excellent Riquewihr (ALSACE) business. Best wines incl MUSCAT les Amandiers, Ries de Riquewihr.

Doudet-Naudin Burgundy merchant and grower at SAVIGNY-LES-BEAUNE. V'yds incl BEAUNE-CLOS DU ROI. Unfashionably dark, long-lived wines, supplied to Berry Bros & Rudd of London, eventually come good.

Dourthe Frères BORDEAUX merchant offering a wide range of ch'x, mainly good CRUS BOURGEOIS, incl CH'X BELGRAVE, MAUCAILLOU, TRONQUOY-LALANDE. Beau-Mayne is their well-made brand.

Doux Sweet.

DRC *See* Romanée-Conti, Domaine de la.

Drouhin, J & Cie Deservedly prestigious Burgundy grower (130 acres) and merchant with highest standards. Cellars in BEAUNE; v'yds in Beaune, CHABLIS, CLOS DE VOUGEOT, MUSIGNY, etc. Drouhin also owns JAFFELIN ET CIE and a v'yd in Oregon. Top wines incl Beaune CLOS DES MOUCHES, GRIOTTE-CHAMBERTIN and PULIGNY-MONTRACHET Les Folatières.

Duboeuf, Georges Top-class BEAUJOLAIS merchant at Romanèche-Thorin. The leader of the region in every sense, with a huge range of admirable wines, incl MOULIN-A-VENT, untypically aged in new oak.

Dubos High-level BORDEAUX *négociant*.

Duclot BORDEAUX *négociant* specializing in top growths. Linked with MOUEIX.

Dujac, Domaine Fashionable burgundy grower (Jacques Seysses) at MOREY-ST-DENIS with v'yds in that village, BONNES-MARES, ECHEZEAUX, GEVREY-CHAMBERTIN, etc. His wines are splendidly vivid and long-lived. Now planting Cab and Chard in COTEAUX VAROIS.

Dulong Highly competent BORDEAUX merchant now breaking all the rules with Rebelle blends.

Durup, Jean One of the biggest CHABLIS growers with 140 acres, including

DOMAINE DE L'EGLANTIERE and admirable Ch de Maligny.

Duval-Leroy Coteaux Champenoise r w; NV; Brut; Vintage Fleur de Champagne Large producer at Vertus with high standards.

Echézeaux Burg r *** 76 78' 79 82 83' 85 86 87 88 89 90 74-acre GRAND CRU between VOSNE-ROMANEE and CLOS DE VOUGEOT. Can be superlative, fragrant, without great weight, eg ENGEL, Gouroux, Jacqueline Jayer, MONGEARD-MUGNERET, Mugneret, Dom de la ROMANEE-CONTI.

The Confrérie des Chevaliers du Tastevin is Burgundy's wine fraternity and the most famous of its kind in the world. It was founded in 1933 by a group of Burgundian patriots, headed by Camille Rodier and Georges Faiveley, to rescue their beloved Burgundy from a period of slump and despair by promoting its inimitable products. Today it regularly holds banquets with elaborate and sprightly ceremonies, for 600 guests, at its headquarters, the Cistercian château in the Clos de Vougeot. The Confrérie has branches in many countries and members among lovers of wines all over the world. See also Tastevin, page 53.

Edelzwicker Alsace w * DYA Modest, light white from mixture of grapes, often fruity and good.

Engel, R Well-known grower of VOSNE-ROMANEE, CLOS DE VOUGEOT, ECHEZEAUX.

Entre-Deux-Mers Bx w dr * DYA Standard dry white BORDEAUX from between the Garonne and Dordogne rivers. Often a good buy, as techniques improve. Ch'x Gournin, Latour-Laguens, Moulin de Launay, ST-BONNET, Séguin, Thieuley.

L'Estandon The VIN ORDINAIRE of Nice (AC COTES DE PROVENCE).

l'Etoile Jura w dr sp (sw) ** Subregion of the Jura known for stylish whites, incl VIN JAUNE, similar to CHATEAU-CHALON; good sparkling.

Faiveley, J Family-owned growers (with 182 acres) and merchants at NUITS-ST-GEORGES, with v'yds in CHAMBERTIN-CLOS DE BEZE, CHAMBOLLE-MUSIGNY, CORTON, MERCUREY, NUITS (150 acres). Consistent high quality recently. 88s are models. Wines for serious ageing.

Faller, Théo Top ALSACE grower at the Domaine Weinbach, Kaysersberg. Concentrated, firm, dry wines needing unusually long ageing.

Faugères Midi r (p w dr) *→*** 88 89 90 Isolated COTEAUX DU LANGUEDOC village with above-average wine. Gained AC status in '82.

Fessy, Sylvain Dynamic BEAUJOLAIS merchant with wide range.

Fèvre, William Excellent CHABLIS grower with the biggest GRAND CRU holding (40 acres). Spices his wines with new oak. One whimsy wine he calls Napa Vallée de France. His label is Domaine de la Maladière.

Fiefs Vendéens Lo r p w dr * DYA Up-and-coming VDQS for light wines from the Vendée, S of the W Loire.

Fitou Midi r ** 85 86 88 89 90 91 Superior CORBIERES red; powerful, ages well. Best from coops at Cascastel, Mont Tuch and Tuchan.

Fixin Burg r ** 78 83 85 86 87 88 89 90 A worthy and under-valued neighbour to GEVREY-CHAMBERTIN. Often splendid reds. Best v'yds: Clos du Chapitre, Les Hervelets, Clos Napoléon. Top growers: Bertheau, CLAIR, Gelin, Gelin-Moulin, FAIVELEY.

Fleurie Burg r *** 88 89 90 91 The epitome of a BEAUJOLAIS CRU: fruity, scented, silky, racy. Top wines from Chapelle des Bois, Chignard, DUBOEUF, Ch de Fleurie, the coop.

Fortant de France Midi r p w * Brand (dressed to kill) of fair quality varietal wines from the neighbourhood of Sète. See Skalli.

Frais Fresh or cool.

Frappé Ice-cold.

Froid Cold.

Fronsac Bx r *→*** 82 83 85 86 88 89' 90 Picturesque area of increasingly fine reds just W of ST-EMILION. Ch'x incl de Carles, DALEM, LA DAUPHINE, Mayne-Vieil, LA RIVIERE, La Valade, La Vieille Cure, Villars. Give them time. See also Canon-Fronsac.

Frontignan Midi br sw ✱ NV   Strong, sweet and liquorous MUSCAT wine of ancient repute.

Gagnard-Delagrange, Jacques Estimable small (13-acre) grower of CHASSAGNE-MONTRACHET, including some MONTRACHET.

Gaillac SW France r p w dr sw sp ✱→✱✱✱ mostly DYA   Ancient area showing signs of new life after generations of dullness. Slightly fizzy Perlé is good value. Reds can age well. Ch Larroze is the quality leader. The major coop at Labastide de Lévis has recently produced some lovely, fruity wines esp from local Mauzac grapes.

Gamay *See* Grapes for red wine (pages 8–9).

Gard, Vin de Pays du The Gard *département* at the mouth of the Rhône makes many of the best VINS DE PAYS; incl the zones Coteaux Flaviens, Pont du Gard, Salaves, Uzège and Vaunage. Watch this area.

Geisweiler et Fils One of the bigger merchant houses of Burgundy, now owned by the Rehs of the Mosel. Cellars and 50 acres of v'yds at NUITS-ST-GEORGES, also 150 acres at Bevy in the HAUTES-COTES DE NUITS and 30 in the COTE CHALONNAISE.

Gevrey-Chambertin Burg r ✱✱✱ 82 83 85 86 87 88 89 90   The village containing the great CHAMBERTIN and many other noble v'yds (eg Cazetiers, Combe au Moine, PREMIERS CRUS CLOS ST-JACQUES, Clos des Varoilles), as well as a considerable number more commonplace. Growers incl BACHELET, Boillot, Damoy, DROUHIN, FAIVELEY, JADOT, Leclerc, LEROY, ROUSSEAU, ROTY, Roumier, TRAPET, Dom des VAROILLES.

Gewürztraminer The speciality grape of ALSACE: perfumed like old roses and often tasting like grapefruit.

Gigondas Rh r p ✱✱ 78 83 84 85 86 88 89 90   Worthy neighbour to CHATEAUNEUF-DU-PAPE. Strong, full-bodied, sometimes peppery wine, eg Dom du Cayron, Dom les Pallières, Dom du Pesquier, Dom Raspail-Ay, Dom St-Gayan, Ch du Trignon.

Gilbey, S A British firm long established as BORDEAUX growers and merchants at CH LOUDENNE in the MEDOC. Now owned by Grand Met.

Giraud, Camille Top small BEAUNE *négociant*. Wines from old vines.

Gisselbrecht, Louis High quality ALSACE shippers at Dambach-la-Ville.

Givry Burg r w dr ✱✱ 83 85 86 87 88 89 90   Underrated COTE CHALONNAISE village: light but tasty and typical burgundy from eg Dom Joblot, Clos Salomon, Baron Thénard.

Gosset NV Brut; Rosé NV; 81 82 83 85 Grande Réserve; Grande Millésime 83; Brut 85; Rosé 85   Small, v old CHAMPAGNE house at AY. Excellent full wines (esp Grande Réserve). Now linked with PHILIPPONNAT.

Goulaine, Château de The ceremonial showplace of MUSCADET; a noble family estate and its appropriate wine.

Goulet, Georges NV; Rosé 85; Crémant Bl de Blancs 83 85   High quality Reims CHAMPAGNE house linked with ABEL LEPITRE. Luxury brand: Cuvée du Centenaire (**79, 82, 83, 85**).

Goût Taste, eg *goût anglais* – as the English like it (ie dry).

Grand Cru One of the top Burgundy v'yds with its own *appellation contrôlée*. Similar meaning in ALSACE but more vague elsewhere. In ST-EMILION the third rank of ch'x, incl about 200 properties.

Grand Roussillon Midi br sw ✱✱ NV   Broad AC for MUSCAT and other sweet, fortified wines (VINS DOUX NATURELS) of E Pyrenees.

Grande Champagne The AC of the best area of COGNAC.

Grande Rue, La Burg r ✱✱✱   Recently-promoted GRAND CRU in VOSNE-ROMANEE, neighbour to ROMANEE-CONTI. Owners, the Lamarche family, could try harder.

Grands-Echézeaux Burg r ✱✱✱✱ 69 71 76 78 79 82 83 85 86 87 88 89 90   Superlative 22-acre GRAND CRU next to CLOS DE VOUGEOT. Viz: DROUHIN, ENGEL, MONGEARD-MUGNERET, Dom de la ROMANEE-CONTI.

Gratien, Alfred and Gratien & Meyer Excellent smaller CHAMPAGNE house (fine, v dry, long-lasting wine: **79, 82, 83, 85**) and its counterpart at SAUMUR on the Loire. (Vg Cuvée Flamme.)

Graves Bx r w ★→★★★★ Large region S of Bordeaux city with excellent soft, earthy reds, and recently, much improved dry whites.

Graves de Vayres Bx r w ★ Part of ENTRE-DEUX-MERS; of no special character.

Griotte-Chambertin Burg r ★★★★ 76 78′ 79 83 85′ 86 87 88 89 90 14-acre GRAND CRU adjoining CHAMBERTIN. Similar wine, but less masculine and more 'tender'. Growers incl DROUHIN, PONSOT.

Grivot, Jean 25-acre COTE DE NUITS domaine, in RICHEBOURG, NUITS PREMIERS CRUS, VOSNE-ROMANEE, CLOS DE VOUGEOT, etc. Top quality.

Gros Plant du Pays Nantais Lo w ✷ DYA Junior cousin of MUSCADET, sharper and lighter; made of the COGNAC grape also known as Folle Blanche, Ugni Blanc, etc.

Guigal, E and M Celebrated growers and merchants of CONDRIEU, COTE ROTIE and HERMITAGE. Since ′85 owners of VIDAL-FLEURY. By ageing single-v′yd Cote Rôtie (La Landonne, La Mouline, La Turque) in new oak Guigal breaks local tradition, and has lost at least one customer as a result.

Guyon, Antonin Considerable domaine at ALOXE-CORTON with fine wines from CHAMBOLLE-MUSIGNY, CORTON, etc, and HAUTES-COTES DE NUITS.

Haut-Benauge Bx w dr ✷ DYA AC for a limited area in ENTRE-DEUX-MERS.

Hautes-Côtes de Beaune Burg r w dr ✷✷ 85 86 87 88 89 90 Appellation for a dozen villages in the hills behind the COTE DE BEAUNE. Light wines, worth investigating. Top growers: Cornu, Mazilly.

Hautes-Côtes de Nuits Burg r w dr ✷✷ 85 86 87 88 89 90 As above, for the COTE DE NUITS. An area on the way up. Top growers: C Cornu, Jayer-Gilles. Also has large BEAUNE coop; good wines from GEISWEILER.

Haut-Médoc Bx r ★→★★★ 70 75 76 78 79 81 82 83 85 86 87 88 89 90 Big AC including all the best areas of the MEDOC. Most of the zone has communal ACs (eg MARGAUX, PAUILLAC). Some excellent châteaux (eg LA LAGUNE) are simply AC HAUT-MEDOC.

Haut-Montravel Dordogne w sw ✷ 88 89 90 Medium-sweet BERGERAC.

Haut Poitou Lo w (r) dr ★→★★ DYA Up-and-coming young AC area S of ANJOU. Cooperative makes vg whites, incl Chard and Sauv Bl.

Heidsieck, Charles NV; 79 81 83 85; Rosé 81 83 Major CHAMPAGNE house of Reims, now controlled by Rémy Martin; also includes Trouillard and de Venoge. Luxury brands: Cuvée Champagne Charlie 81, 82, 83, Blanc des Millésimes 83. Fine quality recently, incl the NV.

Heidsieck, Monopole NV; Rosé; 79 82 83 85 Important CHAMPAGNE merchant and Reims grower now owned by MUMM. Vg luxury brand: Diamant Bleu (76, 79), Diamant Rosé 82, 85.

Henriot NV; Brut Souverain; Bl de Blancs Crémant NV; 79 82 85; Brut Rosé 81 83 85; Cuvée Baccarat 79 82 Old family CHAMPAGNE house linked with VEUVE CLICQUOT in the Möet Hennessy group. Very big dry style. Luxury private brand: Réserve Baron Philippe de Rothschild.

Hérault Midi The biggest v′yd *département* in France with 400,000 hectares of vines. Chiefly *vin ordinaire* but some good COTEAUX DU LANGUEDOC, and, more interestingly, Vins de Pays de l'Hérault breaking new ground.

Hermitage Rh r w dr ✷✷✷ 71 72 78′ 79 80 82 83′ 84 85 86 88 89 90 The 'manliest' wine of France. Dark, powerful and profound. Needs long ageing. The white is heady and golden; now usually made for early drinking, though the best wines mature for many years. Top makers: CHAPOUTIER, CHAVE, DELAS, Grippat, GUIGAL, JABOULET, Sorrel.

Hospices de Beaune Historic hospital in BEAUNE, with excellent v′yds in BEAUNE, CORTON, MEURSAULT, POMMARD, VOLNAY, etc, whose wines are auctioned on the third Sunday of each November.

Hugel Père & Fils The best-known ALSACE growers and merchants. Founded at Riquewihr in 1639 and still in the family. Best wines are sweet: Cuvées Exceptionnelles, SELECTIONS DES GRAINS NOBLES.

Ile de Beauté Name given to VINS DU PAYS from CORSICA. Two-thirds is red.

Impériale BORDEAUX bottle holding 8.5 normal bottles (6.4 litres).

Irancy ('Bourgogne Irancy') Burg r (p) ✹✹ 85 86 88 89 90 Good light red made nr CHABLIS from Pinot N and César. The best vintages are long-lived and mature well. To watch.

Irouléguy SW France r p (w dr) ✹✹ DYA Agreeable local wines, mainly Tannat reds, of the Basque country.

Jaboulet, Paul Old family firm at Tain, leading growers of HERMITAGE (esp La Chapelle ✹✹✹✹) and merchants of other Rhône wines.

Jaboulet-Vercherre & Cie Burgundy merchant house with v'yds (34 acres) in POMMARD, etc, and cellars in BEAUNE. Middling wines.

Jacquart Popular coop-made MARQUE of CHAMPAGNE.

Jadot, Louis Much-respected top quality Burgundy merchant house with v'yds (150 acres) in BEAUNE, esp those of CLAIR-DAU.

Jaffelin Independently run, high quality *négociant*, owned by DROUHIN.

Jardin de la France Name given to VINS DU PAYS of the Loire valley. The great majority is dry white.

Jasnières Lo w dr (r p) ✹✹✹ 76 78 79 82 83 85 86 88 89 90 V rare, dry, rather VOUVRAY-like wine of N TOURAINE.

Jaubertie, Domaine de la English-owned top BERGERAC estate (114 acres). Sumptuous luxury Sauv Bl, Cuvée Mirabelle. Equally fine Reserve red.

Jayer, Henri Tiny VOSNE-ROMANEE domaine acknowledged even by rivals as superlative. (Monsieur J retired in '88.)

Jeroboam In BORDEAUX a 6-bottle bottle (holding 4.5 litres), or triple magnum; in Champagne a double magnum.

Josmeyer Family house at Wintzenheim, ALSACE. Vg long-ageing wines, esp GEWURZ and Pinot Bl.

Juliénas Burg r ✹✹✹ 88 89 90 91 Leading CRU of BEAUJOLAIS: vigorous, fruity wine to keep 2–3 yrs. Growers incl Ch du Bois de la Salle, Dom Bottière, Ch des Capitans, Ch de Juliénas and the coop.

Jura *See* Côtes de Jura.

Jurançon SW France w sw dr ✹✹→✹✹✹ 82 83 85 86 88 89 90 Unusual, high-flavoured and long-lived speciality of Pau in the Pyrenean foothills, at best like wild-flower SAUTERNES. Not to be missed. Both sweet and dry should age well for several yrs. Top growers: Barrère, Chigné, Gaillot, Guirouilh, Lamouroux, Larredya, Ramonteu (Dom Cauhapé). Also the coop's Grain Sauvage.

Kientzheim-Kayserberg Important ALSACE coop for quality as well as style. Esp for GEWURZ.

Kreydenweiss Fine ALSACE grower with 24 acres at Andlau, esp for Pinot G, Pinot Bl and Ries. Top wine: Kastelberg.

Kriter Popular sparkler processed in Burgundy by PATRIARCHE.

Krug Grande Cuvée; Rosé; 64 66 69 71 73 75 76 79 81 82 83 85; Clos du Mesnil Bl de Blancs 79 80 82 Small but supremely prestigious CHAMPAGNE house. Full-bodied v dry wines of superlative quality. Owned by Rémy Martin (but no-one would know).

Kuentz-Bas Top-quality ALSACE grower and merchant at Husseren-les-Châteaux, esp for GEWURZ and Pinot G (Tokay d'Alsace).

Labarde Village just S of MARGAUX, incl in that AC. Best château: GISCOURS.

Labouré-Gontard Makes high-quality CREMANT DE BOURGOGNE at NUITS.

Labouré-Roi Reliable merchant at NUITS-ST-GEORGES. Many fine domaine wines, esp René Manuel's MEURSAULT, Chantal Lescure's Nuits and CLOS DE VOUGEOT. Also vg CHABLIS.

Ladoucette, de Leading producer of POUILLY-FUME, based at CH DE NOZET. Luxury brand: Baron de L. Also SANCERRE Comte Lafond.

Lafarge, Michel 23-acre COTE DE BEAUNE estate, with outstanding VOLNAYS.

Lafon, Domaine des 31-acres top quality Burgundy estate in MEURSAULT, LE MONTRACHET and VOLNAY.

Laguiche, Marquis de Largest owner of LE MONTRACHET. Magnificent wines made by DROUHIN.

Lalande de Pomerol Bx r ✹✹ 82 83 85 86 88 89 90 Neighbour to POMEROL. Wines similar but generally much less mellow. Top châteaux: Les

Annereaux, DE BELAIR, Belles-Graves, La Croix Bellevue, La Croix-St-André, Les Hauts-Conseillants, Les Hauts-Tuileries, Moncets, SIAURAC, TOURNEFEUILLE.

Langlois-Château Producer of sparkling SAUMUR, controlled by BOLLINGER.

Langon The principal town of the S GRAVES/SAUTERNES district.

Lanson Père & Fils Black Label NV; Rosé NV; Red Label 76 79 81 82 83 85 Important CHAMPAGNE house with cellars at Reims. Luxury brands: Noble Cuvée 81, 85. Black Label is a reliable, fresh NV.

Laroche Important grower (238 acres) and dynamic CHABLIS merchant, incl Domaines La Jouchère and Laroche. Also makes Ch de Puligny-Montrachet and blends good non-regional Chard.

Latour, Louis Famous Burgundy merchant and grower with v'yds (120 acres) in BEAUNE, CORTON, etc. Among the best for white wines, esp CHEVALIER-MONTRACHET, CORTON-CHARLEMAGNE, Les Demoiselles, MONTRACHET, good value MONTAGNY, bargain Chard from L'ARDECHE, etc.

Latour de France r (w dr) ★→★★ 88 89 90 New AC in COTES DE ROUSSILLON-VILLAGES.

Latricières-Chambertin Burg r ★★★ 76 78 82 83 85' 86 87 88 89 90 17-acre GRAND CRU neighbour of CHAMBERTIN. Similar wine, but lighter and 'prettier' eg from FAIVELEY, LEROY, PONSOT, TRAPET.

Laudun Rh r p w dr ✻ Village of COTES DU RHONE-VILLAGES. Attractive wines from the coop incl fresh whites. But Dom Palaquié is better.

Laugel, Michel One of the biggest ALSACE merchant houses at Marlenheim.

Laurent-Perrier NV; Rosé Brut; 78 79 81 82 85 Excellent and highly successful family-owned CHAMPAGNE house at Tours-sur-Marne. Luxury brand: Cuvée Grande Siècle (a blend of vintages, and recently released 85). Ultra Brut is best buy. See also Rodet.

Leflaive, Domaine Formerly considered the best of all white burgundy growers, at PULIGNY-MONTRACHET. Best v'yds: Bienvenue-, Chevalier-Montrachet, Clavoillons, Pucelles. Recent wines have lacked staying power.

Leflaive, Olivier Négociant at PULIGNY-MONTRACHET since '84, now with 22 acres of his own, nephew of the above. Reliable whites and reds, incl less famous ACs.

Léognan Bx r w dr ★★★ Leading village of GRAVES with its own AC: PESSAC-LEOGNAN. Best ch'x: DOMAINE DE CHEVALIER, HAUT-BAILLY and MALARTIC-LAGRAVIERE.

Leroy Important NEGOCIANT-ELEVEUR at AUXEY-DURESSES with a growing domaine and the finest stocks of old wines in Burgundy. Part-owners of the Dom de la ROMANEE-CONTI. In '88 bought the 35-acre Noëllat estate in CLOS VOUGEOT, NUITS, ROMANEE-ST-VIVANT, SAVIGNY, etc. Leroy's range, esp of CHAMBERTIN and neighbours, is magnificent.

Lichine, Alexis & Cie Post-war BORDEAUX merchants (formerly owned by the late Alexis Lichine), proprietors of Ch LASCOMBES. No connection with CH PRIEURE LICHINE.

Lie, sur On the lees. MUSCADET is often bottled straight from the vat, without racking or filtering, for maximum freshness.

Limoux Pyr r w dr ✻✻ NV Austerely dry, non-sparkling version of BLANQUETTE DE LIMOUX (sometimes labelled Limoux Nature) and a good claret-like red from the coop: Anne des Joyeuses. Vinavius (88, 89) is oak-aged and even better.

Lirac Rh r p (w dr) ✻✻ 85 86 88 89 90 Next village to TAVEL. Similar wine; the red overtaking the rosé, esp Dom Maby, Dom de la Mordorée, Dom St-Roch, Ch de Segriés.

Listel Midi r p w dr ★→★★ DYA Vast (4,000-acre+) historic estate on the sandy beaches of the Golfe du Lion. Owned by the giant Salins du Midi. Pleasant, light 'vins des sables' incl sparkling. Domaine du Bosquet is a fruity red. Domaine de Villeroy is a fresh BLANC DE BLANCS SUR LIE. Also fruity, almost non-alcoholic PETILLANT; and Ch de Malijay, COTES DU RHONE.

Listrac Bx r ★★→★★★ Village of HAUT-MEDOC next to MOULIS. Best ch'x: CLARKE, Fonréaud, FOURCAS-DUPRE, FOURCAS-HOSTEN.

Long-Depaquit Vg CHABLIS domaine (esp MOUTONNE), owned by BICHOT.

Lorentz Two small, high quality ALSACE houses at Bergheim: Gustave L and Jerome L, have the same management.

Loron & Fils Big-scale Burgundy grower and merchant at Pontanevaux; specialist in BEAUJOLAIS and sound VINS DE TABLE.

Loupiac Bx w sw ★★ 76 79 80 83 85 86 88 89 90 Across the R Garonne from SAUTERNES. Top châteaux: Clos-Jean, Haut-Loupiac, LOUPIAC-GAUDIET, RICAUD, Rondillon.

Ludon HAUT-MEDOC village S of MARGAUX. Best château: LA LAGUNE.

Lugny ('Mâcon-Lugny') Burg r w dr sp ★★ 88 89 90 91 Village next to VIRE with active and good coop. Wine of Les Genevrières v'yd is sold by Louis LATOUR.

Lupé-Cholet & Cie Merchants and growers at NUITS-ST-GEORGES controlled by BICHOT. Best estate wines: Clos de Lupé and Château Gris.

Lussac-St-Emilion Bx r ★★ 82 85 86 88 89 90 NE neighbour to ST-EMILION. Top châteaux incl Barbe Blanche, Bel Air, DU LYONNAT, Tour de Grenat, Villadière. Coop (at PUISSEGUIN) makes pleasant Roc de Lussac.

Macau HAUT-MEDOC village S of MARGAUX. Best château: CANTEMERLE.

Macération carbonique Traditional technique of fermentation with whole bunches of unbroken grapes in a closed vat. Fermentation inside each grape eventually bursts it, giving vivid and v fruity, mild wine for quick consumption. Esp in BEAUJOLAIS; now much used in the MIDI and elsewhere.

Machard de Gramont BURGUNDY family estate: cellars in NUITS and v'yds in BEAUNE, Nuits, POMMARD, SAVIGNY. Extremely well-made reds.

Mâcon Burg r w (p) dr ★★ 88 89 90 91 Southern district of sound, usually unremarkable reds and v tasty, dry (Chard) whites. Wine with a village name (eg Mâcon-Prissé) is better. POUILLY-FUISSE is best AC of the region. *See also* Mâcon-Villages.

Mâcon-Lugny *See* Lugny.

Mâcon Supérieur The same but slightly better, from riper grapes.

Mâcon-Villages Burg w dr ★★→★★★ 88 89 90 91 Increasingly well-made and typical white burgundies. Mâcon-Clessé, MACON-LUGNY, Mâcon-Prissé, MACON-VIRE, are examples.

Mâcon-Viré *See* Mâcon-Villages and Viré.

Macvin Jura w sw ★★ New AC for 'traditional' aperitif made from MARC and grape juice.

Madiran SW France r ★★★ 82 83 84 85 86 88 89 90 Dark, vigorous red from ARMAGNAC, like hard but fruity MEDOC with a hybrid elegance of its own. Ages 5–10 yrs. Top growers: Ch'x d'Arricau-Bordes, d'Aydié, Barréjat, Dom de Bouscassé, Laplace, Montus, Peyros.

Magenta, Duc de Burgundy estate (30 acres) based at CHASSAGNE-MONTRACHET, managed by JADOT.

Magnum A double bottle (1.5 litres).

Mähler-Besse First-class Dutch wine merchants in BORDEAUX, with a share in CH PALMER. Brands incl Cheval Noir.

Maire, Henri The biggest grower/merchant of JURA wines. Not the best.

Maranges Burg r ★★ New ('89) AC for 600-odd acres of S COTE DE BEAUNE, one-third PREMIER CRU.

Marc Grape skins after pressing; also the strong-smelling brandy made from them (*see* Italian 'Grappa').

Marcillac SW France r p ★ DYA Good rustic red from coop Cave de Valady, promoted to AC (too hastily) in '90.

Margaux Bx r ★★→★★★★★ 66 70 75 76 78 79 81 82 83' 85 86 87 88 89 90 Village of the HAUT-MEDOC making the most 'elegant' red BORDEAUX. The AC includes CANTENAC and several other villages as well. Top châteaux include LASCOMBES, MARGAUX, RAUSAN-SEGLA, etc.

Margnat Major producer of everyday VIN DE TABLE.

Marne et Champagne, Ste Recent but huge-scale CHAMPAGNE house, owner (since '91) of LANSON and many smaller brands.

Marque déposée Trademark.

Marsannay Burg p w (r) dr ******* 85 86 87 88 89 90 (rosé DYA) Village nr Dijon with fine, light red and delicate Pinot N rosé. Growers incl CLAIR, JADOT, Quillardet, TRAPET.

Mas de Daumas Gassac Midi r (w dr) ******* 80 81 82 83 84 85 86 87 88 89 90 The one 'first-growth' estate of the LANGUEDOC, producing potent, BORDEAUX-like, largely Cab wines on apparently unique soil. Also Rosé Frisant and since '87 a sumptuous white of blended Chard, Viognier, Petit Manseng, etc. Sensational quality.

Maufoux, Prosper Family firm of burgundy merchants at SANTENAY. Reliable wines, esp whites, keep well. Alias Marcel Amance.

Maury Pyr r sw *→** NV Red VIN DOUX NATUREL from ROUSSILLON.

Mazis (or Mazy) Chambertin Burg r ******* 76 78 82 83 85 86 87 88 89 90 30-acre GRAND CRU neighbour of CHAMBERTIN, sometimes equally potent. Best from FAIVELEY, HOSPICES DE BEAUNE, LEROY, ROTY.

Médoc Bx r ****** 78 82 83 85 86 87 88 89 90 AC for reds of the less good (northern) part of BORDEAUX's biggest and best district. Flavours tend to slight earthiness. HAUT-MEDOC is better. Top châteaux incl POTENSAC, LA TOUR-DE-BY.

Meffre, Gabriel The biggest S Rhône estate, based at GIGONDAS. Includes Ch de Vaudieu, CHATEAUNEUF-DU-PAPE. Variable quality.

Ménétou-Salon Lo r p w dr ****** DYA Attractive light wines from W of SANCERRE: Sauv Bl white, Pinot N red.

Méo-Camuzet V fine domaine in CLOS DE VOUGEOT, NUITS, RICHEBOURG, VOSNE-ROMANEE.

Mercier & Cie NV; 81 82 83 85; Rosé 81 82 83 85; 'Extra Rich' One of the biggest CHAMPAGNE houses at Epernay. Controlled by MOET ET CHANDON. Good commercial quality. Belle d'Or is the premium NV Cuvée.

Mercurey Burg r w dr ****** 83 85 86 87 88 89 90 Leading red wine village of the COTE CHALONNAISE. Good middle-rank burgundy incl more and improving whites. Growers incl Ch de Chamirey, Chanzy, FAIVELEY.

Mercurey, Région de The up-to-date way of referring to the COTE CHALONNAISE.

Métaireau, Louis The ringleader of a group of top MUSCADET growers. Expensive, well-finished wines.

Méthode champenoise The traditional laborious method of putting the bubbles into CHAMPAGNE by refermenting the wine in its bottle.

Meursault Burg w (r) dr *****→****** 78 82 83 85 86 88 89 90 COTE DE BEAUNE village with some of the world's greatest whites: savoury, dry but nutty and mellow. Best v'yds: Charmes, Genevrières, Perrières. Others vg incl Goutte d'Or, Meursault-Blagny, Poruzots, Tillets. Top growers incl AMPEAU, COCHE-DURY, Delagrange, Jobard, LAFON, LATOUR, MAGENTA, Manuel, Matrot, CH DE MEURSAULT, Michelot-Buisson, P Morey, G ROULOT. *See also* Blagny.

Meursault-Blagny *See* Blagny.

Midi General term for the S of France W of the Rhône delta. Dismal reputation, brilliant promise.

Minervois Midi r (p w) br sw *→** 85 86 88 89 90 91 Hilly VDQS area with some of the best wines of the MIDI: lively and full of flavour esp from Dom de Ste-Eulalie, Ch de Gourgazaud and La Livinère. Also sweet MUSCAT de St-Jean de Minervois.

Mis en bouteille au château/au domaine Bottled at the château, at the property or estate. NB *dans nos caves* (in our cellars) or *dans la région de production* (in the area of production) are often used although they mean little.

Moelleux Mellow. Used of the sweet wines of VOUVRAY, etc.

Moët & Chandon NV; Rosé 81 82 85 86 88; Dry Imperial 76 78 81 82 83 85 86 88 Much the biggest CHAMPAGNE merchant and grower, with cellars in Epernay, and sparkling wine branches in Argentina, Australia, Brazil, California and Spain. Consistent quality. Luxury brand: DOM PERIGNON.

Moillard Big family firm (Domaine Thomas-Moillard) of growers and merchants in NUITS-ST-GEORGES, making dark and v tasty wines, incl CLOS DU ROI, CLOS DE VOUGEOT, CORTON, etc.

Mommessin, J Major BEAUJOLAIS merchant. Owner of CLOS DE TART. White wines less successful.

Monbazillac Dordogne w sw ****** 71 75 76 78 79 80 83 85 86 88 89 90 Golden SAUTERNES-style wine from BERGERAC. Can age well. Ch Monbazillac and Ch Septy are best known.

Mondeuse Savoie r ****** DYA Red grape of SAVOIE. Good, vigorous, deep-coloured wine.

Mongeard-Mugneret 40-acre VOSNE-ROMANEE estate. Fine ECHEZEAUX, RICHEBOURG, SAVIGNY, VOSNE PREMIER CRU, VOUGEOT, etc.

Monopole V'yd under single ownership.

Montagne-St-Emilion Bx r ****** 82 83 85 86 88 89 90 NE neighbour of ST-EMILION with similar wines, becoming more important with each year. Top châteaux: St-André-Corbin, Calon, Haut-Gillet, ROUDIER, Teyssier, DES TOURS, VIEUX-CH-ST-ANDRÉ.

Montagny Burg w (r) dr ****** 88 89 90 COTE CHALONNAISE village. Between MACON and MEURSAULT, both geographically and gastronomically. Top producers: Louis LATOUR, Michel, Ch de la Saule, Cave Coop de Buxy.

Montée de Tonnerre Burg w dr ******* 86 88 89 90 91 Famous and excellent PREMIER CRU of CHABLIS.

Monthélie Burg r (w dr) ****→***** 78 82 83 85 86 87 88 89 90 Little-known neighbour and sometimes almost equal of VOLNAY. Excellent fragrant reds. Growers incl BOUCHARD PERE, DROUHIN, Garaudet, Ch de Monthélie (de Suremain), Monthélie-Douhairet.

Montlouis Lo w sw dr (sp) ****** 75 76 78 82 83' 84 85 86 88' 89 90 Neighbour of VOUVRAY. Similar sweet or dry, long-lived wine.

Montrachet Burg w dr ******** 69 71 78 79 81 82 83 84 85 86 87 88 89 90 (Both 't's are silent.) 19-acre GRAND CRU v'yd in both PULIGNY- and CHASSAGNE-MONTRACHET. Potentially the greatest white burgundy: strong, perfumed, intense, dry yet luscious. Top wines from LAFON, LAGUICHE (DROUHIN), RAMONET, Dom de la ROMANEE-CONTI, THENARD.

Montravel *See* Côtes de Montravel.

Mont-Redon, Domaine de Rh r (w dr) ******* 83 85 86 88 89 90 Outstanding 235-acre estate in CHATEAUNEUF-DU-PAPE. Reliable, fairly early-maturing wines.

Moreau & Fils CHABLIS merchant and grower with 175 acres. Also major table wine producer. Best wine: Clos des Hospices (GRAND CRU).

Morey, Domaines 50 acres in CHASSAGNE-MONTRACHET. Vg wines made by family members, incl BATARD-MONTRACHET.

Morey-St-Denis Burg r ******* 76 78 82 83 85 86 87 88 89 90 Small village with four GRANDS CRUS between GEVREY-CHAMBERTIN and CHAMBOLLE-MUSIGNY. Glorious wine, often overlooked. Growers incl Amiot, Castagnier, DUJAC, Groffier, Lignier, PONSOT, ROUSSEAU, Serveau.

Morgon Burg r ******* 85 88 89 90 91 The 'firmest' CRU of BEAUJOLAIS, needing time to develop its rich and savoury flavour. Growers incl Aucoeur, Ch de Bellevue, Desvignes, Janodet, Lapierre, Ch de Pizay.

Moueix, J-P et Cie The leading proprietor and merchant of ST-EMILION, POMEROL and FRONSAC. Châteaux incl LA FLEUR-PETRUS, MAGDELAINE, and part of PETRUS. Now also has a venture in California: *see* Dominus.

Moulin-à-Vent Burg r ******* 85 86 87 88 89 90 91 The 'biggest' and best wine of BEAUJOLAIS; powerful, meaty and long-lived, eventually tasting more like fine Rhône wine. Many good growers.

Moulis Bx r ****→****** Village of the HAUT-MEDOC with its own AC and several Crus Exceptionnels: CHASSE-SPLEEN, MAUCAILLOU, POUJEAUX (THEIL), etc. Wines are growing steadily finer.

Mousseux Sparkling.

Mouton Cadet Best-selling brand of blended red and white BORDEAUX.

Moutonne CHABLIS GRAND CRU *honoris causa*, owned by BICHOT.

Mugnier, J-F 10-acre Ch de Chambolle estate with first-class BONNES-MARES, CHAMBOLLE-MUSIGNY Les Amoureuses, MUSIGNY.

Mumm, G H & Cie NV Cordon Rouge; Crémant de Cramant (NV); 79 82 85; Rosé 82 85 Major CHAMPAGNE grower and merchant owned by Seagram. Luxury brand: René Lalou (79, 82, 85). The Cramant is superb. Cordon Rouge can be pretty tasteless.

Muré, Clos St-Landelin ALSACE merchant at Rouffach with vines in GRAND CRU Vorbourg. Rather stout, weighty wines.

Muscadet Lo w dr ✶✶ DYA Popular, good value, often delicious dry wine from around Nantes in S Brittany. Should never be sharp but should have an iodine tang. Perfect with fish. The best wines are bottled SUR LIE – on their lees.

Muscadet de Sèvre-et-Maine Wine from the central part of the area.

Muscat Distinctively perfumed grape and its (usually sweet) wine, often fortified as VIN DOUX NATUREL. Made dry in ALSACE.

Muscat de Beaumes de Venise *See* Beaumes de Venise.

Muscat de Frontignan Midi br sw ✶✶ DYA Sweet MIDI MUSCAT. Quality improving.

Muscat de Lunel Midi br sw ✶✶ NV Ditto. A small area but good.

Muscat de Mireval Midi br sw ✶✶ NV Ditto, from nr Montpellier.

Muscat de Rivesaltes Midi br sw ✶ NV Sweet MUSCAT from large zone near Perpignan.

Musigny Burg r (w dr) ✶✶✶✶ 69 71 76 78 79 82 83 85 86 87 88' 89 90 25-acre GRAND CRU in CHAMBOLLE-MUSIGNY. Can be the most beautiful, if not the most powerful, of all red burgundies (and a little white). Best growers: DROUHIN, JADOT, LEROY, MUGNIER, ROUMIER, DE VOGÜE.

Nature Natural or unprocessed – esp of still CHAMPAGNE.

Néac Village N of POMEROL. Wines sold as LALANDE DE POMEROL.

Négociant-éleveur Merchant who 'brings up' (ie matures) the wine.

Nicolas, Ets Paris-based wholesale and retail wine merchants controlled by Castel Frères. One of the biggest in France and one of the best.

Noble rot (French pourriture noble, German Edelfäule, Latin Botrytis cinerea) is a form of mould that attacks the skins of ripe grapes in certain vineyards in warm and misty autumn weather.

Its effect, instead of rotting the grapes, is to wither them. The skin grows soft and flaccid, the juice evaporates through it, and what is left is a super-sweet concentration of everything in the grape except its water content.

The world's best sweet table wines are all made of nobly rotten grapes. They occur in good vintages in Sauternes, the Rhine, the Mosel (where wine made from them is called Trockenbeerenauslese), in Tokaji in Hungary, in Burgenland in Austria, and occasionally elsewhere – California included. The danger is rain on pulpy grapes already far gone in noble rot. All too often, particularly in Sauternes, the grower's hopes are dashed by a break in the weather.

Nuits-St-Georges r ✶✶→✶✶✶ 69 71 76 78' 82 83 85' 86 87 88' 89 90 Important wine town: wines of all qualities, typically sturdy and full-flavoured. Name often shortened to 'Nuits'. Best v'yds incl Les Cailles, Clos de Corvées, Les Pruliers, Les St-Georges, Vaucrains, etc. Many growers and merchants esp Clos de l'Arlot, Chevillon, FAIVELEY, Gouges, GRIVOT, LEROY, MACHARD DE GRAMONT, Michelot, RION.

Oisly & Thésée, Vignerons de Go-ahead coop in E TOURAINE (Loire), experimenting successfully with superior grapes, esp Sauv Bl, Cab, and Chard. Blended wines labelled Baronnie d'Aignan. Good value.

Orléanais, Vin d' Lo r p w dr ✶ DYA Small VDQS for light but fruity wines.

Ostertag Little ALSACE domaine at Epfig. Uses new oak for good Pinot N.

Ott, Domaines The most important producer of high-quality PROVENCE wines, incl CH DE SELLE (rosé and red), Clos Mireille (white) and Ch de Romassan (NB Réserve Rouge 85).

Pacherenc du Vic-Bilh SW France w sw * NV   Rare minor speciality of the ARMAGNAC region.

Paillard, Bruno NV; Crémant Bl de Blancs; Rosé; 79 81 83 85   Small but prestigious young CHAMPAGNE house with excellent silky vintage and NV wines at fair prices.

Palette Prov r p w dr **   Near Aix-en-Provence. Aromatic reds and good rosés from CH SIMONE.

Parigot-Richard Producer of vg CREMANT de BOURGOGNE at SAVIGNY.

Pasquier-Desvignes V old firm of BEAUJOLAIS merchants nr BROUILLY.

Patriarche One of the bigger firms of burgundy merchants. Cellars in BEAUNE; also owns CH DE MEURSAULT (100 acres), KRITER, etc.

Patrimonio Corsica r w p dr **→***   Wide range from dramatic chalk hills in N CORSICA. Fragrant reds, crisp whites, fine VINS DOUX NATURELS. Top grower: Gentile.

Pauillac Bx r **→****** 66' 70' 75 76 78' 79 81 82' 83 85' 86' 87 88' 89' 90'   The only village in BORDEAUX (HAUT-MEDOC) with 3 first-growths (Châteaux LAFITE, LATOUR, MOUTON) and many other fine ones, famous for high flavour; v varied in style.

Pécharmant Dordogne r ** 89 90   Usually better-than-typical, light BERGERAC red, with more 'meat'. Top estates: Dom du Haut-Pécharmant, Ch de Tiregand.

Pelure d'oignon 'Onion skin' – tawny tint of certain rosés.

Perlant or Perlé Very slightly sparkling.

Pernand-Vergelesses Burg r (w dr) *** 78 82 83 85 86 87 88 89 90   Village next to ALOXE-CORTON containing part of the great CORTON and CORTON-CHARLEMAGNE v'yds and one other top v'yd: Ile des Vergelesses. Growers incl BONNEAU DU MARTRAY, CHANDON DE BRIAILLES, Delarche, Dubreuil-Fontaine, JADOT, LATOUR, Rapet.

Perrier, Joseph NV; Rosé; 76 79 82 83 85   Family-run CHAMPAGNE house with considerable v'yds at Châlons-sur-Marne. Consistent light and fruity style.

Perrier-Jouet NV; Blason de France NV; 76 79 82 85   Excellent CHAMPAGNE-growers and makers at Epernay, now linked with MUMM. Luxury brands: Belle Epoque (79, 82, 83, 85) in a painted bottle, Blason de France Rosé (NV). Also Belle Epoque Rosé 79 82 85.

Pessac-Léognan New AC for part of N GRAVES, incl the area of most of the GRANDS CRUS. Since '87 the use of Pessac-Léognan alone has been allowed without adding the name Graves.

Pétillant Slightly sparkling.

Petit Chablis Burg w dr ** DYA   Wine from fourth-rank CHABLIS v'yds. Not much character.

Pfaffenheim Top ALSACE coop. Strongly individual wines of all varieties.

Philipponnat NV; Rosé NV; Grand Blanc Vintage 76 81 82 85; Clos des Goisses 76 78 79 82 85   Small family-run CHAMPAGNE house with well-structured wines, esp the remarkable single v'yd Clos Goisses, and charming rosé. Owned by Marie Brizard.

Piat Père & Fils Important merchants of BEAUJOLAIS and MACON wines at Mâcon, now controlled by Grand Metropolitan. V'yds in MOULIN-A-VENT, also CLOS DE VOUGEOT. BEAUJOLAIS, MACON-VIRE in special Piat bottles maintain a fair standard. Piat d'Or is commercial table wine.

Pic, Albert Fine CHABLIS producer, controlled by DE LADOUCETTE.

Pineau de Charente Strong, sweet aperitif made of white grape juice and COGNAC.

Pinot See Grapes for white and red wine (pages 6–9).

Piper-Heidsieck NV; Rosé 79 85; Vintage 76 79 82 85   CHAMPAGNE-makers of old repute at Reims. Rare 76, 79 and Brut Sauvage (79, 85) are far ahead of their other, rather light wines.

Pol Roger NV; 73 75 76 79 82 85; Rosé 75 79 82 85; Blanc de Chardonnay 79 82 85   Top-ranking, family-owned CHAMPAGNE house at Epernay. Particularly good NV White Foil, Rosé, Réserve PR and Chard. Luxury *cuvée*: 'Sir Winston Churchill' 75, 79, 82, 85.

Pomerol Bx r **→→→→** 70 71 75 76 78 79 81 82 83 85 86 88 89 90   Next village to ST-EMILION: similar but more plummy and creamy wines, maturing sooner, reliable and delicious. Top châteaux: LA FLEUR-PETRUS, LATOUR-À-POMEROL, PETRUS, TROTANOY, VIEUX CH CERTAN, etc.

Pommard Burg r *** 69 71 76 78 82 83 85 86 87 88 89 90   The biggest and best-known COTE D'OR village. Few superlative wines, but many potent and distinguished ones. Best v'yds: Epenots, HOSPICES DE BEAUNE, Rugiens *cuvées*. Growers incl Comte Armand, Billard-Gonnet, de Courcel, Gaunoux, LEROY, MACHARD DE GRAMONT, de Montille, Mussy, Ch de Pommard, Pothier-Rieusset.

Pommery NV; Rosé NV; 76 78 79 80 81 82 83 85 87   Very big CHAMPAGNE growers and merchants at Reims, bought by Moët-Hennessy in '91. Wines are much improved. The luxury brand, Louise Pommery (80, 81, 82, 83, 85), is outstanding. Louise Pommery Rosé 82, 83, 85.

Ponsot, J M 25-acre estate in MOREY-ST-DENIS. V high quality.

Pouilly-Fuissé Burg w dr **→*** 88 89 90 91   The best white of the MACON area. At its best (eg Ch Fuissé VIEILLES VIGNES) excellent, but almost always over-priced compared with (eg) CHABLIS.

Pouilly-Fumé Lo w dr **→*** 89 90 91   'Gun-flinty', fruity, often sharp, pale white from the upper Loire, next to SANCERRE. Grapes must be Sauv Bl. Good vintages improve for 2–3 yrs. Top producers incl Bailly, Dagueneau, LADOUCETTE, Redde, Renaud, Saget, Ch de Tracy.

Pouilly-Loché Burg w dr **   Neighbour of POUILLY-FUISSE. Similar wine but little of it.

Pouilly-sur Loire Lo w dr * DYA   Inferior wine from the same v'yds as POUILLY-FUME, but different grapes (Chasselas). Rarely seen today.

Pouilly-Vinzelles Burg w dr ** 88 89 90 91   Neighbour of POUILLY-FUISSE. Similar wine, worth looking for. Value.

Pousse d'Or, Domaine de la 32-acre estate in POMMARD, SANTENAY and esp VOLNAY, where its MONOPOLES Bousse d'Or and Clos des 60 Ouvrées are tannic, powerful and justly famous.

Premier Cru First-growth in BORDEAUX, but the second rank of v'yds (after GRAND CRU) in Burgundy.

Premières Côtes de Blaye Bx r w dr *→** 82 85 86 88 89 90   Restricted AC for better reds of BLAYE. Ch'x include Barbé, LE BOURDIEU, Charron, l'Escadre, Haut-Sociondo, Le Menaudat, Segonzac, La Tonnelle.

Premières Côtes de Bordeaux Bx r w (p) dr sw *→**   Large area E of GRAVES across the R Garonne: a good bet for quality and value, though never brilliant. Châteaux incl Fayau, Gardera, HAUT-BRIGNON, du Juge, Laffitte (*sic*), REYNON, Tanesse. An area to watch.

Prieur, Domaine Jacques 35-acre estate all in top Burgundy sites, incl PREMIER CRU MEURSAULT, VOLNAY, PULIGNY- and even LE MONTRACHET. Disappointing in '80s. Now 50% owned by RODET. To watch.

Primeur 'Early' wine for refreshment and uplift; esp of BEAUJOLAIS.

Prissé *See* Mâcon-Villages.

Propriétaire-récoltant Owner-manager.

Provence *See* Côtes de Provence.

Puisseguin St-Emilion Bx r ** 82 83 85 86 88 89 90   Eastern neighbour of ST-EMILION; wines similar – not so fine but often good value. Ch'x incl La Croix de Berny, LAURETS, Puisseguin, Soleil, Teyssier, Vieux-Ch-Guibeau. Also Roc de Puisseguin from coop.

Puligny-Montrachet Burg w (r) dr **** 78 82 83 85 86 87 88 89 90   Bigger neighbour of CHASSAGNE-MONTRACHET with potentially even more vital and complex, rich, dry whites: but make sure apparent finesse is not the result of over-production. Best v'yds: BATARD-MONTRACHET, Bienvenue-Bâtard-Montrachet, Champ-Canet, CHEVALIER-MONTRACHET,

Clavoillon, Les Combettes, MONTRACHET, Pucelles, etc. Top growers incl AMPEAU, Boillot, BOUCHARD PERE, L Carillon, CHARTRON, DROUHIN, JADOT, LATOUR, LEFLAIVE, Pernot, SAUZET.

Quarts de Chaume Lo w sw *** 75 76 78 79 82 85 86 88 89' 90' Famous 120-acre plot in COTEAUX DU LAYON. Chenin Bl grapes. Immensely long-lived, intense, rich, golden wine, esp Dom des Beaumard, Ch de Bellerive, Ch La Suronde.

Quatourze Midi r w (p) dr * 88 89 90 Minor VDQS area nr Narbonne.

Quincy Lo w dr ** 89 90 Small area making v dry, SANCERRE-style wine of Sauv Bl. Worth trying. Growers: Domaine Mardon, Meunier-Lapha.

Ramonet, Domaine Leading estate in CHASSAGNE-MONTRACHET with 34 acres, incl some MONTRACHET. Vg whites, and red CLOS ST-JEAN.

Rancio Term for the tang of brown, wood-aged fortified wine, esp BANYULS and other VDN. A fault in table wines.

Rasteau Rh r br (p w dr) sw ** 85' 86 88 89 90 Village of S Rhône valley. V sound reds from the Cave des Vignerons. Good, strong, sweet dessert wine is the (fading) local speciality.

Ratafia de Champagne Sweet aperitif made in CHAMPAGNE of 67% grape juice and 33% brandy. Not unlike PINEAU DE CHARENTE.

Récolte Crop or vintage.

Regnié BEAUJOLAIS village between MORGON and BROUILLY, promoted to CRU status in '88. About 1,800 acres. Try DUBOEUF's.

Reine Pédauque, La Burgundy growers and merchants at ALOXE-CORTON.

Remoissenet Père & Fils Fine burgundy merchant (esp for white wines) with a tiny estate at BEAUNE. Give his reds time.

Rémy Pannier Important Loire wine merchant at SAUMUR.

Reuilly Lo w (r p) dr ** 88 89 90 Neighbour of QUINCY with similar wine; also good Pinot G.

Riceys, Rosé des Champ p *** DYA Minute AC in S CHAMPAGNE for a notable Pinot N rosé. Principal producer: A Bonnet.

Richebourg Burg r **** 69 71 76 78 79 82 83 85 86 87 88 89 90 19-acre GRAND CRU in VOSNE-ROMANEE. Powerful, perfumed, fabulously expensive wine, among Burgundy's very best. Top growers: GRIVOT, Gros, MEO-CAMUZET, Dom de la ROMANEE-CONTI.

Riesling See Grapes for white wine (pages 6–8).

Rion, Daniel et Fils 36-acre domaine in Prémeaux (NUITS). Excellent VOSNE-ROMANEE (Les Vignes Rondes, Les Beaumonts) and Nuits PREMIERS CRUS.

Rivesaltes Midi r w br dr sw ** NV Fortified wine of E Pyrenees, some MUSCAT-flavoured. A tradition v much alive, if struggling these days.

Roche-aux-Moines, La Lo w dr sw *** 75 76 78 79 82 83 85 86 88 89' 90' 60-acre v'yd in SAVENNIERES, ANJOU. Intense, strong, fruity/sharp wine needs long ageing.

Rodet, Antonin Substantial burgundy merchant with large (375-acre) estate, esp in MERCUREY (Ch de Chamirey). See also Prieur. Now owned by LAURENT-PERRIER.

Roederer, Louis Brut Premier NV; Rich NV; 71 73 75 76 78 79 81 83 85; Brut Rosé 75 83 85 One of best CHAMPAGNE-growers and merchants at Reims. Reliable NV, plenty of flavour. Luxury brand: Cristal Brut (79, 82, 83, 85, 86), in white glass bottles, needs time. 83 is still young.

Romanée, La Burg r **** 76 78 82 83 84 85 86 87 88 89 90 2-acre GRAND CRU in VOSNE-ROMANEE, just uphill from ROMANEE-CONTI.

Romanée-Conti Burg r **** 66 71 73 76 78 79 80 81 82 83 84 85 86 87 88 89 4.3-acre MONOPOLE GRAND CRU in VOSNE-ROMANEE. The most celebrated and expensive red wine in the world, with hidden reserves of flavour beyond imagination. 85 and 88 are astonishing.

Romanée-Conti, Domaine de la ('DRC') The grandest estate in Burgundy (AXA-owned). Includes the whole of ROMANEE-CONTI and LA TACHE and major parts of ECHEZEAUX, GRANDS ECHEZEAUX, RICHEBOURG, and ROMANEE-ST-VIVANT. Also a v small part of MONTRACHET. Crown-jewel prices. Keep DRC wines for decades.

Romanée-St-Vivant Burg r **** 71 76 78 79 80 82 83 84 85 86 87 88 89 90   23-acre GRAND CRU in VOSNE-ROMANEE. Similar to ROMANEE-CONTI but lighter and less sumptuous. Top growers: DRC and LEROY.

Ropiteau Burgundy wine-growers and merchants at MEURSAULT. Specialists in Meursault and COTE DE BEAUNE wines.

Rosé d'Anjou Lo p ★ DYA   Pale, slightly sweet rosé. CABERNET D'ANJOU *should* be better.

Rosé de Loire Lo p dr ★→★★ DYA   AC for dry Loire rosé (ANJOU is sweet).

Roty, Joseph Small grower of classic GEVREY-CHAMBERTIN, esp CHARMES- and MAZIS-CHAMBERTIN.

Roumier, Georges 35-acre domaine with exceptional BONNES-MARES, CLOS DE VOUGEOT, MUSIGNY, etc.

Rousseau, Domaine A Major burgundy grower famous for CHAMBERTIN, etc, of highest quality. Intense and long-lived.

Rousette de Savoie Savoie w dr ★★ DYA   The tastiest of the fresh whites from S of Lake Geneva.

Roussillon *See* Côtes du Roussillon. 'Grands Roussillons' are VDNS.

Ruchottes-Chambertin Burg r ★★★ 71 76 78 79 82 83 84 85 86 87 88 89 90   7.5-acre GRAND CRU neighbour of CHAMBERTIN. Similar splendid, long-lasting wine of great finesse. Top growers: LEROY, Mugneret, ROUMIER, ROUSSEAU.

Ruinart Père & Fils NV; Rosé 81 82; Bl de Blancs 79 81 85   The oldest CHAMPAGNE house, now owned by Moët-Hennessy, with notably fine, crisp wines. Luxury brand: Dom Ruinart, Blanc de Blancs 81 82 83. NB the vg mature Rosé. Good value.

Rully Burg r w dr (sp) ★★ 88 89 90   Village of the COTE CHALONNAISE famous for sparkling burgundy. Still white and red are light but tasty and good value, esp the whites. Growers incl DELORME, FAIVELEY, Dom de la Folie, Jacquesson.

Sablet Rh r w (p) dr ★★ 89 90   Admirable COTES DU RHONE village, esp Dom de Boissan, Ch du Trignon, Dom de Verquière.

St-Amour Burg r ★★ 88 89 90 91   Northernmost CRU of BEAUJOLAIS: light, fruity, irresistible.

St-André-de-Cubzac Bx r w dr ★→★★ 82 83 85 86 88 89 90   Town 15 miles NE of BORDEAUX, centre of the minor Cubzaguais region. Sound reds have AC BORDEAUX SUPERIEUR. Incl: Domaine de Beychevelle, Ch du Bouilh, CH DE TERREFORT-QUANCARD, CH TIMBERLAY.

St-Aubin Burg w (r) dr ★★ 85 86 88 89 90   Little-known neighbour of CHASSAGNE-MONTRACHET, up a side-valley. A generous number of PREMIERS CRUS give light, firm, quite stylish wines. Also sold as COTE DE BEAUNE-VILLAGES. Top growers: Clerget, JADOT, J Lamy, H Prudhon, Roux, Thomas.

St-Bris Burg w (r) dr ★ DYA   Village W of CHABLIS known for its fruity ALIGOTE, but chiefly for SAUVIGNON DE ST-BRIS. Also making good sparkling burgundy.

St-Chinian Midi r ★→★★ 88 89 90   Hilly area of growing reputation in the COTEAUX DU LANGUEDOC. AC since '82. Tasty southern reds, esp at Berlou.

St-Emilion Bx r ★★→★★★★ 70 71 75 76 78 79 81 82 83 85 86 88 89 90 The biggest top-quality BORDEAUX district (13,000 acres); solid, rich, tasty wines from hundreds of châteaux, incl AUSONE, CANON, CHEVAL BLANC, FIGEAC, MAGDELAINE, etc. Also a vg coop.

St-Estèphe Bx r ★★→★★★★ 75 78 79 81 82 83 85 86 87 88 89 90   Northern village of HAUT-MEDOC. Solid, structured, occasionally superlative wines. Top châteaux: CALON-SEGUR, COS D'ESTOURNEL, MONTROSE, etc, and more notable CRUS BOURGEOIS than any other HAUT-MEDOC commune.

St-Gall Brand name used by Union-Champagne, the vg CHAMPAGNE-growers' coop at AVIZE.

St-Georges-St-Emilion Bx r ★★ 82 83 85 86 88 89 90   Part of MONTAGNE-ST-EMILION with high standards. Best châteaux: Belair-Montaiguillon, Marquis-St-G, ST-GEORGES, Tour du Pas-St-G.

51

St-Joseph Rh r (p w dr) ✴✴ 83 85 86 88 89 90 N Rhône AC of second rank but reasonable price. Vigorous wine often better than CROZES-HERMITAGE esp from CHAPOUTIER, CHAVE, Grippat, JABOULET.

St-Julien Bx r ✴✴✴→✴✴✴✴ 70 75 76 78 79 81 82' 83' 85' 86 87 88' 89' 90' Mid-MEDOC village with a dozen of BORDEAUX's best châteaux, incl three LEOVILLES, BEYCHEVELLE, DUCRU-BEAUCAILLOU, GRUAUD-LAROSE, etc. The epitome of well-balanced red wine.

St-Laurent Village next to ST-JULIEN. AC HAUT-MEDOC.

St-Nicolas-de-Bourgueil Lo r ✴✴ 82 83 85 86 88 89' 90' The next village to BOURGUEIL: the same lively and fruity Cab F red. Top growers: Ammeaux, Cognard, Jamet, Mabilleau, Taluau.

St-Péray Rh w dr sp ✴✴ NV Rather heavy white from the N Rhône, much of it made sparkling. A curiosity worth trying once.

St-Pourçain-Sur-Sioule Central France r p w dr ✴→✴✴✴ DYA The light but venerable local wine of Vichy. Red and rosé made from Gamay and/or Pinot N, the white from Tressalier and/or Chard or Sauv Bl. Recent vintages vastly improved. AC on the way? Top growers: Dom de Bellevue, Roy.

St-Romain Burg r w dr ✴✴ 85 86 88 89 90 Overlooked village just behind the COTE DE BEAUNE. Value, esp for firm, fresh whites. Reds have a clean 'cut'. Top growers: FEVRE, Jean Germain, Gras, LATOUR, LEROY, Thévenin-Monthélie.

St-Sauveur HAUT-MEDOC village just W of PAUILLAC.

St-Seurin-de-Cadourne HAUT-MEDOC village just N of ST-ESTEPHE.

St-Véran Burg w dr ✴✴ 89 90 91 Next-door AC to POUILLY-FUISSE. Similar but better value: real character from the best slopes of MACON-VILLAGES. Try DUBOEUF's.

Ste-Croix-du-Mont Bx w sw ✴✴ 75 76 82 83 86 88 89 90 Neighbour to SAUTERNES with similar golden wine. No superlatives but well worth trying, esp Clos des Coulinats, Ch Loubens, Ch Lousteau Vieil, Ch du Mont. Often a bargain, esp with age.

Salon Le Mesnil 71 73 76 79 81 83 The original Blanc de Blancs CHAMPAGNE, from Le Mesnil. Fine, v dry wine with long keeping qualities. Bought in '88 by LAURENT-PERRIER.

Sancerre Lo w (r p) dr ✴✴✴ 86 88 89 90 91 Very fragrant and fresh Sauv Bl, almost indistinguishable from POUILLY-FUME, its neighbour over the Loire. Top wines can age 5 yrs. Also light Pinot N red (best drunk at 2–3 yrs) and rosé. Top growers incl Bailly, Bonnard, Bourgeois, CORDIER, Cotat, Crochet, Gitton, Pinard and Reverdy.

Santenay Burg r (w dr) ✴✴✴ 78 79 82 83 85 86 87 88 89 90 Very worthy, rarely rapturous, sturdy reds from the S of the COTE DE BEAUNE. Best v'yds: La Comme, Les Gravières, Clos de Tavannes. Top growers: Lequin-Roussot, MOREY, POUSSE D'OR.

Saumur Lo r p w dr sp ✴→✴✴ Versatile district in ANJOU. Fresh, fruity whites, vg CREMANT (producers incl Chapin & Landeiss, Bouvet-Ladubay), pale rosés and increasingly good Cab F reds (*see next entry*).

Saumur-Champigny Lo r 82 85 86 88 89 90 Flourishing 10-village AC for fresh Cab F reds that age remarkably in sunny vintages. Look for Ch de Chaintres, Dom Filliatreau, Ch du Hureau, Dom Ruault, the coop de St-Cyr.

Sauternes Bx w sw ✴✴→✴✴✴✴ 67' 71 75 76' 78 79 80 81 82 83' 85 86' 88' 89' 90 District of 5 villages (incl BARSAC) which make France's best sweet wine: strong (14%+ alcohol), luscious and golden, demanding to be aged. Top châteaux are D'YQUEM, CLIMENS, COUTET, GUIRAUD, SUDUIRAUT, etc. Also producing dry wines which cannot be sold as Sauternes.

Sauvignon Blanc *See* Grapes for white wine (pages 6–8).

Sauvignon de St-Bris Burg w dr ✴✴ DYA A baby VDQS cousin of SANCERRE, from nr CHABLIS. To try.

Sauvion & Fils Ambitious and well-run MUSCADET house, based at the Ch de Cléray. Top wine: Cardinal Richard.

Sauzet, Etienne White burgundy estate at PULIGNY-MONTRACHET. Clearly defined, well-bred wines, at best superb.

Savennières Lo w dr sw *** 75 76 78 82 83 84 85 86 88 89' 90' Small ANJOU district of pungent, long-lived whites, incl Clos du Papillon, COULEE DE SERRANT, Ch d'Epiré, ROCHE-AUX-MOINES.

Savigny-lès-Beaune Burg r (w dr) *** 78 83 85 86 87 88 89 90 Important village next to BEAUNE, with similar well-balanced middle-weight wines, often deliciously bright, lively and fruity. Best v'yds: Dominode, Les Guettes, Marconnets, Serpentières, Vergelesses. Top growers incl BIZE, Camus, CHANDON DE BRIAILLES, CLAIR, Ecard, Girard-Vollot, LEROY, TOLLOT-BEAUT.

Savoie E France r w dr sp ** DYA Alpine area with light, dry wines like some Swiss wines or minor Loires. APREMONT, CREPY and SEYSSEL are best known whites, ROUSSETTE is often more interesting. Also good MONDEUSE red.

Schlumberger ALSACE grower-merchants of luscious wines at Guebwiller.

Schröder & Schÿler Old BORDEAUX merchants, owners of CH KIRWAN.

Sciacarello Red grape of CORSICA's best red and rosé, eg AJACCIO, Sartène.

Sec Literally means dry, though CHAMPAGNE so-called is medium-sweet (and better at breakfast and tea-time than Brut).

Sélection des Grains Nobles Descriptions coined by HUGEL for ALSACE equivalent to German *Beerenauslese*. *Grains nobles* are individual grapes with 'noble rot' (*see* page 47).

Sèvre-et-Maine The *département* containing the best v'yds of MUSCADET.

Seyssel Savoie w dr sp ** NV Delicate, pale, dry white, making v pleasant sparkling wine.

Sichel & Co Two famous merchant houses. In BORDEAUX Peter A Sichel runs Maison Sichel and owns CH D'ANGLUDET and part of CH PALMER. In Germany, Peter M F Sichel (of New York) runs Sichel Söhne, makers of BLUE NUN, and respected merchants.

Sirius Serious oak-aged, blended BORDEAUX from Maison SICHEL.

Skalli Dynamic producer of good wines from Cab, Merlot, Chard, etc, at Sète in the Languedoc. FORTANT DE FRANCE is standard brand. Experimental wines extraordinary.

Soussans Village just N of MARGAUX, sharing its AC.

Sylvaner *See* Grapes for white wine (pages 6–8).

Syrah *See* Grapes for red wine (pages 8–9).

Tâche, La Burg r **** 69 70 71 76 78 79 80 81 82 83 84 85 86 87 88 89 90 15-acre GRAND CRU of VOSNE-ROMANEE and one of the best v'yds on earth: dark, perfumed, luxurious wine. Owned by Dom de la ROMANEE-CONTI.

Taittinger NV; Rosé NV; 73 75 76 78 79 80 82 83 85 86; Collection Brut 78 81 82 83 85 Fashionable Reims CHAMPAGNE growers and merchants with a light touch. Luxury brand: Comtes de Champagne Blanc de Blancs (79, 81, 82, 83, 85). Also vg Rosé (79, 83, 85). Also own Champagne Irroy.

Tastevin, Confrèrie des Chevaliers du Burgundy's colourful and successful promotion society. Wine carrying their Tastevinage label will have been approved by them and will usually be of a fair standard. A *tastevin* is the traditional, shallow, silver wine-tasting cup of Burgundy. *See also* page 39.

Tavel Rh p *** DYA France's most famous, though not her best, rosé: strong and dry. Best growers: Bernard, Maby, Ch de Trinquevedel. Drink v young.

Tempier, Domaine Top grower of BANDOL, with noble reds and rosé.

Thénard, Domaine The major grower of GIVRY, but best known for his substantial portion (4+ acres) of LE MONTRACHET. Could try harder.

Thorin, J Grower and major merchant of BEAUJOLAIS, owner of the Château des Jacques, MOULIN-A-VENT. Recently bought by Racke of Germany.

Thouarsais, Vin de Lo r w dr ✳ DYA Light Gamay and Sauv Bl VDQS area S of SAUMUR.

Tokay d'Alsace *See under* Pinot Gris (Grapes for white wine – pages 6–8).

Tollot-Beaut Stylish burgundy grower with some 50 acres in the COTE DE BEAUNE, incl Beaune Grèves, CORTON, SAVIGNY- (Les Champs Chevrey) and at CHOREY-LES-BEAUNE where he is based.

Touchais, Moulin Extraordinary luscious COTEAUX DU LAYON from spectacular old stocks of the Touchais family. Vintages back to the '20s are like creamy honey.

Touraine Lo r p w dr sw sp ✳→✳✳✳✳ Big mid-Loire province with immense range of wines, incl dry white Sauv, dry and sweet Chenin Bl (eg VOUVRAY), red CHINON and BOURGUEIL, light red Cabs, Gamays and rosés: often bargains. Amboise, Azay-le-Rideau and Mesland are sub-sections of the AC.

Trapet Two domaines in GEVREY-CHAMBERTIN, both good; esp R Trapet.

Trimbach, F E Distinguished ALSACE grower and merchant at Ribeauvillé. Best wines incl the austere Ries Clos Ste-Hune.

Turckheim, Cave Vinicole de Perhaps the best coop in ALSACE. Many fine wines incl GRANDS CRUS from 900+ acres.

Tursan SW France r p w dr ✳ Emerging VDQS in the Landes. Sound reds. Ch de Bachen (✳✳✳), owned by Michel Gérard, guarantees notoriety and suggests an AC on the way.

Vacqueyras Rh r ✳✳ 83 85 86 88 89 90 Neighbour to GIGONDAS and often better value. Try JABOULET's version or Ch de Montmirail.

Val d'Orbieu, Vignerons du Association of some 200 top growers and coops in CORBIERES, COTEAUX DU LANGUEDOC, ROUSSILLON etc with Maison SICHEL, marketing perhaps the leading range of selected AC wines of the MIDI.

Valençay Lo w dr ✳ DYA VDQS neighbour of CHEVERNY: similar, pleasant, sharpish wine.

Val-Joanis, Ch de Prov r p w dr ✳✳ Impressive new estate making vg COTES DU LUBERON wines. To try.

Valréas Rh r (p w dr) ✳✳ 85 86 88 89 90 COTES DU RHONE village with big coop and good, mid-weight reds.

Varichon & Clerc Principal makers and shippers of SAVOIE sparkling wines.

Varoilles, Domaine des Burgundy estate of 30 acres, principally in GEVREY-CHAMBERTIN. Tannic wines with great keeping qualities.

Vaudésir Burg w dr ✳✳✳✳ 78 83 85 86 87 88 89 90 91 Arguably the best of 7 CHABLIS GRANDS CRUS (but then so are the others).

VDQS Vin Délimité de Qualité Supérieure (*see* page 23).

Vendange Harvest.

Vendange tardive Late vintage. In ALSACE equivalent to German *Auslese*, but stronger and usually less fine.

Veuve Clicquot NV (Yellow label); NV Demi-Sec (White Label); 76 78 79 82 83 85 (Gold Label); and Rosé 83 Historic CHAMPAGNE house of the highest standing, now owned by Moët Hennessy. Full-bodied, almost rich wines. Cellars at Reims. Luxury brand: La Grande Dame 79, 83, 85.

Vidal-Fleury, J Long-established shippers and growers of top Rhône wines, esp HERMITAGE and COTE ROTIE. Bought in '85 by GUIGAL.

Vieilles Vignes Old vines – therefore the best wine. Used for such wine by BOLLINGER, DE VOGUE and others.

Viénot, Charles Grower-merchant of good burgundy, owned by BOISSET in NUITS. 70 acres in CORTON, Nuits, RICHEBOURG, etc.

Vieux Télégraphe, Domaine du Rh r (w dr) ✳✳✳ 78' 79 81 83 84 85 86 88 89 90 A leader in fine, vigorous, modern CHATEAUNEUF-DU-PAPE.

Vignoble Area of vineyards.

Vin de garde Wine that will improve with keeping. The serious stuff.

Vin de l'année This year's wine. *See* Beaujolais, Beaujolais-Villages.

Vin de paille Wine from grapes dried on straw mats, consequently v sweet, like Italian *passito*. Esp in the JURA.

Vin de Pays The junior rank of country wines. No one should overlook this category, the most dynamic in France today. Well over 100 vins de pays names have come into active use recently, mainly in the Midi. They fall into three bands: regional (eg Vin de Pays d'Oc for the whole Midi); departmental (eg Vin de Pays du Gard for the Gard département near the mouth of the Rhône), and vins de pays de zone, the most precise, usually with the highest standards. Well-known zonal vins de pays include Coteaux de l'Uzège, Côtes de Gascogne, Val d'Orbieu. Don't hesitate. There are some gems among them, and many charming trinkets.

Vin de Table Standard, everyday table wine, not subject to particular regulations about grapes and origin. Choose *vins de pays*.

Vin Doux Naturel ('VDN') Sweet wine, fortified with wine alcohol, so the sweetness is 'natural', not the strength. The speciality of ROUSSILLON. A *vin doux liquoreux* is several degrees stronger.

Vin Gris 'Grey' wine is v pale pink, made of red grapes pressed before fermentation begins, unlike rosé which ferments briefly before pressing. *Oeil de Perdrix* means much the same; so does 'blush'.

Vin Jaune Jura w dr ✱✱✱ Speciality of ARBOIS: odd yellow wine like *fino* sherry. Normally ready when bottled (at at least 7 yrs old). The best is CHATEAU-CHALON.

Vin nouveau See Beaujolais Nouveau.

Vin Vert A very light, acidic, refreshing white wine, a speciality of ROUSSILLON and v necessary in summer in those torrid parts.

Vinsobres Rh r (p w dr) ✱✱ 85 86 88 89 90 Contradictory name of good S Rhône village. Potentially substantial reds, but many ordinary.

Viré Burg w dr ✱✱ 89 90 91 One of the best white wine villages of MACON. Good wines from Clos du Chapitre, JADOT, Ch de Viré, coop.

Visan Rh r p w dr ✱✱ 88 89 90 One of the better S Rhône villages. Reds much better than whites.

Viticulteur Wine-growor.

Vogüé, Comte Georges de (Now called Dom les Musigny) First-class 30-acre domaine at CHAMBOLLE-MUSIGNY. At best the ultimate BONNES-MARES and MUSIGNY.

Volnay Burg r ✱✱✱ 78 79 82 83 85' 86 87 88 89 90 Village between POMMARD and MEURSAULT: often the best reds of the COTE DE BEAUNE, not strong or heavy but fragrant and silky. Best v'yds: Caillerets, Champans, Clos des Chênes, Clos des Ducs, etc. Best growers: D'ANGERVILLE, HOSPICES DE BEAUNE, LAFARGE, de Montille, POUSSE D'OR.

Volnay-Santenots Burg r ✱✱✱ Excellent red wine from MEURSAULT is sold under this name. Indistinguishable from Premier Cru VOLNAY.

Vosne-Romanée Burg r ✱✱✱→✱✱✱✱ 76 78 79 82 83 85 86 87 88 89 90 The village containing Burgundy's grandest CRUS (ROMANEE-CONTI, LA TACHE, etc). There are (or should be) no common wines in Vosne. Many good growers incl Arnoux, Castagnier, ENGEL, GRIVOT, Gros, JAYER, LATOUR, LEROY, MEO-CAMUZET, MONGEARD-MUGNERET, Mugneret, ROMANEE-CONTI.

Vougeot See Clos de Vougeot.

Vouvray Lo w dr sw sp ✱✱→✱✱✱✱ 76' 78 79 82 83 85 86 88 89' 90' Small district of TOURAINE with v variable wines, at their best intensely sweet and almost immortal. Good dry sparkling. Best producers: Allias, BREDIF, Brisebarre, Foreau, Fouguet, Ch Gaudrelle, Huet, Ch Moncontour, Poniatowski.

Willm, A N ALSACE grower at Barr, with vg GEWÜRZ Clos Gaensbronnel.

'Y' (pronounced *ygrec*) 78 79 80 84 85 86 Dry wine produced occasionally at CH D'YQUEM.

Ziltener, André Swiss burgundy grower and merchant.

Zind-Humbrecht 64-acre ALSACE estate in Thann, Turckheim and Wintzenheim. First-rate single-v'yd wines (esp Clos St-Urbain Ries).

Châteaux
of Bordeaux

After the bounty of three great vintages in a row Bordeaux woke up, on April 22 1991, to see its vineyards decimated by the blackest of frosts. As though in answer to a prayer, the torrent of fine wine which had already almost swamped the market was reduced to a trickle. At this juncture it still remains to be seen how many producers made good wine from their devastated vineyards. After an August of record heat, rain arrived just as some were picking their early Merlot, but after others had safely gathered it in. Vintners' reports vary from 'almost another '89' to 'no wine to sell'. It will be spring 1993 before it is bottled and specific judgements can be recorded.

Over 400 of the best-known châteaux are listed below. Information on the current state of each vintage of most châteaux (whether it is ready to start drinking; whether in its maker's view it is a particular success) is complete up to the 1990 vintage, the eighth good one in ten years, and a close rival to the magnificent '89. The chief danger in a near-perfect year was too many grapes – which top châteaux avoided by bunch-thinning. The great '89s are for the future, and so are the usually less rich but extremely fine '88s. '87 is the youngest year to be generally ready; light, fragrant and delicious. The '86s are for the long haul; the '85s, beautifully mellow and in balance, are already tempting... Never forget, though, that in Bordeaux the making of a vintage is only the prologue to its long history.

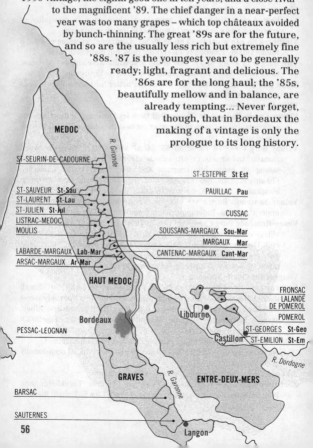

MEDOC

R. Gironde

ST-SEURIN-DE-CADOURNE

ST-ESTEPHE St Est

ST-SAUVEUR St-Sau
ST-LAURENT St-Lau
ST-JULIEN St-Jul
LISTRAC-MEDOC
MOULIS

PAUILLAC Pau

CUSSAC

SOUSSANS-MARGAUX Sou-Mar
MARGAUX Mar
CANTENAC-MARGAUX Cant-Mar

LABARDE-MARGAUX Lab-Mar
ARSAC-MARGAUX Ar-Mar

HAUT MEDOC

FRONSAC
LALANDE
DE POMEROL

Bordeaux

Libourne

POMEROL

PESSAC-LEOGNAN

Castillon

ST-GEORGES St-Geo
ST-EMILION St-Em

R. Dordogne

GRAVES

R. Garonne

ENTRE-DEUX-MERS

BARSAC

SAUTERNES

Langon

Vintages shown in light type should only be opened now out of curiosity to gauge their future. Vintages shown in bold type are deemed (usually by their makers) to be ready for drinking. Remember though that the French tend to enjoy the vigour of young wines, and that many 82s, 83s, 85s and most good 86s have at least another decade of development in front of them. Vintages marked thus ' are regarded as particularly successful for the property in question.

d'Agassac H-Méd r ** 78 82' 83 85 86 88 89 90 Sleeping Beauty 14th-C moated fort. 86 acres v nr Bordeaux suburbs. Same owners as Ch'x CALON-SEGUR and DU TERTRE. Steady.

d'Alesme Mar r ** 75' 78 79 81 82 83 85 86 87 88' 89 90 Tiny (17-acre) third-growth, formerly 'Marquis-d'Alesme'. Better than its reputation.

Andron-Blanquet St-Est r ** 82 83 84 85' 86 88 89 90 Sister château to COS-LABORY. Recent improvements in formerly over-light wine. 40 acres.

L'Angélus St-Em r *** 79' 81 82 83' 85 86 87 88 89' 90' Well-situated classed-growth of 57 acres on the ST-EMILION *côtes* W of the town. Looking vg recently.

d'Angludet Cant-Mar r *** 61 70' 75 76' 78' 79 80 81' 82 83 85 86 87 88' 89' 90 75-acre Cru Exceptionnel of classed-growth quality owned by Peter A Sichel. Lively, fragrant MARGAUX of great style. Value.

d'Archambeau Graves r w dr (sw) ** 85 86 88 89 90 (w) 87 88 90' Up-to-date 54-acre property at Illats. Vg, fruity, dry white; since '85, fragrant barrel-aged reds.

d'Arche Saut w sw ** 79 80 81 82 83' 85 86 88 89 90 classed-growth of 88 acres rejuvenated since '80. Rich, juicy wines.

d'Arcins Central Méd r ** 185-acre property of the Castel family (Castelvin is a best-selling *vin de table*). Sister château to neighbouring Barreyres (160 acres).

d'Armailhac New name ('91) for CH MOUTON-BARONNE-PHILIPPE.

Arnauld H-Méd r ** 45 acres of old vines in Arcins to note.

l'Arrosée St-Em r *** 78 79 81 82 83 85' 86' 87 88 89 90 Substantial 24-acre *côtes* property. Despite its name (which means watered), a top ST-EMILION: opulence and structure.

Ausone St-Em r **** 76' 78 79' 80 81 82' 83' 84 85 86' 87 88 89 90 First-growth with 17 acres (about 2,500 cases) in the best position on the *côtes*, with famous rock-hewn cellars under the v'yd. The firmest, most elegant and subtle St-Emilion. *See also* Ch Belair.

Bahans-Haut-Brion Graves r *** NV and 82 83 85 86' 87 88 89 90 The second-quality wine of CH HAUT-BRION. Worthy of its noble origin.

Balestard-la-Tonnelle St-Em r ** 83 85 86' 87 88 89 Historic 30-acre classed-growth of the plateau. Big flavour; more finesse since '85.

de Barbe Côtes de Bourg r (w) ** 81 82' 83 85 86 87 88 89 90 The biggest (148 acres) and best-known château of the right bank of the Gironde. Good, tasty, light but fruity Merlot red.

Baret Pessac-L r w ** 4,000 cases red, 3,000 white. A famous name recovered from a lull, now managed by M Castéja of BATAILLEY. Looking impressive.

Bastor-Lamontagne Saut w sw ** 75 76 79 81 82 83 85 86 88' 89' 90' Large Bourgeois Preignac property at classed-growth standard, owned by a bank. Excellent, rich wines. NB also their Ch St-Robert at Pujols for red and white GRAVES. 10,000 cases.

Batailley Pau r *** 70 75' 78' 79' 81 82' 83' 85 86 87 88 89 90 The bigger of the famous pair of fifth-growths (with HAUT-BATAILLEY) on the borders of PAUILLAC and ST-JULIEN. 110 acres. Fine, firm, strong-flavoured wine. Home of the Castéja family of BORIE-MANOUX.

Beaumont Cussac, H-Méd r ** 81 82 85 86' 87 88 89' 90' 200-acre+ Cru Bourgeois, well known in France for easily enjoyable and increasingly serious wines. Second label: Ch Moulin d'Arvigny. 35,000 cases. In the same hands as CH BEYCHEVELLE since '87.

Beauregard Pom r *** 79' 81 82' 83 85 86 87 88 89' 90' 32-acre v'yd with pretty 17th-C château nr LA CONSEILLANTE now owned by a bank. Well-made but rather delicate wines to drink quite young.

Beau-Séjour-Bécot St-Em r *** 75 76 78 79 81 82' 83 85 86' 88 89 90' Half of the old Beau-Séjour Premier Grand Cru estate on the W slope of the *côtes*. 45 acres. Controversially demoted in class in '85 but much revved-up since. The Bécots also own CH GRAND-PONTET.

Beauséjour-Duffau-Lagarosse St-Em r *** 82 83 85 86 88 89 90 The other half of the above, 17 acres in old family hands. Coasting in the '70s; a little more grip since '82.

Beau-Site St-Est r ** 75' 78' 79 81 82 83 85 86' 87 88 89 90 55-acre Cru Bourgeois Exceptionnel in same hands as CH BATAILLEY, etc. Quality and substance typical of ST-ESTEPHE.

Belair St-Em r *** 70 71 75' 76' 78 79' 80 82' 83' 85' 86' 88' 89' 90' Sister château and neighbour of AUSONE with 34.5 acres on the *côtes*. Wine a shade softer and less complex. V high standard in recent vintages. Makes a NV, Roc-Blanquant, in magnums only.

de Bel-Air Lalande de Pom r ** 81 82' 83 85 86 87 88 89' The best-known estate of this village just N of POMEROL. Pomerol-style wine. 37 acres.

Bel-Air-Marquis-d'Aligre Soussans-Mar r ** 75' 78 79' 81 82' 85 86 88 89 90 Cru Exceptionnel with 42 acres of old vines giving only 3,500 cases. The owner likes gutsy wine.

Belgrave St-Laurent r ** 81 82 83 85 86' 87 88 89 90' Obscure fifth-growth in ST-JULIEN's back-country. 107 acres. Managed by DOURTHE since '79. 86 shows real promise.

Bellegrave Listrac r ** 82 83 85 86 88 89 90 38-acre Cru Bourgeois making full-flavoured wine with advice from PICHON-LALANDE.

Bel-Orme-Tronquoy-de-Lalande St-Seurin-de-Cadourne (H-Méd) r ** 75' 79' 81 82 85 86 88 89 60-acre Cru Bourgeois N of ST-ESTEPHE. Old v'yd producing tannic wines. More effort now.

Berliquet St-Em r ** 79 81 82 83 85 86 88 89 90 23-acre Grand Cru Classé recently v well run (sold by the ST-EMILION coop).

Bertineau St-Vincent 'Lalande de Pom' r ** 10 acres owned by top oenologist Michel Rolland (*see also* Le Bon Pasteur).

Beychevelle St-Jul r ***→**** 61 70' 75' 78 81 82' 83 84 85' 86' 87 88 89 90 170-acre fourth-growth with the MEDOC's finest mansion. New owners (an insurance company) since '85. Wine of more elegance than power; back in the top flight of ST-JULIEN.

Biston-Brillette Moulis r ** Another attractive MOULIS. 7,000 cases.

Bonalgue Pom r ** Ambitious 2,500-case estate to watch. Les Hautes-Tuileries is sister château.

Bonnet E-Deux-Mers r w dr ** (w) DYA Big-scale producer (600 acres!) of some of the best ENTRE-DEUX-MERS.

Le Bon Pasteur Pom r *** 70 75 76 78 79 80 81 82 83 84 85 86' 87 88 89' 90' Excellent small property (3,500 cases) on the ST-EMILION boundary, owned by consultant oenologist Michel Rolland. Concentrated, sometimes even creamy wines.

Le Boscq St-Est r ** 82 83 85 86 87 88 89' 90 Leading Cru Bourgeois giving excellent value in tasty ST-ESTEPHE.

Le Bourdieu H-Méd r ** 78' 79 81 82 83 85 86 88 89 90' Cru Bourgeois at Vertheuil with sister château Victoria (134 acres in all) known for well-made ST-ESTEPHE-style wines. New owners in '90.

Bourgneuf Pom r **→*** 81 82 83 85' 86 88 89' 90 22-acre v'yd on chalky clay soil, making fairly rich wines with typically plummy POMEROL perfume. 5,000 cases.

Bouscaut Graves r w dr ** 78' 79 81 82' 83 85 86' 88 89 90 Classed-growth at Cadaujac bought in '80 by Lucien Lurton, owner of CH BRANE-CANTENAC, etc. 75 acres red (largely Merlot); 15 acres white. Never yet brilliant, but slowly getting there.

du Bousquet Côtes de Bourg r ** 82 83 85 86 87 88 89 90' Reliable estate with 148 acres, making attractive, solid wine.

Boyd-Cantenac Mar r *** 78' 79 81 82' 83' 85 86' 87 88 89 90 44-acre third-growth often producing attractive wine, full of flavour, if not of third-growth class. *See also* Ch Pouget.

Branaire-Ducru St-Jul r *** 70' 75' 76 78 79' 81 82' 83 84 85 86 87 88 89' 90' Fourth-growth of 125 acres, producing notably spicy and flavoury wine in the '70s. The late '80s have seen a full-scale revival. New owners in '88. Second label: Duluc (since '88).

Brane-Cantenac Cant-Mar r *** 75' 78' 79 81 82' 83 84 85 86' 87 88 89 90 Big (211-acre), well-run second-growth. Rich, even gamey wines of strong character. Same owners as CH'X BOUSCAUT, CLIMENS, DURFORT-VIVENS, VILLEGEORGE, etc. Second labels: Ch'x Baron de Brane, Notton.

du Breuil Cissac r ** 87 88 89 90 Abandoned château bought by owners of CH CISSAC and restored. To follow.

Brillette Moulis r ** 79 81' 82 83 84 85' 86 88 89' 90 70-acre Cru Bourgeois. Reliable and attractive; fulfilling promise.

La Cabanne Pom r ** 79 81 82' 83 85 86 88' 89' 90' Highly regarded 25-acre property nr the great TROTANOY. Recently modernized; expect to hear more. Second wine: Dom de Compostelle. Also Ch Haut-Maillet, POMEROL.

Cadet-Piola St-Em r ** 70' 75' 76 78 79 81 82 83' 84 85' 86 87 88 89' 90 Distinguished little property just N of the town of ST-EMILION. 3,000 cases. CH FAURIE-DE-SOUCHARD has same owner; less robust wine.

	A Bordeaux Label
CHATEAU DUCRU-BEAUCAILLOU **Grand Cru Classé** APPELLATION ST-JULIEN CONTROLLE Mis en Bouteille au Château	A château is an estate – not necessarily with a mansion or a big expanse of vineyard. Reference to the local classification. It varies from one part of Bordeaux to another. The *appellation contrôlée*: look up St-Julien in the France A-Z. 'Bottled at the château' – now the normal practice with classed-growth wines.

Caillou Saut w sw ** 76 78 81 82 83 85 86 87 88' 89' 90 Well-run second-rank 37-acre BARSAC v'yd for firm, fruity wine. Private Cuvée (81, 83, 85, 86, 88, 89') is a top selection.

Calon-Ségur St-Est r *** 70 75 78' 79' 81 82' 83 85' 86' 87 88' 89 90 Big (123-acre) third-growth of great reputation for big, hearty wines; but rather patchy in recent years. (86, 88, 89, 90 look good.)

Cambon-la-Pelouse H-Méd r ** 82 83 85 86 87 88 89 90 Big (145-acre), accessible Cru Bourgeois. A sure bet for fresh, typical MEDOC without wood-ageing.

Camensac St-Laurent r ** 79 81 82' 85 86' 87 88 89 90 149-acre fifth-growth, with the same expert direction as LAROSE-TRINTAUDON. Good, lively, if not exactly classic wines.

Canon Canon-Fronsac r **→**** 81 82 83 85 86' 88 89' 90 Tiny property of Christian MOUEIX. Long-ageing wine.

Canon St-Em r *** 75' 78 79' 80 81 82' 83 85' 86 87 88' 89' 90 Famous first-classed-growth with 44+ acres on the plateau W of the town. Conservative methods; v impressive wine, among best of ST-EMILION.

Canon-la-Gaffelière St-Em r **×- >*** 82 83 85 86' 87 88' 89 90' 47-acre classed-growth on the lower slopes of the *côtes*, under Austrian ownership. Total renovation in '85. Now stylish, meaty, impressive.

Canon-de-Brem Canon-Fronsac r ** 78 81 82' 83 85 86 88 89' 90 One of the top FRONSAC v'yds for vigorous wine. MOUEIX property.

Canon-Moueix Canon-Fronsac r ** 83 85 86 88 89' 90 The latest MOUEIX investment in this rising AC. V stylish wine.

Cantegril Graves r ✱✱ 88 89 90 Stylish, earthy, fragrant red from BARSAC CH DOISY-DAENE.

Cantemerle Macau r ✱✱✱ 61 70' 75' 78 81 82 83' 84 85 86 87 88 89 90 Superb estate at the extreme S of the MEDOC, with a romantic château in a wood and 150 acres of vines. Officially fifth-growth: potentially much higher for its harmony of flavours. Problems hampered quality in late '70s. A new broom (CORDIER) since '81 has fulfilled potential.

Cantenac-Brown Cant-Mar r ✱✱✱ 70 78 79 81 82 83 85 86' 87 88 89 90' Formerly old-fashioned 77-acre third-growth. New owners (same as PICHON-LONGUEVILLE) investing heavily, with J-M Cazes' direction and v promising recent vintages. Big wines. Second label: Canuet.

Capbern-Gasqueton St-Est r ✱✱ 81 82 83 84 85 86 88 89 90 Good 85-acre Cru Bourgeois; same owner as CALON-SEGUR.

Cap-de-Mourlin St-Em r ✱✱ 70' 79' 81 82' 83 84 85 86 87 88 89 90 Well-known 37-acre property of the Cap-de-Mourlin family, owners of CH BALESTARD and CH ROUDIER, MONTAGNE-ST-EM. Rich ST-EMILION.

Carbonnieux Graves r w dr ✱✱✱ 82 83 85 86' 87 88 89' 90' Historic estate at LEOGNAN making rather light reds (since '85 much better). The whites, 50% Sémillon (eg 86, 88, 89, 90, 91), have the structure to age 10 yrs. Ch'x Le Pape and Le Sartre are also in the family.

Cardaillan Graves r ✱✱ The trusty red wine of the distinguished (SAUTERNES) CH DE MALLE.

La Cardonne Blaignan (Méd) r ✱✱ 85 86 87 88 89 90 Large (300-acre+) Cru Bourgeois in the N MEDOC bought in '73 by the Rothschilds of LAFITE and sold in '90. Tough Médoc, best young.

Les Carmes-Haut-Brion Graves r ✱✱ 75 78 79 81' 82' 83 85 86 87 88' 89 90 Small (9-acre) neighbour of HAUT-BRION with higher than Bourgeois standards. Old vintages show its potential. Alas only 1,500 cases.

Caronne-Ste-Gemme St-Laurent r ✱✱→✱✱✱ 75 78 79 81 82' 83 84 85 86 87 88 89' 90 Cru Bourgeois Exceptionnel of 100 acres. Steady quality repays patience. At minor *cru classé* level.

Carteau-Côtes-Daugay St-Em ✱✱ Emerging 5,000-case Grand Cru; to follow for full-flavoured wines maturing fairly early.

du Castéra Méd r ✱✱ 82 83 85 86 87 88 89 90' Historic property at St-Germain (N MEDOC). Recent investment; tasty but not tannic wine.

Certan-de-May Pom r ✱✱✱ 70 75 78 79 81 82' 83' 84 85' 86 87 88 89' 90 Neighbour of VIEUX CHATEAU CERTAN. Tiny property (1,800 cases) with full-bodied, rich and tannic wine, consistently flying v high.

Certan-Giraud Pom r ✱✱✱ 75 79 81 82 83' 85 86 88 89 Small (17-acre) property next to PETRUS, though quarter the depth.

Chambert-Marbuzet St-Est r ✱✱ 66 70 76 78 79 81 82 83 84 85 86 87 88 89' 90' Tiny (20-acre) sister château of HAUT-MARBUZET. Vg predominantly Cab wine, aged in new oak relatively fast but v tastily.

Chantegrive Graves r w dr ✱✱ 82 85 87 88 89 90 (w) 91 215-acre estate, half white, half red; modern GRAVES of high quality. Cuvée Caroline is top white selection, Cuvée Edouard top red. Other labels incl Mayne-Lévêque, Bon-Dieu-des-Vignes.

Chasse-Spleen Moulis r ✱✱✱ 70' 75' 76 78' 79 81' 82' 83' 84 85 86 87 88 89 90 180-acre Cru Exceptionnel of classed-growth quality. Consistently good, usually outstanding, long-maturing wine. Second label: Ermitage de C-S. One of the surest things in Bordeaux.

Chéret-Pitres Graves r w dr ✱→✱✱ Substantial estate in the up-and-coming village of Portets.

Cheval Blanc St-Em r ✱✱✱✱ 64 66 70 71 75' 76 78 79 80 81' 82' 83' 84 85' 86 87 88 89 90 This and AUSONE are the 'first-growths' of ST-EMILION. Cheval Blanc is richer, more full-blooded, intensely vigorous and perfumed, from 100 acres. Delicious young, and lasts almost forever. Second wine: Le Petit Cheval.

Chevalier, Domaine de Graves r w dr ✱✱✱✱ 66 70' 75' 76 78' 79' 80 81' 82' 83 84 85 86' 88' 89 90 Superb small estate of 36 acres at LEOGNAN.

The red is stern at first, richly subtle with age. The white is delicate but matures to rich flavours (79', 81, 82, 83', 84, 85', 87', 88, 89, 90, 91). Changed hands (but not management) in '83.

Chicane Graves r ** 85 86 88 89 90' Satisfying and reliable product of the Langon merchant Pierre Coste. (Domaine de Gaillat is another.) Drink at 2–6 yrs (the Gaillat a little later).

Cissac Cissac r ** 70' 71 75' 76 78' 79 81 82' 83' 84 85 86' 87 88 89 90 A pillar of the bourgeoisie. 80-acre Grand Bourgeois Exceptionnel: steady record for tasty, v long-lived wine. Also, since '87, CH DU BREUIL.

Citran Avensan (H-Méd) r ** 78' 82 83 85 86 88 89' 90 Grand Bourgeois Exceptionnel of 178 acres, bought by Japanese in '87. Major works. 89 is turbo-charged.

Médoc: The Class System
The Médoc has 60 crus classés, ranked in 1855 in five classes. In a separate classification it has 18 Crus Grands Bourgeois Exceptionnels and 41 Crus Grands Bourgeois (which must age their wine in barrels), and 68 Crus Bourgeois. (The terms Grand Bourgeois and Exceptionnel are not acceptable to the EC, and are therefore not used on labels.)

Apart from the first-growths, the five classes of 1855 are now considerably jumbled in quality, with some second-growths at fifth-growth level and vice versa. They also overlap in quality with the Crus Exceptionnels. (Beside the official 18, another 13 châteaux are unofficially acknowledged as belonging to this category.) The French are famous for logic.

Clarke Listrac r (p) ** 82 83 85' 86' 87 88 89' 90 Huge (350-acre) Cru Bourgeois Rothschild development, incl visitor facilities and neighbouring Ch'x Malmaison and Peyrelebade. Still to come: a unique sweet white 'Le Merle Blanc du Ch Clarke'.

Clerc-Milon Pau r *** 73 75' 76 78' 79 80 81 82' 83 84 85 86' 87 88 89 90 Once-forgotten little fifth-growth bought by the late Baron Philippe de Rothschild in '70. Now 73 acres. Not normally thrilling in the '70s (except 70), but vg 85, 86 (esp), and now 88, 89 and 90.

Climens Saut w sw *** 71' 75' 76' 78' 79 80' 81 82 83' 85' 86' 88 89 90' 74-acre classed-growth at BARSAC making some of the most stylish (though not the v sweetest) wine in the world for a good 10 yrs' maturing. A superb 83. (Occasional) second label: Les Cyprès. Same owner as CH BRANE-CANTENAC, etc.

Clinet Pom r ** 83 85 86 87 88 89 90 17-acre property in central POMEROL making tannic wines from old vines. Progress in recent vintages towards a much juicier style.

Clos l'Eglise Pom r *** 75 78 79' 81 83 85 86 88 89' 90 14-acre v'yd on one of the best sites in POMEROL. Fine wine without great muscle or flesh. The same family owns CH PLINCE.

Clos Floridène Graves w dr ** 90' 91 *Tour de force* by one of the best white-wine makers of Bordeaux, Denis Dubourdieu. Oak-aged Sauv to drink young or keep 5 yrs.

Clos Fourtet St-Em r *** 78 79 81 82' 83 85 86 88 89 90 Well-placed 42-acre first-growth on the plateau, with cellars almost in the town. Back on form after a middling patch, but still scarcely resonant. Same owners as BRANE-CANTENAC, CLIMENS, etc.

Clos Haut-Peyraguey Saut w sw ** 78 79 81 83 84 85 86' 87 88 89 90' Tiny production of good, medium-rich wine. The vg Cru Bourgeois Ch Haut-Bommes is in the same hands.

Clos des Jacobins St-Em r ** 75' 78 79 81 82' 83 85 86 87 88 89 90 Well-known and well-run little (18-acre) classed-growth owned by the shipper CORDIER. Wines of notable depth and style.

Clos du Marquis St-Jul r ** 81 82 83 85 86' 87 88 89' 90 The second wine of LEOVILLE-LAS-CASES, cut from the same cloth.

Clos René Pom r *** 75 81 82' 83 85 86 87 88 89 90 Leading château on the W of POMEROL. 38 acres making increasingly concentrated wine. Also sold as Ch Moulinet-Lasserre.

Clos St-Martin St-Em r *** 9 acres in prime spot co-owned with Grandes-Murailles and Côte Baleau; the other two were demoted in the '85 reclassification. A muddle, but taste the wines.

La Closerie-Grand-Poujeaux Moulis r ** 85 86 88 89 90   Small but respected traditional middle-MEDOC. Also owns neighbouring Ch Bel-Air-Lagrave.

La Clotte St-Em r ** 82 83' 85 86 87 88 89 90   Tiny *côtes* Grand Cru with fragrant, supple wine. Drink at the owners' restaurant, La Cadène, in ST-EMILION. Change of winemaker in '90.

Colombier-Monpelou Pau r ** 81 82 83 85 86' 87 88 89 90'   Reliable small Cru Bourgeois made to a fair standard.

La Conseillante Pom r *** 70' 75 79 81' 82' 83 84 85 86 87 88 89   29-acre historic property on the plateau between PETRUS and CHEVAL BLANC. At best some of the noblest and most fragrant POMEROL, worthy of its superb position.

Corbin (Giraud) St-Em r ** 75 79 81 82' 83 85 86 88 89 90   28-acre classed-growth in N ST-EMILION where a cluster of Corbins occupy the edge of the plateau. Top vintages are v rich.

Corbin-Michotte St-Em r ** 75 81 82 83 85 86 88 89 90   Well-run 19-acre property; 'generous' POMEROL-like wine.

Cordeillan-Bages Pau r **   A mere 1,000 cases of full-blooded PAUILLAC from the château-hotel of J-M Cazes (*see* Lynch-Bages).

Cos-d'Estournel St-Est r **** 61 66 70 75' 76' 78' 79 81' 82' 83' 84 85' 86' 87 88' 89' 90'   140-acre second-growth with eccentric chinoiserie tower overlooking CH LAFITE. Always full-flavoured, often magnificent . Now regularly one of best in the MEDOC. Second label: CH DE MARBUZET.

Cos-Labory St-Est r ** 81 82 83 85 86 87 88 89 90   Little-known fifth-growth neighbour of COS-D'ESTOURNEL with 37 acres. Efforts since '85 put it on level with a good ST-ESTEPHE Cru Bourgeois, but with more elegance. ANDRON-BLANQUET is in effect its second wine.

Coufran St Seurin-de-Cadourne (H-Méd) r ** 78' 79 81 82' 83 85 86' 87 88 89 90   Coufran and CH VERDIGNAN, on the northern-most hillock of the HAUT-MEDOC are co-owned. Coufran has mainly Merlot vines; soft, supple wine. 148 acres. Ch Soudars is another, smaller sister.

Couhins-Lurton Graves w dr ** 85 86' 87' 88 89 90 91   Tiny quantity of v fine Sauv wine for maturing.

Coutet Saut w sw *** 67' 70' 71' 73 75' 76 79 81 82 83' 84 85 86' 87 88 89 90'   Traditional rival to CH CLIMENS; 91 acres in BARSAC. Usually slightly less rich; at its best equally fine. Cuvée Madame is a v rich selection of the best. A dry GRAVES is sold under the same name.

Couvent des Jacobins St-Em r ** 75 78 79' 81 82' 83 85 86 87 88 89 90   Well-known 22-acre v'yd adjacent to the town of ST-EMILION in the E. Among the best of its kind. Splendid cellars.

Le Crock St-Est r ** 79 81 82 83 84 85 86 87 88 89 90   Well-situated Cru Bourgeois of 74 acres in the same family as CH LEOVILLE-POYFERRE. Among the many good Crus Bourgeois of the commune.

La Croix Pom r ** 75' 76 79' 81 82 83 85 86 87 88 89 90   Well-reputed property of 32 acres. Appealing, plummy POMEROL with a spine; matures well. Also La C-St-Georges, La C-Toulifaut, Castalot and Clos des Litanies.

La Croix du Casse Pom r ** Sister château of CLINET. 22 acres making easy-drinking POMEROL.

La Croix-de-Gay Pom r *** 75' 79 81 82'83' 85 86 88 89 90   30 acres in best part of the commune. Recently on fine form. Has underground cellars (rare in POMEROL). La Fleur-de-Gay is the best selection.

Croizet-Bages Pau r ** 82' 83 85 86 87 88 89 90   52-acre fifth-growth (lacking a château or a reputation) with the same owners as CH RAUZAN-GASSIES. Wines with growing vigour (at last) since '86. Fine 89.

Croque-Michotte St-Em r ✻✻ 75 81 82' 83 85 86 87 88 89 90   35-acre POMEROL-style classed-growth on the Pomerol border.

de Cruzeaux Graves r w dr ✻✻   100-acre GRAVES-LEOGNAN v'yd recently developed by André Lurton of LA LOUVIERE etc. V high standards; to try. Drink white at 1–3 yrs.

Curé-Bon-la-Madeleine St-Em r ✻✻✻ 75 78 81 82' 83 85 86 88 89 90   Small (12-acre) property among côtes' best; between AUSONE and CANON.

Dalem Fronsac r ✻✻ 82 83 85 86 88 89 90   Leading full-blooded FRONSAC to follow.

Dassault St-Em r ✻✻ 82 83 85 86 88 89 90   Consistent, early-maturing, middle-weight Grand Cru. 58 acres.

La Dauphine Fronsac ✻✻ 85 86 87 88 89 90   Famous old star of FRONSAC rejuvenated by J-P MOUEIX.

Dauzac Labarde-Mar r ✻✻→✻✻✻ 79' 81 82' 83' 84 85 86 87 88 89 90'   Substantial fifth-growth nr the river S of MARGAUX. Doing well since '79; new owner (an insurance company) in '89. 120 acres. 22,000 cases. Second wine: La Bastide Dauzac.

Desmirail Mar r ✻✻→✻✻✻ 82 83' 85 86 87 88 89 90   Third-growth, now 45 acres. A long-defunct name recently revived by the owner of BRANE-CANTENAC. So far wines for drinking young.

Doisy-Daëne Barsac w (r) sw dr ✻✻✻ 76' 78 79 80 81 82 83 85 86 88 89' 90' 91   Forward-looking 34-acre estate making crisp, oaky, dry white and red CH CANTEGRIL as well as notably fine (and long-lived) sweet BARSAC.

Doisy-Dubroca Barsac w sw ✻✻ 75' 76 78 79 81 83 85 86 87 88 89 90'   Tiny (8.5-acre) BARSAC classed-growth allied to CH CLIMENS.

Doisy-Védrines Saut w sw ✻✻✻ 71 75' 76' 78 79 80 81 82' 83' 85 86 88' 89' 90   50-acre classed-growth at BARSAC, nr CLIMENS and COUTET, recently re-equipped. Delicious, sturdy, rich: for keeping. NB the 89.

La Dominique St-Em r ✻✻✻ 75 78 79 81 82' 83 85 86' 87 88 89 90   Fine 45-acre classed-growth next door to CH CHEVAL BLANC, making wine almost as arresting.

Ducluzeau Listrac r ✻✻   Tiny sister property of DUCRU-BEAUCAILLOU. 10 acres, unusually 90% Merlot.

Ducru-Beaucaillou St-Jul r ✻✻✻✻ 61 66 70' 75' 76 78' 79 80 81 82' 83' 84 85' 86' 87 88 89 90   Outstanding second-growth; 120 acres overlooking the river. Second label: La Croix-Beaucaillou. The owner, M Borie, makes classic, cedar-scented claret for v long ageing. *See also* Grand-Puy-Lacoste, Haut-Batailley, Lalande-Borie.

Why do the Châteaux of Bordeaux have such a large section of this book devoted to them? The reason is simple: collectively they form by far the largest supply of high-quality wine on earth. A single typical Médoc château with 150 acres (some have far more) makes approximately 26,000 dozen bottles of identifiable wine each year – the production of two or three California 'boutique' wineries.

The tendency over the last two decades has been for the better-known châteaux to buy more land. Many classed-growths have expanded very considerably since they were classified in 1855. The majority have also raised their sights and invested the good profits of the past decade in better technology.

Duhart-Milon-Rothschild Pau r ✻✻✻ 75' 78 79 81 82' 83 85 86 87 88 89 90   Fourth-growth neighbour of LAFITE under the same management. Maturing vines; increasingly fine quality. 110 acres.

Duplessis-Fabre Moulis r ✻✻ 82 83 85 86 87 88' 89 90   Former sister ch of FOURCAS-DUPRE; since '89 owned by DOURTHE (MAUCAILLOU). To watch.

Durfort-Vivens Mar r ✻✻✻ 78' 79' 81 82' 83 84 85' 86 87 88' 89 90   Relatively small (49-acre) second-growth owned by M Lurton of BRANE-CANTENAC. Recent wines have structure and class.

Dûtruch-Grand-Poujeaux Moulis r ✻✻ 78' 79 81 82' 83 85 86 87 88 89 90

One of the leaders of MOULIS; full-bodied and tannic wines.

de l'Eglise Pom r ✹✹ 79' 81 82' 83 85 86 88 89 90 Small property: stylish, resonant wine distributed by BORIE-MANOUX.

L'Eglise-Clinet Pom r ✹✹✹ 70 71 75 76 78 79 81 82' 83' 84 85' 86 87 88' 89 90 11 acres. Ranked v nr the top; full, fleshy wine. Changed hands in '82; 86 is noble. 1,700 cases. Second label: La Petite Eglise.

L'Enclos Pom r ✹✹ 70 75 76 79 81 82' 83 85 86 87 88 89 90' Respected 26-acre property on the W side of POMEROL, nr CLOS RENE. Big, well-made, long-flavoured wine.

L'Evangile Pom r ✹✹✹ 75' 78 79 82' 83' 84 85' 86 87 88 89 90 33 acres between PETRUS and CHEVAL BLANC. Deep-veined but elegant style. In the same area and class as LA CONSEILLANTE. Bought in '90 by Domaines (Lafite) Rothschild.

de Fargues Saut w sw ✹✹✹ 70' 71' 75' 76' 78 79 80 81 83 85' 86 87 88 89 90 25-acre v'yd by ruined château in same ownership as CH D'YQUEM. Fruity and extremely elegant wines, maturing earlier than Yquem.

Faurie-de-Souchard St-Em r ✹✹ 85 86 88 89 90 Small Grand Cru Classé on the *côtes. See also* Ch Cadet-Piola.

Ferrande Graves r (w dr) ✹✹ 82 83 85 86 87 88 89 90 Major estate of Castres with 100+ acres. Easy, enjoyable red and vg white at 1–4 yrs. Early drinking is fun; the proprietor prefers to wait.

Ferrière Mar r ✹✹ 75 78 79 81 82 83 85 86 87 88 89 90 Phantom third-growth; only 10+ acres. Now in same capable hands as CHASSE-SPLEEN.

Feytit-Clinet Pom r ✹✹ 75' 79 81 82' 83 85' 86 87 88' 89' 90 Little property next to LATOUR-A-POMEROL. Has made some fine, ripe wines. Managed by J-P MOUEIX.

Fieuzal Graves r (w dr) ✹✹✹ 78' 79 81 82' 83 84 85' 86' 87 88 89 90' (w) 91 75-acre classed-growth at LEOGNAN. Finely made, memorable wines of both colours esp since '84. Whites since '85 are 4–8-yr keepers. Second label: Ch le Bonnat.

Figeac St-Em r ✹✹✹✹ 70' 75' 76' 78 79 81 82' 83 84 85' 86 87 88 89 Famous first-growth neighbour of CHEVAL BLANC. 98-acre gravelly v'yd gives one of Bordeaux's most stylish, rich but elegant wines, maturing relatively quickly, but lasting almost indefinitely.

Filhot Saut w sw dr ✹✹✹ 75 76' 79' 82' 83' 85 86' 87 88 89 90' Second-rank classed-growth with splendid château, 148-acre v'yd. Lightish (Sauv) sweet wines for fairly early drinking, a little dry, and red.

La Fleur St-Em r ✹✹ 75 78 79 81 82' 83 85 86 88 89' 90 16-acre *côtes* estate; consistently fruity wines. Now managed by J-P MOUEIX.

La Fleur-de-Gay *See* La Croix-de-Gay.

La Fleur-Pétrus Pom r ✹✹✹ 70 75' 78 79 81' 82 83' 84 85 86 87 88' 89' 90 18-acre v'yd flanking PETRUS and under the same management. Exceedingly fine, plummy wines; POMEROL at its most stylish.

Fombrauge St-Em r ✹✹ 79 81 82' 83 85 86 87 88' 89 90 Major, 120-acre property of St-Christophe-des-Bardes, E of ST-EMILION, with Danish connections. Reliable early-drinking St-Emilion making great efforts. Second label: Ch Maurens.

Fonbadet Pau r ✹✹ 70 76 78 79 81' 82' 83 84 85 86 87 88 89 90' Cru Bourgeois of high repute. 38 acres next to PONTET-CANET. Old vines give solid wine needing long bottle-age. Value.

Fonplégade St-Em r ✹✹ 75 78 79 81 82' 83 85 86 87 88 89 90 48-acre Grand Cru Classé on the *côtes* W of ST-EMILION in another branch of the MOUEIX family. Fragrant and appealing.

Fonréaud Listrac r ✹✹ 78' 79 81 82' 83 85' 86' 87 88 89 90 One of the bigger (96 acres) and better Crus Bourgeois of its area. New broom (and barrels) since '83. *See also* Ch Lestage.

Fonroque St-Em r ✹✹✹ 70 75' 78 79 81 82 83' 85' 86 87 88 89' 90 48 acres on the plateau N of ST-EMILION, J-P MOUEIX property. Big, deep, dark wine that nonetheless opens up quite young.

Les Forts de Latour Pau r ✹✹✹ 70' 75 78' 79 80 81 82' 83 84 85 87 90 The second wine of CH LATOUR; well worthy of its big brother. For long unique in being bottle-aged at least 3 yrs before release; since '90 offered *en primeur* as well. V fine 82.

Fourcas-Dupré Listrac r ★★ 70' 75 78' 79 81 82' 83' 84 85' 86' 87 88 89' 90 A top-class 100-acre Cru Bourgeois Exceptionnel making consistent and elegant wine. To follow. Second label: Ch Bellevue-Laffont.

Fourcas-Hosten Listrac r ★★→★★★ 70 75 78' 79 81 82' 83' 84 85 86' 87 88 89 90 96-acre Cru Bourgeois currently considered the best of its (underestimated) commune. Firm wine with a long life.

Franc-Mayne St-Em r ★★ 85 86 87 88 89' 90 '89 acquisition of AXA Insurance. 18 acres run by J-M Cazes (*see* Lynch-Bages). Expect v high standards. Ch'x La Fleur-Pourret and Petit-Figeac (total 19 acres) are in the same stable.

de France Pessac-L r w ★★ Well-known GRAVES, 65 acres red, 10 white recently replanted. 89 red is notable.

La Gaffelière St-Em r ★★★ 70 78 79 81 82' 83' 85 86' 87 88' 89' 90 61-acre first-growth at the foot of the *côtes* below CH BEL-AIR. Elegant, not rich wines; worth its rank since '82, after a bad patch.

La Garde Graves r (w dr) ★★ 81 82' 83' 84 85 86 88 89 90 Substantial property making reliably sound red.

Le Gay Pom r ★★★ 70 75' 76' 78 79 82' 83' 85 86 88 89' 90 Well-known 14-acre v'yd on N edge of POMEROL. Same owner as CH LAFLEUR, different management since '85. Splendid wine.

Gazin Pom r ★★★ 81 82 83 85 86 87' 88 89 90 Large property (for POMEROL) with 58 acres. Not quite as splendid as its position next to PETRUS but vg results since '86. Second label: Ch l'Hospitalet.

Gilette Saut w sw ★★★ 37 49 53 55 59 61 62 Extraordinary, small Preignac château which stores its sumptuous wines in cask to a great age. Only about 5,000 bottles of each. Ch Les Justices is the sister château.

Giscours Labarde-Mar r ★★★ 70 71' 75' 76 78' 79' 80 81' 82' 83 84 85 86 87 88 89' 90 Splendid 182-acre third-growth S of CANTENAC. Dynamically run with excellent vigorous wine in '70s; recently lighter and patchy.

du Glana St-Jul r ★★ 81 82' 83 85 86 88 89 90 Big Cru Bourgeois in centre of ST-JULIEN. Undemanding; undramatic.

Gloria St-Jul r ★★★ 70' 75' 76 78' 79 80 81 82' 83 84 85 86 87 88 89 90 Outstanding Cru Bourgeois making wine of vigour and finesse, among classed-growths in quality. 110 acres. In '82 the owner, the late Henri Martin, bought CH ST-PIERRE. Recent return to long-maturing style.

Grand-Barrail-Lamarzelle-Figeac St-Em r ★★ 75 78 79' 82' 83 85 86 87 88 89 90 48-acre property near FIGEAC, incl Ch La Marzelle. Well-reputed and popular, if scarcely exciting.

Grand-Corbin-Despagne St-Em r ★★ 70 75 78 79 81 82' 83 85 86 88 89 90' One of the biggest and best Grands Crus on the CORBIN plateau.

Grand-Mayne St Em ★★ 82 83 84 85 86 87 88 89 90 40-acre Grand Cru Classé on W *côtes*. To watch.

Grand-Pontet St-Em r ★★ 82' 83 85 86' 87 88 89 90 35 acres beside CH BEAU-SEJOUR BECOT; like it revitalized since '85.

Grand-Puy-Ducasse Pau r ★★★ 75 78 79 81 82' 83 84 85 86 87 88 89 90 Well-known little fifth-growth bought in '71, renovated and enlarged to 90 acres under expert management. A best buy. Second label: Ch Artiges-Arnaud.

Grand-Puy-Lacoste Pau r ★★★ 70 75 76 78' 79' 81' 82' 83 84 85' 86' 87 88 89 90 Leading fifth-growth famous for excellent, full-bodied, vigorous PAUILLAC. 110 acres among the 'Bages' châteaux, owned by the Borie family of DUCRU-BEAUCAILLOU. Second label: Lacoste-Borie.

Gravas Saut w sw ★★ 83' 85 86 88 89' 90' Small BARSAC property; impressive, firm wine. NB Cuvée Spéciale.

La Grave, Domaine Graves r w dr ★★ 82 83 84 85 86 88 89 Innovative little estate with lively reds made for long life; oak-aged, delicious whites. Made at Ch de Landiras by Peter Vinding-Diers.

La Grave-Trigant-de-Boisset Pom r *** 75' 76' 78 79 81' 82' 83 84 85 86' 87 88 89' 90 Verdant château with small but first-class v'yd owned by Christian MOUEIX. Elegant, beautifully structured POMEROL.

Gressier-Grand-Poujeaux Moulis r *** 70 75' 78 79' 81 82 83' 84 85 86 87 88 89 90 Good Cru Bourgeois, neighbour of CHASSE-SPLEEN. Fine, firm wine with a good track record for repaying patient cellaring.

Greysac Méd r ** 79' 81' 82 83 85 86 88 89 90 Elegant 140-acre property. Easy, early-maturing wines popular in US.

Gruaud-Larose St-Jul r *** 70' 75' 76 78' 79 81 82' 83 84 85 86 87 88 89 90 One of the biggest and best-loved second-growths. 189 acres making smooth, rich, stylish claret. Owned by CORDIER. The excellent second wine is called Sarget de Gruaud-Larose.

Guadet-St-Julien St-Em ** 82 83 85 86 87 88 89 90' Extremely well-made wines from v small Grand Cru Classé.

Guiraud Saut w (r) sw (dr) *** 70' 76 78' 79' 81 82 83' 84 85 86' 87 88 89' 90' Restored classed-growth of top quality. 250+ acres. At best, excellent sweet wine of great finesse, and a small amount of red and dry white. The 86, 88, 89 and 90 will be superb in time.

La Gurgue Mar r ** 79 81 82 83' 84 85' 86 87 88 89 90 Small (30-acre) well-placed property making MARGAUX of the fruitiest sort, by owners of CH CHASSE-SPLEEN. To watch.

Hanteillan Cissac r ** 81 82' 83 85' 86 87 88' 89 90 Large (200-acre+) v'yd renovated since '73. V fair Bourgeois wine. Ch Larrivaux-Hanteillan is second quality. 50,000 cases.

Haut-Bages-Averous Pau r ** 82' 83 85 86 87 88 89 90 The second wine of CH LYNCH BAGES. Delicious easy drinking.

Haut-Bages-Libéral Pau r ** 75 78 81 82' 83 84 85 86' 87 88 89' 90 Lesser-known fifth-growth of 64 acres, in same stable as CHASSE-SPLEEN since '83. The results are excellent, full of PAUILLAC vitality.

Haut-Bages-Monpelou Pau r ** 75' 78 79 81 82' 83 85 86 87 88 89' 90 25-acre Cru Bourgeois stable-mate of CH BATAILLEY on former DUHART-MILON land. Good minor PAUILLAC.

Haut-Bailly Graves r *** 70' 78 79' 80 81' 82 83 84 85 86' 87 88 89 90 70-acre+ estate at LEOGNAN, famous for ripe, round, intelligently made, sometimes 'feminine' wine since '79. Second label: La Parde de H-B.

Haut-Batailley Pau r *** 70' 75' 78' 79 81 82' 83 84 85 86 87 88 89' 90 The smaller section of the fifth-growth BATAILLEY estate: 49 acres. Often in a gentler vein than its sister château, GRAND-PUY-LACOSTE. Second label: La Tour-d'Aspic.

Haut-Bergey Pessac-L r ** 40 acres, largely Cab; fragrant, delicate GRAVES.

Haut-Bommes See Clos Haut-Puyraguey.

Haut-Brignon Premières Côtes r w dr * Big producer of standard wines at Cénac, owned by major CHAMPAGNE coop. Do not confuse with the next!

Haut-Brion Pessac (Graves) r (w) **** 61 64 66 70' 71' 75' 76 78' 79' 80 81 82 83 84 85' 86' 87 88 89' 90' The oldest great château of Bordeaux and the only non-MEDOC first-growth of 1855. 108 acres. Beautifully harmonious, never aggressive wine. Particularly good since '75. A little full dry white in 78, 79, 81, 83, 85, 86, 87, 88, 89, 90, 91. See Bahans-Haut-Brion, La Mission-Haut-Brion.

Haut-Marbuzet St-Est r **→**** 75' 78' 79 80 81 82' 83 84 85 86 87 88 89 90 The best of many good ST-ESTEPHE Crus Bourgeois. 100 acres, 60% Merlot. Second-label châteaux CHAMBERT-MARBUZET, MACCARTHY, MacCarthy-Moula, Tour de Marbuzet are in same hands. New oak gives them all classic style.

Haut-Pontet St-Em r ** 70 75 78 79 81 82' 83 85 86 88 89 90 12-acre v'yd of the *côtes* well deserving its Grand Cru status.

Haut-Quercus St-Em r ** 83 85 86 88 89' 90 Oak-aged coop wine to a v high standard.

Haut-Sarpe St-Em r ** 79 81 82 83' 85 86 87 88 89 90 Grand Cru Classé (6,000 cases) with v elegant château and park. Same owner as CH LA

CROIX, POMEROL.

Hortevie St-Jul r ✹✹ 81 82 83 84 85' 86 87 88 89 90 One of the few ST-JULIEN Crus Bourgeois. This tiny v'yd and its bigger sister, TERREY-GROS-CAILLOU, are shining examples. Needs bottle-age.

Houissant St-Est r ✹✹ 78 79 81 82 83 85 86 87 88 89 90 Typical, robust, well-balanced ST-ESTEPHE Cru Bourgeois Exceptionnel, also called Ch Leyssac; well known in Denmark.

d'Issan Cant-Mar r ✹✹✹ 70 75' 78 79 81 82' 83' 84 85 86 87 88 89 90 Beautifully restored moated château with 75-acre third-growth v'yd well known for fragrant, virile but delicate wine.

Kirwan Cant-Mar r ✹✹✹ 78 79' 81 82' 83' 84 85 86 87 88' 89 90 Well-run 86-acre third-growth owned by SCHRODER & SCHYLER. Mature v'yds giving ever tastier wines.

Labégorce Mar r ✹✹ 75' 78 79 81' 82' 83' 84 85 86 87 88 89 90 Substantial 69-acre property N of MARGAUX producing long-lived wines of true Margaux quality.

Labégorce-Zédé Mar r ✹✹ 75' 78 79 81' 82' 83' 84 85 86' 87 88 89' 90 Outstanding Cru Bourgeois on the road N from MARGAUX. 62 acres. Typical delicate, fragrant Margaux, truly classic since '81. The same family as VIEUX CHATEAU CERTAN. Second label: Domaine Zédé.

Laclaverie See Puygueraud.

Lacoste-Borie The second wine of CH GRAND-PUY-LACOSTE.

Lafaurie-Peyraguey Saut w sw ✹✹✹ 75' 76' 78' 80 81' 82 83' 85 86 87 88 89 90 Fine classed-growth of only 49 acres at BOMMES, belonging to CORDIER. After a lean patch, good, rich and racy wines.

Lafite-Rothschild Pau r ✹✹✹✹ 70' 75' 76 78 79 81' 82' 83 84 85 86' 87 88' 89' 90 First-growth of fabulous style and perfume in its great vintages, which keep for decades. Off form for several yrs but resplendent since '76. Amazing circular cellars opened '87; joint ventures in Chile ('88), California ('89). Second wine: MOULIN-DES-CARRUADES. 225 acres. Also owns CH'X DUHART-MILON, L'EVANGILE, RIEUSSEC.

Lafleur Pom r ✹✹✹ 70' 75' 78 81 82' 83 85 86 88 89' 90 Property of 12 acres just N of PETRUS. Resounding wine of the tannic, less 'fleshy' kind. Same owner as LE GAY. MOUEIX oenology through '90. Second wine: Pensées de Lafleur.

Lafleur-Gazin Pom r ✹✹ 70 75' 78 79 81 82' 83 85' 86 87 88' 89 90 Distinguished small J-P MOUEIX estate on the NE border of POMEROL.

Lafon-Rochet St-Est r ✹✹ 70' 79 81 82 83' 85 86 88 89 90 Fourth-growth neighbour of CH COS D'ESTOURNEL, restored in the '60s and again recently. 110 acres. Rather hard, dark, full-bodied ST-ESTEPHE. Same owner as CH PONTET-CANET. Second label: Numéro 2.

Lagrange Pom r ✹✹✹ 70' 75' 78 81 82' 83 85' 86 87 88 89' 90 20-acre v'yd in the centre of POMEROL run by the ubiquitous house of J-P MOUEIX. Marked improvement in late '80s.

Lagrange St-Jul r ✹✹✹ 70 75 79 81 82 83 84 85' 86' 87 88 89' 90 Formerly run-down third-growth inland from ST-JULIEN, bought by Suntory at the end of '83. 280 acres now in tiptop condition. To follow. Second wine: Les Fiefs de Lagrange (83', 85, 86, 87, 88, 89, 90).

La Lagune Ludon r ✹✹✹ 70' 75' 76' 78' 79 81 82' 83 84 85 86' 87 88' 89' 90' Well-run, ultra-modern 160-acre third-growth in the extreme S of the MEDOC. Attractively rich and fleshy wines; usually brilliant quality.

Lalande-Borie St-Jul r ✹✹ 78 79 81 82 83 85 86 87 88 89 90 A baby brother of the great DUCRU-BEAUCAILLOU created from part of the former v'yd of CH LAGRANGE.

Lamarque Lamarque (H-Méd) r ✹✹ 81' 82 83' 85 86 87 88 89 90 Splendid medieval fortress of the central MEDOC with 113 acres giving admirable and improving wine of high Bourgeois standard.

Lamothe de Bergeron H-Méd r ✹✹ 150 acres at CUSSAC makes 25,000 cases of reliable claret. Run by GRAND-PUY-DUCASSE.

Lanessan Cussac (H-Méd) r ✹✹ 75' 78' 79 81 82 83 84 85 86' 87 88 89 90

Distinguished 108-acre Cru Bourgeois Exceptionnel just S of ST-JULIEN. Can be classed-growth quality. Fine rather than burly.

Langoa-Barton St-Jul r ******* 70' 75' 76 78' 79 81 82' 83 84 85 86' 87 88 89' 90'   49-acre third-growth sister château to LEOVILLE-BARTON. V old family property with impeccable standards, and value. Second wine: Lady Langoa.

Larcis-Ducasse St-Em r ****** 82' 83 85 86 87 88 89 90   The top property of St-Laurent, E neighbour of ST-EMILION, on the *côtes* next to CH PAVIE. 30 acres. Coasting.

Larmande St-Em r ****** 75' 78 79 81 82 83 84 85 86 87 88 89 90   Substantial 54-acre property related to CAP-DE-MOURLIN. Replanted and now making rich, strikingly scented wine.

Laroque St-Em r ****** 75' 78 79 81 82' 83 85 86 88 89 90   Important 108-acre v'yd on the ST-EMILION *côtes* in St-Christophe.

Larose-Trintaudon St-Laurent r ****** 75 79 82 83 85 86 87 88 89 90 The biggest v'yd in the MEDOC: 425 acres. Modern methods make reliable, fruity and charming Cru Bourgeois wine. New management in '89 and second label Larose St-Laurent.

Laroze St-Em r ****** 75' 79 81 82 83 85 86 87 88' 89 90'   Big v'yd (74 acres) on the W *côtes*. Relatively light wines from sandy soil; soon enjoyable. Sometimes excellent.

Larrivet-Haut-Brion Graves (w) ****** 75' 76 79' 81 82' 83 84 85 86 87 88 89 90   Little property at LEOGNAN with perfectionist standards. Also 500 cases of barrel-fermented white to age up to 10 yrs.

Lascombes Mar r (p) ******* 70' 75' 78 79 81 82 83 84 85 86 87 88' 89 90' 240-acre second-growth owned by British brewers Bass-Charrington and lavishly restored. After a poor patch, some new vigour since '82 but still not tasting like a second-growth. Second wine: Ch Segonnes.

Latour Pau r ******** 61 62 64 66 67 70' 71 73 75' 76' 78' 79 80 81' 82' 83 84 85 86' 87 88' 89' 90'   First-growth considered the grandest statement of the MEDOC. Rich, intense and almost immortal in great yrs, almost always classical and pleasing even in weak ones. Some controversy over style in early '80s, but Latour always needs time to show its hand. British-owned (though different company since '89). 150 acres sloping to the R Gironde. Second wine: LES FORTS DE LATOUR.

Latour-Martillac Graves r w dr ****** (r) 81 82' 83 84 85' 86 87 88' 89 90 Small but serious property at Martillac. 10 acres of white grapes; 37 of black. The white can age admirably (85, 86, 87, 88, 89, 90, 91). The owner is resurrecting the neighbouring Ch Lespault.

Latour-à-Pomerol Pom r ******** 70' 76' 79' 81' 82 83 84 85' 86 87 88 89 Top growth of 19 acres under MOUEIX management. POMEROL of great power and perfume, yet also ravishing finesse.

des Laurets St-Em r ****** 75' 78 79 81 82 83 85 86 88 89' 90'   Major property in PUISSEGUIN- and MONTAGNE-ST-EMILION (to the E) with 160 acres (40,000 cases) on the *côtes*. Sterling wine sold by J-P MOUEIX.

Laville-Haut-Brion Graves w dr ******** 78 79 81 82 83 85' 86 87' 88 89' 90 91   A tiny production of one of the v best white GRAVES for long succulent maturing, made at CH LA MISSION-HAUT-BRION.

Léoville-Barton St-Jul r ******* 61 66 70' 75' 76 78' 79 80 81 82' 83 84 85 86 87 88 89 90   90-acre portion of the great second-growth Léoville v'yd in the Anglo-Irish hands of the Barton family for over 150 yrs. Powerful and classic claret; traditional methods and v fair prices. Major investment is raising already v high standards.

Léoville-Las-Cases St-Jul r ******** 61 66 70' 75' 76 78' 79 81 82 83 84 85 86 87 88 89' 90'   The largest portion of the old Léoville estate, adjacent to LATOUR; 210 acres, with one of the highest reputations in Bordeaux. Elegant, complex, powerful, rather austere wines, built for immortality. Second label: CLOS DU MARQUIS, also outstanding.

Léoville-Poyferré St-Jul r ******* 75' 79 81 82 83 84 85 86' 87 88 89 90   For yrs the least outstanding of the Léovilles; since '80 again living up to the great name. 156 acres. Second label: Ch Moulin-Riche.

Lestage Listrac r ✸✸ 81 82' 83 85 86' 87 88 89 90   130-acre Cru Bourgeois in same hands as CH FONREAUD. Light, quite stylish wine, aged in oak since '85. Second wine: Ch Caroline.

Lilian-Ladouys St-Est ✸✸ 89 90   Recent creation: a 50-acre Cru Bourgeois with high ambitions. To watch.

Liot Barsac w sw ✸✸ 75' 82 83 85 86 88 89' 90'   Consistent, fairly light, golden wines from 50 acres.

Liversan St-Sauveur r ✸✸ 81 82' 83 85 86' 87 88 89 90   116-acre Grand Cru Bourgeois inland from PAUILLAC. Change of regime in '84 greatly improved standards. Second wine: Ch Fonpiqueyre.

Livran Méd r ✸✸ 78' 79 81 82' 83 85 86 88 89 90   Big Cru Bourgeois at St-Germain in the N MEDOC. Consistent round wines (half Merlot).

Loudenne St-Yzans (Méd) r ✸✸✸ 82' 83 85 86' 87' 88 89' 90   Beautiful riverside château owned by Gilbeys since 1875. Well-made Cru Bourgeois red and an increasingly delicious dry white from 120 acres. The white is best at 2–3 yrs (89', 90).

Loupiac-Gaudiet Loupiac w sw ✸✸ 85 86 87 88 89 90 91   Reliable source of good value almost-SAUTERNES, just across the R Garonne. 7,500 cases.

La Louvière Graves r w dr ✸✸→✸✸✸ 78 81 82' 83 85 86 87 88 89 90 (w) 87 88 89 90 91   Noble 135-acre estate at LEOGNAN restored by the ubiquitous Lurton family (BRANE-CANTENAC etc). Excellent white for drinking or maturing, and red recently of classed-growth standard.

de Lussac St-Em r ✸✸ 82 83 85 86 88 89' 90   One of the best estates in LUSSAC-ST-EMILION (to the NE).

Lynch-Bages Pau r (w dr) ✸✸✸→✸✸✸✸ 61' 66 70 75' 78' 79 81 82' 83' 84 85' 86' 87 88 89' 90'   Always popular, but now one of PAUILLAC's regular stars. 200 acres making rich, robust wine: deliciously brambly; aspiring to greatness. Recent vintages, esp notable. Second wine: HAUT-BAGES-AVEROUX. From '90, a little intense, oaky white. The owner, J-M Cazes, also directs PICHON-LONGUEVILLE etc for AXA Insurance.

Lynch-Moussas Pau r ✸✸ 75' 78 81 82 83 85 86 87 88 89 90   Fifth-growth restored by the director of CH BATAILLEY since '69. Now 60+ acres and new equipment are making serious wine, gaining depth as the young vines age, but only so far at high Cru Bourgeois level.

du Lyonnat Lussac-St-Em r ✸✸ 82 83 85 86' 88 89 90   120-acre estate with well-distributed, reliable wine.

MacCarthy St-Est r ✸✸   Cru Bourgeois in the same splendid stable as HAUT-MARBUZET.

Macquin-St-Georges St-Em r ✸✸ 85 86 88 89 90   Steady producer of delicious 'satellite' ST-EMILION at ST-GEORGES.

St-Emilion: The Class System
St-Emilion has its own class system, revised in 1985. At the top are 2 Premiers Grands Crus Classés 'A': Châteaux Ausone and Cheval Blanc. Then come 9 Premiers Grands Crus Classés 'B'. 63 châteaux were elected as Grands Crus Classés (they will seek reelection in 1994). Another 170-odd are classed simply as Grands Crus, a rank renewable each year after official tastings. St-Emilion Grand Cru is therefore the very approximate equivalent of Médoc Crus Bourgeois and Grand Bourgeois.

Magdelaine St-Em r ✸✸✸ 70' 71' 73 75 76 78 79 81 82 83' 85' 86 88 89 90   Leading *côtes* first-growth: 28 acres next to AUSONE owned by J-P MOUEIX. Beautifully balanced, full-flavoured wine. On top form.

Magence Graves r w dr ✸✸ w (r) dr   Go-ahead 45-acre property at St-Pierre de Mons, in S GRAVES. Sauv-flavoured dry white, and fruity red. Both age well 2–6 yrs.

Malartic-Lagravière Graves r (w dr) ✸✸✸ 70' 75' 76' 78 79 81 82' 83 85 86' 87 88 89 (w) 81' 82 83 85 86 87' 88 89 90 91   Well-known LEOGNAN classed-growth of 53 acres. Well-structured, rather hard red and a v little excellent fruity Sauv white, hard to resist young, but worth cellaring. Bought in '90 by LAURENT-PERRIER.

Malescasse Lamarque (H-Méd) r ** 78 79' 81 82 83 85 86 87 88 89 90 Renovated Cru Bourgeois with 100 acres in a good situation, owned by M Tesseron of LAFON-ROCHET. Second label: Le Tana de Malescasse.

Malescot-St-Exupéry Mar r *** 70' 75' 78' 79 81 82' 83' 85 86 87 88 89 90 Third-growth of 84 acres. Often tough when young, eventually fragrant and stylish MARGAUX. New consultant from '90 augurs well.

de Malle Saut r w sw dr *** (w sw) 75 76 78 79 80 81' 82 83 85 86' 88 89' 90' Famous, beautiful château with Italian gardens at Preignac. 124 acres. Good sweet and dry white and red (GRAVES) DU CARDAILLAN (**).

de Malleret H-Méd r ** 82 83 85 86 88 89' 90 An aristocrat's domaine. The Comte du Vivier makes 25,000 cases of easy, gentlemanly claret at Le Pian, among forests just N of Bordeaux.

de Marbuzet St-Est r ** 75 78 79 81 82 83 85 86 87 88 89 90 Effectively the second label of CH COS-D'ESTOURNEL: correspondingly well made.

Margaux Mar r (w dr) **** 61 70 78' 79 80 81' 82' 83' 84 85' 86' 87 88 89' 90' First-growth (with 209 acres of vines), the most penetrating and fabulously perfumed of all in its (v frequent) best vintages. Pavillon Rouge (81, 82', 83', 84, 85, 86, 87, 88, 89, 90') is the second wine. Pavillon Blanc is the best white (Sauv) wine of the MEDOC (78, 79, 80, 81, 82, 83, 84, 86, 87, 88, 89, 90, 91).

Marquis-d'Alesme *See* d'Alesme.

Marquis-de-Terme Mar r *** 75' 81' 82 83 85 86' 87 88 89 90 Renovated fourth-growth of 84 acres. Fragrant, fairly lean style has developed since '85.

Martinens Mar r ** 78' 79' 81 82 83 85 86 87 88 89 90 Worthy 75-acre Cru Bourgeois at CANTENAC; new barrels since '89.

Maucaillou Moulis r ** 75' 78 79 81 82 83' 84 85' 86' 87 88 89 90 130-acre Cru Bourgeois with *cru classé* standards, property of DOURTHE family. Full, richly fruity Cap de Haut-Maucaillou is second wine.

Mazeyres Pom r ** Consistent, useful lesser POMEROL. 5,000 cases.

Méaume Bx Supérieur r ** An Englishman's domaine, out of the mainstream, N of POMEROL. Since '80 has built a solid reputation for vg daily claret to age 4–5 yrs. 7,500 cases.

Meyney St-Est r **→**** 75' 78' 79 81 82' 83 84 85 86 87 88 89 90 Big (125-acre) riverside property next door to CH MONTROSE, one of the best of many steady Crus Bourgeois in ST-ESTEPHE. Owned by CORDIER. Second label: Prieur de Meyney.

Millet Graves r w (p) dr ** 82 83 85 86 88 89 90 (w) 91 Useful GRAVES. Second label, Ch Renon: mainly white; drink young.

La Mission-Haut-Brion Graves r **** 61 64 66 71' 74 75' 76 78' 79 80 81 82' 83 84 85' 86 87 88 89' 90' Neighbour and long-time rival to CH HAUT-BRION; since '84 in the same hands. New equipment in '87. Serious, grand, old-style claret for long maturing; 'bigger' wine than Haut-Brion. 30 acres.

Monbousquet St-Em r ** 75 78' 79' 81 82 83 85' 86 88' 89 90 Attractive, early-maturing wine from deep gravel soil: lasts well.

Monbrison Arsac-Mar r ** 81 82 83 84 85 86 87 88' 89' 90 A new name to watch in MARGAUX. Top Bourgeois standards. 4,000 cases plus 2,000 of second label, Ch Cordet.

Montrose St-Est r *** 61 66 70' 75' 76 78' 79 81 82' 83 84 85 86' 87 88 89' 90' 158-acre family-run second-growth well known for deeply coloured, forceful, old-style claret. Vintages between 79–86 (except 82) were lighter, but recent Montrose is almost ST-ESTEPHE's answer to CH LATOUR. Second wine: La Dame de Montrose.

Moulin-à-Vent Moulis r ** 70' 75' 78' 79 81 82' 83 84 85 86 88 89 90' 60-acre property in the forefront of this booming AC. Lively, forceful wine. LA TOUR-BLANCHE (MEDOC) has same owners.

Moulin-des-Carruades The second-quality wine of CH LAFITE.

Moulin du Cadet St-Em ** 75' 81 82' 83 85 86 87 88 89' 90   First-class little v'yd on the *côtes,* owned by MOUEIX.

Moulinet Pom r *** 75 78 79 81 82 83 85 86 87 88' 89 90   One of POMEROL's bigger châteaux, 43 acres on lightish soil; wine lightish also.

Mouton-Baronne-Philippe Pau r *** 70' 75' 78' 79 81 82' 83 84 85 86' 87 88 89 90'   Substantial fifth-growth nurtured by the late Baron Philippe de Rothschild, 125 acres making less rich and luscious wine than MOUTON-R, but still outstanding in its class. *See* d'Armailhac.

Mouton-Rothschild Pau r **** 61 66 70' 71 75' 76 78' 79 81 82' 83 84 85 86' 87 88 89' 90'   Officially a first-growth since '73, though for 40 yrs worthy of the title. 175 acres (87% Cab S) make majestic, rich wine. Also the world's greatest museum of works of art relating to wine. Baron Philippe, the greatest champion of the MEDOC, died in '88, to be succeeded by his daughter Philippine. *See also* Opus One, California.

Nairac Saut w sw ** 73 75 76' 78 79 80 81 82 83' 85 86' 88 89 90'   BARSAC classed-growth with perfectionist owner. Fascinating wines to lay down for a decade.

Nenin Pom r *** 70' 75' 78 83 85' 86 87 88' 89 90   Well-known 66-acre estate; on an upswing since '85.

d'Olivier Graves r w dr ** (r) 82 83 85 86 87 88 89' 90' (w) 91   90-acre classed-growth, surrounding a moated castle at LEOGNAN. 9,000 cases red, 12,000 white. New broom in '89 has upgraded quality drastically.

Les Ormes-de-Pez St-Est r **→**** 75' 78' 79 81' 82' 83' 84 85 86' 87 88 89' 90'   Outstanding 72-acre Cru Bourgeois owned by CH LYNCH-BAGES. Increasingly notable full-flavoured ST-ESTEPHE. A fire in '88 destroyed the CHAI and three-quarters of the '88 crop.

Les Ormes-Sorbet Méd r ** 82 83 85 86 87 88 89 90   Emerging smaller producer of good solid red aged in new oak at Couquèques. A leader of the N MEDOC. Second label: Ch de Conques.

Palmer Cant-Mar r **** 61' 66' 70 71' 75' 76 78' 79' 81 82 83' 84 85 86' 87 88' 89 90   The star château of CANTENAC: a third-growth often on a level just below the first-growths. Wine of power, flesh and delicacy. 110 acres with Dutch, British, French owners. Second wine: Réserve du Général.

Pape-Clément Graves r (w dr) *** 75' 78' 82' 83 84 85' 86' 87 88' 89' 90'   Ancient v'yd at Pessac, with record of seductive, scented, not ponderous reds. Early '80s not up to snuff, but new resolve (and more white) since '85.

de Parenchère r (w) *   Steady supply of supply of useful AC Ste-Foy Bordeaux from handsome château with 125 acres.

Patache d'Aux Bégadan (Méd) r ** 81 82' 83' 85 86 88 89' 90'   90-acre Cru Bourgeois of the N MEDOC. Fragrant, largely Cab wine with the earthy quality of its area.

Paveil (de Luze) Mar r ** 75' 78 79 81 82' 83' 84 85 86' 87 88 89' 90'   Old family estate at SOUSSANS. Small but highly regarded.

Pavie St-Em r *** 75' 78 79' 81 82' 83' 84 85 86' 87 88 89' 90'   Splendidly sited first-growth of 92 acres on the slope of the *côtes.* Typically rich and tasty ST-EMILION, particularly since '86. The family owns the smaller châteaux PAVIE-DECESSE and La Clusière.

Pavie-Decesse St-Em r **   24 acres challenging their big brother (above).

Pavie-Macquin St-Em r ** 75 78 79 82 83 85' 86 87 88 89 90   Reliable 25-acre *côtes* v'yd E of ST-EMILION. New energy since '86.

Pavillon-Cadet St-Em r **   The smallest, not the least, Grand Cru Classé 750 cases.

Pavillon Rouge du Château Margaux *See* Ch Margaux

Pedesclaux Pau r ** 75 78 79 81 82' 83 84 85 86 87 88 89 90'   50-acre fifth-growth on the level of a good Cru Bourgeois. Solid, strong wines that Belgians love. Second labels: Bellerose, Grand-Duroc-Milon.

Petit-Village Pom r *** 75' 78 79 81 82' 83 85 86 88 89' 90'   One of the best-known little properties: 26 acres next to VIEUX CHATEAU CERTAN, same owner as CH PICHON-LONGUEVILLE. Powerful plummy wine.

Pétrus Pom r **** 61 64 66 67 70' 71' 73 75' 76' 78 79' 80 81 82' 83 84 85' 86 88' 89' 90   The great name of POMEROL. 28 acres of gravelly clay giving massively rich and concentrated wine. 95% Merlot vines. Each vintage adds lustre. The price, too, is legendary.

Peyrabon St-Sauveur r ** 75 78 81 82 83 85 86 87 88 89 90   Serious 132-acre Cru Bourgeois popular in the Low Countries. Also La Fleur-Peyrabon (only 12 acres).

Peyreau St-Em r **   Sister château of Clos l'Oratoire.

Peyre-Labade Listrac ** Another LISTRAC Cru Bourgeois to follow since '88.

de Pez St-Est r *** 66 70' 75' 76 78' 79 81 82' 83 84 85 86' 87 88 89 90   Outstanding Cru Bourgeois of 60 acres. As reliable as any of the classed-growths of the village, and nearly as fine. Needs v long storage (eg 66 was ideal in '88.)

Phélan-Ségur St-Est r ** 75' 81 82' 85 86 87 88 89 90   Big and important Cru Bourgeois (125 acres) with some fine old vintages. 83–84 were faulty and had to be withdrawn, but from '86 things have gone well.

Pibran Pau r ** 89 90   Small Cru Bourgeois allied to PICHON-LONGUEVILLE. V classy wine.

Pichon-Longueville (formerly **Baron de Pichon-Longueville**) Pau r *** 78 79' 81 82' 83 85 86' 87 88' 89' 90'   77-acre second-growth whose wines have varied widely. Since '87 owned by AXA Insurance, run by J-M Cazes (LYNCH-BAGES). Revitalized winemaking matches spectacular building programme. Second label: Les Tourelles de Longueville.

Pichon-Lalande (formerly **Pichon-Longueville, Comtesse de Lalande**) Pau r **** 61 66 70' 75' 76 78' 79' 81 82' 83' 84 85' 86' 87 88 89' 90'   Second-growth neighbour to CH LATOUR. 148 acres. Consistently among the v top performers; long-lived wine of fabulous breed for those who like it luscious, even in lesser yrs. Second wine: Réserve de la Comtesse. Rivalry across the road (last entry) is worth watching.

Pique-Caillou Graves r ** 85 86 87 88 89 90   Nr Bordeaux airport. Recently refurbished; delicate, charming wine. Also next-door Ch Chênevert.

Le Pin Pom r *** A mere 6 acres of Merlot, with same owners as VIEUX CHATEAU CERTAN. A perfectionist miniature.

Pindefleurs St-Em r ** 79 81 82' 83 85 86 88 89 90   Steady 25-acre v'yd on the ST-EMILION plateau.

Piron Graves w (r) dr **   Producer of seductively fruity modern white GRAVES at St-Morillon.

de Pitray Castillon r ** 82 83 85 86 87 88 89 90   Substantial (62-acre) v'yd on COTES DE CASTILLON E of ST-EMILION. Good, flavoursome, chewy wines.

Plagnac Méd r ** 79 81 82 83 85 86 88 89 90   Cru Bourgeois at BEGADAN restored by CORDIER. To follow.

Plince Pom r ** 75 79 81 82 83 85 86 88 89 90   Reputable 20-acre property nr Libourne. Attractive, perhaps rather simple wine from sandy soil.

La Pointe Pom r **→*** 81 82 83' 85 86 87 88 89' 90'   Prominent 63-acre estate, well made, but relatively spare of flesh until '86, when a new consultant started work. 89 is terrific. LA SERRE is in the same hands.

Pontac-Monplaisir Graves r (w dr) ** 87 88 89 90   Another GRAVES property offering delicious Sauv Bl white.

Pontet-Canet Pau r *** 70 75' 78' 79' 81 82' 83 85 86 87 88 89 90   One of the biggest classed-growths. 182 acres, neighbour to MOUTON-R. Dragged its feet for many yrs. Current owners (same as LAFON-ROCHET) have re-equipped and shown new resolve since '85. They should make potent, long-lived wines. Second label: Les Hauts de Pontet.

Pontoise-Cabarrus H-Méd r **   Useful and improving Cru Bourgeois at ST-SEURIN. Wines need 5–6 yrs.

Potensac Méd r ** 78' 79 81 82' 83 84 85' 86 87 88 89' 90'   The best-known Cru Bourgeois of the N MEDOC. The neighbouring Châteaux

Lassalle and Gallais-Bellevue belong to the same family, the Delons, owners of LEOVILLE-LAS-CASES. Class shows.

Pouget Mar ** **78 79 81 82' 83 85 86 87 88 89 90** 19-acre v'yd attached to CH BOYD-CANTENAC. In '83 separate CHAIS were built. Similar, rather lighter wines.

Poujeaux (Theil) Moulis r ** **70' 75' 76 78 79' 80 81 82' 83' 84 85' 86 87 88 89' 90'** Family-run Cru Exceptionnel of 120 acres. 20,000-odd cases of characterful, tannic and concentrated wine for a long life. Second label: La Salle de Poujeaux. Also Ch Arnauld.

Prieuré-Lichine Cant-Mar r *** **70 75 78' 81 82' 83' 84 85 86' 87 88 89' 90** 143-acre fourth-growth brought to the fore by the late Alexis Lichine. Excellent, full-bodied and fragrant MARGAUX.

Puy-Blanquet St-Em r ** **75' 81 82' 83 85 86 88 89' 90** The major property of St-Etienne-de-Lisse, E of ST-EMILION, with over 50 acres. Early-maturing St-Em in early '80s; now firming up well.

Puy-Razac St-Em r ** **78 79 81' 82' 83 85 86 88' 89 90** Tiny brother to MONBOUSQUET at the foot of the *côtes* near CH PAVIE.

Puygueraud Côte de Francs r ** **82 83 85 86 87 88 89' 90** Leading château of this rising district. Wood-aged wines of surprising class. Ch Laclaverie (since '85) and Les Charmes-Godard (since '88) follow the same lines.

Rabaud-Promis Saut w sw ** **75 76 78 79 81 83 85 86 88 89 90** 74-acre classed-growth at BOMMES. Little seen outside France.

Rahoul Graves r w dr ** **78' 81 82 83 85 86 87 88 89 90' (w) 85 86' 87 88 89' 90' 91** 37-acre v'yd at Portets making particularly good wine in the '80s from maturing vines; 80% red. White is aged in oak, too.

Ramage-la-Bâtisse H-Méd r ** **82 83' 85 86 87 88 89' 90** Potentially outstanding Cru Bourgeois of 130 acres at ST-SAUVEUR, N of PAUILLAC. Increasingly good since '85. Ch Tourteran is second wine.

Rausan-Ségla Mar r *** **70' 81 82 83' 84 85 86' 88' 89' 90** 106-acre second-growth; famous for its fragrance; a great MEDOC name trying hard to regain its rank since '83. New British owners (and splendid wine) in '89. Second wine: Ch Lamouroux.

Rauzan-Gassies Mar r ** **61 75' 78' 79' 82 83 85 86 87 88 89 90** 75-acre second-growth neighbour of the last with little excitement to report for two decades, now definitely perking up – but still far to go.

Raymond-Lafon Saut w sw ** **75 76 78' 79 80' 81' 82 83 85 86 87 88 89 90** Serious SAUTERNES estate run by the ex-manager of CH D'YQUEM. Splendid wines for long ageing. Among the top Sauternes.

de Rayne-Vigneau Saut w sw *** **71' 76' 78 81 83 85 86' 88 89 90'** 164-acre classed-growth at BOMMES. Standard sweet wine and a little dry Rayne Sec. New equipment in '80: looking better.

Respide-Médeville Graves w (r) dr ** **(w) 86 87 88 89 90 91** One of the better unclassified white wine châteaux. Full-flavoured wines for ageing. (NB 85 Cuvée Kauffman.)

Reynon Premières Côtes r w dr ** **100 acres producing extraordinary dry white from v old Sauv vines (VIEILLES VIGNES: 86, 87, 88, 89, 90', 91). Also CLOS FLORIDENE barrel-fermented white (86, 87', 88, 89', 90, 91) and red since '85, DYA white and serious red (85, 86, 88', 89, 90). Second wine (red): Ch Reynon-Peyrat.

Reysson Vertheuil (H-Méd) r ** **81 82' 83 84 85 86 87 88 89 90** Recently replanted, up-and-coming 120-acre Cru Bourgeois with the same owners as CH CHASSE-SPLEEN. To follow.

Ricaud Loupiac w sw (dr) r ** **81 82 83' 85 86' 88 89 90 91** Substantial grower of almost SAUTERNES-like dessert wine, just across the river. New owners are working hard. It ages well.

Rieussec Saut w sw *** **70 71' 75' 76' 80 81 82 83' 85 86 87 88 89 88 89 90' 91** Worthy neighbour of CH D'YQUEM with 136 acres in Fargues, bought in '84 by the (Lafite) Rothschilds. Not the sweetest; can be exquisitely fine. Also dry 'R' and super-wine Crême de Tête.

Ripeau St-Em r ✱✱ 78 79 81 82 83 85 86 87 88 89 90 Steady Grand Cru in the centre of the plateau. 49 acres.

La Rivière Fronsac r ✱✱ 85' 86 87 88' 89 90 The biggest and most impressive FRONSAC property. Tannic but juicy wines win prizes in youth and stay youthful for a decade.

de Rochemorin Graves r (w dr) ✱✱ 82 83 84 85 86 87 88 89 90 An important restoration at Martillac by the owner of CH LA LOUVIÈRE. 165 acres of maturing vines promise great things.

Romer-du-Hayot Saut w sw ✱✱ 81 82 83 85 86' 88 89 90 A minor classed-growth with a growing reputation.

de Roquetaillade-la-Grange Graves r w dr ✱✱ Substantial estate establishing a name for fine red (S) GRAVES.

Roudier Montagne-St-Em r ✱✱ 75-acre 'satellite' with real flavour.

Rouget Pom r ✱✱ 75' 76' 78 79 81 82' 83 85' 86 88 89 90 Attractive old estate on the N edge of POMEROL. Good, without polish.

Royal St-Emilion Brand name of the important and dynamic growers' coop. *See also* Berliquet, Haut-Quercus.

Ruat-Petit-Poujeaux Moulis r ✱✱ 82 85 86 87 88 89 90 45-acre v'yd gaining in reputation for vigorous wine, to drink in 5–6 yrs.

St-André-Corbin St-Em r ✱✱ 75' 78 79' 81 82' 83 85' 86 87 88 89 90 Considerable 54-acre property in MONTAGNE- and ST-GEORGES-ST-EMILION with a long record of above average wines.

St-Bonnet Méd r ✱✱ 81 82 83 85 86 89 90 Big N MEDOC estate at St-Christoly. V flavoury wine.

St-Estèphe, Marquis de St-Est r ✱ 82 86 88 89 90 The growers' coop; not as interesting as formerly.

St-Georges St-Georges-St-Em r ✱✱ 82 83 85' 86 87 88 89' 90 Noble 18th-C château overlooking the ST-EMILION plateau from the hill to the N. 125 acres; vg wine sold direct to the public.

St-Georges-Côte-Pavie St-Em r ✱✱ 79 81 82 83' 85' 86 88 89' 90' Perfectly placed little v'yd on the *côtes*. Run with dedication (and served by Air France First Class).

St-Pierre St-Jul r ✱✱✱ 70' 75' 78' 79 81' 82' 83' 84 85 86 87 88 89 90 Small (50-acre) fourth-growth many yrs in Belgian ownership; bought in '82 by the late Henri Martin of CH GLORIA. A name to follow.

St-Pierre Graves w (r) dr ✱✱ 85 86 87 88 89 90 91 Mainstream white GRAVES of notable character and flavour.

de Sales Pom r ✱✱✱ 75' 81 82' 83 85 86 87 88 89 90 Biggest v'yd of POMEROL (116 acres), attached to grandest château. Not often poetry, but at least lucid prose. Second labels: Ch Chantalouette and Ch du Delias.

Saransot-Dupré Listrac r (w dr) ✱✱ 86 88 89 90 Small property performing well since '86. Also LISTRAC's only white (?).

Sénéjac H-Méd r (w dr) ✱✱ 75 76' 78 79 81 82' 83' 84 85 86' 87 88 89 90' 60-acre Cru Bourgeois in S MEDOC run with zeal by a New Zealander. All-Sémillon white to age. Second label: Dom de l'Artigue.

La Serre St-Em r ✱✱ 81 82 83 85 86 87 88' 89 90 Small Grand Cru, same owner as LA POINTE. Fresh approach since '86.

Siaurac Lalande de Pom r ✱✱ Substantial, consistent; nr POMEROL. 57 acres.

Sigalas-Rabaud Saut w sw ✱✱✱ 71 75 76' 78 80 82 83' 85 86 88' 89' 90' 91 The lesser part of the former Rabaud estate: 34 acres in BOMMES, making first-class sweet wine in a fresh, grapey style.

Siran Labarde-Mar r ✱✱✱ 61 66 70 75' 78' 79 81' 82' 83 84 85 86 87 88 89 90 74-acre property of *cru classé* quality. Elegant, long-lived wines.

Smith-Haut-Lafitte Graves r (w dr) ✱✱ 82' 85 86 88 89 90 (w: age 2–3 yrs) Classed-growth at Martillac restored in the '70s. New British owners (same as RAUSAN-SEGLA) in '89. 122 acres (14 of white). White is light and fruity; the red just light. Recent efforts have improved matters.

Sociando-Mallet H-Méd r ✱✱ 70 75 78 79 81 82 83 84 85 86 88 89 90 Splendid Cru Grand Bourgeois at ST-SEURIN in the north. 65 acres. Conservative, big-boned wines to lay down.

Soudars H-Méd r ** Sister to COUFRAN; a good new Cru Bourgeois getting into its stride.

Soutard St-Em r **→*** 70' 71 75' 76 78' 79 80 81 82' 83 84 85' 86 87 88' 89 90 Excellent reliable 48-acre classed-growth. Potent, long-lived wine.

Suduiraut Saut w sw *** 67 70 75 76' 78 79' 81 82' 83' 84 85 86 88' 89 90' One of the best SAUTERNES – though rarely super-rich. Over 173 acres of the top class. Selection: Cuvée Madame (82, 83, 86).

du Tailhas Pom r ** 5,000 cases POMEROL of the lighter kind, not far from FIGEAC.

Taillefer Pom r ** 70 75 78 79 81 82' 83 85 86 87 88' 89 90 24-acre property on the edge of POMEROL owned by another branch of the MOUEIX family (*see also* Fonplégade). Give it time.

Talbot St-Jul r (w) *** 70' 75' 78' 79 81 82' 83 84 85 86' 87 88' 89 90 Important 240-acre fourth-growth, sister château to GRUAUD-LAROSE. Wine similarly attractive: rich, satisfying, reliable and good value. Vg second label: Connétable Talbot. White is called Caillou Blanc.

Tayac Soussans-Mar r ** 81 82 83 85 86 87 88 89 90 MARGAUX's biggest Cru Bourgeois. Reliable if not noteworthy.

de Terrefort-Quancard Bx r w dr ** 82 85 86 87 88 89 90 Huge producer of good value wines at ST-ANDRE-DE-CUBZAC on the road to Paris. Rocky subsoil contributes to surprising quality. 33,000 cases.

Terrey-Gros-Caillou St-Jul r ** 79 82 83 85 86' 87 88 89' 90 Sister château to HORTEVIE; equally noteworthy.

du Tertre Arsac-Mar r *** 70' 75 78 79' 81 82' 83' 85 86 87 88' 89' Fifth-growth, isolated S of MARGAUX; restored to excellence by the owner of CALON-SEGUR. Fragrant and long-lived.

Tertre-Daugay St-Em r *** 78 79 81 82' 83' 85 86 87 88 89 90 Small, spectacularly sited Grand Cru. Restored to its proper place since purchase in '78 by the owner of LA GAFFELIERE.

Le Tertre-Rôteboeuf St-Em *** 85 86 87 88 89 90 A new star making concentrated, even dramatic, largely Merlot wine since '83. The 'roast beef' of the name gives the idea.

Thieuley E-Deux-Mers r p w dr ** 85 86 88 89 90 Substantial supplier, esp of *clairet* (rosé) and grapey Sauv. But reds are aged in oak.

Timberlay Bx r (w dr) * 82 85 86 88' 89 90 The biggest property of ST-ANDRE-DE-CUBZAC; 185 acres. Pleasant light wines.

Toumilon Graves r w dr ** Little château in St-Pierre-de-Mons to note. Fresh and charming red and white.

La Tour-Blanche Saut w (r) sw *** 75' 76 81' 82 83' 85 86 87 88 89' 90 Historic leader of SAUTERNES, now a government wine college. Since '83 better and better.

La Tour-de-By Bégadan (Méd) r ** 79' 81 82' 83 85' 86 87 88' 89' 90' V well run 144-acre Cru Bourgeois in the N MEDOC steadily increasing its reputation for sturdy, impressive yet appealing wine.

La Tour-Carnet St-Laurent r ** 79 81 82' 83 85 86 87 88 89' 90 Fourth-growth with medieval fortress, reborn after total neglect. Lightish wine (much bolder since '86). Second wine: Sire de Comin.

La Tour-Figeac St-Em r ** 75 81 82' 83 85 86 88 89 90 34-acre Grand Cru between CH FIGEAC and POMEROL, not quite showing the form that such a site suggests.

La Tour-Haut-Brion Graves r *** 70 78 79 81 82' 83 85 86 87 88 89 90 Formerly second label of CH LA MISSION-HAUT-BRION. Up to '83 a plainer, v tannic wine for long life. Now a separate v'yd, and easier wines.

La Tour-Haut-Caussan Méd r ** Ambitious, small (23-acre) estate at Blaignan attracting attention.

La Tour-du-Haut-Moulin Cussac (H-Méd) r ** 82 83 85 86 87 88 89 Conservative producer of intense, slightly rustic wines.

La Tour-de-Mons Soussans-Mar r ** 70' 75' 78 81 82' 83 85 86' 87 88' 89' 90' Distinguished Cru Bourgeois of 87 acres, 3 centuries in the same family. After a dull patch, 6 good vintages in a row.

La Tour-du-Pin-Figeac St-Em r ** 26-acre Grand Cru worthy of restoration.

La Tour-du-Pin-Figeac-Moueix St-Em r ** 81 82 83 85 86 88' 89 90 Another 26-acre section of the same old property, owned by a branch of the famous MOUEIX family. Looking good, not inspired.

La Tour-St-Bonnet Méd r ** 81 82' 83 85 86 87 88 89 90 Consistently well-made N MEDOC from St-Christoly. 100 acres.

Tournefeuille Lalande de Pom r ** 81' 82' 83' 85 86 88 89 90' Best-known château of NEAC. 43 acres making v sound wine.

des Tours Montagne-St-Em r ** 82 83 85 86 88 89 90 Spectacular château with modern 170-acre v'yd. Sound, easy wine.

Toutigeac, Domaine de E-Deux-Mers r (w dr) * 89 90 (w) 91 Enormous producer of useful Bordeaux at Targon.

Tronquoy-Lalande St-Est r ** 70 75 78 79 81 82' 83 85 86 88 89 90 40-acre Cru Bourgeois making typical high-coloured ST-ESTEPHE needing long ageing. Distributed by DOURTHE.

Troplong-Mondot St-Em r **→** 82' 83 85' 86 87 88' 89' 90 70 acres well sited on the *côtes* above CH PAVIE (and with the same owners). To follow. Second wine: Mondot.

Trotanoy Pom r **** 61' 70' 71' 73 75' 76' 78 79' 81 82 83 84 85' 86 87 88 89 90 Sometimes the second POMEROL after PETRUS, from the same stable. Only 27 acres; but a glorious, fleshy, perfumed wine.

Trottevieille St-Em r *** 79' 81 82' 83 85' 86 87 88 89 90 Grand Cru of 27 acres on the *côtes*. Dragged its feet for yrs. Same owners as BATAILLEY have raised their sights since '83. To watch.

Le Tuquet Graves r w dr ** 85 86 88 89 90 (w) 91 Big estate at Beautiran. Light, fruity wines; the white better.

Verdignan Méd r ** 81 82 83 85 86 87 88 89' 90 Substantial Grand Bourgeois sister property to CH COUFRAN. More Cab than Coufran: Jack Sprat and his wife.

Vieux Château Certan Pom r *** 71 75 78 79 81 82' 83 84 85 86' 87 88' 89 90 Traditionally rated close to PETRUS in quality, but totally different in style; almost HAUT-BRION build. 34 acres. Same (Belgian) family owns LABEGORCE-ZEDE and tiny POMEROL, Le Pin. *See also* Puygueraud.

Vieux-Château-St-André St-Em r ** 79' 81 82' 83 85' 86 87 88' 89 90 Small v'yd in MONTAGNE-ST-EMILION owned by the leading winemaker of Libourne. To follow. 2,500 cases.

Villegeorge Avensan r ** 81 82 83' 85 86 87' 88 89 90 24-acre Cru Exceptionnel to the N of MARGAUX; same owner as BRANE-CANTENAC. Enjoyable, rather tannic wine. Sister ch: Duplessis (Hauchecorne).

Villemaurine St-Em r ** 82' 83 84 85' 86 88 89 90 Small Grand Cru with splendid cellars, well sited on the *côtes* by the town. Firm wine with a high proportion of Cab.

Vray-Croix-de-Gay Pom r *** 75' 81 82' 83 85 86 87 88 89 V small, ideally situated v'yd in the best part of POMEROL.

Yon-Figeac St-Em r ** 81 82 83 85 86 88 89 59-acre Grand Cru to follow for savoury and scented wine.

d'Yquem Saut w sw (dr) **** 67' 71' 73 75' 76' 77 78 79 80 81 82 83' 84 85 86' 87 88' (89' 90' 91 to come) The world's most famous sweet-wine estate. 250 acres making only 500 bottles per acre of v strong, intense, luscious wine, kept 4 yrs in barrel. Most vintages improve for at least 15 yrs. Also dry Ygrec in 78, 79, 80, 84, 85, 86 (v little), 87, 88.

More Bordeaux châteaux are listed under Canon-Fronsac, Côtes de Bourg, Côtes-de-Castillon, Côtes de France, Fronsac, Lalande de Pomerol, Loupiac, Premières Côtes de Blaye, Premières Côtes de Bordeaux, St-André-de-Cubzac, Ste-Croix-du-Mont in the A–Z of France, pages 22–55.

Switzerland has no truly great wines, but almost all (especially whites) are enjoyable and satisfying – and very expensive. Switzerland has some of the world's most efficient and productive vineyards; costs are high and nothing less is viable. All the most important are in French-speaking areas, along the south-facing slopes of the upper Rhône valley and Lake Geneva, respectively the Valais and the Vaud. Wines from German- and Italian-speaking zones (*see* map) are mostly drunk locally. Wines are known by place names, grape names and legally controlled type names. A full Swiss appellation régime is likely in the future, to be discussed at cantonal and federal level.

Aigle Vaud w dr **✮✮→✮✮✮✮** Principal village of CHABLAIS S of MONTREUX. Dry CHASSELAS whites at best strong and well-balanced.

Amigne Traditional white grape of the VALAIS, performing especially well around VETROZ. Full-bodied, tasty wine, often made sweet.

Arvine Another old VALAIS white grape, sometimes called Petite Arvine, made both dry and sweet. Makes elegant, long-lasting wines with a characteristic salty finish.

Auvernier Neuchâtel r p w dr (sp) **✮✮** Village S of NEUCHÂTEL, known for meaty Pinot N, prickly CHASSELAS and OEIL-DE-PERDRIX.

Blauburgunder The German-Swiss name for Pinot N, only permitted red variety in German-speaking Switzerland.

Bonvin Old-established growers and merchants at SION.

Bünder Herrschaft The 'gentlemen's villages' of Malans, Jenins, Maienfeld and Fläsch, producing serious BLAUBURGUNDER; also Pinot G, Chard and FREISAMER (often late-picked). Generally worth their high price.

Chablais Vaud w (r) dr **✮✮→✮✮✮✮** Subsection of the VAUD v'yd between Ollon and MONTREUX. Good whites (CHASSELAS) and increasingly impressive reds (Pinot N). Best villages: AIGLE, Bex, Ollon, VILLENEUVE, YVORNE.

Chasselas The principal white grape of French-speaking areas, neutral in flavour which enables it to take on remarkable local character. Known as FENDANT in the VALAIS and PERLAN round Geneva.

Clevner (or Klevner) Name for BLAUBURGUNDER used around L Zürich.

Completer Rare, old, late-ripening white variety grown in Graubünden and around L Zürich.

Cornalin Old red VALAIS grape making tannic, long-lasting wines.

Cortaillod Neuchâtel r (p w) **✮✮** Small village S of NEUCHÂTEL making good

CHASSELAS and OEIL DE PERDRIX, but esp famous for its Pinot N.

Côte, La Subsection of VAUD v'yds, between Lausanne and Nyon, generally considered to produce the lightest wines of the area.

Dézaley Vaud w dr ✱✱✱ Best-known and most scenic v'yd of LAVAUX, between Lausanne and MONTREUX. Steep S slopes to the lake make fine, strong, fruity CHASSELAS.

Dôle Valais r ✱✱ VALAIS appellation for a blend of (at least 51%) Pinot N with GAMAY. Dôle Blanche is a v lightly pressed rosé.

Dorin Vaud w dr ✱→✱✱ Obsolescent name for CHASSELAS wine in the VAUD, the equivalent of FENDANT. Most wines are known by village names.

Epesses Vaud w r dr ✱✱ Well-known lake village of LAVAUX producing good dry CHASSELAS.

Ermitage VALAIS name for white wine from MARSANNE grapes. Rich, concentrated and full-bodied, usually dry. Best area around FULLY.

Fendant Valais w dr ✱→✱✱ The VALAIS appellation for CHASSELAS, giving a whole range of wines. Better ones now have village names appended (FULLY, SION, etc).

Flétri and **Mi-flétri** Terms used (particularly in the VALAIS) to indicate a sweet wine made from 'withered' grapes late-harvested.

Freisamer (or Freiburger) A cross between Sylvaner and Pinot G, planted in German-speaking Switzerland and on L Morat.

Frisan CHASSELAS of VALAIS not up to appellation FENDANT standard.

Fully Village nr Martigny making excellent ERMITAGE, FENDANT and GAMAY.

Gamay The Beaujolais grape; pretty thin wine except around Martigny.

Glacier, Vin du Almost legendary oxidized white made in the Val d'Anniviers and offered by the thimbleful to visiting dignitaries.

Goron DOLE that fails to make the grade.

Hallau Largest wine-growing commune of German-speaking Switzerland.

Hammel Huge domaine and merchant at Rolle, LA COTE, with wide range.

Heida Old VALAIS white grape also known as Païen, thought to be a relation of either SAVAGNIN (from the Jura) or of Traminer.

Herrschaft Grisons r (w sw) ✱→✱✱ District nr border of Austria and Liechtenstein. Small amount of light Pinot N reds and a few sweet whites.

Himbertscha Antique VALAIS white grape giving clean-tasting, acidic wine.

Humagne Old VALAIS grape. Some red Humagne is sold: decent country wine. The strong white is a rare speciality.

Johannisberg VALAIS name for Sylvaner, which can make excellent, stiff, dense and high-flavoured dry wine like Germany's Frankenwein.

Lausanne, Ville de Producer of fine wines in surroundng villages for centuries (eg Clos des Moines, LA COTE; Clos des Abbayes, LAVAUX). Now incl late-harvest Chard.

Lavaux Vaud r w dr ✱→✱✱✱ Subsection of VAUD v'yd on N shore of L Geneva between MONTREUX and LAUSANNE, famous for lively and generous CHASSELAS. Best-known *crus* are DEZALEY and Calamin.

Légèrement doux Most Swiss wines are dry. Any with measurable sugar must be labelled thus or as '*avec sucre residuel*'.

Malvoisie VALAIS name for Pinot G. Wonderful late-picked sweet wines.

Mandement Geneva r w (p) dr ✱ Wine district W of Geneva making light reds, chiefly GAMAY, and whites (PERLAN) plus some Chard and Aligoté.

Marsanne The white grape of Hermitage on the French Rhône, used in the VALAIS to make ERMITAGE.

Merlot Bordeaux red grape used to make the better wine of Italian-speaking Switzerland (TICINO). *See also* Viti.

Mont d'Or, Domaine du Valais w dr sw ✱✱✱✱ Well-sited property near SION, producing rich, concentrated wines. Notable JOHANNISBERG, ARVINE and DOLE.

Montreux The town's v'yds make some of th best CHASSELAS of the VAUD: juicy, ripe and resonant.

Neuchâtel r p w dr sp ✱→✱✱✱ City and canton on N shore of the lake. Its

Pinot N can be memorable; nervy CHASSELAS is quickly forgotten.

Nostrano Word meaning 'ours', applied to lesser red wine of TICINO, made from native and Italian grapes (Bondola, Freisa, Barbera, etc).

Oeil de Perdrix Pale rosé from Pinot N.

Orsat, Caves SA Long-established house at Martigny making fine domaine and village-named wines (FENDANT, DOLE, GAMAY, HUMAGNE Rouge, Pinot N etc). Their Primus Classicus ARVINE is highly esteemed.

Orsat, J A & P A newly formed company making good village-named wines, incl FENDANT and SYRAH.

Perlan Name for boring CHASSELAS grown in the Geneva area.

Provins The excellent central coop of the VALAIS.

Rèze Very old, rare VALAIS grape, rumoured to be in VIN DU GLACIER.

Riesling-Sylvaner Swiss name for Müller-T, the only permitted white variety in N and E Switzerland.

Rivaz Vaud r w dr ** One of the better-known villages of LAVAUX.

St Saphorin Vaud w dr ** One of the principal villages of LAVAUX. Firm, fruity CHASSELAS.

Salvagnin A VAUD blend of Pinot N and GAMAY (*see also* Dôle).

Savagnin Swiss name for the Traminer. Called Païen in the VALAIS.

Schafiser Bern w (r) dr *→** Dry, light CHASSELAS from either Schafis or neighbouring Twann on shores of L Bienne (Bierlersee).

Schenk, SA Huge Swiss wine firm with estates in YVORNE, Mont-sur-Rolle, Vinzel and Féchy, and holdings in Burgundy, Spain, Italy, Midi, US, etc.

Sion Valais w dr *→*** Capital and wine centre of the VALAIS. FENDANT de Sion is famous.

Sierre Important wine-growing centre of the VALAIS, with good red.

Spätburgunder Alternative name for BLAUBURGUNDER (Pinot N).

Syrah Rhône red grape increasingly and encouragingly planted in the VALAIS.

Testuz, V & P Respected VAUD growers and merchants in DEZALEY, with v'yds in AIGLE, EPESSES, ST-SAPHORIN and YVORNE.

Thurgau E Switzerland canton beside Bodensee. BLAUBURGUNDER and RIES-SYLVANER; best v'yds: Arenenberg, Ottoberg, Weinfelden.

Ticino Italian-speaking S Switzerland growing principally MERLOT. Some recent trials with Cab S, Sauv Bl, Sém, Pinot G.

Twanner *See* Schafiser.

Valais The Rhône Valley from the Grimselpass round to St Gingolph on L Geneva. Its N side is an admirable, dry, sunny and sheltered v'yd, planted with CHASSELAS, Pinot N, GAMAY and many specialities unique to the area (AMIGNE, ARVINE, Carnalin, ERMITAGE, HEIDA, HIMBERTSCHA, HUMAGNE, Lafnetscha).

Vaud Region of L Geneva, whose N shore is Switzerland's largest vyd and in places as good as any. Main wines are SALVAGNIN, good CHASSELAS and Pinot N.

Vétroz Valais w (r) dr ** Top village near SION particularly famous for AMIGNE.

Vevey Town nr MONTREUX with a famous wine festival once every 30-odd yrs. The last was in '77.

Vin du Glacier *See* Glacier, Vin du.

Villeneuve One of the best villages in CHABLAIS: good CHASSELAS and Pinot N.

Vin-Union Genève Big growers' coop at Satigny in the MANDEMENT.

Viti Ticino r ** Legal designation of better quality TICINO red, made of MERLOT and with at least 12% alcohol.

Yvorne One of the best villages of CHABLAIS, famous for its CHASSELAS.

Italy

Switzerland

VALLE D'AOSTA

M

Turin

PIEDMONT

LIG

Geno

1992 may turn out in retrospect to have been the turning point in the reputation and fortunes of the Italian wine industry, whose genial chaos has always tended to mask its real values and qualities. January 23 saw the enactment of a completely revised version of the seriously discredited DOC legislation, which for 30 years has caused confusion among consumers and militated against both quality and innovation.

The Goria Law, named for the Minister of Agriculture who wound up a decade of debate, is intended to end all the old anomalies, but especially that by which a *vino da tavola*, officially the lowest grade of wine clasification, was frequently a much better (and more expensive) wine than one made within the statutory requirements of a DOC – or even a DOCG, formerly the most elevated appellation available (*see* page 87).

Eventually (though this may take years) the new laws will bring Italian appellations very close in spirit to those of France, where all the stress is on geography. They are also intended (like the French laws) to discourage the marketing of high quality wines simply by grape variety name.

The Goria Law is most graphically represented by a pyramid, whose base is the humble *vino da tavola*. No geographical (or varietal) claims can be made at this level: only a brand name. The next level is a new institution, intended to mirror the French *vin de pays* and known as IGT (*Indicazione Geografica Tipica*). IGTs can use the geographical name and the grape name (strictly in that order). Above the IGT come the DOC and DOCG. In these bands the label can carry information as specific as a single vineyard (*vigna*) name – but only by sacrificing quantity for quality.

Thus the highest rank in the pyramid will be a *vigna* wine from within a DOCG zone. But whereas the rank of DOCG was formerly limited to a dozen famous areas, it will now become the right of any DOC which has performed well enough for five years. Conversely a DOC which functions poorly will lose its rank (some 50 are already threatened). Even more radically, an outstanding proprietorial wine 'which does honour to Italy' may be eligible for its own DOCG.

A distinct advantage of the pyramid system is that producers in a DOC zone can decide at vintage time how high they are going to pitch their wine. Self-discipline can give them the right to the top appellation; high yields and lower concentration will automatically demote him down the pyramid.

There is very much more detail to the Goria Law, and much that only experience will finally determine, but it is a convincingly bold attempt to sort out the minestrone of the old system. No doubt the German government will pay due heed.

Meanwhile, as always, the best advice is to be bold. Do not cling limply to familiar names: look for distinctive labels on distinctive bottles. But be prepared to pay more for quality.

The following abbreviations are used in the text.

Ab Abruzzi	**F-VG** Friuli-Venezia Giulia	**Pie** Piedmont
Ap Apulia	**Lat** Latium	**Sar** Sardinia
Bas Basilicata	**Lig** Liguria	**Si** Sicily
Cal Calabria	**Lom** Lombardy	**T-AA** Trentino-Alto Adige
Cam Campania	**Mar** Marches	**Tus** Tuscany
E-R Emilia-Romagna		**Umb** Umbria
		VdA Valle d'Aosta
		Ven Veneto

Abbazia di Rosazzo A leading estate of COLLI ORIENTALI. White Ronco delle Acacie and Ronco di Corte and red Ronco dei Roseti are vg single-v'yd wines.

Abboccato Semi-sweet.

Adanti Umbrian maker of vg red SAGRANTINO DI MONTEFALCO; VDT BIANCO D'ARQUATA and Rosso d'Arquata, an outstanding BARBERA-Canaiolo-MERLOT blend. Also good CAB S.

Aglianico del Vulture Bas DOC r dr (s/sw sp) ★★★ 82 85 86 87 88 90 91 Among the best wines of S Italy. Ages well to rich aromas. Called *vecchio* after 3 yrs, RISERVA after 5. Top grower: Fratelli D'Angelo (also makes vg pure Aglianico VDT Canneto).

Alba Major wine centre of PIEDMONT.

Albana di Romagna E-R DOCG w dr s/sw (sp) ★★ DYA Italy's first DOCG for white wine, though no-one seems to know why. Produced for centuries in Romagna from Albana grapes. Cold fermentation now robs it of what little character it had. Fattoria PARADISO makes some of the best. AMABILE is often better than dry. Fattoria ZERBINA's botrytis-affected PASSITO is outstanding.

Alcamo Si DOC w dr ★ Soft, neutral whites. Rapitalà is the best brand.

Aleatico Excellent red Muscat-flavoured grape, chiefly of the south.

Aleatico di Gradoli Lat DOC r sw fz ★★ Aromatic, fruity; alcohol 17.5%. Made nr Viterbo.

Aleatico di Puglia Ap DOC r sw fz ★★ ALEATICO grapes make good dessert wine in limited quantities. 2 distinct types have 15% or 18.5% alcohol.

Alezio Ap DOC p (r) dr ★★ 88 89 90 91 Recent DOC at Salento, esp for delicate rosé. Top grower: Calò.

Allegrini Top-quality producer of Veronese wines, incl VALPOLICELLA from prime new v'yds, and vg AMARONE.

Altare Reputed small producer of BAROLO and BARBERA VDT Vigna Larigi.

Altesino Highly regarded estate producing BRUNELLO DI MONTALCINO and VDT Palazzo Altesi.

Alto Adige T-AA DOC r p w dr sw sp ★★→★★★ A DOC covering some 19 different wines, usually named after their grape varieties, in 33 villages around Bolzano. This largely German-speaking region is often called Südtirol.

Ama, Castello di Modern CHIANTI CLASSICO estate nr Gaiole. San Lorenzo, Bertinga, La Casuccia and Bellavista are excellent top wines. Vg CHARD, SAUV, MERLOT (Vigna L'Apparita).

Amabile Semi-sweet, but usually sweeter than ABBOCCATO.

Amaro Bitter. When prominent on a label the content is a 'bitters'.

Amarone High-octane version of VALPOLICELLA; potent, dry, impressive and long-lived. *See also* Recioto.

Anghelu Ruju Port-like version of Sardinian CANNONAU from SELLA & MOSCA.

Anselmi, Roberto A leader in SOAVE with his single-v'yd Capitel Foscarino and exceptional sweet dessert RECIOTO dei Capitelli.

Antinori, Marchesi L & P Immensely influential, long-established Tuscan house of the highest repute producing first-rate CHIANTI (esp PEPPOLI, Tenute Marchese Antinori and Badia a Passignano), and ORVIETO. Distinguished for pioneering new VDT styles, eg TIGNANELLO, SOLAIA, CERVARO DELLA SALA. The Marchese Piero A could be called the Voice of Italy in world wine circles. *See also* Prunotto.

Aquileia F-VG DOC r w dr ★★ 88 89 90 91 12 varietal wines from around town of Aquileia. Good REFOSCO.

Argusto Oak-aged DOLCETTO from BANFI.

Arneis Pie w dr ★★ DYA Revival of this ancient grape variety is much in vogue. Now DOC under Roero, a zone N of Alba. Good producers incl Blangé (Ceretto), CASTELLO DI NEIVE, Bruno GIACOSA, Angelo Negri, VIETTI.

Artimino Ancient hill-town W of Florence, known for its DOCG CARMIGNANO.

Assisi Umb r (w dr) ★★ DYA Rosso and Bianco di Assisi are v attractive VDT. Drink cool.

Asti Major wine centre of PIEDMONT.

Asti Spumante Pie DOC w sp ** NV Sweet and v fruity Muscat sparkling wine. Low in alcohol.

Avignonesi MONTEPULCIANO house with range of excellent wines incl VINO NOBILE, blended red Grifi, first-rate CHARD, SAUV BL, MERLOT and superlative VIN SANTO.

Azienda agricola/agraria A farm producing crops, often incl wine.

Azienda/casa vinicola Wine firm using bought-in grapes and/or wines.

Azienda vitivinicola A (specialized) wine estate.

Badia a Coltibuono *** Fine CHIANTI-maker at Gaiole with a restaurant and collection of old vintages. Also produces VDT SANGIOVETO (82, 83, 85, 86, 88, 90).

Banfi (Castello or Villa) The production department of the biggest US importer of Italian wine. Huge plantings at MONTALCINO, incl Syrah, PINOT N, CAB, CHARD, are part of a drive for quality plus quantity. BRUNELLO is proving excellent. Centine is ROSSO DI MONTALCINO. In PIEDMONT Banfi produces vg sparkling Banfi Brut, Principessa GAVI, BRACCHETTO D'ACQUI, Pinot G.

Barbacarlo Lom r dr sw sp ** 88 89 90 91 Delicate wines with typical bitter-almond taste, from OLTREPO PAVESE.

Barbaresco Pie DOCG r dr ***→**** 78 79 82 85 86 87 88 89 90 Neighbour of BAROLO from the same grapes but lighter, ageing sooner. At best deep, palate-cleansing, subtle and fine. At 4 yrs becomes RISERVA. Best producers incl CERETTO, GAJA, Bruno GIACOSA, Marchesi di Gresy, Produttori del B, PRUNOTTO, Alfredo Roagna, Bruno Rocca.

Barbera Dark, acidic, red grape, the second most planted in Italy after SANGIOVESE; a speciality of PIEDMONT also used in Lombardy, Emilia-Romagna and other northern provinces. Its best wines are:

Barbera d'Alba Pie DOC r dr ** 85 86 87 88 89 90 91 Tasty, tannic, fragrant red. SUPERIORE can age 7 yrs or more. Round ALBA, NEBBIOLO is sometimes added to make a VDT (*barrique*-aged 100% Barbera is also VDT). Top producers incl A CONTERNO, GAJA, PRUNOTTO.

Barbera d'Asti Pie DOC r dr ** 82 85 86 87 88 89 90 91 For real Barbera-lovers: solely Barbera grapes, tangy and appetizing, drunk young or aged up to 7 yrs. Top producers incl Brema, Carnevale, Chiarlo, Scarpa, Trinchero.

Barbera del Monferrato Pie DOC r dr *→** 88 89 90 91 Easy-drinking Barbera from a large area in the province of Alessandria and ASTI. Pleasant, slightly fizzy, sometimes sweetish.

Barberani Leading ORVIETO producer; Calcaia is sweet, botrytis-affected.

Barco Reale Tus DOC r dr ** New DOC for junior wine of CARMIGNANO, with same grapes; VDT since '82.

Bardolino Ven DOC r (p) dr ** DYA Pale, light, slightly bitter red from E shore of Lake Garda. Bardolino CHIARETTO is even paler and lighter. Top makers: GUERRIERI-RIZZARDI, Fratelli Zeni.

Barolo Pie DOCG r dr ***→**** 78 79 82 85' 86 88 89 90 Small area S of Turin with one of the highest-rated Italian red wines, dark, rich, alcoholic (min 13°), dry but deep in flavour. From NEBBIOLO grapes. Ages for up to 15 yrs (RISERVA after 5). Best producers incl ALTARE, CERETTO, Clerico, CONTERNO, CORDERO, FONTANAFREDDA, GIACOSA, Elio Grasso, Giovanni Manzone, Marcarini, MASCARELLO, PIO CESARE, PRUNOTTO, RATTI, Rinaldi, ROCCHE DEI MANZONI, Sandrone, VIETTI, VOERZIO.

Bava ASTI firm with well-presented range of sound PIEDMONT wines.

Bellavista Franciacorta estate rivalling CA' DEL BOSCO for fine, brisk and subtle sparkling wines. Also notable Crémant. Good VDT reds from CAB and PINOT N.

Berlucchi, Guido Italy's biggest producer of sparkling METODO CLASSICO, at FRANCIACORTA. Steady quality.

Bertani Well-known producers of quality Veronese wines (VALPOLICELLA, VALPANTENA, SOAVE, etc), incl aged AMARONE and white VDT Catullo.

Bianco White.

Bianco d'Arquata Umb w dr ✹✹ 88 89 90 91 *See* Adanti.

Bianco di Custoza Ven DOC w dr (sp) ✹✹ DYA Twin of SOAVE from W of Verona; often rivals or surpasses it in quality.

Bianco di Pitigliano Tus DOC w dr ✹ DYA A soft, fruity, lively wine near Grosseto.

Biancolella Ischia's best white is a VDT from D'AMBRA.

Bianco Vergine della Valdichiana Tus DOC w dr ✹ DYA Pale, dry, light wine from Arezzo. But what music in the name.

Bigi, Luigi & Figlio Famous producers of ORVIETO and other wines of Umbria and Tuscany. Their TORRICELLA v'yd produces vg dry Orvieto.

Biondi-Santi The original producer of BRUNELLO in MONTALCINO (Siena). His Il Greppo v'yd is only 45 acres. Prices are v high but ancient vintages unique.

Boca Pie DOC r dr ✹✹ 85 86 88 89 90 91 From same grape as BAROLO (NEBBIOLO) in N of PIEDMONT. Look for Poderi ai Valloni.

Bolla Famous Veronese firm producing VALPOLICELLA, SOAVE, etc. Top wines: Castellaro (one of the v best Soaves), Creso (red and white), Jago.

Bonarda Minor red grape (alias Croatina) widely grown in PIEDMONT and Lombardy.

Bonarda (Oltrepò Pavese) Lom DOC r dr ✹✹ 89 90 91 Soft, fresh, often FRIZZANTE red from S of Pavia.

Bosca, Luigi PIEDMONT producers of ASTI SPUMANTE and Vermouths.

Boscarelli, Poderi Small estate with vg VINO NOBILE DI MONTEPULCIANO.

Brachetto d'Acqui Pie DOC r sw (sp) ✹✹ DYA Sweet, sparkling red with enticing Muscat aroma.

Bramaterra Pie DOC r dr ✹✹ 82 85 86 88 89 90 A stylish addition to PIEDMONT's reds. NEBBIOLO grapes predominate.

Breganze Ven DOC ✹→✹✹✹ 82 83 85 86 87 88 90 A catch-all for many varieties around Vicenza. CAB and PINOT BL are best. Top producer: MACULAN.

Bricco dell'Uccellone Pie r dr ✹✹✹ 82 85 86 87 88 89 90 91 *Barrique*-aged BARBERA from the Braida firm of the late Giacomo Bologna. Bricco della Bigotta and Ai Suma are others.

Bricco Manzoni Pie r ✹✹✹ 82 85 89 90 91 Excellent blend of NEBBIOLO and BARBERA from Monforte d'Alba.

Brindisi Ap DOC r ✹✹→✹✹✹ Strong NEGROAMARO red. Best is Patriglione from Taurino.

Brunello di Montalcino Tus DOCG r dr ✹✹✹→✹✹✹✹ 82 83 85 86 89 With BAROLO, Italy's most celebrated red wine. Strong, full-bodied, high-flavoured and long-lived. After 5 yrs is called RISERVA. Produced for over a century 25 miles S of Siena. Noted producers incl ALTESINO, BANFI, Fattoria dei Barbi, BIONDI-SANTI, CAPARZO, Case Basse, Castello, Cebaiona, Col d'Orcia, COSTANTI, LISINI, Poggio Antico, Il POGGIONE, Salvioni. *See also* Rosso di Montalcino.

Brusco dei Barbi Tus r dr ✹✹ 88 89 90 91 Lively variant on BRUNELLO, using old CHIANTI GOVERNO method.

Bukkuram Celebrated MOSCATO DI PANTELLERIA from De Bartoli.

Ca'del Bosco FRANCIACORTA estate making some of Italy's v best sparkling wine, CHARD, and excellent reds (PINOT N, Maurizio ZANELLA).

Cabernet Sauvignon Much used in NE Italy and increasingly (esp in VDT) in Tuscany and the south.

Cafaggio, Villa A solid CHIANTI CLASSICO estate with a good red VDT called Solatio Basilica.

Caldaro or Lago di Caldaro T-AA DOC r dr ✹→✹✹ DYA Alias KALTERERSEE. Light, soft, slightly bitter-almond red. CLASSICO from a smaller area is better. From S of Bolzano.

Caluso Passito Pie DOC w sw (fz) ✹✹✹ Made from Erbaluce grapes left to partly dry; delicate scent, velvety taste. Tiny production from a large area. Best from Vittorio Borrato.

Cannonau di Sardegna Sar DOC r (p) dr s/sw ** 88 89 90 91   Cannonau (Grenache) is Sardinia's basic red grape; its wine often formidably strong (min 13.5% alc for DOC), but always mild in flavour.

Cantina Cellar or winery.

Cantina Sociale Growers' coop.

Capannelle Good producer of Tuscan VDT (formerly CHIANTI CLASSICO), though overrated and (like a number of its class) overpriced.

Caparzo, Tenuta MONTALCINO estate with excellent BRUNELLO La Casa; also CHARD and red blend Ca'del Pazzo.

Capezzana, Tenuta di (or Villa) The Tuscan estate (W of Florence) of the ancient Contini Bonacossi family. Excellent CHIANTI Montalbano and CARMIGNANO. Also a Bordeaux-style red, GHIAIE DELLA FURBA.

Carpenè Malvolti Leading producer of classic PROSECCO and other sparkling wines at Conegliano, Veneto.

Capri Cam DOC r w p *   Widely abused name of the famous island. Better to drink ISCHIA.

Carema Pie DOC r dr ** 82 85 86 88 89 90   Old speciality of N PIEDMONT. Best from Luigi Ferrando (or the CANTINA SOCIALE).

Carignano del Sulcis Sar DOC r p dr **→***   Well-structured wine with capacity for ageing. Best: Terre Brune from CANTINA SOCIALE di Santadi.

Carmignano Tus DOCG r (p br) *** 82 83 85 86 88 90   Section of CHIANTI using 10% CAB to make reliably good, and some v fine, wine. *See* Capezzana.

Carso F-VG DOC r w dr DYA   DOC nr Trieste incl good MALVASIA. Terrano del C is a soft REFOSCO-like red. Top grower: Edy Kante.

Casa fondata nel... Firm founded in...

Castel del Monte Ap DOC r p w dr **   85 86 88 90 91   Dry, fresh, well-balanced southern wines. The red becomes RISERVA after 3 yrs. Rosé most widely known. RIVERA's Il Falcone stands out.

Castel San Michele T-AA r dr ** 85 86 87 88 90   A good red made of CAB and MERLOT grapes by the Trentino Agricultural College nr Trento. Also the name of a good white from Incrocio Manzoni.

Castellare Small but admired CHIANTI CLASSICO producer with first-rate SANGIOVESE VDT I Sodi di San Niccoló and sprightly GOVERNO del Castellare, a modern version of old-style CHIANTI.

Castell'in Villa Vg CHIANTI CLASSICO estate.

Castello d'Albola Famous CHIANTI CLASSICO estate owned by ZONIN.

Castello della Sala ANTINORI's estate at ORVIETO. Borro is the regular white. Top wine is Cervaro della Sala: CHARD and GRECHETTO aged in oak (87, 88, 90, 91).

Castello di Cacchiano First-rate CHIANTI CLASSICO estate at Gaiole.

Castello di Neiv A good producer of BARBARESCO, in the castle where Louis Oudart pioneered NEBBIOLO as dry red wine in 1850s.

Castello di San Polo in Rosso CHIANTI CLASSICO estate with first-rate red VDT Cetinaia (aged in standard casks, not *barriques*).

Castello di Uzzano Famous old CHIANTI CLASSICO estate at Greve.

Castello di Volpaia First-class CHIANTI CLASSICO estate at Radda, making VDT reds Balifico, which contains CAB, and COLTASSALA.

Càvit (Cantina Viticoltori) Group of good quality coops near Trento. Wines incl MARZEMINO, CAB, PINOTS N, BL and G, Nosiola. Top wines: Brume di Monte (red and white) and sparkling Graal.

Cellatica Lom DOC r dr ** 88 89 90   Blended light red with slightly bitter aftertaste.

Cerasuolo Ab DOC p dr **   The ROSATO version of MONTEPULCIANO D'ABRUZZO.

Cerasuolo di Vittoria Si r dr *→*** 87 88 89 90   Cherry-red from southernmost Sicily, best made by COS. Giuseppe Coria makes a fine matured non-DOC version.

Ceretto High-quality grower of v expensive BARBARESCO (called Bricco Asili), BAROLO (Bricco Rocche), top BARBERA D'ALBA (Piana).

Cervaro *See* Castello della Sala.

Cerveteri Lat DOC w dr s /sw ★ DYA Sound wines produced NW of Rome between Bracciano and the sea.

Chardonnay Has recently joined permitted varieties for several N Italian DOCs. Most of the best (eg ANTINORI, FELSINA, GAJA, LUNGAROTTI) are still only VDT.

Chianti Tus DOCG r dr ★→★★★ 85 86 88 90 91 The lively local wine of Florence. Fresh but warmly fruity when young, still sometimes sold in straw-covered flasks. Mostly made to drink young. Of the subdistricts, RUFINA and Colli Fiorentini can make CLASSICO-style RISERVAS. Montalbano, Colli Senesi, Aretini and Pisani make lighter wines.

Chianti Classico Tus DOCG r dr ★★→★★★★ 85 86 87 88 89 90 91 (Riserva) 83 85 86 88 90 Senior Chianti from the central area. Its old, pale, astringent style is becoming rarer as top estates opt for either darker, tannic wines or softer and fruitier ones. Outstanding producers incl AMA, FELSINA, FONTERUTOLI, FONTODI, ISOLE E OLENA, San Giusto. Members of the Consorzio use the badge of a black rooster, but several top firms do not belong.

Chianti Putto Tus DOCG r dr ★→★★ Chianti from a league of producers outside the CLASSICO zone. The neck-label, a pink cherub, is now rarely seen.

Chiaretto Rosé (the word means 'claret') produced esp around L. Garda. *See* Bardolino, Riviera del Garda.

Cinqueterre Lig DOC w dr sw pa ★ Fragrant, fruity white made nr La Spezia. The PASSITO is known as SCIACCHETRA (★★→★★★).

Cinzano Major Vermouth company also known for its ASTI SPUMANTE from PIEDMONT, and Florio MARSALA. Owns MONTALCINO estate of Col d'Orcia.

Cirò Cal DOC r (p w) dr ★★ 85 86 87 88 89 90 91 V strong red; fruity white (to drink young). Top wines: Ronco dei Quattroventi and single-v'yd Donna Madda from San Francesco.

Classico Term for wines from a restricted area within the limits of a DOC. By implication, and often in practice, the best of the district. Applied to sparkling wines, it denotes the champagne method.

Collavini, Cantina Quality producer of COLLIO, COLLI ORIENTALI and GRAVE DEL FRIULI wines: PINOT G, RIES, MERLOT, PINOT N and sparkling.

Colle Picchioni Estate S of Rome making the best MARINO white; also red (CAB-MERLOT) VDT, Vigna del Vassallo, perhaps Latium's best.

Colli Hills. Occurs in many wine-names.

Colli Albani Lat DOC w dr s /sw (sp) ★→★★ DYA Soft fruity wine of the Roman hills.

Colli Berici Ven DOC r w p dr ★★ 86 88 90 CAB is the best wine of these hills S of Vicenza.

Colli Bolognesi E-R DOC r p w dr ★★ DYA (w) 85 86 87 88 90 From hills SW of Bologna. 8 wine types, with 6 grape varieties. TERRE ROSSE is top estate.

Colli del Trasimeno Um DOC r w dr ★★ 85 86 87 88 90 Often lively wines from the province of Perugia.

Colli Euganei Ven DOC r w dr s/sw (sp) ✻ DYA A DOC applicable to 7 wines produced SW of Padua. Red is adequate; white and sparkling are soft and pleasant.

Colli Orientali del Friuli F-VG DOC r w dr sw ★★→★★★★ 88 89 90 91 20 different wines (18 named after their grapes) are produced under this DOC on the hills E of Udine. Whites esp are vg.

Colli Piacentini E-R DOC r p w dr ★→★★ DYA DOC incl traditional GUTTURNIO and MONTEROSSO VAL D'ARDA among 11 types grown round Piacenza. Good fizzy MALVASIA.

Collio (Goriziano) F-VG DOC r w dr ★★→★★★ 88 89 90 91 19 different wines, 17 named after their grapes, from a small area between Udine and Gorizia nr the former Yugoslav border. Vg whites.

Coltassala Tus r dr ★★★ 82 83 85 86 87 88 90 Notable VDT red of SANGIOVESE from the ancient CHIANTI CLASSICO estate of CASTELLO DI VOLPAIA at Radda.

Coltiva-Gruppo Italiano Vini Complex of coóps and wineries, apparently the world's third largest producer. Sells 10% of all Italian wine, incl eg BIGI, FOLONARI, FONTANA CANDIDA, LAMBERTI, MELINI, Negri...

Conterno, Aldo and Giacomo Highly regarded growers of BAROLO, etc, with separate estates at Monforte d'Alba.

Contratto PIEDMONT firm known for ASTI SPUMANTE, BAROLO, etc.

Copertino Ap DOC r (p) dr ** 85 86 87 88 89 90 91 Savoury, age-worthy dark red of NEGROAMARO from the heel of Italy. Look for the RISERVA from the coop.

Cordero di Montezemolo-Monfalletto Tiny producer of good BAROLO.

Cori Lat DOC w r dr sw * DYA Soft and well-balanced wines made 30 miles S of Rome.

Cortese di Gavi See Gavi. (Cortese is the grape.)

Cortese (Oltrepò Pavese) Lom DOC w dr ★→★★ DYA Delicate, fresh white from W Lombardy.

Corvo-Duca di Salaparuta Si r w dr ★★→★★★ Popular Sicilian wines. Sound dry reds, pleasant soft whites. Excellent new *barrique* red called Duca Enrico (85, 86, 87, 88, 89, 90).

Costanti, Conti Tiny estate producing top quality BRUNELLO DI MONTALCINO.

D'Ambra Top producer of ISCHIA and other wines of that island.

Darmagi Pie r dr ★★★★ 82 83 85 86 87 88 89 90 91 CAB S grown in a choice plot in BARBARESCO by GAJA has become PIEDMONT's most discussed and admired VDT red.

Decugnano dei Barbi Top ORVIETO estate with an ABBOCCATO version known as 'Pourriture Noble', and a good red VDT.

Under the laws in place up to 1992 (see Introduction, page 80) the top category of Italian wine was DOCG, denominazione di origine controllata e garantita. It was awarded only to certain wines from top quality zones which were bottled and sealed with a government seal by the producer. The first five areas to be 'guaranteed' were Barolo, Barbaresco, Brunello di Montalcino, Chianti and Vino Nobile di Montepulciano. The sixth (and first white) was Albana di Romagna, for no discernible reason. Then came Carmignano, Torgiano, Gattinara and Sagrantino. But it should be remembered that many of Italy's best wines are not yet covered by the DOC system and are officially only vino da tavola (referred to here as vdt). Examples are Bricco Manzoni, Sassicaia, Tignanello, Venegazzù, etc, etc.

Di Majo Norante Lone star of Molise on the Adriatic with vg Biferno DOC MONTEPULCIANO and white Falanghina under the Ramitello label. Also lighter, more aromatic Molí. Fine value. To watch for new ideas.

Dolce Sweet.

Dolceacqua See Rossese di Dolceacqua.

Dolcetto Popular low-acid red grape of PIEDMONT, yielding the everyday wine of BAROLO and BARBARESCO-producing areas and giving its name to the following:

Dolcetto d'Acqui Pie DOC r dr * DYA Pale, quick-maturing table wine from S of ASTI.

Dolcetto d'Alba Pie DOC r dr ** 89 90 91 Among the best Dolcetti, with a trace of bitter almond.

Dolcetto di Diano d'Alba Pie DOC ** 89 90 91 A rival to Dolcetto d'Alba; often more potent.

Dolcetto di Dogliani Pie DOC r ** 89 90 91 Often regarded as the top Dolcetto subregion.

Dolcetto di Ovada Pie DOC r dr ** 88 89 90 91 Reputedly the sturdiest and longest-lived of Dolcetti.

Donnafugata Si r w ** Zesty white (best are Vigna di Gabri, Damaskino). Also sound red.

Donnaz VdA DOC dr ** 85 86 88 89 90 A mountain NEBBIOLO, fragrant, pale and faintly bitter. Aged for a statutory 3 yrs. Now part of the

VALLE D'AOSTA regional DOC.

Duca Enrico *See* Corvo-Duca di Salaparuta.

Elba Tus r w dr (sp) ★ DYA   The island's white is drinkable with fish. Decent dry red.

Enfer d'Arvier VdA DOC r dr ★★ 88 89 90 91   Alpine speciality (*see* Donnaz); pale, pleasantly bitter, light red.

Enoteca Wine library. There are many; the impressive original being the Enoteca Italiana of Siena. Also used for wine shops or restaurants.

Erbaluce di Caluso *See* Caluso Passito.

Est! Est!! Est!!! Lat DOC w dr s/sw ★ DYA   Soft, fruity white from Montefiascone, N of Rome, that has traded for centuries on its odd-ball name.

Etna Si DOC r p w dr ★—→★★ 88 89 90 91   Wine from the volcanic slopes. The red is warm, full, balanced and can age well; the white is distinctly grapey. *See* Villagrande.

Falerio dei Colli Ascolani Mar DOC w dr ⬛ DYA   Made nr Ascoli Piceno. Pleasant, fresh, fruity; a summer wine.

Falerno del Massico Cam DOC r w dr ★★ 88 89 90 91   As Falernum, the best-known wine of ancient times. Strong red from AGLIANICO, fruity white from Falanghina. Good producer: Villa Matilde.

Fara Pie DOC r dr ★★ 85 86 88 89 90   Good NEBBIOLO wine from Novara, N PIEDMONT. Fragrant; worth ageing. Small production. Best is Dessilani's Caramino.

Faro Si DOC r dr ★★ 87 88 89 90 91   Strong Sicilian red from the Straits of Messina. Made only (and rather well) by Bagni.

Favorita Pie w dr ★—→★★   Dry, fruity white making friends in BAROLO country. From eg Negro, Sant'Orsola, VOERZIO.

Fazi-Battaglia Well-known producer of VERDICCHIO, etc. VDT white Le Moie is pleasant. Also owner of Fassati, impressive producer of VINO NOBILE DI MONTEPULCIANO.

Felluga Brothers Livio and Marco (Russiz SUPERIORE) have separate companies in the COLLIO and COLLI ORIENTALI. Both highly esteemed.

Felsina-Berardenga CHIANTI CLASSICO estate with famous RISERVA Vigna Rancia and VDT Fontalloro.

Ferrari Firm making some of Italy's best dry sparkling wines nr Trento, Trentino-Alto Adige. Giulio Ferrari RISERVA is best.

Fiano di Avellino Cam w dr ★★—→★★★ 89 90 91   Considered the best white of Campania. Smooth, pale, dry but not otherwise remarkable. MASTROBERARDINO's Vignadora is best.

Fiorano Lat r w dr s/sw ★★ 85 86 88 89 90 91   Interesting Roman reds of CAB and MERLOT, whites of Sémillon.

Flaccianello della Pieve *See* Fontodi.

Florio The major producer of MARSALA, controlled by CINZANO.

Foianeghe T-AA r (w) ★★ 85 86 88 89 90   Trentino CAB-MERLOT red to age 7–10 yrs. White is PINOT BL-CHARD-TRAMINER.

Folonari Large run-of-the-mill merchant of Lombardy.

Fontana Candida One of the biggest producers of FRASCATI. Single-v'yd Santa Teresa stands out.

Fontanafredda One of the biggest producers of PIEDMONTESE wines, incl BAROLO from single v'yds and a range of ALBA DOCs. Also vg sparkling wines.

Fonterutoli High quality CHIANTI CLASSICO estate at Castellina with noted VDT Concerto and RISERVA Ser Lapo.

Fontodi Rising CHIANTI CLASSICO estate producing one of Italy's most highly regarded VDT in Flaccianello della Pieve.

Franciacorta Pinot Lom DOC w (p) dr (sp) ★★—→★★★   Pleasant soft white and some vg sparkling wines made of PINOTS BL, N or G and CHARD. CA'DEL BOSCO is outstanding. BELLAVISTA, Cavalleri and Monte Rossa also vg.

Franciacorta Rosso Lom DOC r dr ★★ 85 86 88 89 90 91   Lightish red of mixed CAB and BARBERA from Brescia.

Frascati Lat DOC w dr s/sw sw (sp) *→*** DYA   Best-known wine of the Roman hills: should be soft, ripe, golden, tasting of whole grapes. Most is disappointingly neutral today: look for dated wines from small producers (eg Conte Zandotti, Villa Simone, or single-v'yd Santa Teresa from FONTANA CANDIDA). The sweet version is known as Cannellino.

Freisa Pie r dr s/sw sw (sp) ** DYA   Sometimes sweet, often FRIZZANTE red, said to taste of raspberries and roses. With enough acidity it can be highly appetizing.

Frescobaldi Ancient noble family, leading pioneers of CHIANTI at NIPOZZANO, E of Florence. Also white POMINO and PREDICATO SAUV BL (Vergena) and CAB (Mormoreto). *See also* Montesodi.

Friuli-Venezia Giulia The NE province on the former Yugoslav border. Many wines; the DOCs COLLIO and COLLI ORIENTALI include most of the best.

Frizzante [fz] Semi-sparkling. Used to describe wines such as LAMBRUSCO.

Gaja Old family firm at BARBARESCO with inspired direction of Angelo G. Top quality (and price) PIEDMONT wines, esp BARBARESCO (single v'yds Sorì Tildin, Sorì San Lorenzo, Costa Russi). Now setting trends with excellent CHARD (Gaja & Rey 85, 86, 87, 88, 89, 90), CAB (DARMAGI) and SAUV BL. Vignarey is excellent BARBERA.

Galestro Tus w dr *   V light grapey white from eponymous shaley soil in CHIANTI country.

Gambellara Ven DOC w dr s/sw (sp) * DYA   Neighbour of SOAVE. Dry wine similar. Sweet (known as RECIOTO DI GAMBELLARA) agreeably fruity. Also VIN SANTO.

Gancia Famous ASTI SPUMANTE house from PIEDMONT, also produces vermouth and dry sparkling wines. New Torrebianco estate in Apulia is making good VDT whites: CHARD, SAUV, PINOT BL.

Garganega Principal white grape of SOAVE.

Garofoli, Gioacchino Quality leader of the Marches (nr Ancona). Notable style in VERDICCHIO Macrina and Serra Fiorese; also *champenoise*. ROSSO CONERO Piancarda and Grosso Agontano are outstanding.

Gattinara Pie DOCG r dr **→*** 82 85 86 88 89 90   V tasty big-scale BAROLO-type red from N PIEDMONT, made from NEBBIOLO, locally known as Spanna. Best are Monsecco and single-v'yd wines from Antoniola. Other good producers: Nervi, Travaglini.

Gavi (or Cortese di Gavi) Pie w dr **→*** 89 90 91 (usually DYA)   At best substantial, subtle, dry white of CORTESE grapes. La Scolca is best known, Castello di Tassarolo top quality, La Giustiniana and Tenuta San Pietro admirable. But high prices are rarely justified.

Ghemme Pie DOC r dr **→*** 82 85 86 88 89 90   Neighbour of GATTINARA, rival in quality but rare. Best is Antichi Vigneti di Cantalupo.

Ghiaie della Furba Tus r dr *** 85 86 88 89 90   Bordeaux-style VDT CAB blend from the admirable Tenuta di CAPEZZANA, CARMIGNANO.

Giacobazzi Well-known producers of LAMBRUSCO nr Modena.

Giacosa, Bruno Inspired loner making excellent BARBARESCO, BAROLO and other PIEDMONT wines at Neive. Outstanding ARNEIS white.

Girò di Cagliari Sar DOC r dr sw *   A formidably alcoholic red, most sympathetic when some of its sugar content is left unfermented.

Goldmuskateller Aromatic grape made into irresistible dry white, esp by TIEFENBRUNNER.

Governo Old Tuscan custom, enjoying mild revival from some producers, in which dried grapes/musts are added to young wine to induce secondary fermentation and give a slight prickle. Must be declared on label and sold within 1 yr of harvest. *See* Brusco dei Barbi, Castellare.

Gradi Degrees (of alcohol), ie percent by volume.

Grai, Giorgio Merchant/consultant to top ALTO ADIGE and other estates.

Grattamacco Top Tuscan producer on coast outside classic centres (nr SASSICAIA S of Bolgheri). Vg Grattamacco SANGIOVESE-CAB blend.

Grave del Friuli F-VG DOC r w dr ✷✷ 88 89 90 91 A DOC covering 15 different wines, 14 named after their grapes, from nr the former Yugoslav border. Good MERLOT and CAB.

Gravner COLLIO estate encompassing a range of superb whites, led by CHARD and SAUV.

Grechetto White grape with more flavour than the ubiquitous TREBBIANO, increasingly used in Umbria.

Greco di Bianco (or Greco di Gerace) Cal DOC w sw ✷✷ 86 87 88 89 90 91 An original smooth and fragrant dessert wine from Italy's toe. *See also* Mantonico.

Greco di Tufo Cam DOC w dr (sp) ✷✷✷ 89 90 91 One of the best whites of the south, fruity and slightly 'wild' in flavour. A character. MASTROBERARDINO makes single-v'yd Vignadangelo.

Grignolino d'Asti Pie DOC r dr ✷ DYA Pleasant, lively, standard wine of PIEDMONT.

Grumello Lom DOC r dr ✷✷ 82 85 86 88 89 90 NEBBIOLO wine from VALTELLINA, can be delicate (or meagre).

Guerrieri-Gonzaga Top producer in TRENTINO; esp VDT San Leonardo, ✷✷✷ CAB-MERLOT blend.

Guerrieri-Rizzardi Top producer of BARDOLINO and other Veronese wines from various family estates.

Gutturnio dei Colli Piacentini E-R DOC r dr (s/sw) ✷✷ 88 89 90 91 Full-bodied BARBERA-BONARDA blend from the hills of Piacenza. Can age admirably.

Inferno Lom DOC r dr ✷✷ 82 85 86 88 89 90 Similar to GRUMELLO and, like it, classified as VALTELLINA SUPERIORE.

Ischia Cam DOC w (r) dr ✷→✷✷ DYA The wine of the island off Naples. Slightly sharp white SUPERIORE is best of the DOC. But top producer D'Ambra makes better VDT whites BIANCOLELLA and Forestera and red PER'E PALUMMO.

Isole e Olena Top CHIANTI CLASSICO estate with fine red VDT Cepparello. Vg VIN SANTO.

Isonzo F-VG DOC r w dr ✷✷ 88 89 90 91 DOC covering 19 wines (17 varietals) in the extreme northeast. Best whites and CAB (esp from Stelio Gallo) compare with top COLLIO wines.

Jermann Estate in COLLIO producing top-ranked VDT, incl singular VINTAGE TUNINA oak-aged white blend.

Kalterersee German name for Lago di CALDARO.

Lacryma (or Lacrima) Christi del Vesuvio Cam r p w (fz) dr (sw) ✷→✷✷ 88 89 90 91 Famous but usually ordinary wines in great variety from Vesuvius. (DOC is Vesuvio.) MASTROBERARDINO makes the only good example.

Lageder, Alois The lion of the Bolzano DOCs: SANTA MADDALENA, etc. Exciting wines, incl barrel-aged CHARD and CAB Löwengang. Single-v'yd SAUV BL is called Lehenhof, PINOT BL Haberlehof, PINOT G Benefizium Porer. Also Portico dei Leoni CHARD.

Lago di Caldaro *See* Caldaro.

Lagrein T-AA DOC r p dr ✷✷→✷✷✷ 85 86 88 89 90 A Tyrolean grape with a bitter twist. Good fruity wine – at best v appetizing. The rosé is called Kretzer, the dark Dunkel.

Lamberti Substantial producers of SOAVE, VALPOLICELLA, BARDOLINO, etc at Lazise on the E shore of Lake Garda. NB LUGANA and VDT Turà.

Lambrusco DOC (or not) r p (w) s/sw ✷ DYA Bizarre, highly popular fizzy red (or white), generally drunk *secco* (dry) in Italy but best known in its sweet version in the USA.

Lambrusco di Sorbara E-R DOC r (w) dr s/sw sp ✷✷ DYA The best of the Lambruscos. From nr Modena.

Lambrusco Grasparossa di Castelvetro E-R DOC r dr r s/sw sp ✷✷ DYA Often rivals the foregoing. Acidic: good with rich food.

Lambrusco Salamino di Santa Croce E-R DOC r dr s/sw sp ✷ DYA Similar to above. Fruity smell, high acidity and a thick 'head'.

Langhe The hills of central PIEDMONT, home of BAROLO, BARBARESCO, etc. Candidate for its own DOC. The name is seen on many VDT.

Latisana F-VG DOC r w dr ✶✶ 88 89 90 91 DOC for 13 varietal wines from some 50 miles NE of Venice. Particularly good TOCAI FRIULANO.

Leone de Castris Large but variable producer of Apulian wines with an estate at SALICE SALENTINO, near Lecce.

Lessona Pie DOC r dr ✶✶ 85 86 88 89 90 Soft, dry, claret-like wine produced in the province of Vercelli from NEBBIOLO, Vespolina and BONARDA grapes.

Liquoroso Means strong and usually sweet (whether fortified with alcohol or not), eg Tuscan VIN SANTO.

Lisini Small estate producing some of the finest recent vintages of BRUNELLO.

Locorotondo Ap DOC w dr (sp) ✶ DYA Pleasantly fresh southern white.

Lugana Lom DOC w dr (sp) ✶✶✶ DYA One of the best white wines of S Lake Garda: fragrant, smooth, full of body and flavour. Visconti is the best producer.

Lungarotti The leading producer of TORGIANO wine, with cellars, hotel and wine museum nr Perugia. Also some of Italy's best CHARD (Miralduolo and Vigna I Palazzi) and PINOT G.

Maculan The top producer of DOC BREGANZE. Also Torcolato, dessert VDT (✶✶✶) and Prato di Canzio (CHARD, PINOT BL and PINOT G).

Malvasia Important white or red grape for luscious wines, incl Madeira's Malmsey. Used all over Italy for dry and sweet, still and sparkling wines. An outstanding mature example is TORRICELLA.

Malvasia di Bosa Sar DOC w dr sw ✶✶ 87 88 89 90 91 A wine of character. Strong, aromatic finish.

Malvasia di Cagliari Sar DOC w dr s/sw sw ✶✶ 88 89 90 91 Interesting, strong, Sardinian wine, fragrant and slightly bitter.

Malvasia di Casorzo d'Asti Pie DOC r sw sp ✶✶ DYA Fragrant, grapey, sweet red, sometimes sparkling.

Malvasia di Castelnuovo Don Bosco Pie DOC r sw (sp) ✶✶ DYA Interrupted fermentation gives very sweet aromatic red.

Malvasia delle Lipari Si DOC w sw (pa fz) ✶✶✶ 86 87 88 89 90 91 Among the very best Malvasias, aromatic and rich, from the volcanic Lipari or Aeolian Islands N of Sicily. Top producer: Carlo Hauner.

Malvoisie de Nus VdA DOC w dr s/sw ✶✶✶ Rare Alpine white, with a deep bouquet of honey. Small production and high reputation. Can age remarkably well.

Mandrolisai Sar DOC r p dr ✶ 89 90 91 A CANNONAU blend at a lower strength and more approachable style.

Manduria (Primitivo di) Ap DOC r s/sw (fz dr sw) ✶✶ 88 89 90 91 Heady red, naturally strong but often fortified. From nr Taranto. Primitivo is a southern grape related to Zinfandel.

Mantonico Cal w dr sw fz ✶✶ 85 86 87 88 89 90 91 Fruity, deep amber dessert wine from Reggio Calabria. Can age remarkably well. *See also* Greco di Bianco.

Marino Lat DOC w dr s/sw (sp) ✶✶ DYA A neighbour of FRASCATI with similar wine, often a better buy. Look for COLLE PICCHIONI brand.

Marrano Umb w dr ✶✶✶ Pungent white from GRECHETTO grapes grown by BIGI nr ORVIETO.

Marsala Si DOC br dr s/sw sw fz ✶✶→✶✶✶ NV Sherry-type wine invented by the Woodhouse Brothers from Liverpool in 1773; excellent aperitif or for dessert, but mostly used in the kitchen. The dry ('virgin'), sometimes made by the *solera* system, must be 5 yrs old. Top producers: FLORIO, Pellegrino, RALLO, VECCHIO SAMPERI.

Martina Franca Ap DOC w dr (sp) ✶ DYA Rather neutral southern white, cousin to LOCOROTONDO.

Martini & Rossi Well-known vermouth and sparkling wine house, also famous for its splendid wine museum in Pessione, nr Turin.

Marzemino (del Trentino) T-AA DOC r dr ★→★★★ 89 90 91   Pleasant local red of Trento. Fruity; slightly bitter taste. *See* Cávit.

Mascarello The name of 2 top producers of BAROLO etc: Bartolo M and Giuseppe M & Figli.

Masi, Agricola Well-known, conscientious and reliable specialist producers of VALPOLICELLA, RECIOTO, SOAVE, etc, incl fine red Campo Fiorin and vg single-v'yd AMARONE.

Mastroberardino The leading wine producer of Campania (by far). Wines incl FIANO DI AVELLINO, GRECO DI TUFO, LACRYMA CHRISTI and TAURASI.

Melini Long-established, important producers of CHIANTI CLASSICO at Poggibonsi.

Melissa Cal DOC r w dr ★★ 87 88 89 90 91   Mostly made from (red) Gaglioppo grapes in Catanzaro. Delicate, balanced, can age rather well. CIRO is virtually identical.

Meranese di Collina T-AA DOC r dr ★ DYA   Light red of Merano, known in German as Meraner Hügel.

Merlot Adaptable red Bordeaux grape widely grown in NE Italy and elsewhere. Top Tuscan producers (AMA, AVIGNONESI, ORNELLAIA) make the best. Merlot DOCs include the following:

Merlot dell'Alto Adige T-AA ★★→★★★   Good growers: Haas, Schreckbichl.

Merlot di Aprilia Lat DOC r dr ★ 89 90 91   Harsh at first, softer after 2–3 yrs.

Merlot Colli Berici Ven DOC r dr ★→★★ 88 90   Pleasantly light and soft. Campo del Lago VDT from Villa dal Ferro is one of Italy's best Merlots.

Merlot Colli Orientali del Friuli F-VG DOC r dr ★★ 88 89 90 91   Pleasant herby character, best at 2–3 yrs (RISERVA). Some ages well, notably Vigne dal Leon.

Merlot Collio Goriziano F-VG DOC r dr ★★ 88 89 90 91   Grassy scent, slightly bitter taste. Best at 2–3 yrs.

Merlot Grave del Friuli F-VG DOC r dr ★★ 88 89 90 91   Pleasant light wine, usually best at 1–2 yrs, but potentially a keeper.

Merlot Isonzo F-VG DOC r dr ★★ 88 90 91   A DOC in Gorizia. Dry, herby, agreeable wine.

Merlot Lison-Pramaggiore Ven DOC r dr ★★ 86 88 90 91   A cut above most other Merlots. RISERVA after 2 yrs.

Merlot del Piave Ven DOC r dr ★★ 88 90 91   Sound, tasty red, usually best at 2–4 yrs.

Merlot del Trentino T-AA DOC r dr ★ 86 88 89 90   Full flavour, slightly grassy scent; RISERVA after 2 yrs. (ALTO ADIGE has better; esp from Margreid and Siebeneich v'yds.)

Metodo classico or tradizionale Terms increasingly in use to identify champagne-method sparkling wines. (*See also* Classico.)

Monica di Cagliari Sar DOC r dr sw (fz dr sw) ★★ 89 90 91   Strong, spicy red, often fortified and comparable with Spanish Málaga. Monica is a Sardinian grape.

Monica di Sardegna Sar DOC r dr ★ 89 90 91   Dry version of the above, not fortified.

Monsanto Esteemed CHIANTI CLASSICO estate, esp for Il Poggio v'yd.

Montalcino Small town in the province of Siena, Tuscany, famous for its deep red BRUNELLO and lighter ROSSO DI MONTALCINO.

Monte Vertine Top estate at Radda in CHIANTI. ★★★ VDT Le Pergole Torte (100% SANGIOVETO) and Sodaccio (Sangioveto plus Canaiolo). Also fine VIN SANTO.

Montecarlo Tus DOC w dr r ★★ DYA (w)   One of Tuscany's best whites, smooth and delicate; TREBBIANO blended with a range of better grapes. Now applies to a CHIANTI-style red too (eg Rosso di Cercatoia).

Montecompatri Colonna Lat DOC w dr s/sw ★ DYA   A neighbour of FRASCATI. Similar wine.

Montefalco Umb DOC r dr sw ★★ 87 88 89 90   M Rosso is standard red, SAGRANTINO (named for the grape) has sweetness and bite. ADANTI's Rosso d'Arquata VDT stands out.

Montepulciano An important red grape of central-east Italy as well as the famous Tuscan town.

Montepulciano, Vino Nobile di *See* Vino Nobile di Montepulciano.

Montepulciano d'Abruzzo (or Molise) Ab (or Mol) DOC r p dr ** 85 87 88 89 90 91   At its best one of Italy's tastiest reds, full of flavour and warmth, from the Adriatic coast round Pescara. *See also* Cerasuolo, Valentini.

Monterosso (Val d'Arda) E-R DOC w dr sw (sp) * DYA   Agreeable minor white from Piacenza (DOC COLLI PIACENTINI).

Montesodi Tus r *** 82 83 85 86 88 90   Tip-top CHIANTI Rufina RISERVA from FRESCOBALDI.

Morellino di Scansano Tus DOC r *→***   Local SANGIOVESE of the Maremma, the S Tuscan coast. Starting to stir. Fattorie Le Pupille is good.

Moscadello di Montalcino Tus DOC w sw (sp) ** DYA   Traditional wine of MONTALCINO, much older than BRUNELLO. White, sweet, fizzy MOSCATO. Good producers: BANFI, Il POGGIONE.

Moscato Fruitily fragrant grape grown all over Italy.

Moscato d'Asti Pie DOC w sw sp ** NV   Low-strength, sweet, fruity sparkler, delicious from Bera, Carbonere, Dogliotti, Gatti, Rivetti, Saracco, Vignaioli di Santo Stefano. ASTI SPUMANTE is the (theoretically) superior version

Moscato dei Colli Euganei Ven DOC w sw (sp) ** DYA   Golden wine, fruity and smooth, from nr Padua.

Moscato (Oltrepò Pavese) Lom DOC w sw (sp) * DYA   The Lombardy equivalent of MOSCATO D'ASTI. Rarely as good.

Moscato di Pantelleria Si DOC w sw (sp) (fz pa) ****   Italy's best Muscat, from the island of Pantelleria off the Tunisian coast; rich, fruity and aromatic. Ages well. Top wine: BUKKURAM.

Moscato di Sorso Sennori Sar DOC w sw (fz) * DYA   Strong, golden dessert wine from Sassari, N Sardinia.

Moscato di Trani Ap DOC w sw fz ***   Another golden dessert wine, sometimes fortified, with a 'bouquet of faded roses'. NB unfortified version from Fratelli Nugnes.

Müller-Thurgau Makes wine to be reckoned with in Trentino-Alto Adige and FRIULI, esp TIEFENBRUNNER's Feldmarschall.

Nasco di Cagliari Sar DOC w dr sw (fz dr sw) **   Sardinian speciality with light, bitter taste, high alcoholic content.

Nebbiolo The best red grape of PIEDMONT and Lombardy.

Nebbiolo d'Alba Pie DOC r dr s/sw (sp) ** 85 86 87 88 89 90 91   Like lightweight BAROLO; sometimes easier to appreciate than the more powerful classic wine. ROERO is a new DOC from N of ALBA.

Negroamaro Literally 'black bitter'; Apulian red grape with potential for quality. *See* Copertino.

Nipozzano, Castello di The FRESCOBALDI estate E of Florence producing MONTESODI CHIANTI. The most important outside the CLASSICO zone.

Nosiola (Trentino) T-AA DOC w dr sw ** DYA   Light, fruity white from dried Nosiola grapes. Also good Vin Santo. Best from Pravis: Le Frate.

Nozzole Famous estate, owned by RUFFINO, in the heart of CHIANTI CLASSICO N of Greve. Also good CAB.

Nuragus di Cagliari Sar DOC w dr * DYA   Lively Sardinian white, not too strong.

Oliena Sar r dr **   Interesting strong fragrant CANNONAU red; a touch bitter.

Oltrepò Pavese Lom DOC r w dr sw sp *→**   DOC applicable to 14 wines produced in the province of Pavia, mostly named after their grapes. Top growers incl Cabanon, Doria, Mairano, Tenuta Mazzolino, Monsupello, Montelio.

Ornellaia Tus *** 85 86 87 88 89 90 91   New estate of Lodovico ANTINORI nr Bolgheri on Tuscan coast. To watch for CAB-MERLOT and SAUV BL called Poggio delle Gazze. Also Masseto, vg straight Merlot (**87**, 88, 89, 90, 91).

Orvieto Umb DOC w dr s/sw **→*** DYA   The classical Umbrian golden white, smooth and substantial, formerly rather dull but recently more interesting, esp in sweet versions. O CLASSICO is better. Only the finest examples (eg BIGI, BARBERANI, DECUGANO DEI BARBI) age well. But *see* Castello della Sala.

Pagadebit di Romagna E-R DOC w dr s/sw DYA Pleasant traditional 'payer of debts' from around Bertinoro.

Paradiso, Fattoria Century-old family estate near Bertinoro (E-R). Good ALBANA and PAGADEBIT and unique red BARBAROSSA. Vg SANGIOVESE.

Parrina Tus r w dr ** 89 90 91 Light red and fresh, appetizing white from S Tuscany.

Pasolini Dall'Onda Noble family with estates in CHIANTI Colli Fiorentini and Romagna, producing fine traditional-style wines.

Passito [pa] Strong sweet wine from grapes dried on the vine or indoors.

Pelaverga Pie r dr ** 88 89 90 91 Pale red with spicy perfume from this old variety. Best is from Verduno; others incl Alessandria, Bel Colle.

Peppoli Estate owned by ANTINORI, producing excellent CHIANTI CLASSICO in a full, round, youthful style – first vintage 85.

Per'e Palummo Cam r dr ** 89 90 91 Appetizing, light, tannic red from the island of ISCHIA.

Petit Rouge VdA ** 88 89 90 91 Good, dark, lively REFOSCO-like red. Part of VALLE D'AOSTA DOC.

Piave Ven DOC r w dr ** 88 90 (w DYA) Flourishing DOC covering 8 wines, 4 red and 4 white, named after their grapes. CAB, MERLOT and RABOSO reds all need ageing.

Picolit (Colli Orientali del Friuli) F-VG DOC w s/sw sw *** 88 90 Delicate, well-balanced, very sweet dessert wine with exaggerated reputation. Ages up to 6 yrs, but wildly overpriced.

Piedmont (Piemonte) The most important Italian region for quality wine. Turin is the capital, ASTI and ALBA the wine centres. *See* Barbera, Barbaresco, Barolo, Dolcetto, Grignolino, Moscato, etc.

Pieropan Outstanding producer of SOAVE that deserves its fame.

Pigato New DOC under Riviera Ligure di Ponente Often outclasses VERMENTINO as Liguria's finest white, with rich texture and structure.

Pighin, Fratelli Solid producers of COLLIO and GRAVE DEL FRIULI.

Pinot Bianco Popular grape in NE, esp good for sparkling wine.

Pinot Bianco (Alto Adige) T-AA DOC w dr ** DYA Italy's best and longest-lived wine of this variety.

Pinot Bianco (dei Colli Berici) Ven DOC w dr ** DYA Straight, satisfying dry white.

Pinot Bianco (Colli Orientali del Friuli) F-VG DOC w dr ** DYA Good white; smooth rather than showy.

Pinot Bianco (Collio Goriziano) F-VG DOC w dr ** DYA Similar to above.

Pinot Bianco (Grave del Friuli) F-VG DOC w dr ** DYA Not normally up to the standard of the last two.

Pinot Grigio Tasty, low-acid white grape increasingly popular in NE Italy. Best from ALTO ADIGE, COLLIO. Also in eg Tuscany (from AMA, BANFI).

Pinot Grigio (Collio Goriziano) F-VG DOC w dr ** DYA Fruity, soft, agreeable dry white. The best age well.

Pinot Grigio (Grave del Friuli) F-VG DOC w dr ** DYA Second choice to COLLIO or COLLI ORIENTALI.

Pinot Grigio (Oltrepò Pavese) Lom DOC w dr (sp) * DYA Lombardy's Pinot G is usually at least adequate.

Pinot Nero T-AA DOC r dr ** 85 86 88 89 90 91 Pinot Nero (Noir) gives lively, burgundy-scented, light wine in much of NE Italy, incl TRENTINO and esp ALTO ADIGE. Vg results from Cantina Sociale Colterenzio-Schreckbichl, Castelfeder, Haas, Niedrist. RISERVA after 2 yrs. Also fine sparkling.

Pio Cesare A producer of top-quality red wines of PIEDMONT, incl BAROLO.

Podere Il Palazzino Small estate with admirable CHIANTI CLASSICO and VDT Grosso Sanese.

Poggione, Tenuta Il Perhaps the most consistent estate for BRUNELLO and ROSSO DI MONTALCINO.

Pojer & Sandri Top producers of TRENTINO VDT MULLER-T and CHARD.

Pomino Tus DOC w (r) (br) dr ★★★ 85 86 87 88 90 Fine white, partly CHARD (Il Benefizio is 100%) and a SANGIOVESE-CAB-MERLOT-PINOT N blend. Also Vin Santo. From FRESCOBALDI.

Predicato Name for 4 kinds of VDT from central Tuscany, illustrating the current headlong rush from tradition. P del Muschio is CHARD and PINOT BL; P del Selvante is SAUV BL; P di Biturica is CAB S with SANGIOVESE, P di Cardisco is SANGIOVESE straight. RUFFINO's Cabreo brand wines are examples.

Primitivo di Apulia *See* Manduria.

Prosecco di Conegliano-Valdobbiadene Ven DOC w dr s/sw (sp) ★★→★★★ DYA Popular sparkling wine of the NE. Slight fruity bouquet, the dry pleasantly bitter, the sweet fruity; the best are known as Superiore di Cartizze. Carpené-Malvolti is leading producer, now challenged by Canevel, Cardinal, Nino Franco, Pino Zardetto and others.

Prunotto, Alfredo Very serious ALBA company with vg BARBARESCO, BAROLO, NEBBIOLO, etc. Now controlled by ANTINORI.

Querciabella Up-coming CHIANTI CLASSICO estate with excellent red VDT Camartina and a dream of a white VDT, Bâtard Pinot (PINOT BL and G).

Quintarelli, Giuseppe True artisan producer of VALPOLICELLA, RECIOTO and AMARONE, at the top in both quality and price.

Raboso del Piave (now DOC) Ven r dr ★★ 83 85 86 88 90 Powerful, sharp, interesting country red; needs age.

Rallo, Nuova A leader in MARSALA with first class Vergine, and other wines.

Ramandolo *See* Verduzzo Colli Orientali del Friuli.

Ramitello *See* Di Majo Norante.

Rampolla, Castello dei Top CHIANTI CLASSICO estate at Panzano; also excellent CAB-based VDT Sammarco.

Rapitalà *See* Alcamo.

Ratti, Renato Maker of vg BAROLO and other ALBA wines. The late Signor Ratti (d '88) was a highly respected leader of the PIEDMONT industry.

Ravello Cam r p w dr ★★ 88 89 90 91 Among the best wines of Campania: full dry red, fresh white. Caruso is the best-known brand. Episcopio-Vuillemier makes better wines.

Recioto Wine made partly of half-dried grapes. Speciality of Veneto since the great days of the Venetian empire.

Recioto di Gambellara Ven DOC w s/sw sp ★ DYA Sweetish golden wine, often half-sparkling.

Recioto di Soave Ven DOC w s/sw (sp) ★★ 86 87 88 90 SOAVE made from selected half-dried grapes; sweet, fruity, fresh, slightly almondy; high alcohol. Top makers: ANSELMI, PIEROPAN.

Recioto della Valpolicella Ven DOC r s/sw sp ★★ 85 86 88 90 Strong, late-harvested red, sometimes sparkling. 'Amabile' is sweet.

Recioto della Valpolicella Amarone Ven DOC r dr ★★★★ 79 81 83 85 86 88 90 Dry version of the above; strong concentrated flavour, rather bitter. Impressive and expensive. Now properly called just Amarone.

Refosco (Colli Orientali del Friuli) F-VG DOC r dr ★★ 86 88 90 Full-bodied dry red; RISERVA after 2 yrs. Refosco is said to be the same grape as the Mondeuse of Savoie (France).

Refosco (Grave del Friuli) F-VG DOC r dr ★★ 86 87 88 90 Similar to above but slightly lighter.

Regaleali Si w r p ★★ 86 87 88 89 90 91 Perhaps the best Sicilian table wines, produced between Palermo and Caltanissetta to the SE.

Ribolla (Colli Orientali del Friuli) F-VG DOC w dr ★ DYA Clean and fruity NE white.

Ricasoli Famous Tuscan family, 'inventors' of CHIANTI, whose Chianti

Classico is named after their BROLIO estate and castle.

Riecine Tus r (w dr) ★★★ First-class CHIANTI CLASSICO estate at Gaiole, started 20 yrs ago by an Englishman, John Dunkley. Also VDT La Gioia di Riecine.

Riesling Formerly referred to Italian Ries (R Italico or Welschriesling). German (Rhine) Riesling, now ascendant, is R Renano.

Riesling (Alto Adige) DOC w dr ★★ 89 90 91 Can often be Italy's best RIES.

Riesling (Oltrepò Pavese) Lom DOC w dr (sp) ★★ The Lombardy version, quite light and fresh. Occasionally sparkling. Keeps well. Made of both types of RIES.

Riesling (Trentino) T-AA DOC w dr ★★ DYA Delicate, slightly acid, v fruity.

Riserva Wine aged for a statutory period, usually in barrels.

Riunite One of the world's largest coop cellars nr Reggio Emilia, producing huge quantities of LAMBRUSCO and other wines.

Rivera Reliable winemakers at Andria, near Bari, with good red Il Falcone and CASTEL DEL MONTE rosé. Also Vigna al Monte label.

Riviera del Garda Chiaretto Ven, Lom DOC p dr ★★ DYA Charming, cherry-pink, fresh and slightly bitter, from SW Garda.

Riviera del Garda Rosso Ven DOC r dr ★★ 88 90 91 Red version of the above; ages surprisingly well.

Rocche dei Manzoni, Podere Go-ahead estate at Monforte d'Alba. Excellent BAROLO, BRICCO MANZONI, ALBA wines and Valentino Brut sparkling.

Roero DOC r ★★ 90 91 New name for a drink-me-quick NEBBIOLO from ALBA. Can be delicious.

Ronco del Gnemiz Tiny property with outstanding COLLI ORIENTALI DOCs and VDT CHARD made in *barriques*.

Rosa del Golfo Ap p dr ★★ DYA An outstanding VDT rosé of ALEZIO.

Rosato Rosé.

Rosato del Salento Ap p dr ★→★★ DYA Strong but refreshing southern rosé from round Brindisi.

Rossese di Dolceacqua Lig DOC r dr ★★ 89 90 91 Well-known, fragrant light red of the Riviera, as clean as claret.

Rosso Red.

Rosso Cònero Mar DOC r dr ★★★ 85 86 88 89 90 91 Some of the best MONTEPULCIANO (varietal) reds of Italy, eg Garofoli's Grosso Agontano, Moroder's RC Riserva, Umani Ronchi's Cumaro and San Lorenzo.

Rosso d'Arquata *See* Adanti.

Rosso delle Colline Lucchesi Tus DOC r dr ★→★★ 88 89 90 91 Produced round Lucca but not greatly different from CHIANTI.

Rosso di Montalcino Tus DOC r dr ★★→★★★ 87 88 89 90 91 Recent DOC for younger wines from BRUNELLO grapes. Still variable but potentially a winner if the many good producers are not too greedy over prices.

Rosso di Montepulciano Tus DOC r dr ★★ 90 91 Equivalant of the last for junior VINO NOBILE, recently introduced and yet to establish a style.

Rosso Piceno Mar DOC r dr ★→★★ 88 89 90 91 Adriatic red with a touch of style. Can be SUPERIORE from classic zone nr Ascoli. Best producers: Cocci Grifoni, Villamagna, Villa Pigna.

Rubesco The excellent popular red of LUNGAROTTI; *see* Torgiano.

Rubino di Cantavenna Pie DOC r dr ★★ DYA Lively red, principally BARBERA, from a well-known coop SE of Turin.

Ruchè di Castagnole Monferrato DOC r (sw) ★★★ Blend of BARBERA and GRIGNOLINO, barrel-aged and aromatic.

Rufina Important subregion of CHIANTI in the hills E of Florence.

Ruffino Perhaps the biggest and best known of all CHIANTI merchants, at Pontassieve. RISERVA Ducale and Santedame are the top wines. NB new PREDICATO wines and CAB Il Pareto.

Sagrantino di Montefalco Umb DOCG r sw ★★ 90 91 A little dry and even less sweet red. *See also* Montefalco.

Salice Salentino Ap DOC r ★★ 83 85 86 87 88 89 90 91 Strong red from

NEGROAMARO grapes. RISERVA after 2 yrs; smooth when mature. Top makers: Francesco Candido, De Castris, Taurino, Vallone.

San Felice Rising star in CHIANTI with fine CLASSICO Poggio Rosso. Also red VDT Vigorello and PREDICATO di Biturica.

Sangiovese or Sangioveto Principal red grape of Italy, esp Tuscany. Many forms incl the noble BRUNELLO (of MONTALCINO) and Prugnolo Gentile (of MONTEPULCIANO), also the following:

Sangiovese d'Aprilia Lat DOC r p dr ★ DYA Strong dry rosé from S of Rome.

Sangiovese di Romagna E-R DOC r dr ★★ 85 86 87 88 89 90 91 Pleasant standard red; gains character with a little age.

San Giusto a Rentennano One of the best CHIANTI CLASSICO producers. Delicious but v rare VIN SANTO. Excellent VDT red Percarlo.

San Severo Ap DOC r p w dr ★ Sound, neutral southern wine; not particularly strong.

Santa Maddalena T-AA DOC r dr ★★ 90 91 Typical Schiava Tyrolean red. Slightly almondy.

Santa Margherita The Veneto winery that popularized PINOT G, now on a broad base with many good wines.

Sassella (Valtellina) Lom DOC r dr ★★★ 82 85 86 88 89 90 Considerable NEBBIOLO wine, tough when young. Known since Roman times; mentioned by Leonardo da Vinci. Neighbour to INFERNO etc.

Sassicaia Tus r dr ★★★★ 75 78 82 83 84 85 86 87 88 89 90 91 Outstanding pioneer CAB, Italy's best, from the Tenuta San Guido of the Incisa family, at Bolgheri nr Livorno.

Sauvignon Sauv Bl: used in NE, perhaps best at TERLANO, ALTO ADIGE. Vg in COLLIO and COLLI ORIENTALI.

Sauvignon (Colli Berici) Ven DOC w dr ★ DYA Fresh white from nr Vicenza.

Sauvignon (Colli Orientali del Friuli) F-VG DOC w dr ★★ 89 90 91 Full, smooth, freshly aromatic NE white.

Sauvignon (Collio Goriziano) F-VG DOC w dr ★★ 89 90 91 V similar to the last; slightly higher alcohol.

Savuto Cal DOC r p dr ★★ 89 90 91 Fragrant, juicy wine from the provinces of Cosenza and Catanzaro.

Schiava High-yielding red grape of Trentino-Alto Adige with characteristic bitter aftertaste, used for Lago di CALDARO, SANTA MADDALENA, etc.

Sciacchetrà *See* Cinqueterre.

Secco Dry.

Sella & Mosca Major Sardinian growers and merchants at Alghero. Their port-like Anghelu Ruju is good. Also pleasant white TORBATO and delicious, light, fruity VERMENTINO Cala Viola.

Selvapiana RUFINA estate owned by Giuntini family. Top wine is RISERVA Bucerchiale.

Settesoli Sicilian growers' coop with range of sometimes vg table wines.

Sforzato (Valtellina) Lom DOC r dr ★★★ 79 82 83 85 86 88 89 90 Valtellina equivalent of RECIOTO AMARONE made with partly dried grapes. Velvety, strong, ages remarkably well. Also called Sfursat.

Sizzano Pie DOC r dr ★★ 85 86 87 88 89 90 Attractive, full-bodied red produced at Sizzano in the province of Novara, mostly from NEBBIOLO. Ages up to 10 yrs.

Soave Ven DOC w dr ★★→★★★ DYA Famous, if not very characterful, Veronese white. Fresh with v attractive texture. Standards are rising (at last). S CLASSICO is more restricted and better. Top growers are ANSELMI, BOSCAINI, PIEROPAN. *See also* Bolla.

Solaia Tus r ★★★★ 78 79 82 83 85 86 88 90 V fine Bordeaux-style VDT of CAB S and a little SANGIOVESE from ANTINORI, first made in '78 and extraordinarily influential.

Solopaca Cam DOC r w dr ★★ 88 89 90 91 Up-and-coming from nr Benevento; rather sharp when young, the white soft and fruity.

Sorni T-AA r w dr ** DYA Made in the province of Trento. Light, fresh and soft. Drink young.

Spanna *See* Gattinara.

Spumante Sparkling, as in sweet ASTI or many good dry wines, incl both METODO CLASSICO (best from TRENTINO, ALTO ADIGE, FRANCIACORTA) and tank-made cheapos.

Squinzano Ap DOC r p dr * 85 86 87 88 89 90 91 Strong southern red from Lecce. RISERVA after 2 yrs.

Stravecchio Very old.

Südtirol The local name of German-speaking ALTO ADIGE.

Superiore Wine that has undergone more ageing than normal DOC and contains 1% more alcohol.

Taurasi Cam DOC r dr *** 79 80 82 83 85 86 87 88 89 90 91 The best Campanian red, from MASTROBERARDINO of Avellino. Harsh when young. RISERVA after 4 yrs. Radici (since '86) is Mastroberardino's top estate bottling.

Tedeschi, Fratelli Leading small producer of VALPOLICELLA, RECIOTO and AMARONE. Vg Capitel San Rocco red and white VDT.

Terlano T-AA DOC w dr **→*** 90 91 A DOC for 8 white wines from the province of Bolzano, named by their grapes, esp outstanding SAUV. Terlaner in German.

Teroldego Rotaliano T-AA DOC r p dr **→*** 86 88 89 90 91 The attractive local red of Trento. Blackberry-scented; slight bitter aftertaste; can age v well. Top maker: Foradori.

Terre di Ginestra Si w dr ** Good white VDT from Cataratto, grown SW of Palermo.

Terre Rosse Distinguished small estate nr Bologna. CAB, CHARD, SAUV BL, PINOT G, etc, are the best of the region.

Tiefenbrunner Leading grower of some of the very best ALTO ADIGE white and red wines at Schloss Turmhof, Kurtatsch (Cortaccio).

Tignanello Tus r dr *** 77 79 82 83 85 86 88 90 Pioneer and still leader of the new style of Bordeaux-inspired Tuscan reds, made by ANTINORI.

Tocai Friulano (Collio) ** 89 90 NE Italian white grape; no relation of Hungarian or Alsace Tokay. Light dry wine. The Tocais of the COLLI ORIENTALI DEL FRIULI and COLLIO GORIZIANO are best.

Tocai di Lison Ven DOC w dr ** DYA From E Veneto, delicate scent, faintly fruity taste. CLASSICO is better.

Tocai (Colli Berici) Ven DOC w dr * DYA A more modest wine altogether.

Tocai (Grave del Friuli) F-VG DOC w dr ** DYA Similar to TOCAI DI LISON; generally rather milder.

Tocai di San Martino della Battaglia Lom DOC w dr ** DYA Small production S of Lake Garda. Light, slightly bitter.

Torbato di Alghero Sar w dr (pa) ** DYA Good N Sardinian table wine. Top maker: SELLA & MOSCA.

Torgiano (Rubesco di) Umb DOCG r w dr *** 82 83 85 87 88 90 The creation of the LUNGAROTTI family. Excellent red from nr Perugia, comparable with top CHIANTI CLASSICO. Rubesco is the standard quality. RISERVA Vigna Monticchio is superb; keep 10 yrs. VDT San Giorgio involves CAB to splendid effect. White Torre di Giano, of TREBBIANO and GRECHETTO, also ages well. *See also* Lungarotti.

Torricella Tus w dr *** 83 85 86 87 88 90 Remarkable, aged, soft, buttery MALVASIA dry white from Brolio.

Toscana Tuscany.

Traminer Aromatico T-AA DOC w dr **→*** DYA Delicate, aromatic, rather soft Gewürz.

Trebbiano The principal white grape of Tuscany, found all over Italy. Ugni Blanc in French. Rarely remarkable unless blended.

Trebbiano d'Abruzzo Ab, Mol DOC w dr *→** DYA Gentle, rather neutral, slightly tannic. From round Pescara. VALENTINI is much the best producer (also of MONTEPULCIANO D'ABRUZZO).

Trebbiano d'Aprilia Lat DOC w dr ★ DYA Heady, mild-flavoured, rather yellow. From S of Rome.

Trebbiano di Romagna E-R DOC w dr s/sw (sp) ★ DYA Clean, pleasant white from nr Bologna.

Trentino T-AA DOC r w dr sw →★★★ DOC for as many as 20 different wines, mostly named after their grapes. Best are CHARD, PINOT BL, MARZEMINO and esp VIN SANTO.

Umani Ronchi A leading producer of quality wines of the Marches; notably VERDICCHIO (Casal di Serra and Villa Bianchi) and ROSSO CONERO (Cumaro and San Lorenzo).

Valcalepio Lom DOC r w dr ★ 90 91 From nr Bergamo. Pleasant red; lightly scented, fresh white.

Valdadige T-AA DOC r w dr s/sw ★ Name for the simple wines of the Adige valley – in German 'Etschtaler'.

Val d'Arbia Tus DOC w dr ★→★★ DYA Another DOC for a pleasant white and VIN SANTO from CHIANTI country.

Valentini, Edoardo Outstanding traditionalist maker of TREBBIANO and MONTEPULCIANO D'ABRUZZO.

Valgella (Valtellina) Lom DOC r dr ★★ 82 85 86 88 89 90 One of the VALTELLINA NEBBIOLOS: good dry red. RISERVA at 4 yrs.

Valle d'Aosta/Vallée d'Aosta VdA DOC Regional DOC for 15 Alpine wines incl DONNAZ. A mixed bag.

Valle Isarco T-AA DOC w dr ★→★★ 89 90 91 A DOC applicable to 5 varietal wines made NE of Bolzano. Outstanding MULLER-T, SYLVANER.

Valpantena Valley in the VALPOLICELLA zone. Rival to CLASSICO. *See* Bertani.

Valpolicella Ven DOC r dr ★→★★★ 88 89 90 91 Attractive light red from nr Verona; most attractive when young. Delicate, nutty scent, slightly bitter taste. (None of this is true of Valpolicella sold in litre and bigger bottles.) CLASSICO more restricted; SUPERIORE has 12% alcohol and 1 yr of age. Best wines from ALLEGRINI, MASI, QUINTARELLI.

Valtellina Lom DOC r dr ★★→★★★ 85 86 88 89 90 91 A DOC for tannic wines made principally from Chiavennasca (NEBBIOLO) grapes in the province of Sondrio, N Lombardy. V SUPERIORE are GRUMELLO, INFERNO, SASSELLA, VALGELLA.

Vecchio Samperi Si ★★★ The outstanding estate of MARSALA today, although not DOC. A dry aperitif not unlike *amontillado* sherry. The owner, De Bartoli, also makes DOC Marsalas.

Velletri Lat DOC r w dr s/sw ★★ 89 90 91 Agreeable Roman dry red and smooth white. Drink young.

Vendemmia Harvest or vintage.

Venegazzù Ven r w dr sp ★★★ 82 83 85 86 87 88 89 90 91 Remarkable rustic Bordeaux-style red produced from CAB grapes nr Treviso. Rich bouquet, soft, warm taste. 'Della Casa' is best quality. Also sparkling.

Verdicchio dei Castelli di Jesi Mar DOC w dr (sp) ★→★★★ DYA Ancient, famous and v pleasant fresh pale white from nr Ancona, dating back to the Etruscans. CLASSICO is more restricted. Traditionally comes in amphora-shaped bottles; today also standard bottles, notably from Brunori, Bucci, GAROFOLI, Monteschiavo, UMANI RONCHI; also FAZI-BATTAGLIA.

Verdicchio di Matelica Mar DOC w dr (sp) ★★ DYA Similar to the last, though less well known. Bigger wines than Jesi.

Verdiso Rare native white grape of NE Italy, used with PROSECCO.

Verduzzo (Colli Orientali del Friuli) F-VG DOC w dr s/sw sw ★★ 88 89 90 Full-bodied white from a native grape. The best sweet is called Ramandolo. Top maker: Giovanni Dri.

Verduzzo (del Piave) Ven DOC w dr ★ DYA A dull little white.

Vermentino Lig w dr DOC ★★ DYA The best seafood white of the Riviera: from Pietra Ligure and San Remo. DOC is Riviera Ligure di Ponente. *See* Pigato.

Vermentino di Gallura Sar DOC w dr ★★ DYA Soft, dry, rather strong white from N Sardinia.

Vernaccia di Oristano Sar DOC w dr (sw) (fz) ******* 75 78 81 83 85 87 88 Sardinian speciality, like light sherry, a touch bitter, full-bodied and interesting. SUPERIORE with 15.5% alcohol and 3 yrs of age. Top producer Contini also makes ancient *solera* wine Antico Gregori.

Vernaccia di San Gimignano Tus DOC w dr (fz) ****** 90 91 Should be a distinctive, strong, high-flavoured wine from nr Siena. Michelangelo's favourite. Much today is light and bland, but there are signs of improvement. Try Teruzzi & Puthod, Falchini or (old-style) Pietrafitta. RISERVA after 1 yr.

Vernaccia di Serrapetrona Mar DOC r s/sw sp ****** DYA From Macerata; aromatic, with pleasantly bitter aftertaste.

Vernatsch German for SCHIAVA.

Vicchiomaggio Important CHIANTI CLASSICO estate near Greve.

Vietti Excellent small producer of some of PIEDMONT's most characterful wines, incl BAROLO. At Castiglione Falletto in province of Cuneo.

VIDE An association of better-class Italian producers for marketing their estate wines from many parts of Italy.

Vigna A single vineyard –*see* Introduction, page 80.

Vignamaggio Historic, beautiful and vg CHIANTI CLASSICO estate nr Greve.

Villagrande Imposing old estate on the slopes of Mt Etna, Sicily. DOC ETNA.

Vino da arrosto 'Wine for roast meat', ie good, robust, dry red.

Vino da pasto 'Mealtime wine', ie nothing special.

Vino da tavola [vdt] 'Table wine': intended to be the humblest class of Italian wine, with no specific geographical or other claim to fame, but recently the category to watch (with reasonable circumspection and a wary eye on the price) for top-class wines not conforming to DOC regulations. New laws introduced in '92 to phase out this situation (*see* Introduction, page 80).

Vino Nobile di Montepulciano Tus DOCG r dr ******* 82 83 85 86 87 88 90 91 Impressive CHIANTI-like red with bouquet and style, rapidly making its name and fortune. RISERVA after 3 yrs. Best estates incl AVIGNONESI, Bindella, BOSCARELLI, Le Casalte, Fattoria del Cerro, Contucci, Poliziano, Talosa, Tenuta Trerose, Valdipiatta.

Vino novello Italy's equivalent of France's *primeurs* (as in Beaujolais).

Vinsanto or **Vin(o) Santo** Term for certain strong, sweet wines esp in Tuscany: usually PASSITO. Can be v fine, esp in Tuscany and Trentino.

Vin Santo di Gambellara Ven DOC w sw ****** Powerful, velvety, golden; made near Vicenza and Verona.

Vin Santo Toscano Tus w s/sw ****→***** Aromatic bouquet, rich and smooth. Aged in v small barrels called *caratelli*. Can be astonishing.

Vintage Tunina F-VG w dr ******* 88 89 90 91 A notable blended COLLIO white from the JERMANN estate.

Voerzio, Roberto Young pace-setter in BAROLO producing refreshing wines.

VQPRD Often found on the labels of DOC wines to signify *vini di qualità prodotti in regioni delimitate*.

Zagarolo Lat DOC w dr s/sw ****** DYA Neighbour of FRASCATI, similar wine.

Zanella, Maurizio Owner of CA'DEL BOSCO. His name is on top CAB-MERLOT blend, one of Italy's best (85, 86, 87, 89, 90, 91).

Zerbina, Fattoria New leader in Romagna with best ALBANA DOCG to date (a rich PASSITO), good SANGIOVESE and a *barrique*-aged Sangiovese-CAB VDT called Marzeno di Marzeno.

Zibibbo Si w sw ****** Fashionable MOSCATO of island of Pantelleria.

Zonin One of Italy's biggest privately owned estates and wineries, based at GAMBELLARA, with DOC VALPOLICELLA etc. Other large estates are at ASTI and in CHIANTI, San Gimignano and FRIULI. Also at Barboursville, Virginia, USA.

Germany

The earth is moving in Germany. There is now a distinct feeling that two decades of drift in Germany's cellars may be coming to an end. They began with the 1971 Wine Laws, which encouraged low standards, over-production and confusing (not to say misleading) labelling. Demoralization, greed and fraud made matters worse. And so did the weather: 12 years with only two good vintages.

1988 seems to have been a turning point. Three fine vintages have been matched by a new determination among young winemakers. Germany's best growers have at last resolved to ignore the laws that encourage inflation of quantity and dilution of quality, and make the best wine they can, many of them in a style that has not been seen for half a century. They have turned their backs on flowery, sugar-watery wines. Most are now being made dry or close to dry, with sweetness reserved as the exception, for *Spätlesen* and *Auslesen* and not always even for these. Growers are experimenting with *barrique*-ageing (though not of Riesling) to open up new stylistic possibilities and supply top restaurants. On the home market, these fine, dry wines are all the rage, abroad they have yet to be fully understood.

Officially, all German wines are classified according to the ripeness of their grapes. Most German wine (like most French) needs sugar added before fermentation to make up for missing sunshine and increase its strength. But unlike in France, wine from grapes ripe enough not to need extra sugar is made and sold as a separate product. The term is *Qualitätswein mit Prädikat*, or QmP. Within this top category, natural sugar content is expressed by traditional terms in ascending order of ripeness: *Kabinett*, *Auslese*, *Spätlese*, *Beerenauslese*, *Trockenbeerenauslese*.

Qualitätswein bestimmter Anbaugebiete (QbA), the second level, is for wines that needed additional sugar before fermentation. The third level, *Tafelwein*, has no pretensions to quality.

Though there is very much more detail in the laws, this is the gist of the quality grading. It differs completely from the French system in ignoring geographical difference. There are no Grands Crus, no VDQS. In theory all any German vineyard has to do to make the best wine is to grow the ripest grapes.

The law distinguishes only between degrees of geographical exactness. In labelling quality wine the growers or merchants are given a choice. They can (and generally always will) label the relatively small quantities of their best wine with the name of the precise vineyard or *Einzellage*. Germany has about 2,600 *Einzellage* names. Obviously only particularly good ones are famous enough to help sell the wine. Therefore the 1971 law created a second class of vineyard name: the *Grosslage*. A *Grosslage* is a group of neighbouring *Einzellagen* of supposedly similar character. Because there are fewer *Grosslage* names, and far more wine from each, they have the advantage of familiarity. The law was thus responsible for confusing the public, and the industry has suffered as a result.

The following abbreviations of regional names are used in the text.

Bad	Baden	**Na**	Nahe
Frank	Franken	**Rhg**	Rheingau
M-M	Mittel-Mosel	**Rhh**	Rheinhessen
M-S-R	Mosel-Saar-Ruwer	**Rhpf**	Rheinpfalz
		Würt	Württemberg

Thirdly, growers or merchants (more likely the latter) may choose to sell their wine under a regional name: the word is *Bereich*. To cope with the vast demand for 'Bernkasteler' or 'Niersteiner' or 'Johannisberger' these world-famous names have been made legal for considerable districts. 'Bereich Johannisberg' is the whole of the Rheingau. By this logic the whole of the Médoc could be Margaux. Beware the *Bereich*.

More and more growers and estates are now working out their own simplified labelling system to avoid confusion and clutter. Some use the village name only, not mentioning the vineyard, or indeed omit even this and sell top wines under their brand name alone in the Italian fashion. It is after all, and in Germany above all, the producer that counts most.

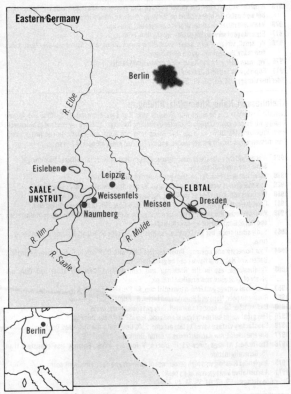

Recent vintages

Mosel-Saar-Ruwer

Mosels (including Saar and Ruwer wines) are so attractive young that their keeping qualities are not often enough explored, and wines older than about 7 yrs are unusual. But well-made Riesling wines of *Kabinett* class gain from 3 or more in bottle, *Spätlese* by up to 10 yrs or so, and *Auslese* and *Beerenauslese* by anything from 10–20 yrs.

As a rule, in poor yrs the Saar and Ruwer make sharp, thin wines, but in the best years they can surpass the whole world for elegance and thrilling, steely 'breed'.

1991 A difficult and diverse vintage. Bad frost damage in Saar and Ruwer, but many *Spätlesen* in Mittelmosel.

1990 Superb vintage, though small. Many QmP wines will be classics.

1989 Large and outstandingly good, with noble rot giving many *Auslesen*, etc. Saar best; Mittelmosel overproduced.

1988 Excellent vintage. Much ripe QmP, esp in Mittelmosel. For long keeping.

1987 Rainy summer but warm Sept/Oct. 90% QbA wines, crisp and lively, to drink soon.

1986 Fair Riesling year despite autumn rain: 13% QmP wines, mostly *Kabinett*. For drinking.

1985 A modest summer but beautiful autumn. 40% of harvest was QmP. Riesling vintage from best v'yds, incl *Eiswein*. Many need keeping.

1984 A late and rainy year. Two-thirds QbA, one-third *Tafel-* or *Landwein*. Almost no QmP. But good acidity means some wines (esp Mittelmosels) have kept well.

1983 The best between 76 and 88; 31% *Spätlese, Auslesen* few but fine. No hurry to drink.

1982 A huge ripe vintage marred by rain which considerably diluted the wines. Most is plain QbA but good sites made *Kabinett, Spätlese* and *Auslese*. Drink up.

1981 A wet vintage but some good Mittelmosels up to *Spätlese*. Also *Eiswein*. Drinking well.

1980 A terrible summer. Some pleasant wines but little more. Avoid.

1979 A patchy vintage after bad winter damage. But several excellent *Kabinetts* and better. Light but well-balanced wines should be drunk up. *Auslesen* will still improve.

1978 V late and rather small. Generally to be avoided. Drink up.

1977 Big vintage of serviceable quality, mostly QbA. Drink up.

1976 Vg small vintage, with some superlative sweet wines and almost no dry. Most wines now ready; the best will keep a while longer.

1975 Vg; many *Spätlesen* and *Auslesen*. Almost all now ready.

1971 Superb, with perfect balance. At its peak.

Older fine vintages: 64, 59, 53, 49, 45.

Rheinhessen, Nahe, Rheinpfalz, Rheingau

Even the best wines can be drunk with pleasure after 2 or 3 yrs, but *Kabinett*, *Spätlese* and *Auslese* Riesling wines gain enormously in character by keeping for longer. Rheingau wines tend to be longest-lived, improving for 10 yrs or more, but wines from the Nahe and Palatinate can last as long. Rheinhessen wines usually mature sooner, and dry Franken wines are best at 3–6 yrs.

1991 A good middling vintage in most regions, though light soils in Pfalz suffered from drought. Some fine wines will emerge.

1990 Small but exceptionally fine. High percentage of QmP to lay down.

1989 Summer storms reduced crop in Rheingau. Vg quality elsewhere, up to *Auslese* level.

1988 Not quite so outstanding as the Mosel, but comparable with 83. Drinking well.

1987 Good average quality: lively, round and fresh. 80% QbA, 15% QmP. Now drinking well.

1986 Well-balanced Rieslings, mostly QbA but some *Kabinett* and *Spätlese*, esp in Rheinhessen and Nahe. Good botrytis wines in Rheinpfalz.

1985 Sadly small crops, but good quality, esp Riesling. Average 65% QmP. Successful wines need time.

1984 Poor flowering and ripening. Three-quarters QbA, with QmP only in Rheinhessen, Rheinpfalz, Baden and Nahe. But flavour can be good. Drink soon.

1983 Vg Rieslings, esp in the Rheingau and central Nahe. Generally about half QbA, but plenty of *Spätlesen*, now excellent to drink.

1982 A colossal vintage gathered in torrential rain. All 82s should be drunk up.

1981 Rheingau poor, Nahe and Rheinhessen better, Rheinpfalz best. Drink up.

1980 Bad weather from spring to autumn. Only passable wines. Avoid.

1979 Few great wines but many typical and good, esp in Palatinate. Drink up.

1978 Satisfactory vintage saved by late autumn. 25% QmP, but v few *Spätlesen*. Drink up.

1977 Big and useful; few *Kabinett* wines or better. Drink up.

1976 The richest vintage since 21 in places. V few dry wines. Balance less consistent than 75. Generally mature.

1975 A splendid Riesling yr, a high percentage of *Kabinett* and *Spätlesen*. Drink soon.

1971 A superlative vintage, now at its peak.

Older fine vintages: 69, 67, 64, 59, 53, 49, 45.

NB On the German vintage notation

Vintage notes after entries in the German section are given in a different form from those elsewhere, to show the style of the vintage as well as its quality. Three styles are indicated:

Bold type (eg **90**) indicates classic, super-ripe vintages with a high proportion of natural (QmP) wines, including *Spätlese* and *Auslese*.

Normal type (eg 91) indicates 'normal' successful vintages with plenty of good wine but no great preponderance of sweeter wines.

Italic type (eg *84*) indicates cool vintages with generally poor ripeness but a fair proportion of reasonably successful wines, tending to be over-acid. Few or no QmP wines, but correspondingly more selection in the QbA category. Such wines sometimes mature better than expected.

Where no mention is made the vintage is generally not recommended, or most of its wines have passed maturity.

Achkarren Bad w (r) ✶✶ Well-known village on the KAISERSTUHL, esp for SILVANER, RULANDER. Best site: Schlossberg. Good wines from DR HEGER and coop.

Adelmann, Graf Grower with 37 acres at Kleinbottwar, WURTTEMBERG. Uses the name 'Brussele'. Light reds; good dry RIES.

Ahr Ahr r ✶→✶✶ 76 83 85 87 88 **89 90 91** Germany's best-known red-wine area, S of Bonn. Very light, pale SPATBURGUNDER, esp from STATE DOMAIN

Kloster Marienthal, Meyer-Näkel.

Amtliche Prüfungsnummer *See* Prüfungsnummer.

Anheuser Name of two growers of the NAHE, August (★★) and Paul (★★★).

APNr Abbreviation of AMTLICHE PRUFUNGSNUMMER.

Assmannshausen Rhg r ★→★★★ **71 75 76 83 85 87 88 89 90 91** RHEINGAU
village known for its pale, sometimes sweet reds. Top v'yd:
Höllenberg. Grosslagen: Steil and Burgweg. Growers incl the STATE
DOMAIN at ELTVILLE, August Kesseler, Robert König, von MUMM.

Auslese Specially selected wine with high natural sugar content; the best
often affected by 'noble rot' and correspondingly unctuous in flavour.

Avelsbach M-S-R (Ruwer) w ★★★ **71 75 76 83 85 87 88 89 90 91** Village nr
TRIER. Supremely delicate wines. Growers: BISCHOFLICHE WEINGUTER,
Staatliche Weinbaudomäne (*see* Staatsweingut). Grosslage: Römerlay.

Ayl M-S-R (Saar) w ★★★ **71 75 76 83 85 87 88 89 90 91** One of the best
villages of the SAAR. Top v'yds: Herrenberger, Kupp. Grosslage:
SCHARZBERG. Growers incl BISCHOFLICHE WEINGUTER, LAUER, Wagner.

Bacchus Modern highly perfumed grape variety, best for sweet wines.

Bacharach Romantic old town, a tourist centre of the MITTELRHEIN.

Bacharach (Bereich) ★→★★ District name for the S MITTELRHEIN v'yds
downstream from the RHEINGAU. Steely, racy wines, some v pleasant.
Growers incl Toni JOST, Ratzenberger.

Baden Huge SW area of scattered wine-growing. The style is substantial,
relatively low in acid, well adapted for mealtimes. Good Pinots etc and
SPATBURGUNDER, less RIES. Best areas: KAISERSTUHL, ORTENAU.

Badische Bergstrasse/Kraichgau (Bereich) Widespread district of N
BADEN. RIES and RULANDER are best.

Badischer Winzerkeller New name for the ZBW, Germany's (and
Europe's) biggest coop, at BREISACH; 25,000 members with 12,000
acres, producing 80% of BADEN's wine at all quality levels.

Badisches Frankenland (Bereich) Minor district name of N BADEN;
FRANKEN-style wines.

Bad Dürkheim Rhpf w (r) ★★→★★★ **76 83 85 86 87 88 89 90 91** Main town
of the MITTELHAARDT, with the world's biggest barrel (converted into a
tavern). Scene of a vast and ancient September wine festival, the
'Wurstmarkt'. Top v'yds: Hochbenn, Michelsberg, Spielberg.
Grosslagen: Feuerberg, Hochmess, Schenkenböhl. Top growers:
BURKLIN-WOLF, RITZ-RITTER, KARST, KOEHLER-RUPRECHT, Schäfer.

Bad Kreuznach Nahe w ★★→★★★ **75 76 79 83 85 86 87 88 89 90 91** Main
town of the NAHE with some of its best wines. Many fine v'yds, incl
Brückes, Kahlenberg, Krötenpfuhl, Steinweg. Grosslage: Kronenberg.
Growers incl ANHEUSER, Finkenauer, PLETTENBERG.

Balbach Erben, Bürgermeister One of the best-known NIERSTEIN growers.
44 acres, 80% RIES. Best v'yds: Ölberg, Pettenthal.

Barriques A few German growers are experimenting with fashionable
new-oak small-barrel ageing. A quick route to notoriety and higher
prices, it can be positive for SPATBURGUNDER, Weissburgunder or
Grauburgunder, but generally disfigures RIES.

Bassermann-Jordan 117-acre MITTELHAARDT family estate with many of the
best v'yds in DEIDESHEIM, FORST, RUPPERTSBERG, etc. 100% RIES and a
formidable track-record.

Becker, J B Dedicated family estate and brokerage house at WALLUF. 30
acres in ELTVILLE, MARTINSTHAL, Walluf.

Beerenauslese Extremely sweet and luscious wine from selected
exceptionally ripe individual bunches, their sugar and flavour usually
concentrated by 'noble rot'. Very rare and expensive.

Bereich District within an *Anbaugebiet* (region). The word on a label
should be treated as a warning. As a rule do not buy. *See* Introduction
and under *Bereich* names, eg Bernkastel (Bereich).

Bergweiler-Prüm Erben (Dr Pauly-Bergweiler), Zach, Weingut Fine 27-
acre estate based at BERNKASTEL. V'yds there and in WEHLEN, etc. Also

Nicolay wines from URZIG and ERDEN.

Bernkastel M-M w **→**** 71 75 76 79 83 *84* 85 86 87 88 89 90 91 Top wine town of the MITTELMOSEL; the epitome of RIES. Best v'yds: Bratenhöfchen, Doctor (8 acres), Graben. Grosslagen: Badstube (***) and Kurfürstlay (**). Top growers incl BERGWEILER-PRUM, FRIEDRICH WILHELM GYMNASIUM, KERPEN, Lay, LAUERBURG, LOOSEN, PRUM, Studert-Prüm, THANISCH, WEGELER-DEINHARD.

Bernkastel (Bereich) Wide area of deplorably mixed quality but hopefully flowery character. Includes all the MITTELMOSEL.

Bingen Rhh w **→*** 71 75 76 83 85 87 88 89 90 91 Town on Rhine and NAHE with fine v'yds, incl Scharlachberg. Grosslage: Sankt Rochuskapelle. Top grower: VILLA SACHSEN.

Bingen (Bereich) District name for W RHEINHESSEN.

Bischöfliche Weingüter Famous M-S-R estate at TRIER, a union of the cathedral properties with 2 other famous charities, the Bischöfliches Priesterseminar and the Bischöfliches Konvikt. 260 acres of top v'yds, esp in SAAR and RUWER, but wines recently disappointing.

Blankenhornsberg Well-known KAISERSTUHL estate; 62 acres at IHRINGEN.

Blue Nun The best-selling brand of LIEBFRAUMILCH, from SICHEL.

Bocksbeutel Flask-shaped bottle used for FRANKEN wines.

Bodenheim Rhh w ** Village nr NIERSTEIN with delicate wines, esp from Silberberg. Top growers: Kühling-Gillot, Liebrecht.

Bodensee (Bereich) Minor district of S BADEN, on Lake Constance.

Brauneberg M-M w *** 71 75 76 83 85 86 87 88 89 90 91 Village nr BERNKASTEL with 750 acres. Excellent full-flavoured RIES. Best v'yd: Juffer. Grosslage: Kurfürstlay. Growers incl BERGWEILER, FRITZ HAAG, WILLI HAAG, Paulinshof, RICHTER.

Breisach Baden Frontier town on RHINE nr KAISERSTUHL. Seat of the largest German coop, the BADISCHER WINZERKELLER.

Breisgau (Bereich) Minor district of BADEN, just N and E of KAISERSTUHL. Best known for very pale pink WEISSHERBST.

Breuer, Weingut G Family estate of 36 acres in RUDESHEIM, with 6 acres of Berg Schlossberg setting the pace for the district. Brilliant quality and new ideas, incl sparkling wine (87) blended from RIES plus Pinots Bl and G. *See also* Scholl & Hillebrand.

Buhl, Reichsrat von Historic RHEINPFALZ family estate. 250+ acres in DEIDESHEIM, FORST, RUPPERTSBERG, etc. Recently leased by Japanese firm.

Bundesweinprämierung The German State Wine Award, organized by DLG (*see below*): gives great (Grosse), silver or bronze medallion labels.

Bürgerspital zum Heiligen Geist Ancient charitable estate at WURZBURG. 333 acres in Würzburg, RANDERSACKER, etc, make often magnificent, rich, dry wines, esp from SILVANER.

Bürklin-Wolf, Dr Great RHEINPFALZ family estate. 247 acres in WACHENHEIM. FORST, DEIDESHEIM and RUPPERTSBERG. Vg 89s.

Castell'sches, Fürstlich Domänenamt Historic 142-acre princely estate in STEIGERWALD. Noble FRANKEN wines: SILVANER, RIESLANER. Also SEKT.

Chardonnay A small acreage of Chard has been experimentally, and sometimes illegally, planted – eg on an island in the Rhine. BADEN might prove suitable.

Charta Organization of top RHEINGAU estates making dry RIES. Wines made to far higher standards than dismally permissive laws require.

Christoffel, J J Tiny domaine in ERDEN, GRAACH, WEHLEN, URZIG. Polished RIES.

Crusius 30-acre family estate at TRAISEN, NAHE. Vivid RIES from Bastei, Rotenfels and SCHLOSSBOCKELHEIM. Felsenberg can age v well. Also good SEKT and freshly fruity SPATBURGUNDER dry rosé.

Dahlem Erben, Dr Long-established 67-acre estate in OPPENHEIM.

Deidesheim Rhpf w (r) **→**** 71 75 76 83 85 86 87 88 89 90 91 Biggest top-quality wine village of RHEINPFALZ with 1,000 acres. Rich, high-flavoured, lively wines. Top v'yds incl Grainhübel, Hohenmorgen, Kalkofen, Leinhöhle, etc. Grosslagen: Hofstück (**), Mariengarten

(★★★). Top growers: BASSERMANN-JORDAN, Biffar, BURKLIN-WOLF, DEINHARD, FITZ-RITTER, Von BUHL.

Deinhard Famous old Koblenz merchants and growers of top-quality wines in RHEINGAU, MITTELMOSEL, RUWER and RHEINPFALZ (*see* Wegeler-Deinhard), also makers of vg SEKT (brand name: Lila). Launched in '88 the Heritage range of single-village (DEIDESHEIM, HOCHHEIM, etc) TROCKEN wines. Leaders in both quality and new ideas.

Deinhard, Dr 62-acre family estate in DEIDESHEIM with many of best v'yds.

Deutscher Tafelwein TAFELWEIN from Germany (only).

Deutsches Weinsiegel A quality seal (ie neck label) for wines which have passed a statutory tasting test. Seals are: yellow = dry, green = medium-dry, red = medium-sweet.

Deutsche Weinstrasse Popular tourist road of the S PALATINATE, Bockenheim to SCHWEIGEN.

DLG (Deutsche Landwirtschaftgesellschaft) The German Agricultural Society at Frankfurt. Awards national medals for quality.

Dhron *See* Neumagen-Dhron.

Diabetiker Wein Wine with minimal residual sugar (less than 4 g/l); thus suitable for diabetics – or those who like *very* dry wine.

Diel auf Burg Layen, Schlossgut Fashionable 30-acre NAHE estate; known for ageing RULANDER and Weissburgunder in French BARRIQUES. Also traditional RIES.

Dienheim Rhh w ★★ 76 83 85 87 88 **89** 90 91 Southern neighbour of OPPENHEIM. Mainly run-of-the-mill wines.

Dom German for 'cathedral'. Wines from the famous TRIER cathedral properties have 'Dom' before the v'yd name.

Domäne German for 'domain' or 'estate'. Sometimes used alone to mean the 'State domain' (STAATLICHE WEINBAUDOMANE).

Dönnhoff, Weingut Hermann 23-acre NAHE estate with exceptionally fine RIES from KREUZNACH, NIEDERHAUSEN, Oberhausen, etc.

Durbach Baden w (r) ★★→★★★ 76 83 85 87 88 89 90 91 Village with 775 acres of the best v'yds of BADEN. Top growers: H Männle, von Neveu, SCHLOSS STAUFENBERG, Wolf-Metternich. Choose their KLINGELBERGERS (RIES) and KLEVNERS (TRAMINER). Grosslage: Fürsteneck.

Edel Means 'noble'. *Edelfäule* means 'noble rot': the condition which gives the greatest sweet wines (*see* page 47).

Egon Müller zu Scharzhof Top SAAR estate of 32 acres at WILTINGEN. Its delicate, racy SCHARZHOFBERGER RIES are among the world's greatest wines, esp in vintages that produce AUSLESEN. The best *Auslesen* are given gold capsules. 89s and 90s are sublime. Le Gallais is a second estate in Hiltinger Braune Kupp.

Eiswein Wine made from frozen grapes with the ice (ie water content) rejected, thus v concentrated in flavour and sugar, of BEERENAUSLESE ripeness or more. Rare and v expensive. Sometimes produced as late as January or February following the vintage. Alcohol content can be as low as 5.5%. High acidity gives them v long life.

Eitelsbach Ruwer w ★★→★★★ 71 75 76 83 85 87 88 89 90 91 RUWER village now part of TRIER, incl superb KARTHÄUSERHOFBERG estate. Grosslage: Römerlay.

Elbling Traditional but generally inferior grape widely grown on upper MOSEL but capable of great freshness and vitality in the best conditions (eg at Nittel in the OBERMOSEL).

Elbtal Sachsen. Former E German wine region of 750 acres on the outskirts of Dresden and Meissen. MULLER-T dominant; also Weissburgunder, TRAMINER etc. Schloss Wackerbarth makes top SEKT, Graf von Wackerbarth.

Eltville Rhg w ★★→★★★ 71 75 76 83 85 86 87 88 **89** 90 91 Major wine town with cellars of RHEINGAU STATE DOMAIN, FISCHER and von SIMMERN estates. Excellent wines. Top v'yd: Sonnenberg. Grosslage: Steinmächer.

Enkirch M-M w ★★→★★★ 71 76 83 85 87 88 **89** 90 91 Minor MITTELMOSEL village, often overlooked but with lovely, light, tasty wine. Grosslage: Schwarzlay. Top v'yds: Batterieberg, Zeppwingert. Top grower: IMMICH-BATTERIEBERG.

Erbach Rhg w ***→**** 71 76 83 85 86 87 88 89 90 91 One of the best parts of the RHEINGAU with powerful, perfumed wines, incl the great MARCOBRUNN; other top v'yds: Schlossberg, Siegelsberg. Major estates: SCHLOSS REINHARTSHAUSEN, SCHLOSS SCHONBORN. Also BECKER, KNYPHAUSEN, RESS, von SIMMERN, etc.

Erben Word meaning 'heirs', often used on old-established estate labels.

Erden M-M w **→**** 71 75 76 83 *84* 85 86 87 88 89 90 Village between Urzig and Kröv with full-flavoured, vigorous wine. Top v'yds: Prälat, Treppchen. Grosslage: Schwarzlay. Growers incl BISCHOFLICHE WEINGUTER, Stefan Ehlen, LOOSEN, Meulenhoff, MONCHHOF, Nicolay.

Erzeugerabfüllung Bottled by the producer.

Escherndorf Frank w **→**** 76 83 87 88 89 90 91 Important wine town near WURZBURG. Similar tasty dry wine. Top v'yds: Berg, Lump. Grosslage: Kirchberg. Growers incl JULIUSSPITAL.

Eser, Weingut August 20-acre RHEINGAU estate at OESTRICH. V'yds also in HALLGARTEN, RAUENTHAL (esp Rottenberg), WINKEL, etc. Model wines.

Filzen M-S-R w **→*** 76 83 85 87 88 89 90 91 Small SAAR village nr WILTINGEN. Grower to note: Piedmont.

Fischer, Weingut Dr 60-acre estate of generally high quality at OCKFEN, incl whole of 25-acre WAWERNER Herrenberg.

Fischer Erben, Weingut 18-acre RHEINGAU estate at ELTVILLE with highest traditional standards. Long-lived classic wines.

Fitz-Ritter High-profile BAD DURKHEIM estate. 54 acres, fine RIES.

Forschungsanstalt *See* Hessische Forschungsanstalt für Wein-Obst-& Gartenbau

Forst Rhpf w **→**** 71 75 76 83 85 86 87 88 89 90 91 MITTELHAARDT village with 500 wines of Germany's best v'yds. Ripe, richly fragrant, full-bodied but subtle wines. Top v'yds: Jesuitengarten, Kirchenstück, Ungeheuer. Grosslagen: Mariengarten, Schnepfenflug. Top growers: BASSERMANN-JORDAN, Georg Mosbacher, Heinrich Spindler.

Franken Franconia: region of excellent, distinctive, dry wines, esp SILVANER, always bottled in round-bellied flasks. The centre is WURZBURG. Bereich names: MAINDREIECK, STEIGERWALD. Top producers: BURGERSPITAL, JULIUSSPITAL, WIRSCHING, etc.

Freiburg Baden w (r) *→*** DYA Wine centre in N of MARKGRAFLERLAND. Good GUTEDEL.

Freinsheim Rhpf w r ** Well-known village of MITTELHAARDT with high proportion of RIES. Earthy, spicy wines. Top grower: LINGENFELDER.

Friedrich Wilhelm Gymnasium Superb 111-acre charitable estate based in TRIER with v'yds in BERNKASTEL, GRAACH, OCKFEN, TRITTENHEIM, ZELTINGEN, etc, all M-S-R. Sound wines and good value.

Fuhrmann *See* Pfeffingen.

Gallais Le *See* Egon Müller.

Geheimrat 'J' Brand-name of vg, dry RIES SPATLESE from WEGELER-DEINHARD, OESTRICH, since '85. Epitomizes new thinking.

Geisenheim Rhg w **→**** 71 76 83 85 86 87 88 89 90 91 Village famous for Germany's leading wine school and fine aromatic wines. Best v'yds incl Kläuserweg, Rothenberg. Grosslagen: Burgweg, Erntebringer. Many top growers (eg SCHLOSS SCHONBORN) have v'yds here.

Gemeinde A commune or parish.

Gewürztraminer (or Traminer) Spicy grape, speciality of Alsace, used a little in Germany, esp RHEINPFALZ, RHEINHESSEN and BADEN.

Gimmeldingen Rhpf w *→** 76 83 85 87 88 89 90 91 Village just S of MITTELHAARDT. At their best, similar wines. Grosslage: Meerspinne. Top grower: MULLER-CATOIR.

Goldener Oktober Brand of RHINE and MOSEL blends from ST-URSULA.

Graach M-M w **→*** 71 75 76 83 *84* 85 86 87 88 89 90 91 Small village between BERNKASTEL and WEHLEN. Top v'yds: Domprobst, Himmelreich, Josephshöfer. Grosslage: Münzlay. Many top growers incl: KESSELSTATT, LOOSEN, PRUM, Willi Schaefer, Weins-Prüm etc.

Grans-Fassian Fine 25-acre MOSEL estate at Leiwen. V'yds there and in PIESPORT, TRITTENHEIM.

Remember that vintage information for German wines is given in a different form from the ready/not ready distinction applying to other countries. Read the explanation on page 104.

Grosslage *See* Introduction, page 101.

Grosvenor, G & M Wine-brokers of JOHANNISBERG and exporters of many fine estate wines.

Gunderloch Currently top-rated 30-acre NACKENHEIM estate. 70% RIES. Best wines are N Rothenbert, but all are vg.

Guntersblum Rhh w ★→★★ 76 83 85 88 89 90 91 Big wine town S of OPPENHEIM. Grosslagen: Krötenbrunnen, Vogelsgärten. Top growers: DAHLEM, RAPPENHOF.

Guntrum, Louis Fine 164-acre family estate in NIERSTEIN, OPPENHEIM, etc, and merchant house with high and reliable standards. Fine SILVANERS and GEWURZ as well as RIES.

Gutedel German word for the Chasselas grape, used in S BADEN.

Gutsverwaltung Estate administration.

Haag, Fritz and Willi Two small, high quality estates at BRAUNEBERG. Fritz H is in the v top league.

Haardt, Reinholdt Small estate emerging as one of the best in PIESPORT.

Halbtrocken Medium-dry (literally 'semi-dry'). Containing less than 18 but more than 9 grams per litre unfermented sugar. An increasingly popular category of wine intended for meal-times, often better balanced than TROCKEN. All CHARTA wines are *halbtrocken*.

Hallgarten Rhg w ★★→★★★ 71 76 83 85 86 87 88 89 90 91 Small wine town behind HATTENHEIM. Robust, full-bodied wines. Top v'yds incl Hendelberg, Jungfer, Schönhell. Grosslage: Mehrhölzchen. Growers incl DEINHARD, ESER, LOWENSTEIN, WEIL.

Hallgarten, House of Well-known London-based wine merchant.

Hattenheim Rhg w ★★→★★★★ 71 75 76 83 85 87 88 89 90 91 Superlative 500-acre wine town. V'yds incl Nussbrunnen, Mannberg, Pfaffenberg, STEINBERG (ORTSTEIL), Wisselbrunnen, etc. Grosslage: Deutelsberg. MARCOBRUNN lies on the ERBACH boundary. Many fine estates incl KNYPHAUSEN, SCHLOSS SCHONBORN, von SIMMERN, STATE DOMAIN, etc.

Heger, Dr Some of BADEN's best SPATBURGUNDER reds come from old vines on this 28-acre IHRINGEN estate.

Heilbronn Würt w r ★→★★ 76 83 85 87 88 89 90 91 Wine town with many small growers and a big coop. Seat of DLG competition. Top growers: Amalienhof, Drautz-Able, Heinrich.

Hessen, Prinz von Wide-ranging 75-acre estate in JOHANNISBERG, .WINKEL, KIEDRICH and ELTVILLE. An under-achiever.

Hessische Bergstrasse w ★★→★★★ 76 83 85 87 88 89 90 91 Formerly W Germany's smallest wine region (1,000 acres), N of Heidelberg. Pleasant RIES from STATE DOMAIN v'yds in Bensheim, Bergstrasser Coop, Heppenheim and Stadt Bensheim.

Hessische Forschungsanstalt für Wein-Obst-& Gartenbau Germany's top wine school and research establishment, at GEISENHEIM, RHEINGAU. Good wines incl reds. The name on the label is Forschungsanstalt.

Heyl zu Herrnsheim Leading 72-acre NIERSTEIN estate, 60% RIES, with an impeccable record.

Hochgewächs A superior level of QBA RIES, esp in MOSEL-SAAR-RUWER.

Hochheim Rhg w ★★→★★★ 71 75 76 79 83 *84* 85 86 87 88 89 90 91 600-acre wine town 15 miles E of main part of RHEINGAU. Similar fine wines with an earthy intensity and fragrance of their own. Top v'yds:

Domdechaney, Hölle, Kirchenstück, Königin Viktoria Berg (12-acre monopoly of Hupfeld of OESTRICH, sold only by DEINHARD). Grosslage: Daubhaus. Growers incl Aschrott, Hupfeld, Franz KUNSTLER, RESS, SCHLOSS SCHONBORN, WERNER.

Hock English term for Rhine wine, derived from HOCHHEIM.

Hövel, Weingut von Exceptional SAAR estate at OBERMOSEL (Hütte has 12-acre monopoly) and in SCHARZHOFBERG.

Huesgen, Adolph Important merchant house at TRABEN-TRARBACH.

Huxelrebe Modern, very aromatic grape variety, mainly for sweet wines.

Ihringen Bad r w ★→★★★ 83 85 86 87 88 89 90 91 One of the best villages of the KAISERSTUHL, BADEN. Proud of its SPATBURGUNDER red, WEISSHERBST and vg SILVANER. Top growers: Blankenhornsberg, Heger, Stigler.

Ilbesheim Rhpf w ★→★★★ 83 85 87 88 89 90 91 Base of important growers' coop of SUDLICHE WEINSTRASSE. *See also* Schweigen.

Immich-Batterieberg The top estate of ENKIRCH. 15 acres. Sole owner of Batterieberg v'yd.

Ingelheim Rhh r or w ★ 85 88 89 90 91 Town opposite the RHEINGAU historically known for SPATBURGUNDER.

Iphofen Frank w ★★→★★★ 75 76 *83* 85 87 88 89 90 91 Village E of WURZBURG. Superb top v'yd: Julius-Echter-Berg. Grosslage: Burgweg. Growers: JULIUSSPITAL, Ruck, STAATLICHER HOFKELLER, Wirsching.

Jahrgang Year – as in 'vintage'.

Johannisberg Rhg w ★★→★★★★ 71 75 76 *83* 85 86 87 88 89 90 91 260-acre village with superlative, subtle RIES. Top v'yds incl Hölle, SCHLOSS JOHANNISBERG, Klaus, etc. Grosslage: Erntebringer. Many good growers. But beware 'Bereich Johannisberg' wines (*see* next entry).

Johannisberg (Bereich) District name for the entire RHEINGAU.

Johner, Karl-Heinz Tiny BADEN estate at Bischoffingen in the front line for new-look SPATBURGUNDER and oak-aged Weissburgunder.

Josephshöfer Fine v'yd at GRAACH, the sole property of von KESSELSTATT.

Jost, Toni Perhaps the top estate of the MITTELRHEIN. 25 acres, mainly RIES, in BACHARACH and also in the RHEINGAU.

Juliusspital Ancient religious charity at WURZBURG with 374 acres of top FRANKEN v'yds. Look for its SILVANERS.

Kabinett The term for the lightest category of natural, unsugared (QMP) wines. Low in alcohol (average 7–9%) but capable of sublime finesse. Do not hurry to drink.

Kaiserstuhl-Tuniberg (Bereich) One of the top districts of BADEN. Villages incl ACHKARREN, IHRINGEN.

Kallstadt Rhpf w (r) ★★→★★★ 76 83 85 86 87 88 **89** 90 91 Village of N MITTELHAARDT. Fine, rich wines. Top v'yds: Annaberg, Saumagen. Grosslagen: Feuerberg, Kobnert. Growers incl Henninger, KOEHLER-RUPRECHT, Schüster.

Kammerpreismünze See Landespreismünze.

Kanzem M-S-R (Saar) w ★★★ 71 75 76 83 85 87 88 **89** 90 91 Small neighbour of WILTINGEN. Top v'yds: Altenberg, Sonnenberg. Grosslage: SCHARZBERG. Growers incl Othegraven, Reverchon. Best is J P Reinert.

Karlsmühle The hotelier of MERTESDORF, making top-grade RUWERS in Felsberg, Lorenzhof and Maüerchen.

Karst, Weingut Johannes Very sound 18-acre BAD DURKHEIM estate. Owner Heinz K is the ringleader of the Wurstmarkt wine fair.

Karthäuserhofberg Top RUWER estate of 46 acres at Eitelsbach. Easily known by bottles with only a neck-label. Recently back on top form, esp with Gold Capsule AUSLESEN.

Kasel M-S-R (Ruwer) w ★★→★★★ 71 75 76 83 85 86 87 88 **89** 90 91 Village with wonderfully attractive, light wines. Best v'yd: Nies'chen. Grosslage: Römerlay. Top growers: KARLSMUHLE, von KESSELSTATT, WEGELER-DEINHARD.

Keller Wine cellar.

Kellerei Winery.

Kerner Modern grape variety, earlier-ripening than RIES, of fair quality but without the inbuilt harmony of Ries.

Kerpen, Weingut Heribert Tiny top-class estate in BERNKASTEL, GRAACH, SONNENUHR, WEHLEN.

Kesselstatt, von The biggest private MOSEL estate, 600 yrs old. Some 150 acres in GRAACH, KASEL, Mennig, PIESPORT, WILTINGEN, etc, plus substantial rented or managed estates, making light, mostly fruity Mosels. Now belongs to Günther REH (Leiwen). Excellently run since '87.

Kesten M-M w *→*** 71 75 76 83 85 86 87 88 89 90 91 Neighbour of BRAUNEBERG. Best wines (from Paulinshofberg v'yd) similar. Grosslage: Kurfürstlay. Top growers: DEINHARD, Paulinshof.

Kiedrich Rhg w **→**** 71 76 83 *84* 85 86 87 88 89 90 91 Neighbour of RAUENTHAL; almost as splendid and high-flavoured. Top v'yds: Gräfenberg, Sandgrub, Wasseros. Grosslage: Heiligenstock. Growers incl: FISCHER, KNYPHAUSEN, SCHLOSS GROENESTEYN, STATE DOMAIN, WEIL, etc.

Klevner (or Clevner) Red Klevner (synonym, Blauer Frühburgunder) grown in WURTTEMBERG is supposedly either a mutation of Pinot N or Italian Chiavenna, an early-ripening black Pinot. Also an ORTENAU (BADEN) synonym for TRAMINER.

Klingelberger BADEN term for the RIES, esp at DURBACH.

Kloster Eberbach Glorious 12th-C Cistercian Abbey at HATTENHEIM, RHEINGAU, whose monks planted the STEINBERG. Now STATE DOMAIN property and HQ of the German Wine Academy.

Klüsserath M-M w **→*** 76 83 85 88 89 90 91 Minor MOSEL village, good yrs worth trying. Best v'yds: Bruderschaft, Königsberg. Grosslage: St-Michael. Top growers: FRIEDRICH WILHELM GYMNASIUM, Kirsten.

Knyphausen, Weingut Freiherr zu Noble 50-acre estate on former Cistercian land in ELTVILLE, ERBACH, HATTENHEIM, KIEDRICH and MARCOBRUNN. Top RHEINGAU wines, many dry.

Koehler-Ruprecht Highly-rated little (22-acre) estate; the top grower in KALLSTADT, RHEINPFALZ. Ultra-traditional winemaking, v long-lived wine.

Kraichgau Small BADEN region S of Heidelberg. Best-known wines are from village of Wiesloch.

Kreuznach (Bereich) District name for the entire northern NAHE. *See also* Bad Kreuznach.

Kröv M-M w *→*** 88 89 90 91 Popular tourist resort famous for its Grosslage name: Nacktarsch, meaning 'bare bottom'. Wines to avoid.

Künstler, Franz Outstanding 12.5-acre HOCHHEIM estate, esp for H Kirchenstück and model CHARTA wines.

Landespreismünze Prizes for quality at state, rather than national, level. Considered by some more discriminating than DLG medals.

Landwein A category of better quality TAFELWEIN (the grapes must be slightly riper) from 15 designated regions. It must be TROCKEN or HALBTROCKEN. Similar in intention to France's *Vin de Pays*.

Lauerburg One of the 4 owners of the famous Doctor v'yd, with 10 acres, all in BERNKASTEL. Often excellent, racy wines.

Liebfrauenstift 26-acre v'yd in city of Worms; origin of 'LIEBFRAUMILCH'.

Liebfraumilch A much abused name, accounting for 50% of all German wine exports – much to the detriment of Germany's better products. Legally defined as a QBA 'of pleasant character' from RHEINHESSEN, RHEINPFALZ, NAHE or RHEINGAU, of a blend with at least 51% Riesling, SILVANER, KERNER or MULLER-T. Most is mild, semi-sweet wine from RHEINHESSEN and RHEINPFALZ. The rules now say it must have more than 18 grams per litre unfermented sugar. Sometimes v cheap and of inferior quality, depending on brand or shipper. Its definition makes a mockery of the term 'Quality Wine'.

Lieser M-M w *→** 71 76 83 85 86 87 88 89 90 91 Little-known neighbour of BERNKASTEL. Lighter wines. Best v'yds: Niederberg-

Helden, Schlossberg. Grosslage: Kurfürstlay.

Lingenfelder, Weingut Small, innovative estate at Grosskarlbach, RHEINPFALZ, making Germany's best burgundy-style SPATBURGUNDER and full-bodied RIES, etc.

Loosen, Weingut Dr 20-acre St-Johannishof estate in BERNKASTEL, ERDEN, GRAACH, URZIG, WEHLEN. Lovely quality in recent vintages.

Lorch Rhg w (r) *→** **71 76** 83 85 87 88 **89 90** 91 At extreme W end of RHEINGAU. Some fine light RIES, more like MITTELRHEIN wines. Best growers: Altenkirch, von Kanitz.

Löwenstein, Fürst 66-acre FRANKEN estate: classic, dry, powerful wines. 45-acre HALLGARTEN property is rented by MATUSCHKA-GREIFFENCLAU.

Maindreieck (Bereich) District name for central part of FRANKEN, incl WURZBURG.

Marcobrunn Historic RHEINGAU v'yd; one of Germany's best. *See* Erbach.

Markgräflerland (Bereich) District S of Freiburg, BADEN. Typical GUTEDEL wine can be delicious refreshment when drunk v young, but best wines are the -burgunders: Weiss-, Grau- and SPAT-.

Martinsthal Rhg w **→*** **71 75 76** 83 85 86 87 88 89 **90** 91 Little-known neighbour of RAUENTHAL. Top v'yds: Langenberg, Wildsau. Grosslage: Steinmächer. Growers incl: BECKER, Diefenhardt.

Matuschka-Greiffenclau, Graf Erwein Owner of the ancient SCHLOSS VOLLRADS estate and tenant of the Weingut Fürst LOWENSTEIN at HALLGARTEN, now in a joint venture with Suntory at the WEIL estate. A principal spokesman for German high quality wine, dedicated to dry wines and their combination wth food.

Maximin Grünhaus M-S-R (Ruwer) w **** **71 75 76** 79 83 *84* 85 86 87 88 89 90 91 Supreme RUWER estate of 80 acres at MERTESDORF. Wines of firm elegance to mature 20 yrs+.

Mertesdorf *See* Maximin Grünhaus and Karlsmühle.

Mittelhaardt The north-central and best part of RHEINPFALZ, incl DEIDESHEIM, FORST, RUPPERTSBERG, WACHENHEIM, largely planted with RIES.

Mittelhaardt-Deutsche Weinstrasse (Bereich) District name for the northern and central parts of RHEINPFALZ.

Mittelheim Rhg w **→*** **71 75 76** 83 *84* 85 86 87 88 89 **90** 91 Relatively minor village between WINKEL and OESTRICH. Grosslage: Honigberg. Top grower: WEGELER-DEINHARD.

Mittelmosel The central and best part of the MOSEL, incl BERNKASTEL, PIESPORT, WEHLEN, etc. Its best sites are (or should be) entirely RIES.

Mittelrhein Northern Rhine area of domestic importance, incl BACHARACH and Boppard. Some attractive, steely RIES.

Mönchhof, Weingut Top quality, 12-acre estate in ERDEN, URZIG, WEHLEN and ZELTINGEN.

Morio-Muskat Stridently aromatic grape variety now on the decline.

Mosel The TAFELWEIN name of the area. All quality wines from the area must be labelled MOSEL-SAAR-RUWER. (Moselle is the French – and English – spelling for this beautiful river.)

Moselland, Winzergenossenschaft The biggest coop of the M-S-R, based at BERNKASTEL, incl Saar-Winzerverein at WILTINGEN. Its 5,200 members produce 25% of the M-S-R wines, but nothing above average.

Mosel-Saar-Ruwer (M-S-R) 31,000-acre QUALITATSWEIN region between TRIER and Koblenz. Incl MITTELMOSEL, RUWER, SAAR and lesser areas. Grows more RIES than any other region on earth.

Müller-Catoir Leading estate of NEUSTADT, RHEINPFALZ, with 40 acres and many varieties, incl barrel-aged reds.

Müller zu Scharzhof, Egon *See* Egon Müller

Müller-Thurgau Fruity, early-ripening, usually low-acid grape variety; the commonest in RHEINPFALZ and RHEINHESSEN, NAHE, BADEN and FRANKEN, and increasingly planted in all areas, incl MOSEL; generally to the detriment of quality.

Mumm, von 173-acre estate in JOHANNISBERG, RUDESHEIM, etc. Under the same control as SCHLOSS JOHANNISBERG, but scarcely up to the same standard.

Münster Nahe w ★→★★★ 71 75 76 83 85 86 87 88 89 90 91 Best village of N NAHE, with fine, delicate wines. Grosslage: Schlosskapelle. Top growers: Kruger-Rumpf, STATE DOMAIN.

Nackenheim Rhh w ★→★★★ 75 76 83 85 86 87 88 89 90 91 Neighbour of NIERSTEIN; best wines (Rothenberg) similar. Grosslagen: Spiegelberg (★★★), Gutes Domtal (★). Top growers: GUNDERLOCH, GUNTRUM.

Nahe Tributary of the Rhine and high quality wine region. Balanced, fresh and clean but full-, even earthy-flavoured wines; the best are RIES. Two BEREICHE: KREUZNACH and SCHLOSS BOCKELHEIM.

Nahesteiner Brand name of new NAHE HALBTROCKEN blend of RIES, SILVANER and MÜLLER-T. V sound standard: not too dry.

Neckerauer, Weingut Klaus Out-of-the-way but distinguished 40-acre estate at Weissenheim-am-Sand, on sandy soil in N PFALZ. Impressive but unpredictable range.

Neef M-S-R w ★→★★ 71 76 83 85 87 88 89 90 91 Village of lower MOSEL with one fine v'yd: Frauenberg.

Neipperg, Graf von 71-acre top WÜRTTEMBERG estate at Schwaigern, esp known for red wines and TRAMINER.

Nell, von (Weingut Thiergarten) 40-acre family estate at TRIER and AYL.

Neumagen-Dhron M-M w ★→★★ 71 75 76 83 85 86 87 88 89 90 91 Neighbour of PIESPORT. Top v'yd: Hofberger. Grosslage: Michelsberg.

Neustadt Central town of RHEINPFALZ, with a famous wine school.

Niederhausen Nahe w ★★→★★★★ 71 75 76 83 *84* 85 86 87 88 89 90 91 Neighbour of SCHLOSS BOCKELHEIM and HQ of the NAHE STATE DOMAIN. Wines of grace and power. Top v'yds incl: Hermannsberg, Hermannshöhle, Steinberg. Grosslage: Burgweg. Top growers: CRUSIUS, DONNHOFF, Hehner-Kilz, Schneider, STATE DOMAIN.

Germany's quality levels

The official range of qualities in ascending order are as follows:

1) Deutscher Tafelwein: *sweetish light wine of no special character.*
2) Landwein: *dryish Tafelwein with some regional style.*
3) Qualitätswein: *dry or sweetish wine with sugar added before fermentation to increase its strength, but tested for quality and with distinct local and grape character.*
4) Kabinettwein: *dry or dryish natural (unsugared) wine of distinct personality and distinguishing lightness. Can be very fine.*
5) Spätlese: *stronger, often sweeter than Kabinett. Full-bodied. The trend today is towards drier or even completely dry Spätlese.*
6) Auslese: *sweeter, sometimes stronger than Spätlese, often with honey-like flavours, intense and long.*
7) Beerenauslese: *very sweet and usually strong, intense; can be superb.*
8) Eiswein: (Beeren- or Trockenbeerenauslese) *concentrated, sharpish and very sweet. Extraordinary and everlasting.*
9) Trockenbeerenauslese: *intensely sweet and aromatic; alcohol slight.*

Niederwalluf See Walluf.

Nierstein (Bereich) Large E RHEINHESSEN district of v mixed quality.

Nierstein Rhh w ★→★★★ 71 75 76 83 *84* 85 86 87 88 89 90 91 Famous but treacherous name. 1,300 acres incl superb v'yds: Hipping, Olberg, Pettenthal, etc, and their Grosslagen: Rehbach, Spiegelberg, Auflangen. Ripe, aromatic wines with great 'elegance'. But beware Grosslage Gutes Domtal: no guarantee of anything. Growers to choose incl BALBACH, H Braun, GUNDERLOCH, GUNTRUM, HEYL ZU HERRNSHEIM, St-Anthony, G A Schneider, Seebrich, Strub.

Nobling New white grape variety giving light, fresh wine in BADEN, esp MARKGRÄFLERLAND.

Norheim Nahe w ★→★★★ 71 76 79 83 *84* 85 86 87 88 89 90 91 Neighbour

113

of NIEDERHAUSEN. Top v'yds: Kafels, Kirschheck, Klosterberg. Grosslage: Burgweg. Growers: P ANHEUSER, CRUSIUS.

Novum Completely new style of wine from SICHEL, softened by malolactic fermentation. Aromatic, gentle, full and versatile.

Oberemmel M-S-R (Saar) w **→*** 71 75 76 83 85 86 87 88 89 90 Next village to WILTINGEN. V fine wines from Hütte, Rosenberg, etc. Grosslage: SCHARZBERG. Top growers: von HOVEL, von KESSELSTADT.

Obermosel (Bereich) District name for the upper MOSEL above TRIER. Generally uninspiring wines from the ELBLING grape, unless v young.

Ockfen M-S-R (Saar) w **→*** 71 75 76 83 85 86 87 88 89 90 91 200-acre village with superb, fragrant, austere wines. Top v'yd: Bockstein. Grosslage: SCHARZBERG. Growers incl: DR FISCHER, FRIEDRICH WILHELM GYMNASIUM, Wagner, ZILLIKEN.

Oechsle Scale for sugar content of grape juice (*see* page 19).

Oestrich Rhg w **→*** 71 75 76 83 *84* 85 86 87 88 89 90 91 Big village; variable but capable of splendid RIES AUSLESE. V'yds incl: Doosberg, Klosterberg, Lenchen. Grosslage: Gottesthal. Major grower: WEGELER-DEINHARD.

Oppenheim Rhh w *→*** 71 75 76 83 *84* 85 86 87 88 89 90 91 Town S of NIERSTEIN with a famous 13th-C church. Best wines (Kreuz, Sackträger) similar. Grosslagen: Guldenmorgen (***), Krötenbrunnen (*). Growers incl: Baumann, DAHLEM, GUNTRUM.

Ortsteil Independent part of a community allowed to use estate and v'yd name without the village name, eg STEINBERG, SCHLOSS JOHANNISBERG.

Ortenau (Bereich) District just S of Baden-Baden. Good KLINGELBERGER (RIES), SPATBURGUNDER and RULANDER. Top village: DURBACH.

Palatinate English for RHEINPFALZ.

Perlwein Semi-sparkling wine.

Pfalz *See* Rheinpfalz.

Pfeffingen, Weingut Messrs Fuhrmann and Eymael make outstanding RIES and SCHEUREBE on 26 acres of UNGSTEIN.

Piesport M-M w **→**** 71 75 76 83 *84* 85 86 87 88 89 90 91 Tiny village with famous vine amphitheatre, gives (at best) glorious, gentle, fruity RIES. Top v'yd: Goldtröpfchen. Treppchen, on flatter land, is altogether inferior. Grosslage: Michelsberg (mainly MULLER-T). Incl: Reinhold Haardt, Reuscher-Haardt, KESSELSTATT, Weller-Lehnert.

Plettenberg, von Fine 100-acre NAHE estate at BAD KREUZNACH. Wines recently v 'commercial'.

Pokalwein Wine by the glass. A *pokal* is a big glass.

Portugieser Second-rate red-wine grape now often used for WEISSHERBST.

Prädikat Special attributes or qualities. *See* QmP.

Prüfungsnummer The official identifying test-number of a quality wine.

Prüm, J J Superlative and legendary 34-acre MOSEL estate in BERNKASTEL, GRAACH, WEHLEN, ZELTINGEN. Delicate but long-lived wines, esp in Wehlener SONNENUHR.

Prüm Erben, S A Small, separate part of the Prüm family estate for WEHLENERS etc – but not in the class of the above.

Qualitätswein bestimmter Anbaugebiete (QbA) The middle quality of German wine, with sugar added before fermentation (as in French 'chaptalisation'), but controlled as to areas, grapes, etc.

Qualitätswein mit Prädikat (QmP) Top category, incl all wines ripe enough to be unsugared, from KABINETT to TROCKENBEERENAUSLESE. *See* Introduction, page 101.

Randersacker Frank w **→*** 76 *83* 86 87 88 89 90 91 Leading village for distinctive dry wine. Top v'yds incl Teufelskeller. Grosslage: Ewig Leben. Growers incl BURGERSPITAL, STAATLICHER HOFKELLER, JULIUSSPITAL and Schmitt.

Rappenhof, Weingut 90-acre RHEINHESSEN estate at Alsheim with wide range of varieties and techniques, incl BARRIQUE-aged CHARD and deep-coloured SPATBURGUNDER.

Rauenthal Rhg w ✯✯✯→✯✯✯✯ 71 75 76 83 *84* 85 86 87 88 **89 90 91**
Supreme village for spicy, complex wine. Top v'yds incl: Baiken,
Gehrn, Wulfen. Grosslage: Steinmächer. Growers: ESER, SCHLOSS
REINHARTSHAUSEN, SCHLOSS SCHONBORN, von SIMMERN, STATE DOMAIN.

Reh, Franz & Sohn Thriving wine merchant at Leiwen (MOSEL) with 2 small
estates.

Ress, Balthasar RHEINGAU grower with 50 acres of good land, cellars in
HATTENHEIM. Also runs SCHLOSS REICHARTSHAUSEN. Variable wines; highly
original artists' labels.

Restsüsse Unfermented grape sugar remaining in (or more often added to)
wine to give it sweetness. New TROCKEN wines have v little, if any.

Rheinart Erben 26-acre SAAR estate known for its OCKFENER Bockstein.

Rheinburgengau (Bereich) District name for MITTELRHEIN v'yds around the
Rhine gorge. Wines with 'steely' acidity needing time to mature.

Rheinfront, Winzergenossenschaft The leading NIERSTEIN coop, with way
above average standards.

Rheingau The best v'yd region of the Rhine W of Wiesbaden. 7,000 acres.
Classic, substantial but subtle RIES. BEREICH name for the whole region:
JOHANNISBERG.

Rheinhessen Vast region (61,000 acres of v'yds) between Mainz and
Worms, bordered by the river NAHE, most second-rate, but incl top
wines from NIERSTEIN, OPPENHEIM etc.

Rheinhessen Silvaner (RS) New uniform label for dry wines from SILVANER
– designed to give a modern quality image to the region.

Rheinpfalz 56,000-acre v'yd region S of RHEINHESSEN (*see* Mittelhaardt and
Südliche Weinstrasse.) This and Rheinhessen are the chief sources of
LIEBFRAUMILCH. Grapes ripen to relatively high degrees. The classics
are rich wines, with TROCKEN and HALBTROCKEN increasingly
fashionable (and well made).

Rhodt Village of SUDLICHE WEINSTRASSE with well-known coop. Agreeable,
fruity wines. Grosslage: Ordensgut.

Richter, Weingut Max Ferd 37-acre MITTELMOSEL family estate, based at
Mülheim. Fine barrel-aged RIES from: BRAUNEBERG (Juffer), GRAACH,
Mülheim (Helenenkloster), WEHLEN.

Rieslaner Cross between SILVANER and RIES; has made fine AUSLESEN in
FRANKEN, where most is grown.

Riesling The best German grape: fine, fragrant, fruity, long-lived. Only
CHARD can compete as the world's best white grape.

Roseewein Rosé wine made of red grapes fermented without their skins.

Rotwein Red wine.

Rüdesheim Rhg w ✯✯→✯✯✯✯ 71 75 76 79 *81* 82 83 *84* 85 86 87 88 **89 90 91**
Rhine resort with 650 acres of excellent v'yds; the 3 best called
Rüdesheimer Berg... Full-bodied wines, fine-flavoured, often
remarkable in 'off' vintages. Grosslage: Burgweg. Most top RHEINGAU
estates own some Rüdesheim v'yds.

Rüdesheimer Rosengarten RUDESHEIM is also the name of a NAHE village
near BAD KREUZNACH. Do not be misled by the ubiquitous blend going by
this name. It has nothing to do with RHEINGAU Rüdesheim.

Ruländer PINOT GRIS: grape giving soft, full-bodied wine, alias
Grauburgunder. Best in BADEN and S RHEINPFALZ.

Ruppertsberg Rhpf w ✯✯→✯✯✯ 75 76 83 *84* 85 86 87 88 89 **90 91** Southern
village of MITTELHAARDT. Top v'yds incl Hoheburg, Linsenbusch,
Reiterpfad. Grosslage: Hofstück. Growers incl BASSERMANN-JORDAN, von
BUHL, BURKLIN-WOLF, DEINHARD.

Ruwer Tributary of MOSEL nr TRIER. V fine, delicate but well-structured
wines. Villages incl EITELSBACH, KASEL, MERTESDORF.

Saale-Unstrut Former E German wine region, 1,000 acres around the
confluence of these two rivers at Naumburg, nr Leipzig. Terraced
v'yds of WEISSBURGUNDER, SILVANER, GUTEDEL, etc and red PORTUGIESER and
SPATBURGUNDER have Cistercian origins.

Saar Tributary of MOSEL S of RUWER. Brilliant, austere, 'steely' RIES. Villages incl AYL, OCKFEN, SERRIG, WILTINGEN (SCHARZHOFBERG). Grosslage: SCHARZBERG. Many fine estates.

Saar-Ruwer (Bereich) District covering these 2 regions.

St-Ursula Well-known merchants at BINGEN.

Salm, Prinz zu Owner of SCHLOSS WALLHAUSEN and President of VDP.

Salwey, Weingut Leading BADEN estate at Oberottweil, esp for SPATBURGUNDER and RULANDER.

Scharzberg Grosslage name of WILTINGEN and neighbours.

Scharzhofberg M-S-R (Saar) w ★★★★ 71 75 76 83 85 86 87 **88 89 90** 91 Superlative 67-acre SAAR v'yd: austerely beautiful wines, the perfection of RIES. Do not confuse with above. Top estates: von HOVEL, von KESSELSTADT, EGON MULLER.

Schaumwein Sparkling wine.

Scheurebe Fruity grape of high quality (and RIES parentage) used in RHEINHESSEN and RHEINPFALZ.

Schillerwein Light red or rosé QBA, speciality of WURTTEMBERG (only).

Schlossböckelheim Nahe w ★★→★★★★ 71 75 76 79 83 *84* 85 86 87 **88 89 90** 91 Village with the best NAHE v'yds, incl Felsenberg, Kupfergrube. Firm yet delicate wine. Grosslage: Burgweg. Top growers: A ANHEUSER, CRUSIUS, DONHOFF, STATE DOMAIN.

Schlossböckelheim (Bereich) District name for the whole S NAHE.

Schloss Groenesteyn Top-grade RHEINGAU estate (80 acres) in KIEDRICH and RUDESHEIM, owned by Baron von Ritter zu Groenesteyn. Not on top form.

Schloss Johannisberg Rhg w ★★★★ 76 79 83 *84* 85 86 87 **88 89 90** 91 Famous RHEINGAU estate of 86 acres owned by Prince Metternich and the Oetker family. The 'first-growth' of the Rhine, back on form since '88 after going through a less brilliant spell. Wines incl fine SPATLESE and KABINETT TROCKEN, yet one feels still more could be achieved with this great v'yd.

Schloss Reichartshausen 10-acre HATTENHEIM v'yd run by RESS.

Schloss Reinhartshausen Fine 175-acre estate in ERBACH, HATTENHEIM, Kiedrich, etc. Changed hands in '87. The mansion is now a hotel.

Schloss Salem 188-acre estate of Margrave of BADEN near L Constance in S Germany. MULLER-T and WEISSHERBST.

Schloss Schönborn One of the biggest and best RHEINGAU estates, based at HATTENHEIM. Full-flavoured wines, at best excellent. Also vg SEKT.

Schloss Staufenberg 69-acre DURBACH estate of the Margrave, BADEN. Best wines are KLINGELBERGER.

Schloss Vollrads Rhg w ★★★→★★★★ 71 76 83 85 86 87 **88 89 90** 91 Great estate at WINKEL since 1300. 116 acres producing generally dry and austere RHEINGAU RIES. TROCKEN and HALBTROCKEN wines are the speciality; some would like to see rather less austerity. The owner, Graf MATUSCHKA-GREIFFENCLAU, leads the 'German wine with food' campaign, rents the LOWENSTEIN estate and runs DR WEIL.

Schloss Wallhausen The 25-acre NAHE estate of the Prinz zu SALM, one of Germany's oldest. 65% RIES. Vg TROCKEN.

Schmitt, Gustav Adolf Merchant house with fine old 250-acre family estate at NIERSTEIN. Has fallen behind the times.

Schoppenwein Café (or bar) wine: ie wine by the glass.

Schubert, von Owner of MAXIMIN GRUNHAUS.

Schwarzer Adler, Weingut The Keller brothers make some of BADEN's best GRAUBURGUNDER and WEISSBURGUNDER, also SPATBURGUNDER, on 35 acres at Oberbergen.

Schweigen Rhpf w ★→▩▩ 85 86 87 88 **89 90** 91 Southernmost RHEINPFALZ village with important coop, Deutsches WEINTOR. Grosslage: Guttenberg.

Sekt German (QBA) sparkling wine, best when RIES is on the label. *Sekt* bA is the same thing but from a specified area.

Selbach-Oster 15-acre ZELTINGEN estate now among MITTELMOSEL leaders.

Serrig M-S-R (Saar) w **→*** 71 75 76 83 85 86 87 **88 89 90** 91 Village known for 'steely' wine, excellent in sunny yrs. Top growers: STATE DOMAIN, VEREINIGTE HOSPITIEN. Grosslage: SCHARZBERG. Growers also incl Schloss Saarstein, Bert SIMON.

Sichel, Söhne H Famous wine merchants of London and Mainz with new KELLEREI in Alzey, RHEINHESSEN. Owners of BLUE NUN LIEBFRAUMILCH and creators of revolutionary NOVUM.

Silvaner The third most-planted German white grape, usually underrated, best in FRANKEN and the KAISERSTUHL. But look for good Silvaners from RHEINHESSEN, too.

Simmern, Langwerth von Top 120-acre family estate at ELTVILLE. Famous v'yds: Baiken, Mannberg, MARCOBRUNN, etc. Some of the v best, most elegant RHEINGAU RIES.

Simon, Weingut Bert One of largest SAAR estates. 80 acres: KASEL, SERRIG.

Sonnenuhr Sundial. Name of several v'yds, esp one at WEHLEN.

Spätburgunder Pinot Noir: the best red-wine grape in Germany, esp in BADEN and WURTTEMBERG and, increasingly, RHEINPFALZ – though its wines are not widely appreciated outside the country.

Spätlese Late Harvest. One better (stronger/sweeter) than KABINETT. Wines to age *at least* 3 yrs. Dry *Spätlesen* can be v fine.

Staatlicher Hofkeller The Bavarian STATE DOMAIN. 287 acres of finest FRANKEN v'yds with spectacular cellars under the great baroque Residenz at WURZBURG.

Staatsweingut (or Staatliche Weinbaudomäne) The State wine estate or domain, the principal of which are: KLOSTER EBERBACH, SCHLOSS-BOCKELHEIM, TRIER.

State Domain *See* Staatsweingut.

Steigerwald (Bereich) District name for E part of FRANKEN.

Steinberg Rhg w ***→**** 71 75 76 79 83 *84* 85 86 87 88 89 90 91 Famous 79-acre walled v'yd at HATTENHEIM planted by Cistercians 700 yrs ago. Now property of the STATE DOMAIN, ELTVILLE.

Steinwein Wine from WURZBURG's best v'yd, Stein. In the past the term was loosely used for all Franconian wine.

Stolleis, Peter Estate at NEUSTADT. Enthusiast for intense GEWURZ, lively WEISSBURGUNDER, etc.

Stuttgart Chief city of WURTTEMBERG, producer of some pleasant wines (esp RIES), recently beginning to be exported.

Südliche Weinstrasse (Bereich) District name for the S RHEINPFALZ. Quality has improved tremendously in the last 25 yrs.

Tafelwein Table wine. The *vin ordinaire* of Germany. Frequently blended with other EC wines. But DEUTSCHER TAFELWEIN must come from Germany alone. (*See also* Landwein.)

Thanisch, Weingut Wwe Dr H 16-acre BERNKASTEL family estate of top quality, incl part of Doctor v'yd.

Traben-Trarbach M-M w ** 76 83 85 86 87 88 89 90 91 Major wine town of 800 acres, 87% of it RIES. Top v'yds incl Gaispfad, Schlossberg, Ungsberg-Pfarrwingert, Würzgarten. Grosslage: Schwarzlay. Top grower: RICHTER.

Traisen Nahe w *** 71 75 76 79 83 85 86 87 88 89 90 91 Small village incl superlative Bastei and Rotenfels v'yds, making RIES of great concentration and class. Top grower: CRUSIUS.

Traminer *See* Gewürztraminer.

Trier M-S-R w **→*** Important wine city of Roman origin, on the MOSEL, adjacent to RUWER, now incl AVELSBACH and EITELSBACH. Grosslage: Römerlay. The big Mosel charitable estates have their cellars here.

Trittenheim M-M w ** 71 75 76 83 85 88 89 90 91 Attractive light wines from the S end of the MITTELMOSEL. Top v'yds were Altärchen, Apotheke; but they now incl second-rate flat land. Grosslage: Michelsberg. Top growers: GRANS-FASSIAN, Milz.

Trocken 'Dry'. By law trocken *on a label means with a maximum of 9 grams per litre unfermented sugar. The new wave in German winemaking completely upsets the old notion of sweetness balancing acidity and embraces an austerity of flavour that can seem positively Lenten. It is much harder to make good dry wines in German conditions, and non-initiates should not expect to fall in love at first sip. To be good,* trocken *wines need substantial body or alcohol; more than most Kabinett wines have to offer.* Halbtrockens *are friendlier.* Spätlesen *(or QbA) make the best* trocken *wines.* Auslese trocken *sounds like a contradiction in terms – and usually tastes like one. Do not be confused by the apparent link with* Trockenbeerenauslesen *(see below): they are unrelated.*

Trockenbeerenauslese The sweetest and most expensive category of German wine, extremely rare and with concentrated honey flavour, made from selected shrivelled grapes affected by 'noble rot' (botrytis). TBA for short. *See also* Edel. *Edelbeerenauslese* would be a less confusing name for these wines.

Trollinger Common red grape of WURTTEMBERG; locally v popular.

Ungstein Rhpf w ✶✶→✶✶✶ 71 75 76 83 85 86 87 88 89 90 91 MITTELHAARDT village with fine, harmonious wines. Top v'yd: Herrenberg. Top growers: BASSERMANN-JORDAN, FITZ-RITTER, PFEFFINGEN, K Schäfer. Grosslagen: Honigsäckel, Kobnert.

Urzig M-M w ✶✶✶ 71 75 76 83 85 86 87 88 89 90 91 Village famous for lively, spicy wine. Top v'yd: Würzgarten. Grosslage: Schwarzlay. Growers incl: Christoffel-Berres, MONCHHOF.

Valckenberg, P J Major merchants at Worms, with Madonna LIEBFRAUMILCH and a small estate producing good RIES. Also dry Ries.

VdP Verband Deutscher Prädikats und Qualitätsweingüter, an association of premium growers. President: Prinz zu SALM.

Vereinigte Hospitien 'United Hospitals'. Ancient charity at TRIER with large holdings in PIESPORT, SERRIG, TRIER, WILTINGEN, etc; but wines recently below top class.

Verwaltung Administration (of property/estate etc).

Villa Sachsen 67-acre BINGEN estate belonging to Nestlé Co.

Wachenheim Rhpf w ✶✶✶→✶✶✶✶ 71 75 76 79 83 *84* 85 86 87 88 89 90 91 840 acres, incl exceptionally fine RIES. V'yds incl Böhlig, Gerümpel, Mandelgarten, Rechbächel. Top grower: BURKLIN-WOLF. Grosslagen: Mariengarten, Schenkenböhl, Schnepfenflug.

Waldrach M-S-R (Ruwer) w ✶✶ 75 76 83 87 88 89 90 91 Some charming light wines. Grosslage: Römerlay.

Walluf Rhg w ✶✶ 75 76 79 83 *84* 85 87 88 89 90 91 Neighbour of ELTVILLE; formerly Nieder- and Ober-Walluf. Underrated wines. Grosslage: Steinmächer. Growers incl BECKER.

Walporzheim Ahrtal (Bereich) District name for the whole AHR valley.

Walthari-Hof Much-discussed estate at Edenkoben, RHEINPFALZ, making wine without recourse to sulphur dioxide.

Wawern M-S-R (Saar) w ✶✶→✶✶✶ 71 75 76 83 85 87 88 89 90 91 Small village with fine RIES. Grosslage: SCHARZBERG.

Wegeler-Deinhard 136-acre RHEINGAU estate. V'yds: GEISENHEIM, MITTELHEIM, OESTRICH, RUDESHEIM, WINKEL, etc. Consistent quality; dry SPATLESE, classic AUSLESE, finest EISWEIN. Also 67 acres in MITTELMOSEL, incl major part of BERNKASTELER Doctor (WEHLENER SONNENUHR etc), 46 acres in MITTELHAARDT (DEIDESHEIM, FORST, RUPPERTSBERG). *See also* GEHEIMRAT 'J'.

Wehlen M-M w ✶✶✶→✶✶✶✶ 71 75 76 83 85 86 87 89 90 91 Neighbour of BERNKASTEL with equally fine, somewhat richer wine. Top v'yd: SONNENUHR. Top growers: KERPEN, LOOSEN, PRUM, WEGELER-DEINHARD, Weins-Prüm. Grosslage: Münzlay.

Weil, Dr Fine 84-acre estate at KIEDRICH, now owned by Suntory of Japan and MATUSCHKA-GREIFFENCLAU.

Weinbaugebiet Viticultural region. For TAFELWEIN (eg MOSEL, RHEIN, SAAR).

Weingut Wine estate.

Weinkellerei Wine cellars or winery. *See* Keller.

Weinstrasse Wine road. Scenic route through v'yds. Germany has several, the most famous the Deutsche Weinstrasse in RHEINPFALZ.

Weintor, Deutsches *See* Schweigen.

Weissherbst V pale pink wine of QBA standard or above, from a single variety, even occasionally BEERENAUSLESE, the speciality of BADEN, RHEINPFALZ and WURTTEMBERG. Currently fashionable in Germany.

Werner, Domdechant Fine 25-acre family estate on the best slopes of HOCHHEIM. 95% RIES.

Werner Klein (Mosbacher Hof) 25-acre estate, 90% RIES, in FORST and DEIDESHEIM. Good TROCKEN wines.

Wiltingen Saar w **→**** 71 75 76 83 85 86 87 88 89 90 91 The centre of the SAAR. 790 acres. Beautiful, subtle, austere wine. Top v'yds incl Braune Kupp, Braunfels, Klosterberg, SCHARZHOFBERG (ORTSTEIL). Grosslage (for the whole SAAR): SCHARZBERG. Top growers: EGON MULLER, LE GALLAIS, VON KESSELSTATT, etc.

Winkel Rhg w ***→**** 71 75 76 79 83 *84* 85 86 87 88 89 90 91 Village famous for fragrant wine, incl SCHLOSS VOLLRADS. V'yds incl Hasensprung, Jesuitengarten, Grosslagen: Erntebringer, Honigberg. Growers incl DEINHARD, Prinz von HESSEN, von MUMM, RESS, SCHLOSS SCHONBORN, etc.

Winningen M-S-R w ** Village of lower MOSEL nr Koblenz, producing some fine delicate RIES. Top v'yds: Röttgen, Uhlen. Growers: von Heddesdorf, Heymann-Löwenstein, Richter.

Wintrich M-M w **→*** 71 75 76 83 85 86 87 88 89 90 91 Neighbour of PIESPORT; similar wines. Top v'yds: Grosser Herrgott, Ohligsberg, Sonnenseite. Grosslage: Kurfürstlay.

Remember that vintage information for German wines is given in a different form from the ready/not ready distinction applying to other countries. Read the explanation on page 104.

Winzergenossenschaft Wine-growers' cooperative, often making sound and reasonably priced wine. Referred to in this text as 'coop'.

Winzerverein The same as the above.

Wirsching, Hans Well-known estate in IPHOFEN, FRANKEN. Robust, full-bodied wines. 100 acres in top v'yds: Julius-Echter-Berg, Kalb, etc.

Wonnegau (Bereich) District name for S RHEINHESSEN.

Württemberg Vast S area, little known for wine outside Germany. Some good RIES esp from Neckar valley. Also TROLLINGER.

Würzburg Frank **→**** 71 76 81 *83* 85 86 87 88 89 90 91 Great baroque city on the Main, centre of Franconian (FRANKEN) wine: fine, full-bodied and dry. Top v'yds: Innere, Leiste, Pfaffenberg, Stein. No Grosslage. *See also* Maindreieck. Top growers: BURGERSPITAL, JULIUSSPITAL, STAATLICHER HOFKELLER.

Zell M-S-R w *→** 76 83 85 86 87 88 89 90 91 The best-known lower MOSEL village, esp for its Grosslage: Schwarze Katz ('Black Cat'). RIES on steep slate gives aromatic light wines.

Zell (Bereich) District name for whole lower MOSEL from Zell to Koblenz.

Zeltingen M-M w **→**** 71 75 76 79 83 *84* 85 86 87 88 89 90 91 Important MOSEL village next to WEHLEN. Typically lively, crisp RIES. Top v'yds. Schlossberg, SONNENUHR. Grosslage: Münzlay. Many estates hold v'yds here, the best being PRUM, SELBACH-OSTER.

Zilliken, Forstmeister Geltz Former estate of the Prussian royal forester at Saarburg and OCKFEN, SAAR. Old-style RIES wines for maturing.

Zwierlein, Freiherr von 55-acre family estate in GEISENHEIM. 100% RIES. Top v'yds: Kläuserweg, Rothenberg.

Spain & Portugal

The following abbreviations are used in the text.

Alen Alto Alentejo	**Cas-León** Castilla-León	**R Alt** Rioja Alta
Alg Algarve	**Cat** Catalonia	**R Ala** Rioja Alavesa
And Andalucía	**Est** Estremadura	**R B** Rioja Baja
Ara Aragón	**Ext** Extremadura	
B Al Beira Alta	**Gal** Galicia	**Trás-os-M**
B Lit Beira Littoral	**Lev** Levante	Trás-os-Montes
Cas-La M Castilla-La	**Min** Minho	
Mancha	**Nav** Navarra	**g** vino generoso
		res reserva

Since 1986, when Spain and Portugal joined the European Community, their wine industries have boomed in both quality and variety. Modern ideas have arrived to enrich (and often replace) their traditions. The continuing state of ferment is highly productive, and some splendid new wines have appeared, both in their few traditional quality areas, and in former bulk-wine regions.

Currently in Spain (apart from sherry country), Catalonia, Rioja, Navarra, Rueda and Ribera del Duero still hold most interest; in Portugal (apart from port and madeira) Bairrada, the Douro, the Ribatejo, Alentejo and Estremadura, and the Minho. In Portugal especially, new delimited ('VQPRD') areas are tending to overshadow such old appellations as eg Dão.

The listing here includes the best and most interesting types and regions of each country, whether legally delimited or not. Geographical references (*see map*) are to the autonomies and demarcated regions (DOs) of Spain, and provinces of Portugal.

Sherry, port and madeira are listed separately on pages 134–140.

Spain

AGE, Bodegas Unidas R Alt r w (p) dr sw res ★→★★ 73 74 75 78 80 81 82 83 84 85 Large BODEGA making a wide range of wines. Red MARQUES DE ROMERAL and Siglo Gran Reserva are best.

Alavesas, Bodegas R Ala r (w dr) res ★★→★★★ 73 74 75 76 78 80 81 83 84 85 86 87 Pale orange-red Solar de Samaniego was always one of the most delicate of the soft, fast-maturing Alavesa wines. But quality since '83 has been seriously variable; some wines excessively light.

Albariño Aromatic, high-quality white grape of Galicia and its wine. The Zona del Albariño, together with the Contado de Tea and El Rosal, has recently been demarcated under the name Rías Baixas. Its cold-fermented wines are some of Spain's best, at appropriate prices.

Alella Cat r w (p) dr sw ★★ Small demarcated region just N of Barcelona. Pleasantly fresh, fruity wines. *(See Marfil, Marqués de Alella, Parxet.)*

Alicante Lev r (w) ★ Demarcated region: wines still tend to be earthy and overstrong.

Almendralejo Ext r w ★ Commercial wine centre of the Extremadura. Much of its wine is distilled to make the spirit for fortifying sherry. *See* Lar de Barros.

Aloque Cas-La M r ▓ DYA A light (though not in alcohol) variety of VALDEPEÑAS, made by fermenting together red and white grapes.

Alvear And g ★★★ The largest producer of excellent sherry-like aperitif and dessert wines in MONTILLA-MORILES.

Ampurdán, Cavas del Cat w p r dr res sp ★→★★ Producers of big-selling white Pescador, red Cazador table wines and *cuve close* sparklers.

Año Year: 4° Año (or Años) means 4 yrs old when bottled. Common on labels in the past, but now being discontinued in favour of vintage years, or terms such as CRIANZA.

Bach, Masia Cat r p w dr sw res ★★→★★★ 70 74 78 80 81 82 83 85 Spectacular villa-winery nr SAN SADURNI DE NOYA, owned by CODORNIU. Formerly known for luscious, oaky, white Extrísimo Bach; now, for dry white Extrísimo and good red RESERVAS.

Banda Azul R Alt r ★★ 75 76 80 81 84 85 86 Big-selling CRIANZA wine, from Bodegas PATERNINA.

Barril, Masia Cat r res br ★★→★★★ 81 83 86 87 88 Tiny family estate in DO PRIORATO: powerful fruity reds – the 83 was 18°! – and superb RANCIO.

Berberana, Bodegas R Alt r (w dr) res ★→★★★ 64 66 70 73 74 75 76 78 80 81 82 83 84 85 86 87 The fruity, full-bodied reds are best: the young Carta de Plata, the 84, 85 Carta de Oro CRIANZA, the velvety RESERVAS.

Berceo, Bodegas R Alt r w dr p res ★★→★★★ Sister-cellar is HARO of BODEGAS GURPEGUI. Gonzalo de Berceo Gran Reserva is vg.

Beronia, Bodegas R Alt r w dr res ★★→★★★ 73 75 77 78 80 81 82 83 84 85 87 Small modern BODEGA making reds in traditional oaky style, and fresh 'modern' whites. Owned by Gonzalez Byass (*see under* Sherry).

Bilbainas, Bodegas R Alt r (p) w dr sw sp res ★★→★★★ 66 69 70 72 73 75 76 78 81 82 83 84 85 Large BODEGA in HARO. Wide and reliable range includes dark Viña Pomal, lighter Viña Zaco, Vendimia Especial RESERVAS and Royal Carlton CAVA.

Blanco White.

Bodega Spanish for 1) a wineshop; 2) a concern occupied in the making, blending and/or shipping of wine; and 3) a cellar.

Campanas, Las *See* Vinícola Navarra.

Campo Viejo, Bodegas R Alt r (w dr) res ★→★★★ 70 71 73 75 76 78 80 81 82 83 84 85 Branch of Bodegas y Bebidas, one of Spain's largest wine companies. Makes the popular and tasty young San Asensio and some big, fruity red RESERVAS, esp Marqués de Villamagna.

Can Rafols de Caus Cat r w dr ★★ 84 85 86 Young, small PENEDES BODEGA, growing its own fruity estate Cab S and pleasant white blend of Chard, Xarel-lo and Chenin Bl.

Cañamero Ext w ★ Remote village nr Guadalupe whose wines grow FLOR and acquire a sherry-like taste.

Caralt, Cavas Conde de Cat sp r w res ★★ 73 78 80 81 82 83 84 85 86 CAVA wines from an outpost of FREIXENET; also pleasant still wines.

Cariñena Ara r (p w) ✸ Demarcated region and large-scale supplier of strong everyday wine, dominated by coops. Now being invigorated (and its wines lightened) by modern technology.

Casar de Valdaiga Cas-León r w dr ★★ Fruity red made by Pérez Camares in EL BIERZO N of LEON.

Castellblanch Cat sp ★★ PENEDES CAVA firm, owned by FREIXENET. Currently much praised for Brut Zéro and slightly sweeter Cristal Seco.

Castillo Ygay 25 34 42 62 68 See Marqués de Murrieta

Cava The official term for any Spanish sparkling wine made by the champagne method, and the DO covering the areas up and down Spain where it is made.

Cenalsa Nav r w dr ★★ Large firm blending and maturing coop-made wines and shipping a range from NAVARRA, incl a flowery, new-style white and a fruity red, Agramont.

Cenicero Wine township in the RIOJA ALTA with ancient Roman origins.

Cepa Wine or grape variety.

Cervera, Lagar de Gal w dr ★★★ DYA Makers of a dry and elegant ALBARIÑO with pronounced bubbles.

Chacolí w (r) ★ DYA Alarmingly sharp, often fizzy, wine from the Basque coast now possessing its own DO, which applies to all 116 acres! It contains only 9–11% alcohol.

Chaves, Bodegas Gal w dr ★★→★★★ 89 90 (DYA) Small family firm making good, fragrant, slightly acidic ALBARIÑO.

Chivite, Bodegas Julián Nav r (p) w dr sw res ★★ 81 82 83 84 86 87 88 Biggest BODEGA in NAVARRA, producing full-bodied, fruity red wines and a flowery, well-balanced white. See Gran Feudo.

Clarete Traditional term, now banned by the EC, for light red wine (occasionally dark rosé).

Codorníu Cat sp ★★→★★★ One of the two largest firms in SAN SADURNI DE NOYA making good CAVA. Non Plus Ultra is matured. Many prefer the fresher Ana de Codorníu, the Première Cuvée Brut (86/7) and the Chard (86).

Compañía Vinícola del Norte de España (CVNE) R Alt r w (p) dr sw res ★★→★★★ 66 70 73 74 75 76 78 80 81 82 83 84 85 86 87 Top RIOJA BODEGA. The CRIANZA is among the best young red RIOJAS, and Monopole one of the best slightly oaky whites. Excellent red Imperial and Viña Real RESERVAS. CVNE is pronounced 'coonay'.

Conca de Barberá Cat w (r p) dr Demarcated region growing Parellada grapes for making CAVA, shortly to be incorporated in the DO PENEDES. Its best wine is TORRES MILMANDA Chard.

Consejo Regulador Official organization for the defence, control and promotion of a DENOMINACION DE ORIGEN.

Contino R Ala r res ★★★★ 74 75 76 78 80 81 82 84 85 Superior single-v'yd red made by a subsidiary of COMPAÑIA VINICOLA DEL NORTE DE ESPAÑA.

Corral, Bodegas R Alt r (p w dr) res ★★→★★★ 73 75 78 80 81 85 Long-established BODEGA now in improved new premises at Navarrete. Best known for red Don Jacobo.

Cosecha Crop or vintage.

Cosecheros Alaveses R Ala r ★★ 87 88 89 Up-and-coming coop, esp for good, young, unoaked red Artadi.

Criado y embotellado por... Grown and bottled by...

Crianza Literally 'nursing', the ageing of wine. New or unaged wine is *sin crianza* or *joven* (young). Wines labelled *crianza* must be at least 2 yrs old, of which 1 yr is spent in barrel, and must not be released before the third yr.

Cumbrero See Montecillo, Bodegas.

De Muller Cat br (r w dr) ****→***** Old TARRAGONA firm specializing in altar wines, making a good PRIORATO and superb v old *solera*-aged dessert wines, perhaps Spain's most sumptuous, incl Priorato DULCE and PAXARETE. Also fragrant Moscatel Seco.

Denominación de Origen Officially regulated wine region (*see* page 120).

Diaz e Hijos, Jesús Cas-La M w dr p r res ****→***** 86 87 Unoaked reds from this small BODEGA near Madrid win many prizes and have been compared with those of RIOJA and Catalonia.

Domecq R Ala r (w dr) res ****→***** 73 74 76 78 80 81 82 83 84 85 88 RIOJA outpost of sherry firm. Best wines are the fruity red Domecq Domain, exceptional in '76, and Marqués de Arienzo RESERVAS.

Dulce Sweet.

Elaborado y añejado por... Made and aged by...

El Bierzo Cas-León Region N of LEON newly demarcated in '90. *See* Casar de Valdaiga, Palacio de Arganza.

El Coto, Bodegas R Ala r (w dr) res ****→***** 70 75 76 78 80 81 82 84 85 86 87 88 BODEGA best known for light, soft red El Coto and Coto de Imaz.

Espumoso Sparkling (but *see* Cava).

Evena Nav Government-funded research station revolutionizing NAVARRA wines. Run by Javier OCHOA.

Fariña, Bodegas Cas-León r res w dr ****→***** 82 85 86 Rising star of new DO TORO: good spicy reds. Gran Colegiata ls cask-aged; Colegiata not.

Faustino Martínez R Ala r w (p) dr res ****→***** 64 70 72 73 74 75 76 78 80 81 82 83 85 86 Good reds; light, fruity white Faustino V. Gran Reserva is Faustino I. Do not be put off by the repellent fake-antique bottles.

Felix Solis Cas-La M r ****** BODEGA in VALDEPEÑAS setting a new pace with oak-aged reds, Viña Albali, RESERVAS (78, 83) and fresh white.

Ferrer, José L Mallorca r res ****** 78 80 84 85 86 The best-known BODEGA of Mallorca, at Binissalem. Second best known is Vinos Oliver, at Felanitx.

Fillaboa, Granxa Gal w dr ******* DYA Small, newly established firm making perhaps the most delicately fruity wine from ALBARIÑO.

Flor A floating yeast peculiar to *fino* sherry and certain other wines that oxidize slowly and tastily under its influence.

Franco-Españolas, Bodegas R Alt r w dr sw res ***→**** 64 70 73 74 75 76 78 79 81 82 85 Reliable wines from LOGROÑO. Bordón is a fruity red. The semi-sweet white Diamante is a favourite in Spain.

Freixenet Cavas Cat sp ****→***** Large producer of CAVA, rivalling CODORNIU in size through many acquisitions. Range of good sparkling wines, notably its Cordon Negro in black bottles, Brut Nature and Reserva Real. Also owns Gloria Ferrer in California and the champagne house of Henri Abelé in Reims. Paul Cheneau is a low-price brand.

Generoso Aperitif or dessert wine rich in alcohol.

Gonzalez y Dubosc, Cavas Cat sp ****** A branch of the sherry giant Gonzalez Byass. Pleasant sparkling wines exported as 'Jean Perico'.

Gran Feudo Nav w dr res ****→***** Brand name of fragrant white, refreshing rosé, soft, plummy red; the best-known wines from CHIVITE.

Gran Vas Pressurized tanks (French *cuves closes*) for making cheap sparkling wines; also used to describe this type of wine.

Gurpegui, Bodegas R B r (p w dr) res ***→**** 88 89 Large family firm making inexpensive wines from the RIOJA BAJA, labelled as Viñadrian, incl a fresh rosé. *See also* Berceo.

Haro The wine centre of the RIOJA ALTA, a small but stylish old town.

Hill, Cavas Cat dr w r sp res ****→***** 83 84 86 Old PENEDES firm making fresh dry white Blanc Cru, good Gran Civet and Gran Toc reds and a delicate Reserva Oro Brut CAVA.

Huelva And r w br ***→**** Demarcated region W of Cádiz. White table wines and sherry-like GENEROSOS, formerly an important resource of Jerez for blending.

Irache, SL Nav r p (w dr) res ****** 64 70 73 78 81 82 87 Well-known BODEGA making sound everyday reds.

Jean Perico *See* Gonzalez y Dubosc.

Jerez de la Frontera The capital city of sherry (*see* page 137).

Joven (vino) Young, unoaked wine.

Jumilla Lev r (w dr p) ★→★★ Demarcated region in the mountains N of Murcia. Its overstrong (up to 18%) wines are being lightened by earlier picking and better winemaking, esp by French-owned Bodegas VITIVINO, eg their Altos de Pío.

Juvé y Camps Cat sp ★★→★★★ Family firm aiming for and achieving top quality CAVA, made only with free-run juice, esp Reserva de la Familia.

Labastida, Cooperativa Vinícola de R Ala r res ★★ Makers of v drinkable Manuel Quintano, fruity, well-balanced Montebuena, Gastrijo and Castillo Labastida RESERVAS and Gran Reservas, and a tasty, fresh, dry white.

Laguardia Picturesque walled town at the centre of the RIOJA ALAVESA.

Lagunilla, Bodegas R Alt r ★★ 73 75 78 81 82 83 84 85 Modern firm owned by the British Grand Met Co. Easy, oaky, light reds incl Viña Herminia and Gran Reserva.

Lan, Bodegas R Alt r (p w) res ★★→★★★ 70 73 75 78 80 81 82 85 86 Huge modern BODEGA, lavishly equipped and making aromatic red RIOJAS, incl the good Lanciano and Lander and fresh white Lan Blanco.

Lar de Barros Ext r res ★★→★★★ 83 84 87 Meaty RESERVAS from Bodegas Inviosa, the first wines from remote Extremadura to make their mark outside Spain. Also Lar de Larres Gran Reservas 80, 82, 84.

La Rioja Alta, Bodegas R Alt r w (p) dr (sw) res ★★→★★★ 64 68 70 73 76 78 80 81 82 83 84 85 86 Excellent wines, esp red CRIANZA Viña Alberdi, velvety Ardanza Reserva, lighter Araña Reserva, splendid Reserva 904 and marvellous Reserva 890. Now making only RESERVAS and Gran Reservas.

León Cas-León r p w ★→★★ 78 81 82 83 84 Northern region to watch. Its wines can be fruity, dry and refreshing, esp those from Vinos de León, the former unfortunately named VILE (eg the young Coyanza, more mature Palacio de Suzman, and full-blooded Don Suero RESERVA). *See also* El Bierzo.

León, Jean Cat r w dr res ★★★ 74 75 77 78 79 80 81 82 83 84 Small firm owned by a Los Angeles restaurateur. Good oaky Chard, deep, full-bodied Cab that repays long bottle-ageing, though less so since '80.

Logroño First town of the RIOJA region. HARO has more charm (and BODEGAS).

López de Heredia R Alt r w (p) dr sw res ★★→★★★ 64 68 70 73 76 78 80 81 82 83 84 85 Superb old-established BODEGA in HARO with exceptionally long-lasting, v traditional wines. Viña Tondonia reds and whites are delicate and fine; Viña Bosconia fine and beefy.

López Hermanos Málaga ★★ Large BODEGA for commercial MALAGA wines, incl popular Málaga Virgen and Moscatel Flor de Málaga.

Los Llanos Cas-La M r (p w dr) res ★★ 75 78 81 82 One of the growing number of VALDEPEÑAS BODEGAS to age wine in oak. Señorío de Los Llanos Gran Reserva was remarkably seductive in '89, although recent bottles have shown inconsistency. To watch. Also a clean and fruity white, Armonioso.

Magaña, Bodegas Nav r res ★★→★★★ 80 81 82 83 Tiny young BODEGA making vigorous red with Merlot (vines bought from Pétrus), Cab S.

Málaga And br sw ★★→★★★ Demarcated region around city of Málaga. At their best, its dessert wines can come close to tawny port. *See* Scholtz.

Majorca JOSE FERRER, Miguel Oliver and Jaume Mesquida make the only wines of any interest on the island. On the whole, drink Catalan.

Mancha, La Cas-La M r w ★ Large demarcated region N and NE of VALDEPEÑAS. Mainly white wines, the reds lacking the liveliness of the best Valdepeñas, but showing signs of improvement. To watch.

Marfil Cat r (p) w ★★ Brand name of Alella Vinícola (Bodegas Cooperativas), oldest-established and v traditional producer in ALELLA. Means 'ivory'.

Marqués de Alella Cat w dr (sp) **→**** 86 87 88 89 (DYA)   Light and fragrant white ALELLA wines from PARXET, some from Chard, made by modern methods. Also CAVA.

Marqués de Cáceres, Bodegas R Alt r p w dr res **→**** 70 73 75 76 78 80 81 82 83 87   Good red RIOJAS made by modern French methods from CENICERO (R Alt) grapes; also a surprisingly light and fragrant white (DYA); and new oak-aged white.

Marqués de Griñon Cas-La M r w dr *** (r) 82 83 84 85   Enterprising nobleman making v fine Cab nr Toledo, S of Madrid. Also refreshing white from Verdejo grapes in RUEDA.

Marqués de Monistrol, Bodegas Cat w r sp (dr sw) res ** 75 77 78 80 82   Old BODEGA now owned by Martini & Rossi. Refreshing whites, esp the Vin Nature, a good red RESERVA and an odd sweet red wine.

Marqués de Murrieta R Alt r p w dr res ***→***** 34 42 52 60 62 64 68 70 73 74 75 76 78 79 80 81 82 83 84 85   Historic, much-respected BODEGA near LOGROÑO making some of the best of all RIOJAS. Makes soft and fruity red Etiqueta Blanca; superb red CASTILLO YGAY; an 'old-style' oaky white – dry, fruity and worth bottle-ageing (eg currently Blanco Ygay 70); and a wonderful old-style ROSADO.

Marqués de Riscal R Ala r (p w dr) res **→**** 64 65 68 71 73 75 76 78 80 81 82 83 84 85 86   The best-known BODEGA of the RIOJA ALAVESA. Its red wines are relatively light and dry. Old vintages are v fine; some more recent ones have disappointed; current ones are back on form, and Baron de Chirel, 50% Cab S, new in '86, is magnificent. Its whites from RUEDA, incl a vg Sauv Bl, are some of the best from this region.

Marqués de Romeral R Alt r w dr ** 76 78 80   Everyday Romeral and Gran Reserva are both vg value.

Marqués del Puerto R Alt r (p w dr) res **→**** 73 76 78 80 81 83 84 86   Small concern, founded as Bodegas López Agos and now owned by Bodegas y Bebidas, making red RESERVA Señorío de Agos, highly praised in Spain.

Rioja Vintages

It used to be the custom to cross-blend vintages in Rioja to maintain a degree of consistency. Today at least 85% of each wine must be of the year on the label, although Rioja as a whole still shows less vintage variation than eg Bordeaux. The best vintages of the last 40 years have been: 52, 55, 64, 68, 70, 73, 76, 78, 80, 81, 82, 83, 85, 86, 87, 88, 89 and 90. (Those in bold type were outstanding.)

* Riojas are generally put on the market when they are ready to drink. The best reservas of the best vintages, however, have very long lives and improve with more bottle-age. The best 70s are still at their peak.*

Martínez-Bujanda R Ala r p w dr res *** 70 73 75 78 80 81 84 85 86 87 88 89   Refounded ('85) family-run RIOJA BODEGA, remarkably equipped. Excellent wines, incl fruity SIN CRIANZA and irresistible ROSADO as well as noble Valdemar RESERVAS.

Martínez Lacuesta R Alt r res *→*** 70 73 76 84 85 86 87   For long a main supplier to Iberia airlines, Lacuesta has bounced back with first-rate Campeador 80, 81 and 83.

Mascaró, Cavas Cat sp (w r dr) **→****   Maker of some of the best Spanish brandy, good sparkling wine, lemony, refreshing dry white Viña Franca, and good (85) Anima Cab S.

Mauro, Bodegas Cas-León r *** 80 81 83 84 85 86   Young BODEGA in Tudela del Duero nr Valladolid with vg round, fruity Tinto del País (Tempranillo) red. Not DO, as it is made by Bodegas Sainz in RUEDA.

Méntrida Cas-La M r w *   Demarcated region W of Madrid, source of everyday red wine.

Milmanda **** 86 88 89   *See* Conca de Barberá, Torres.

Monopole *See* Compañía Vinícola del Norte de España (CVNE).

Montánchez Ext r g ★   Village near Mérida whose red wines grow FLOR yeast like *fino* sherry.

Montecillo, Bodegas R Alt r w (p) res ★★★ 75 76 78 80 81 82 84 85 88   'State of the art' RIOJA BODEGA owned by Osborne (*see* Sherry). Red and fresh dry white Cumbrero are among the best CRIANZA wines. Viña Monty is the worthy RESERVA. Gran Reserva Especial is first rate.

Montecristo, Bodegas ★★   Well-known brand of MONTILLA-MORILES wines.

Monterrey Gal r ★   Region near the N border of Portugal; strong wines like those of VERIN.

Montilla-Moriles And g ★★→★★★   Demarcated region nr Córdoba. Its crisp, sherry-like *fino* and *amontillado* contain 14–17.5% natural alcohol and remain unfortified. At best, singularly toothsome aperitifs.

Rioja's Characteristic Style

To the Spanish palate the taste of luxury in wine is essentially the taste of (American) oak. Oak contains vanillin: hence the characteristic vanilla flavour of all traditional Spanish table wines of high quality – exemplified by the reservas of Rioja (red and white). Fashion swung (perhaps too far) against the oaky flavour of old Rioja whites but the pendulum is swinging back, although to subtler oak flavours than in the old days. The marriage of ripe fruit and oak in red Rioja is still highly appreciated.

Muga, Bodegas R Alt r (w) (sp) res ★★★ 70 73 75 76 78 80 81 82 84 85 86   Small family firm in HARO, making some of RIOJA's best reds by strictly traditional methods. Wines are light but highly aromatic, with long, complex finish. The best is Prado Enea. Whites and CAVA less good.

Navajas, Bodegas R Alt r w dr res ★★→★★★ 82 83 85 87   Small firm with bargain reds, fruity and full-bodied.

Navarra Nav r p (w) ★→★★★   Demarcated region; mainly rosés and sturdy reds, but now well launched on stylish Tempranillo, Cab S reds, with some RESERVAS up to RIOJA standards. *See* Cenalsa, Chivite, Magaña, Ochoa, etc.

Nuestro Padre Jésus del Perdón, Coop de Cas-La M r w dr ★→★★ 85 86   DYA   Look for bargain fresh white Lazarillo and more than drinkable Yuntero; 100% Cencibel (alias Tempranillo) aged in oak.

Ochoa Nav w p r res ★★→★★★ 82 84 85 87 88   Small family BODEGA now producing an excellent white, but better known for its well-made red and rosé wines, incl outstanding 100% Tempranillo, 100% Cab S, and a blend of both.

Olarra, Bodegas R Alt r (w p) res ★★→★★★ 70 73 75 76 78 80 81 82 83 84 85 87   Vast modern BODEGA nr LOGROÑO, one of the showpieces of RIOJA, making good red and white wines and excellent Cerro Añon RESERVAS. Since '81, Añares is the top *reserva*.

Palacio, Bodegas R Ala w p r dr res ★★→★★★ 70 73 81 82 85 87   Glorioso was for a long time one of the best of RIOJA RESERVAS. After Seagram bought the BODEGA in '72 it went to pieces, but is now much improved.

Palacio de Arganza Cas-León r p (w dr) res ★★→★★★ 58 65 70 74 76 79 80 83 85   Best-known BODEGA in the new DO of EL BIERZO, between LEON and Galicia. The somewhat variable red Almena del Bierzo is well worth trying.

Palacio de Fefiñanes Gal w res ★★★   Famous for untypical ALBARIÑO. No bubbles and oak-aged 3–5 yrs.

Parxet Cat sp ★★★   Makers of excellent fresh, fruity CAVA and elegant MARQUES DE ALELLA whites from ALELLA.

Paternina, Bodegas R Alt r w (p) dr sw res ★→★★★ 28 59 67 68 71 73 75 76 78 82 83 86   A household name, esp for BANDA AZUL red and Banda Dorada white. The Conde de los Andes label was fine; 64, 70, 73 were outstanding, but recent vintages have been disappointing. Most consistent red is Viña Vial.

Paxarete Traditional, intensely sweet, dark brown, almost chocolatey speciality of TARRAGONA. Not to be missed. *See* De Muller.

Pazo Gal r p w dr ✱✱ DYA Brand name of the RIBEIRO coop, whose wines are akin to *vinhos verdes*. Rasping red is the local favourite. Pleasant, slightly fizzy Pazo and Xeito whites are safer; Viña Costeira has quality.

Peñafiel Cas-León r w dr res ✱✱ 64 74 76 79 80 82 83 85 86 87 89 Village on R Duero nr Valladolid. Best wines: fruity reds from Bodega Ribero Duero, incl tasty Protos RESERVA. Tastes, however, not always agreeable.

Penedès Cat r w dr sp ✱→✱✱✱ Demarcated region including Vilafranca del Penedès, SAN SADURNI DE NOYA and SITGES. *See also* Torres.

Perelada Cat w (r p) sp ✱✱ In the demarcated region of Ampurdán on the Costa Brava. Best known for sparkling, both CAVA and GRAN VAS.

Pérez Pascuas Hermanos Cas-León r (p) res ✱✱✱ 81 83 85 86 87 89 Immaculate tiny family BODEGA in RIBERA DEL DUERO. In Spain its fruity and complex red Viña Pedrosa is rated one of the country's best.

Pesquera Cas-León r ✱✱✱ 80 82 84 85 86 87 RIBERA DEL DUERO red made in small quantity by Alejandro Fernandez. Robert Parker has rated it on a level with Bordeaux Grands Crus. Janus is a special (even more expensive) bottling.

Piqueras, Bodegas Cas-La M r ✱✱ 82 83 Small family BODEGA with some of LA MANCHA's best reds, incl Castillo de Almansa CRIANZA and Marius Gran Reserva.

Priorato Cat br r dr ✱✱✱ 85 Demarcated region, an enclave of TARRAGONA, known for alcoholic RANCIO wines and also for splendidly full-bodied, almost black reds, often used for blending, but at its brambly best one of Spain's triumphs. Lighter, blended Priorato is a good carafe wine in Barcelona. *See* De Muller, Scala Dei, Barril.

Protos *See* Peñafiel.

Raimat Cat r w p sp ✱✱✱→✱✱✱✱ (Cab) 76 81 82 83 84 85 86 87 88 Thrillingly clean, structured and highly promising wines from the new DO of Costers del Segre nr Lérida, planted by CODORNIU with Cab, Chard and other foreign vines. Also a good 100% Chard CAVA.

Rancio Maderized (brown) white wine.

Real Divisa, Bodegas R Alt r res ✱✱✱ 73 80 81 82 85 86 Small and picturesque old BODEGA at Abalos, one of the few in RIOJA growing all its own fruit. Noted for its Marqués de Legarda RESERVAS.

Remélluri La Granja R Ala r res ✱✱✱ 74 76 79 80 81 83 84 85 Small estate (since '70), making vg traditional red RIOJAS.

René Barbier Cat r w dr res ✱✱ 83 85 Owned by FREIXENET, known for fresh white Kraliner and red RB RESERVAS.

Reserva Good quality wine matured for long periods. Red *reservas* must spend at least 1 yr in cask and 2 in bottle; *gran reservas* 2 in cask and 3 in bottle. Thereafter many continue to mature for decades.

Ribeiro Gal r w (p) dr ✱→✱✱ Demarcated region on N border of Portugal making wines similar in style to Portuguese *vinho verde* – and others.

Ribera del Duero Historic demarcated region E of Valladolid, now revealed as excellent for Tinto Fino (Tempranillo) reds. Vintages are somewhat variable and prices high. *See* Peñafiel, Pérez Pascuas, Pesquera, Torremilanos, Vega Sicilia. Also Mauro.

Rioja Cas-León r p w sp ✱→✱✱✱✱ 64 66 68 70 73 75 76 78 80 81 82 83 85 86 87 88 89 90 This upland region along the R Ebro in the N of Spain produces most of the country's best table wines in some 60 *bodegas de exportación*. It is subdivided into 3 areas:

Rioja Alavesa N of the R Ebro, the Rioja Alavesa produces fine red wines, mostly light in body and colour but particularly aromatic.

Rioja Alta S of the R Ebro and W of LOGROÑO, the Rioja Alta grows most of the finest, best-balanced red and white wines; also some rosé.

Rioja Baja Stretching E from LOGROÑO, the Rioja Baja makes coarser red wines, high in alcohol and often used for blending.

Riojanas, Bodegas R Alt r (w p) res ✶✶→✶✶✶ 34 42 56 64 66 68 70 73 74 75 76 78 80 81 82 83 84 85   Old BODEGA making good traditional Viña Albina. Its Monte Real RESERVAS are big and mellow.

Rioja Santiago R Alt r (p w dr sw) res ✶→✶✶✶ 78 81 83 84 87   BODEGA at HARO with brands incl the biggest-selling bottled SANGRIA (it belongs to Pepsi Cola). Its top reds, Condal and Gran Enologica, are respectable.

Rosado Rosé.

Rovellats Cat sp ✶✶→✶✶✶   Small family firm making only good (and expensive) CAVAS, stocked in some of Spain's best restaurants.

Rovira, Pedro Cat r p br w dr sw res ✶→✶✶   Large firm with BODEGAS in the DOs TARRAGONA, Terra Alta and PENEDES, making beverage, aperitif and dessert wines.

Rueda Cas-León br w dr ✶→✶✶   Small historic demarcated area W of Valladolid. Traditional producer of FLOR-growing, sherry-like wines with up to 17° alcohol, now making fresh whites, incl those of the MARQUES DE RISCAL and MARQUES DE GRIÑON. Its secret weapon is the Verdejo grape.

Ruiz, Santiago Gal w dr ✶✶✶ DYA   Small but prestigious BODEGA, now owned by Bodegas LAN, in the new Galicia DO Rías Baixas, whose ALBARIÑO is one of the v best.

Salceda, Bodegas Viña R Ala r res ✶✶→✶✶✶ 73 75 78 80 81 82 83 84 85 86   Makes fruity, light but well-balanced red wines.

Sangre de Toro Brand name for a rich-flavoured red from TORRES.

Sangría Cold red wine cup traditionally made with citrus fruit, fizzy lemonade, ice and brandy. But too often repulsive commercial fizz.

Sanlúcar de Barrameda Centre of the Manzanilla district (*see* Sherry).

San Sadurní de Noya Cat sp ✶✶→✶✶✶   Town S of Barcelona, hollow with cellars where dozens of firms produce CAVA. Standards can be v high, though the flavour (of Parellada and other grapes) is quite different from that of champagne.

San Valero, Bodega Cooperativa Ara r p (w) res ✶→✶✶ 85 86 87   Large CARIÑENA coop with some modern wines. Good red CRIANZA Monte Ducay; fresh Perçebal ROSADO with slight spritz; and good value, young, unoaked Don Mendo red.

Sarría, Señorío de Nav r (p w dr) res ✶✶→✶✶✶ 64 73 74 75 76 78 81 82 84 85   Model estate BODEGA nr Pamplona producing wines up to RIOJA standards.

Scala Dei, Cellers de Cat r res ✶✶→✶✶✶ 76 78 80 82 85 87   One of the few BODEGAS in tiny DO PRIORATO. Wines (esp Gran Reserva) are full-bodied reds, some oak-aged. Less alcohol recently.

Scholtz, Hermanos And br ✶✶→✶✶✶   Makers of the best MALAGA, including dry 10-yr-old *amontillado,* excellent Moscatel and traditional Dulce y Negro. Best of all is the dessert Solera Scholtz 1885.

Seco Dry.

Segura Viudas, Cavas Cat sp ✶✶→✶✶✶   CAVA of PENEDES. Buy the Brut Vintage (83), Aria or RESERVA Heredad.

Serra, Jaume Cat (w dr) r res ✶✶→✶✶✶ 84 85   PENEDES firm making fruity, well-balanced reds.

Sin Crianza *See* Crianza.

Sitges Cat w sw ✶✶   Coastal resort S of Barcelona formerly noted for its dessert wine made from Moscatel and Malvasia grapes. Only one maker, Celler Robert, survives.

Somontano Newly demarcated region in the foothills of the Pyrenees. Best-known BODEGAS are the old French-established Lalanne (nb Viña San Marcos red from Moristel, Tempranillo and Cab S; white from Macabeo and Chard), and Coop Somontano de Sobrarbe (nb Montesierra range and oak-aged Señorío de Lazán).

Tarragona Cat r w dr sw br ✶→✶✶✶   1) Table wines from the demarcated region; of little note. 2) Dessert wines from the firm of DE MULLER.

Tinto Red.

Toro Cas-León r ★→★★ Demarcated region 150 miles NW of Madrid, traditionally making over-powerful (up to 16°) red wines, but now producing some tasty, balanced reds. *See* Bodegas Fariña.

Torremilanos Cas-León r res ★→★★ 76 79 81 82 83 85 86 87 88 Label of Bodegas López Peñalba, a fast-expanding family firm near Aranda de Duero. Their red Tinto Fino (Tempranillo) wines are lighter and more RIOJA-like than most. Also labelled 'Peñalba'.

Torres, Bodegas Cat r w p dr s/sw res ★★→★★★★ 64 70 71 73 74 75 76 77 78 79 80 81 82 83 84 85 86 87 88 Distinguished family firm making most of the best table wines of PENEDES, and a flagship for the whole of Spain. Wines are flowery white Viña Sol, Green Label Fransola Sauv Bl and Parellada, and Gran Viña Sol, MILMANDA oak-fermented Chard, semi-dry aromatic Esmeralda, Waltraud Ries, red Tres Torres and Gran Sangre de Toro, superlative Gran Coronas (Cab) RESERVAS, fresh and soft Los Torres Merlot and Santa Digna Pinot N. Mas Borres is a new 100% Pinot N. The family also has v'yds in Chile and California.

Utiel-Requeña Lev r p (w) Demarcated region W of Valencia. Sturdy reds and chewy *vino de doble pasta* for blending; also light, fragrant rosé.

Valbuena Cas-León r ★★★ 75 76 77 78 79 80 82 83 84 85 Made with the same grapes as VEGA SICILIA but sold when either 3 or 5 yrs old. Best at about 10 yrs. Some prefer it to its older brother.

Valdeorras Gal r w dr ★→★★ Demarcated region E of Orense. Dry and (at best) refreshing wines.

Valdepeñas Cas-La M r (w) ★→★★ Demarcated region nr the border of Andalucía. Its mainly red wines, though high in alcohol, can be surprisingly soft in flavour. Some superior wine (eg LOS LLANOS and FELIX SOLIS) is oak-matured.

Valencia Lev r w ★→★★ Demarcated region exporting vast quantities of clean and drinkable table wine; also refreshing whites, esp Moscatel.

Vallformosa, Masia Cat dr w p r sp res ★★→★★★ 80 84 Good PENEDES wine; a fresh, dry, white Gran Blanc, good Vall Fort red and Vall RESERVAS.

Vega de la Reina Cas-León w dr r res ★★★ 78 80 81 82 RUEDA BODEGA making complex, old-style, oaky reds with something of the quality of the famous VEGA SICILIA.

Vega Sicilia Cas-León r res ★★★★ 41 48 53 59 60 61 62 64 66 67 69 72 73 75 76 79 80 One of the v best Spanish wines, full-bodied, fruity, piquant, rare and fascinating. Up to 16% alcohol. *See also* VALBUENA.

Vendimia Vintage.

Verín Gal r ★ Town near N border of Portugal. Its wines are the strongest from Galicia, without a bubble, and with up to 14% alcohol.

Viña Literally, a vineyard. But wines such as Tondonia (LOPEZ DE HEREDIA) are not necessarily made only with grapes from the v'yd named.

Viña Pedrosa *See* Pérez Pascuas.

Viña Toña Cat w dr ★★→★★★ DYA Clean, fresh and fruity white of Xarel-lo from small firm Celler R Balada. Justifiably high reputation in Spain

Vinícola de Castilla Cas-La M r p w dr ＊83 89 One of the largest firms in LA MANCHA. Red and white Castillo de Alhambra are palatable. Top wines: Cab S and Cencibel (Tempranillo), Señorío de Guadianeja Gran Reservas.

Vinícola Navarra Nav w p r dr res ★★ 78 82 84 Old-established BODEGA making thoroughly traditional NAVARRA wines. The best is the reliable Castillo de Tiebas.

Vinival, Bodegas Lev r w p ★ Huge Valencian consortium marketing the most widely drunk wine in the region, Torres de Quart (rosé best).

Vino comun/corriente Ordinary wine.

Vitivino, Bodegas Lev r ★★→★★★ 88 The French J-L Gadeau has stirred JUMILLA with peachy Altos de Pío from local Monastrell grapes.

Yecla Lev r w ★ Demarcated region N of Murcia. Its ailing cooperative, La Purisima, was once Spain's biggest. Best to avoid its wine.

Ygay *See* Marqués de Murrieta.

Portugal

For port and madeira see pages 134-140.

Abrigada, Quinta de Est r w dr res ✶✶ Family estate: characterful light whites and cherry-like PERIQUITA.

Adega A cellar or winery.

Alentejo r (w) ✶→✶✶ Vast tract of S Portugal with only sparse v'yds nr the Spanish border, but rapidly emerging potential for excellent wine. To date the great bulk of its wine has been coop-made. Estate wines from ROSADO FERNANDES, Herdade de MOUCHAO, Quinta do CARMO and ESPORAO have potency and style. Best coops are at Redondo, BORBA and REGUENGOS DE MONSARRAZ. Growing excitement here.

Algarve Alg r w ✶ Demoted DO in the holiday area. With a few exceptions its wines are nothing to write home about.

Aliança, Caves B Lit r w dr sp res ✶✶→✶✶✶ Large BAIRRADA-based firm making champagne-method sparkling. Reds and whites incl good Bairrada wines and mature DAOS. Aliança Tinta Velha is the best-selling red in Portugal.

Almodovar, Casa Agricola Alen w dr r res ✶✶ 84 86 87 The whites of this ADEGA at Vidigueira are better known, but its reds can also be worth trying.

Amarante Subregion in the VINHOS VERDES area. Rather heavier and stronger wines than those from farther north.

Arruda, Adega Cooperativa de B Al r res ✶ Vinho Tinto Arruda is a best buy. But avoid the *reserva*.

Aveleda, Quinta da Douro w dr ✶✶ DYA A first-class VINHO VERDE made on the Aveleda estate of the Guedes family of MATEUS fame. Sold dry in Portugal but sweetened for export.

Azeveda, Quinta de Min w dr ✶✶ DYA Superior VINHO VERDE from SOGRAPE. 100% Loureiro grapes.

Bacalhoa, Quinta da Est r res ✶✶✶ 81 82 83 84 85 87 88 American-owned estate near SETUBAL, famous for harmonious, fruity, mid-weight Cab S, vinified by João PIRES.

Bairrada B Lit r w dr sp ✶→✶✶ 66 70 75 76 77 78 79 82 85 87 Demarcated region producing excellent red GARRAFEIRAS. Also good sparkling by the champagne method. Now an export hit.

Barca Velha ('Ferreirinha') Trás-os-M r res ✶✶✶✶ 57 64 65 66 78 Perhaps Portugal's best red, made in v limited quantity in the high DOURO by the port firm of Ferreira. Powerful, resonant wine with deep bouquet, still unchallenged by younger rivals.

Barrocão, Cavas do B Lit r w dr res ✶→✶✶✶ Based in the BAIRRADA; blends good red DAOS and makes first-rate old Bairrada GARRAFEIRAS (60, 64).

Basto A subregion of the VINHOS VERDES area on the R Tamego, producing more astringent red wine than white.

Borba Alen r ✶→✶✶✶ Small VQPRD area nr Evora, making some of the best wine from ALENTEJO.

Borba, Adega Cooperativa de Est r (w dr) res ✶→✶✶ 82 84 87 88 89 Leading ALENTEJO coop modernized with stainless steel and oak by EC funding. Big fruity *vinho de ano* red and vg 82 *reserva*.

Borges & Irmão Merchants of port and table wines at Vila Nova de Gaia, incl GATAO and (better) Gamba VINHOS VERDES, sparkling Fita Azul.

Branco White.

Braga Subregion of the VINHOS VERDES area, good red and white.

Buçaco B Al r w (p) res ✶✶✶✶ (r) 51 53 57 58 60 63 67 70 72 75 77; (w) 56 65 66 70 72 75 Legendary speciality of the Palace Hotel at Buçaco nr Coimbra, not seen elsewhere. At best incredible quality.

Bucelas Est w dr ✶✶✶ 79 84 Tiny demarcated region just N of Lisbon. Caves VELHAS make aromatic wines with 11–12% alcohol. Reliable, not dramatic.

Camarate, Quinta de Est r ★★ 74 78 80 82 83 84 85 86 87 90 Notable red from FONSECA, S of Lisbon, incl detectable proportion of Cab S.

Campos da Silva Olivera, JC B Al r res ★★ 84 85 Small ADEGA with v fruity estate DAO, Sete Torres Reserva.

Carcavelos Est br sw ★★★ normally NV Minute demarcated region W of Lisbon. Excellent but rare sweet aperitif or dessert wines average 19% alcohol and resemble honeyed MADEIRA. For yrs the only producer was the ADEGA Regional; now João PIRES has joined in.

Carmo, Quinta do Alen w r dr res ★★★ 86 87 88 89 Small and beautiful ALENTEJO ADEGA, bought in '92 by the Rothschilds of Lafite. 125 acres, plus cork forests (cut small). Ferments its wines in marble *lagares*. Fresh, dry white, but best is the fruity, harmonious red.

Cartaxo Ribatejo r w ★ A district in the RIBATEJO N of Lisbon, now a VQPRD area making everyday wines popular in the capital.

Carvalho, Ribeiro & Ferreira B Al r w res ★★→★★★ Large merchants blending and bottling SERRADAYRES and excellent RIBATEJO GARRAFEIRAS.

Casa Ferreirinha Tras-os-M r res ★★★ The second wine to BARCA VELHA, made in less than ideal vintages.

Casa da Insua B Al r w ★★ One of the very few single-estate wines of the DAO area (though not DO), made for the proprietors by FONSECA with a proportion of Cab S in an old cellar re-equipped and modernized.

Casa de Sezim Min w dr ★★→★★★ DYA One of the best estate-bottled VINHOS VERDES from a member of the new association of private producers, APEVV.

Casal García Douro w dr ★★ DYA One of the biggest-selling VINHOS VERDES in Portugal, made at AVELEDA.

Casal Mendes Min w dr ★★ DYA The VINHOS VERDES from Caves ALIANÇA.

Casaleiro Trademark of Caves Dom Teodosio-João T Barbosa, who make a variety of standard wines: DAO, VINHOS VERDES, etc.

Cepa Velha Min w (r) dr ★★★ Brand name of Vinhos de Monção. Their Alvarinho is one of the best VINHOS VERDES.

Clarete Relatively light red wine.

Colares Est r ★★★ TOTB (the older the better) Small demarcated region on the sandy coast W of Lisbon. Its antique-style dark red wines, rich in tannin, are from vines that have never suffered from phylloxera. Drink the oldest available: it needs at least 10 yrs (*see* Paulo da Silva).

Conde de Santar B Al r (w dr) res ★★→★★★ 70 73 78 85 86 Estate-grown DAO, later matured and sold by the port firm of Cálem. *Reservas* are fruity, full-bodied and exceptionally smooth.

Consumo (vinho) Ordinary wine.

Corval, Quinta do Trás-os-M r ★★ Estate near Pinhão making good light CLARETES.

Côtto, Quinta do Trás-os-M r w dr res ★★→★★★ 82 85 90 Pioneer table wines from port country; red Grande Escolha and Q do Côtto are dense, fruity, tannic wines that will repay long keeping. Also port.

Dão B Al r w res ★★ 69 70 71 74 75 80 83 85 Demarcated region round the town of Viseu on the R Mondego. Produces some of Portugal's best-known, but often disappointing, table wines: solid reds of some subtlety with age; substantial dry whites. Most sold under brand names.

Doce (vinho) Sweet wine.

Douro The northern river whose valley produces port and some of Portugal's most exciting new table wines. *See* Barca Velha, Quinta do Côtto, and others. Watch this space.

Esporão, Herdade do Alen w dr r ★★ 87 Owners Finagra SA spent $10 million on their space-age winery, and planting 900 acres. Their light, fresh Roupeiro white and 87 red, with a touch of Cab S, are pleasant but pricey.

Espumante Sparkling.

Esteva Trás-os-M r ★→★★ 87 DYA V drinkable young DOURO red from the port firm of Ferreira.

Evelita Trás-os-M r ✱→✱✱✱ 75 79   Reliable middle-weight red made near VILA REAL by REAL COMPANHIA VINICOLA DO NORTE DE PORTUGAL. Ages well.

Fonseca, JM da Est r w dr sp res ✱✱→✱✱✱   Venerable firm in Azeitão nr Lisbon, with one of the longest and best ranges in Portugal, incl dry white Pasmados, Portalegre and Quinta de Camarate; red PERIQUITA, PASMADOS, Quinta de CAMARATE, TERRAS ALTAS DAO; and famous dessert Moscatel de SETUBAL. Fonseca also owns ROSADO FERNANDES and makes the wines for CASA DA INSUA.

Fonseca Internacional, JM da Est p ✱   Formerly part of the last, now owned by Grand Met. Produces LANCERS rosé and a surprisingly drinkable sparkling Lancers Brut made by a continuous process of Russian invention.

Gaeiras Est r ✱✱   Dry, full-bodied, well-balanced red made nr Obidos.

Garrafeira The 'private reserve' wine of a merchant, aged for a minimum of 2 yrs in cask and 1 in bottle, but often much longer. Usually their best, though traditionally often of indeterminate origin.

Gatão Min w dr ✱✱ DYA   Standard VINHO VERDE from BORGES & IRMAO; fragrant but sweetened.

Gazela Min w dr ✱✱ DYA   A new VINHO VERDE made at Barcelos by SOGRAPE since AVELEDA estate went to a different branch of the Guedes family.

Generoso Aperitif or dessert wine rich in alcohol.

Grão Vasco B Al r w res ✱✱ 70 73 75 78 80 81 82 83 85 87   One of the best brands of DAO, from a new high-tech ADEGA at Viseu. Fine red *reservas*; fresh young white (DYA). Owned by SOGRAPE.

Lagosta Min w dr ✱ DYA   VINHO VERDE from the REAL COMPANHIA VINICOLA DO NORTE DE PORTUGAL.

Lancers Est p w sp ✱   Sweet carbonated rosé and sparkling white extensively shipped to the USA by FONSECA INTERNACIONAL.

Lima Subregion in N of VINHOS VERDES area, for mainly astringent red wines.

Madeira Island br dr sw ✱✱→✱✱✱✱   Source of famous aperitif and dessert wines. *See* pp 135-141.

Maduro (vinho) A mature table wine – as opposed to a VINHO VERDE.

Mateus Rosé Trás-os-M p (w) ✱   World's biggest-selling medium-sweet carbonated rosé, made by SOGRAPE at VILA REAL and Anadia in BAIRRADA.

Monção N subregion of the VINHOS VERDES area on R Minho, producing the best of them from the Alvarinho grape.

Morgadio de Torre Min w dr ✱✱ DYA   A top VINHO VERDE from SOGRAPE. Largely Alvarinho.

Mouchão, Herdade de Alen r res ✱✱✱ 74   Perhaps the best ALENTEJO estate, ruined in the '75 uprising; recently replanted. A little 74 just released.

Pacheca, Quinta da Trás-os-M r w ✱✱ 82   Superior DOURO table wines, estate-grown, -made and -bottled. Unfortunately not free of faults.

Palacio de Brejoeira Min w (r) dr ✱✱✱   Outstanding estate-made VINHO VERDE from MONÇAO, with astonishing fragrance and full, fruity flavour.

Pancas, Quinta de Est r res ✱✱ 87   Red to watch from Alenquer district N of Lisbon.

Pasmados V tasty FONSECA red from the ALENTEJO.

Paulo da Silva, Antonio Bernardino Est r (w dr) res ✱✱→✱✱✱ 68 70 74 77 80 83 84 85   His COLARES Chita is one of the v few of those classics still made (by the ADEGA Regional).

Penafiel Subregion in the S of the VINHOS VERDES area.

Periquita Est r ✱✱ 71 74 77 78 80 82 84 85 86 87 88   One of Portugal's most enjoyable robust reds, made by FONSECA at Azeitão S of Lisbon. Periquita is a grape much grown in ALENTEJO.

Pinhel B Al w (r) sp ✱   VQPRD region E of the DAO, making similar white, mostly sparkling.

Pires, João Est r w dr sp res ✱✱→✱✱✱   One of the best-equipped and best-run wineries in Portugal. Wines incl the delicious João Pires Branco (Moscato), Catarina containing Chard, dry white and red Santa Marta, red Santo Amaro made by *macération carbonique*, TINTO DE ANFORA,

Quinta da BACALHOA, dessert SETUBAL, *méthode champenoise* João Pires Bruto, and now CARCAVELOS.

Planalto Douro w dr ** Good white wine from SOGRAPE.

Ponte de Lima, Cooperativa de Min r ** Maker of one of the best bone-dry *red* VINHOS VERDES, and first-rate dry and fruity white.

Porta dos Cavalheiros B Al **→*** 75 80 83 85 One of the best red DAOS, matured by Caves SAO JOAO in BAIRRADA.

Quinta Estate.

Raposeira B Al sp ** One of the best-known Portuguese sparklers made by the *méthode champenoise* at Lamego. Ask for the Bruto. An outpost of Seagram.

Real Companhia Vinícola do Norte de Portugal Giant of the port trade *(see* page 138), also produces EVELITA, LAGOSTA, etc.

Redondo *See* Alentejo.

Reguengos de Monsarraz, Cooperativa de Alen r (w dr) res ** 82 83 86 87 Important coop making steadily better wines since modernization, the best of them red.

Ribatejo Region on R Tagus N of Lisbon. Several good GARRAFEIRAS etc.

Ribeirinho, Quinta de B Lit r sp **→*** 80 85 Luis Pato makes some of the best estate-grown BAIRRADA wines: fruity red and fresh *méthode champenoise* sparkling.

Rosado Rosé.

Rosado Fernandes, José de Sousa Alen r res *** 71 75 79 83 86 Small firm recently acquired by FONSECA, making the most sophisticated of the full-bodied wines from the ALENTEJO, fermenting them in pottery *anforas* and ageing them in oak.

São Claudio, Quinta de Min w dr *** DYA Estate at Esposende: perhaps the best VINHO VERDE outside MONÇÃO.

São João, Caves B Lit r w dr sp res **→*** 75 76 78 80 82 83 One of the best firms in the BAIRRADA, known for its fruity and full-bodied reds and PORTA DOS CAVALHEIROS DAOS. Also fizz.

Seco Dry.

Serradayres Est r (w) res * Blended RIBATEJO table wines from CARVALHO, RIBEIRO & FERREIRA. Usually sound and v drinkable; recently too tart.

Setúbal Est br *** Small demarcated region S of the R Tagus, where FONSECA make a highly aromatic dessert Muscat, 6 and 20 yrs old.

Sogrape Sociedad Comercial dos Vinhos de Mesa de Portugal. Largest wine concern in the country, making VINHOS VERDES, DÃO, MATEUS ROSE, VILA REAL red, etc, and now owners of Ferreira port.

Solar dos Boucas VINHO VERDE estate acquired by port house Quinta do Noval. 70 acres. Dry, aromatic wine is a model.

Terras Altas B Al r w res ** 75 76 78 79 80 82 83 84 85 87 88 Good DAO wines made by FONSECA.

Tinto Red.

Tinto de Anfora Est r ** 78 80 81 82 84 85 86 87 Deservedly popular juicy and fruity red from João PIRES. Repays at least 5 yrs in bottle.

Torres Vedras Est r w dr * Area N of Lisbon famous for Wellington's 'lines'. Major supplier of bulk wine; one of biggest coops in Portugal.

Velhas, Caves B Lit r w dr res **→*** Only maker of BUCELAS; also good DAO and (80) Romeira GARRAFEIRAS.

Vila Real Trás-os-M r *→** Town in the demarcated DOURO region, now making some good reds.

Verde Green (*see* Vinhos Verdes).

Vinhos Verdes Min and Douro r * w dr *→*** Demarcated region between R Douro and N frontier with Spain, producing 'green wines': wine made from barely ripe grapes and (originally) undergoing a special secondary fermentation to leave it with a slight sparkle. Today the fizz is usually just added CO_2. Ready for drinking in spring after harvest, it may be white or red. 'Green wine' is not an official term.

Sherry, Port & Madeira

The original authentic sherries of Spain, ports of Portugal and madeiras of Madeira are listed below. References to their many imitators in South Africa, California, Australia, Cyprus and Argentina will be found under those countries. (NB 'British Sherry' is a cynical theft of the name to describe a drink made of dehydrated must and water – not legally wine at all; far less sherry. What is the EC for if not to stop such piracy?)

The map on page 120 locates the port and sherry districts. Madeira is an island 400 miles out in the Atlantic from the coast of Morocco, a port of call for west-bound sailing ships: hence its historical market in North America.

In this section most of the entries are shippers' names followed by a brief account of their wines. The names of wine types are included in the alphabetical listing.

Abad, Tomas Small sherry *bodega* owned by LUSTAU. Vg light FINO.

Almacenista Individual matured but unblended sherry; high quality, usually dark, dry wines for connoisseurs. Often superb quality and value. *See* Lustau.

Amontillado In general use means medium sherry; technically means a FINO which has been aged in the *bodega* beyond its normal span to become more powerful and pungent. The best are natural dry wines.

Amoroso Type of sweet sherry, v similar to a sweet OLOROSO.

Barbadillo, Antonio Much the largest SANLUCAR firm, with a range of 50-odd MANZANILLAS and sherries mostly excellent of their type, incl Sanlúcar FINO, superb SOLERA *manzanilla* PASADA, *fino* de Balbaina, Príncipe AMONTILLADO. Also young Castillo de San Diego table wines.

Barbeito Shippers of good-quality madeira, one of the last independent family firms in the business. Wines include aperitif Island Dry, superior Crown range and rare vintage wines, eg MALMSEY 1901 and the latest, BUAL 1960.

Barros Almeida Large family-owned port house with several brands (incl Feuerheerd, KOPKE), making an excellent 20-yr-old TAWNY and many COLHEITAS.

Bertola Sherry shippers, best known for their Bertola CREAM SHERRY.

Blandy Historic family firm of madeira shippers. Duke of Clarence Malmsey is their most famous. 10-year-old *reservas* (VERDELHO, BUAL, MALMSEY) are superior. Source of many glorious old vintages.

Blázquez Sherry *bodega* at JEREZ (owned by DOMECQ) with outstanding FINO, Carta Blanca, and Carta Oro AMONTILLADO *al natural* (unsweetened).

Bobadilla Large JEREZ *bodega*, best known for v dry Victoria FINO and Bobadilla 103 brandy, esp among Spanish connoisseurs. Also excellent sherry vinegar.

Brown sherry British term for a style of inexpensive dark sweet sherry.

Bual One of the best grapes of madeira, making a soft, smoky, sweet wine, not usually as rich and sweet as MALMSEY.

Burdon English-founded sherry *bodega* owned by CABALLERO. Light FINO, Don Luis AMONTILLADO and raisiny Heavenly Cream are top lines.

Burmester Old, small, family-owned port house with fine, soft, sweet 20-yr-old TAWNY; also vg range of COLHEITAS. Vintages: **50 55 58 60 63 75 77 83 85**.

Caballero Important sherry shippers at PUERTO DE SANTA MARIA, best known for Pavon FINO, Mayoral Cream OLOROSO, excellent BURDON sherries and PONCHE orange liqueur.

Cálem Old family-run Portuguese house with a fine reputation, esp for vintage wines. Owns the excellent Quinta da Foz (**80 82 84 87**). Vintages: **50 58 60 63 70 75 77 80 83 85**. Good light TAWNY and exceptional range of COLHEITAS; **48 50 52 57 60 62**.

Churchill The only recently founded port shipper, already respected for excellent vintages **82** and **85**. Also a vg CRUSTED. Quinta da Agua Alta is Churchill's single-QUINTA port: **87**.

Cockburn British-owned port shippers with a range of good wines incl the v popular and fruity Special Reserve. Fine vintage port from v high v'yds can look deceptively light when young, but has great lasting power. Vintages: **55 60 63 67 70 75 83 85**.

Colheita Vintage-dated port of a single yr, but aged at least 7 winters in wood: in effect a vintage TAWNY. The bottling date is also shown on the label.

Cossart Gordon Leading firm of madeira shippers founded 1745, best known for their Good Company range of wines but also producing 5-yr-old Reservas, old vintages (latest, **52**) and SOLERAS (esp superb SERCIAL Duo Centenary).

Côtto, Quinta do Single-v'yd port from Miguel Champalimaud, best-known of a new wave of grower-bottlers up the Douro. Vg vintage **82**. *See also* Portugal.

Cream Sherry A style of amber sweet sherry made by sweetening a blend of well-aged OLOROSOS. It originated in Bristol.

Croft One of the oldest firms shipping vintage port: 300 yrs old in '78. Bought early this century by Gilbey's. Well-balanced vintage wines tend to mature early (since 66). Vintages: **55 60 63 66 70 75 77 82 85**; and lighter vintage wines under the name of their Quinta da Roeda in several other years (**78 80 83 87**). Distinction is their most popular blend. MORGAN is a small separate company (*see also* Delaforce). Also now in the sherry business with Croft Original (PALE CREAM). Particular (medium), Delicado (FINO, also medium), and good PALO CORTADO.

Crusted Term for a vintage-style port, but usually blended from several vintages not one, bottled young and aged in bottle, so forming a 'crust' in the bottle. Needs decanting.

Delaforce Port shippers owned by CROFT, best known in Germany. His Eminence's Choice is an extremely pleasant TAWNY; VINTAGE CHARACTER is also good. Vintage wines are v fine, among the lighter kind: **55 58 60 63 66 70 75 77 82 85**; Quinta da Côrte in **78 80 84 87**.

Delgado Zuleta Old-established SANLUCAR firm best known for its marvellous La Goya MANZANILLA PASADA.

Diez-Merito SA Fast-growing JEREZ firm owned by Bodegas INTERNACIONALES specializing in 'own-brand' sherries. Latest acquisition is Zoilo Ruiz-Mateos, formerly part of the ill-fated Rumasa empire. Its own FINO Imperial and OLOROSO Victoria Regina are excellent. DON ZOILO wines are superb.

Domecq Giant family-owned sherry *bodegas* at JEREZ, famous also for Fundador brandy. Double Century Original OLOROSO is their biggest brand, La Ina their excellent FINO. Other famous wines incl Celebration Cream, Botaina (old AMONTILLADO) and the magnificent Rio Viejo (v dry *amontillado*) and Sibarita (PALO CORTADO). Recently introduced a range of wonderful old SOLERA sherries (Sibarita, Amontillado 51-1A and Venerable OLOROSO). Now also in Rioja.

Don Zoilo Luxury sherries, incl velvety FINO, sold by DIEZ-MERITO.

Dow Old name used on the British and US markets by the port shippers Silva & Cosens, well known for their relatively dry but nonetheless splendid vintage wines, said to have a faint 'cedarwood' character. Also vg VINTAGE CHARACTER and Boardroom, a 15-yr-old TAWNY. Quinta do Bomfim is their single-QUINTA port. Vintages: **55 60 63 66 70 72 75 77 80 83 85**. Dow, GOULD CAMPBELL, GRAHAM, QUARLES HARRIS, SMITH WOODHOUSE and WARRE all belong to the Symington family.

Dry Fly A household name in the UK, this crisp, nutty AMONTILLADO is made in JEREZ for its British proprietors, Findlater, Mackie, Todd & Co.

Dry Sack *See* Williams & Humbert.

Duff Gordon Sherry shippers best known for their El Cid AMONTILLADO. Also good FINO Feria and Nina Dry OLOROSO. Owned by OSBORNE.

Duke of Wellington A luxury range of sherries from Bodegas INTERNACIONALES.

Eira Velha, Quinta da Small port estate with old-style vintage wines shipped by COCKBURN. Vintages: **72 78 80 82 85 87.**

Ferreira The biggest Portuguese-owned port growers and shippers (since 1751), recently bought by Sogrape (*see* Portugal). Well known for old TAWNIES and juicily sweet, relatively light vintages: **60 63 66 70 75 77 78 80 82 83 85 87.** Also Dona Antónia Personal Reserve and splendidly rich tawny Duque de Bragança.

Fino Term for the lightest and finest of sherries, completely dry, v pale and with great delicacy. *Fino* should always be drunk cool and fresh: it deteriorates rapidly once opened. TIO PEPE is the classic example.

Flor The characteristic natural yeast which gives FINO its unique flavour.

Fonseca Guimaraens British-owned port shipper of stellar reputation, connected with TAYLOR'S. Robust, deeply coloured vintage wine, among the v best. Vintages: Fonseca **70 75 77 80 83 85**; Fonseca Guimaraens **76 78**. Quinta do Panascal **78** is a new single-QUINTA wine. Also delicious VINTAGE CHARACTER Bin 27.

Forrester Port shippers and owners of the famous Quinta da Boa Vista, now owned by Martini & Rossi. Their vintage wines tend to be round, 'fat' and sweet, good for relatively early drinking. Baron de Forrester is vg TAWNY. Vintages: (Offley Forrester) **60 62 63 66 67 70 72 75 77 80 82 83 85 87.**

Garvey Famous old sherry shippers at JEREZ. Their finest wines are deep-flavoured FINO San Patricio, Tio Guillermo Dry AMONTILLADO and Ochavico Dry OLOROSO. San Angelo Medium *amontillado* is the most popular. Also Bicentenary PALE CREAM.

Gonzalez Byass Enormous family-run firm shipping the world's most famous and one of the very best FINO sherries: TIO PEPE. Other brands incl La Concha Medium AMONTILLADO, Elegante Dry *fino*, San Domingo PALE CREAM, Nectar CREAM and Alfonso Dry OLOROSO. AMONTILLADO del Duque is on a higher plane, as are Matusalem and Apostoles: respectively sweet and dry old *olorosos* of rare quality.

Gould Campbell *See* Smith Woodhouse.

Graham Port shippers famous for some of the richest, sweetest and best of VINTAGE PORTS, largely from their own Quinta dos Malvedos. Also excellent brands, incl Six Grapes RUBY, LATE-BOTTLED, and 10- and 20-yr-old TAWNIES. Vintages: **55 58 60 63 66 70 75 77 80 83 85.**

Guita, La Famous old SANLUCAR *bodega* (owned by Perez Marin) and its v fine MANZANILLA PASADA. Also vg vinegar.

Harvey's Probably the largest sherry firm, having bought PALOMINO and de TERRY and having links with BOBADILLA and GARVEY. World-famous Bristol shippers of Bristol Cream and Bristol Milk sweet sherries, Club AMONTILLADO and Bristol Dry, which are medium, Luncheon Dry and Bristol FINO, which are not v dry, and Tico, an odd sweet *fino*. More to the point is their very good '1796' range of high quality sherries. Harvey's also control COCKBURN.

Henriques & Henriques Well-known independent madeira shippers of Funchal. The style of their wide range is rich and toothsome. It also includes a good dry aperitif , Ribeiro Seco; and v fine old *reservas*.

Hildalgo, Vinícola Ol¢ SANLUCAR family firm best known for vg pale MANZANILLA La Gitana.

Internacionales, Bodegas Once the pride of the now-defunct Rumasa company and incorporating such famous houses as BERTOLA, VARELA and DIEZ-MERITO, Internacionales is now the cornerstone of a new empire embracing Paternina and Franco-Españolas in Rioja. Its best-known sherries are the DUKE OF WELLINGTON range.

Jerez de la Frontera Centre of the sherry industry, between Cádiz and Seville in S Spain. The word 'sherry' is a corruption of the name, pronounced in Spanish 'hereth'. In French, Xérès.

Kopke The oldest port house, founded by a German in 1638. Fair quality vintage wines (**63 66 70 74 75 77 78 80 82 83 85 87 89**) and vg COLHEITAS.

Late-bottled vintage (LBV) Port of a single vintage kept in wood for twice as long as VINTAGE PORT (about 5 yrs), therefore lighter when bottled and ageing quicker. A real LBV will 'throw a crust' like vintage port. Few (eg WARRE, SMITH WOODHOUSE) qualify.

Leacock One of the oldest madeira shippers. The basic St John range is v fair; 10-yr-old Special Reserve MALMSEY and 13-yr-old BUAL are excellent.

Sherry, Port, Madeira and Food

By a quirk of fashion the wines of sherry, madeira and to some extent port are currently being left on the sidelines by a world increasingly hypnotized by a limited range of 'varietal' wines. Yet all three include wines with every quality of 'greatness', and far more gastronomic possibilities than the world seems to realize. It is notorious that for the price of eg a bottle of top-class white burgundy you can buy three of the very finest fino sherry, which with many dishes (see Wine & Food) will make an equally exciting accompaniment. Mature madeiras give the most lingering farewell of any wine to a splendid dinner. Tawny port is a wine of many uses, wonderful at sea. Perhaps it is because the New World cannot rival these Old World classics that they are left out of the headlines.

Lomelino Tarquinio Madeira shippers once famous for their collection of antique wines. Standard range is Dom Henriques, top range is Imperial.

Lustau One of the largest family-owned sherry *bodegas* in JEREZ, making many wines for other shippers, but with a vg Dry Lustau range (particularly the FINO and OLOROSO) and Jerez Lustau PALO CORTADO. Pioneer shippers of excellent ALMACENISTA and 'landed age' wines; AMONTILLADOS and *olorosos* aged in elegant bottles before shipping. *See also* Abad.

Macharnudo One of the best parts of the sherry v'yds, N of JEREZ, famous for wines of the highest quality, both FINO and OLOROSO.

Madeira Wine Company In 1913 all the British madeira firms (26 in total) amalgamated to survive hard times. Remarkably, three generations later, their wines, though cellared together, preserve their house styles.

Malmsey The sweetest form of madeira; dark amber, rich and honeyed yet with madeira's unique sharp tang.

Manzanilla Sherry, normally FINO, which has acquired a peculiar, bracing, salty character from being kept in *bodegas* at Sanlúcar de Barrameda, on the Guadalquivir estuary nr JEREZ.

Manzanilla Pasada A mature MANZANILLA half-way to an AMONTILLADO-style wine. At its best (eg La GUITA) one of the most appetizing sherries.

Marqués del Real Tesoro Old sherry firm, famous for MANZANILLA and AMONTILLADO, bought by the enterprising José Estevez. Shrugging off the current slump in sales he has built a spanking new *bodega* – the first in years.

Martinez Gassiot Port firm, subsidiary of COCKBURN, known esp for excellent, rich and pungent Directors 20-yr-old TAWNY, CRUSTED and LATE-BOTTLED VINTAGE.

Medina A SANLUCAR family *bodega* doing well; linking with small companies to become a major exporter.

Morgan A subsidiary of CROFT port, best known in France.

Niepoort Small (Dutch) family-run port house with long record of fine vintages (45 55 60 63 66 70 75 77 78 80 82 83 85) and exceptional COLHEITAS.

Noval, Quinta do Great Portuguese port house making intensely fruity, structured and elegant vintage port; a few ungrafted vines still at the QUINTA make a small quantity of Nacional – extraordinarily dark, full and slow-maturing wine. Also vg 20-yr-old TAWNY. Vintages: 55 58 60 63 66 67 70 75 78 82 85.

Offley Forrester *See* Forrester.

Oloroso Style of sherry, heavier and less brilliant than FINO when young, but maturing to greater richness and pungency. Naturally dry, but generally sweetened for sale, as CREAM.

Osborne Enormous Spanish firm with well-known brandy but also good sherries incl FINO QUINTA, Coquinero dry AMONTILLADO, 10 RF (or Reserva Familiae) OLOROSO. *See also* Duff Gordon.

Pale Cream Popular style of pale sherry made by sweetening FINO, pioneered by CROFT's Original.

Palo Cortado A style of sherry close to OLOROSO but with some of the character of an AMONTILLADO. Dry but rich and soft. Not often seen.

Palomino & Vergara Historic sherry shippers of JEREZ bought in '86 by HARVEY'S, best known for Palomino CREAM, Medium and Dry. Best wine: FINO Tio Mateo.

Pasada Style of FINO or MANZANILLA which is close to AMONTILLADO: a stronger, drier wine without FLOR character.

Ponche An aromatic *digestif* made with old sherry and brandy, flavoured with herbs and orange, and presented in eye-catching silvered bottles. *See* Caballero and de Soto.

Poças Junior Family port firm specializing in TAWNIES and COLHEITAS.

Puerto de Santa María Second city and port of the sherry area, with important *bodegas*.

PX Short for Pedro Ximénez, the grape part-dried in the sun used in JEREZ for sweetening blends.

Quarles Harris One of the oldest port houses, since 1680, now owned by the Symingtons *(see* Dow). Small quantities of LBV, mellow and well balanced. Vintages: 60 63 66 70 75 77 80 83 85.

Quinta Portuguese for 'estate'. Also used to denote vintage ports which are usually, but not invariably, from the estate's v'yds, made in good but not exceptional vintages.

Rainwater A fairly light, not very sweet blend of madeira – traditionally popular in N America.

Ramos-Pinto Dynamic small port house specializing in single-QUINTA TAWNIES of style and elegance.

Real Companhia Vinícola do Norte de Portugal AKA Royal Oporto Wine Co and Real Companhia Velha; the largest port house, with a long political history. Many brands and several QUINTAS, incl Quinta dos Carvalhos which makes TAWNIES and COLHEITAS. Vintage wines generally dismal.

Rebello Valente Name used for the VINTAGE PORT of ROBERTSON. Their vintage wines are light but elegant and well balanced, maturing rather early. Vintages: 55 60 63 66 67 70 72 75 77 80 83 85.

La Riva Distinguished firm of sherry shippers, now controlled by DOMECQ, making one of the best FINOS, Tres Palmas, among many good wines.

Rivero, JM The famous CZ brand of the oldest sherry house now belongs to Antonio Núñez, who makes and markets Rivero sherries as well as his own.

Robertson Subsidiary of SANDEMAN, shipping REBELLO VALENTE VINTAGE, LBV, Robertson's Privateer Reserve, Game Bird TAWNY, 10-yr-old Pyramid and 20-yr-old Imperial. Vintages: 63 66 67 70 72 75 77 80 83 85.

Rozes Port shippers controlled by Moët Hennessy. RUBY v popular in

France; also TAWNY. Vintages: **63 67 77 78** 81 83 85 87.

Ruby The youngest (and cheapest) style of port: simple, sweet and red. The best are vigorous and full of flavour. Others can be merely strong and rather thin.

Rutherford & Miles Madeira shippers with one of the best known of all BUAL wines: Old Trinity House. Also Old Custom House SERCIAL and Old Artillery House MALMSEY. All are relatively rich in style.

Sanchez Romate Family firm in JEREZ since 1781. Best known in Spanish-speaking world, esp for its brandy, Cardinal Mendoza. Makes good sherry – FINO Cristal, OLOROSO Don Antonio, AMONTILLADO NPU ('Non Plus Ultra').

Passing the Port
Vintage port is almost as much a ritual as a drink. It always needs to be decanted with great care (since the method of making it leaves a heavy deposit in the bottle). The surest way of doing this is by filtering it through clean muslin or a coffee filter-paper into either a decanter or a well-rinsed bottle. All except very old ports can safely be decanted the day before drinking. A week may not be too long. At table the decanter is traditionally passed from guest to guest clockwise. Vintage port can be immensely long-lived. Particularly good vintages older than those mentioned in the text include 04, 08, 11, 20, 27, 34, 35, 45, 50.

Sandeman Giant of the port trade and a major figure in the sherry one, owned by Seagram. Founder's Reserve is their well-known VINTAGE CHARACTER; TAWNIES are much better. Vintage wines are at least adequate – some of the old vintages were superlative (**55 60 63 66 67 70 75 77 80 82 85**). Of the sherries, Medium Dry AMONTILLADO is best-seller, Don FINO is vg, and a new range of wonderful luxury dry old sherries incl Royal Ambrosante, Imperial Corregidor, Royal Esmerelda. Not to be missed.

Sanlúcar Seaside sherry-town (*see* Manzanilla).

Sercial Madeira grape for the driest of the island's wines – a good aperitif.

Shortridge Lawton MADEIRA shippers with v dry Reserva SERCIAL and v tangy 10-yr-old Special Reservas.

Smith Woodhouse Port firm founded in 1784, now owned by the Symington family *(see* Dow). Gould Campbell is a subsidiary. Relatively light and easy wines incl His Majesty's Choice 20-yr-old, Old Lodge TAWNY. Vintages (v fine): **60 70 75 77 80 83 85**.

Solera System used in making both sherry and (in modified form) madeira, also some port. It consists of topping up progressively more mature barrels with slightly younger wine of the same sort, the object being to attain continuity in the final wine. Most commercial sherries are blends of several *solera* wines.

Soto, José de Best known for inventing PONCHE, this family firm also makes a range of good sherries, esp Dry OLOROSO.

Tawny A style of port aged for many yrs in wood (in contrast to VINTAGE PORT, which is aged in bottle) until tawny in colour. Many of the best are 20-yr-old. Low-price tawnies are blends of red and white ports. Taste the difference.

Taylor, Fladgate & Yeatman (Taylor's) Perhaps the best port shippers, particularly for their full, rich, long-lived VINTAGE wine and TAWNIES of stated age (40-yr-old, 20-yr-old, etc). Their Vargellas estate is said to give Taylor's its distinctive scent of violets. Vintages: **55 60 63 66 70 75 77 80 83 85**. Quinta de Vargellas is shipped unblended in certain (lesser) vintages (**67 72 74 76 78**). Also now Terra Feita single-QUINTA wine (82). Their LBV is also better than most.

Terry, Fernando A de Magnificent *bodega* at PUERTO DE SANTA MARIA with an undistinguished range of sherries (but famous brandies), bought in '86 by HARVEY'S.

Tio Pepe The most famous of FINO sherries *(see* Gonzalez Byass).

Valdespino Famous family-owned *bodega* at JEREZ, owner of the Inocente v'yd, making the excellent aged FINO of the same name. Tio Diego is their dry AMONTILLADO, Solera 1842 an OLOROSO, Del Carrascal their best *amontillado.* Matador is the name of their popular range.

Varela Sherry shippers best known for their Medium and CREAM.

Verdelho Madeira grape making fairly dry but soft wine without the piquancy of SERCIAL. A pleasant aperitif. Some glorious old vintage wines.

Vintage Character Somewhat misleading term used for a good quality, full and meaty port like a first-class RUBY, made by a version of the SOLERA system. Lacks the splendid 'nose' of VINTAGE PORT.

Vintage Port The best port of exceptional vintages is bottled after only 2 yrs in wood and matures very slowly, for up to 20 yrs or even more, in its bottle. It always leaves a heavy deposit and therefore needs decanting.

Warre Probably the oldest of all British port shippers (since 1670), now owned by the Symington family *(see* Dow). Fine, elegant, long-maturing vintage wines, a good TAWNY, Nimrod, and VINTAGE CHARACTER Warrior, and excellent LBV. Their single-v'yd Quinta da Cavadinha is a new departure. Vintages: **55 58 60 63 66 70 75 77 80 83 85**.

White Port Port made of white grapes, golden in colour. Formerly made sweet, now more often dry: a fair aperitif but a heavy one.

Williams & Humbert Famous and first-class sherry *bodega,* recently bought by Antonio BARBADILLO. Dry Sack (medium AMONTILLADO) is their best-seller. Pando is an excellent FINO. Canasta CREAM and Walnut BROWN are good in their class. Dos Cortados is their famous dry old OLOROSO.

Wisdom & Warter Not a magic formula for free wine, but an old *bodega* with good sherries, esp fine MANZANILLA La Guapa.

Masters of Wine

The Institute of Masters of Wine was founded in London in 1953 to provide an exacting standard of qualification for the British wine trade. A small minority pass its very stiff examinations, even after rigorous training, both theoretical and practical. (They must be able to identify wines 'blind', know how they are made, and also know the relevant EC and Customs regulations.) In all, only 162 people have qualified to become Masters of Wine. Twenty 'Masters' are women.

In 1988 the Institute, aided by a grant from the Madame Bollinger Foundation, opened its examinations for the first time to non-British candidates. The first to pass was a New Zealander. 'Master of Wine' (MW) should eventually become the equivalent of a Bachelor of Arts degree in the worldwide wine trade.

England

The English wine industry started again in earnest in the late 1960s after a pause of some 400 years. Well over a million bottles a year are now being made from some 2,500 acres; almost all white and generally Germanic or similar to Alsace in style (some more Loire-like), many from new German and French grape varieties designed to ripen well in cool weather. Natural acidity is often high, which means that good examples have a built-in ability (and need) to age. Four years is a good age for many, and up to ten for some. The annual Gore-Browne Trophy and medals are awarded for the best English wine. The English Vineyards Association (EVA) seal is worn by wines which pass quality tests. Since 1991 non-hybrid English wines may be labelled as 'Quality Wine', taking them into the European Community quality bracket for the first time. Beware 'British Wine', which is neither British nor wine, and has nothing to do with the following.

Adgestone nr Sandown (Isle of Wight)   Prize-winning 8.5 acre v'yd on chalky hill site. Vines are Müller-T, Reichensteiner, Seyval Bl. First vintage: 70. Light, fragrant, dryish wines age exceedingly well.

Ashburnham nr Battle (Sussex)   19 acres, planted '84, of Bacchus, Optima and Gutenborner. Medal winners in '89. Bought TENTERDEN in '91.

Astley Stourport-on-Severn (Worcestershire)   4.5 acres producing good Kerner. Won prizes for its 85s.

Avalon Shepton Mallet (Somerset)   Organically grown grapes. 2.3 acres.

Bardingley Staplehurst (Kent)   Red and rosé wines are the specialities of this 2.5-acre v'yd.

Barkham Manor Vineyard Uckfield (Sussex)   34 acres of Müller-T, Kerner, etc, planted '85–'87.

Barton Manor East Cowes (Isle of Wight)   10-acre v'yd producing an aromatic, medium-dry blend. Consistently good. Now an acre of Gewürz under plastic tunnels.

Beaulieu nr Lymington (Hampshire)   4.6-acre v'yd, principally of Müller-T, established in '60 by the Gore-Browne family on old monastic site.

Biddenden nr Tenterden (Kent)   20-acre mixed v'yd planted in '70, making crisp, medium-dry white of Müller-T and Ortega; also a rosé with Pinot N and a Reichensteiner sparkler. Makes wine for other growers, and good cider.

Bishops Waltham Bishops Waltham (Hampshire)   10.2 acres: Madeleine-Angevine, Reichensteiner and Schönburger.

Breaky Bottom nr Lewes (Sussex)   Good dry wines, esp Seyval Bl, from 5.5-acre v'yd. Has achieved a semi-cult following.

Bruisyard nr Saxmundham (Suffolk)   10 acres of Müller-T making medium-dry wines since '76.

Cane End Reading (Berkshire)   12 acres; wines made at CHILTERN VALLEY.

Carden Park nr Malpas (Cheshire)   7-acre v'yd in large 'leisure park' nr Welsh Marches. Good Seyval Bl.

Carr Taylor Vineyards nr Hastings (Sussex)   21 acres, planted '74. Gutenborner, Huxelrebe, Reichensteiner and Kerner. Also a Kerner-Reichensteiner *méthode champenoise* and Pinot N rosé. Exports to France.

Chiddingstone Edenbridge (Kent)   28-acre v'yd with stress on dry, French-style wines. *Barrique*-ageing is used.

Chilford Hundred Linton (nr Cambridge)   21 acres of Müller-T, Schönburger, Huxelrebe, Siegerrebe and Ortega making fairly dry wines since '74.

Chilsdown nr Chichester (Sussex) 10 acres of Müller-T, Reichensteiner and Seyval Bl making full, dry, French-style white since '74.

Chiltern Valley Wines Hambleden (Oxfordshire) Small modern winery drawing on 3 acres of own v'yds high up on the chalk, and neighbouring growers; producing 4 white wines, incl fine *liquoreux*. Gold medal in '88. Impressive quality.

Cranmore Cranmore (Isle of Wight) 5-acre v'yd planted with Müller-T and Gutenborner.

Denbies Wine Estate Ranmore Common (Surrey) 250-acre venture using mix of German varieties and advice from Trier. England's biggest v'yd, with first harvest in '89.

Ditchling nr Hassocks (Sussex) 5-acre v'yd well reputed for consistency. Good Müller-T. Leased to ROCK LODGE.

Elham Valley nr Canterbury (Kent) 2-acre v'yd: Kerner, Madeleine-Angevine, Seyval Bl, good Müller-T.

Elmham Park nr East Dereham (Norfolk) 6-acre v'yd belonging to a wine merchant/fruit farmer, producing Müller-T, Madeleine-Angevine, etc. Mosel-style light, dry, flowery wines. First vintage: 74. Also makes a fine dry cider.

Fonthill Salisbury (Wiltshire) 9.5 acres; wines made at LAMBERHURST, winning medals.

Gamlingay nr Sandy (Bedfordshire) 8.5 acres of Müller-T, Reichensteiner and Scheurebe since '70.

Halfpenny Green Stourbridge (W Midlands) 3 acres of vines planted with Huxelrebe, Reichensteiner and Seyval Bl.

Hambledon nr Petersfield (Hampshire) The first modern English v'yd, planted in '51 on a chalk slope with advice from Champagne. Grapes are Chard, Pinot N and Seyval Bl. Now 15.4 acres. Fairly dry wines.

Harden Farm Penshurst (Kent) 18 acres of Schönburger, Bacchus, Reichensteiner, Regner and Huxelrebe.

Headcorn (Kent) 10-acre medal-winning v'yd: Seyval Bl, Huxelrebe, etc.

Helions Vineyard Helion's Bumpstead (Essex) One acre, 50/50 Müller-T and Reichensteiner; vg dry wine.

High Weald Winery Lenham (Kent) No vines, but an influential winemaker (proprietor Christopher Lindlar) for several growers.

Lamberhurst Priory nr Tunbridge Wells (Kent) England's leading winery, with 55 acres, planted '72. Largely Müller-T, Seyval Bl and Reichensteiner. Production capacity approx half a million bottles, incl winemaking for several other v'yds. Also makes Horam Manor, 4.4 acres at Heathfield, Sussex. A regular prize-winner. *Méthode champenoise* and 89 Schönburger are latest news.

Leeford Vineyards nr Battle (Sussex) 35-acre v'yd producing wines under Saxon Valley label.

Loddiswell Kingsbridge (Devon) 6 acres of vines with an acre planted under plastic tunnels. Grapes incl Müller-T, Seyval Bl and Reichensteiner.

Moorlynch nr Bridgewater (Somerset) 11 acres produce award-winning wines from an idyllic farm.

New Hall nr Maldon (Essex) 87 acres of mixed farm planted with Huxelrebe, Müller-T and Pinot N. Experimental reds.

Nutbourne Manor nr Pulborough (Sussex) 12.5 acres: elegant and tasty Schönburger, Bacchus and Huxelrebe. Sussex Reserve is a new blend. Good wines made by HIGH WEALD.

Penshurst nr Tunbridge Wells (Kent) 12 acres of the usual varieties, in production since '76.

Pilton Manor nr Shepton Mallet (Somerset) 19-acre hillside v'yd, chiefly Müller-T and Seyval Bl, planted '66.

Plumpton Agricultural College nr Lewes (Sussex) 2-acre experimental v'yd at college for winemakers.

Pulham nr Norwich (Norfolk) 12.6-acre v'yd planted '73; principally

Müller-T, Auxerrois and experimental Bacchus. Award-winning wines using Magdalen label.

Queen Court Faversham (Kent) 7-acre brewery-owned v'yd of Müller-T.

Rock Lodge nr Haywards Heath (Sussex) 3-acre v'yd of Müller-T and Reichensteiner making dry white since '70, *méthode champenoise* and Late Harvest. *See also* Ditchling.

St-George's Waldron, Heathfield (E Sussex) 15 acres, planted '79. Müller-T etc and some Gewürz. Well-publicized young venture has sold wine to Japan and elsewhere.

Sandhurst Cranbrook (Kent) A family-owned mixed farm with 8.5 acres of vines and 80 acres of hops, plus apple orchards, cereals and sheep.

Sedlescombe Robertsbridge (Sussex) 5.5 acres: claims to be England's first organic v'yd.

Sharpham Totnes (Devon) 5 acres of vines. Wines made at THREE CHOIRS.

Shawsgate Framlingham (Suffolk) 17 well-found acres incl Chard. Wins awards.

Staple nr Canterbury (Kent) 7 acres, mainly Müller-T. Some Huxelrebe and Reichensteiner. Dry and fruity wines of fine quality.

Tenterden nr Tenterden (Kent) 17 acres, planted '77. Six wines from v dry to sweet, incl Müller-T, oak-aged Seyval Bl ('91 Gore-Browne Trophy winner), Gutenborner, rosé and sparkling. *See* Ashburnham.

Thames Valley Twyford (Berkshire) 17-acre v'yd of Müller-T, Pinot N, Schönburger, etc. Some serious reds and Late Harvests.

Three Choirs nr Newent (Gloucestershire) 45 acres of Müller-T, Seyval Bl, Schönburger, Reichensteiner. Successful award-winning wines incl Bacchus Dry and Huxelrebe.

Westbury nr Reading (Berkshire) 12.5 acres of a mixed farm. 11 varieties since '75, incl England's first Pinot N red and Müller-T-Seyval.

Wickham nr Shedfield (Hampshire) 9.5-acre v'yd: incl Bacchus, Faberrebe, Schönburger, Seyval Bl.

Wootton nr Wells (Somerset) 6-acre v'yd of Schönburger, Müller-T, Seyval Bl, etc, making consistently good, fresh, fruity wines since '73.

The current trend towards 'low-alcohol' wines and beers, from which most alcohol has been removed by artificial means, should be a golden opportunity for wines that are naturally lower in alcohol than the 12 or 13 degrees expected in most table wines. Germany is the prime example; England is another. Their best wines, with plenty of fruity acidity, do not need high alcohol to make an impact. They are today's logical choice.

Luxembourg

Luxembourg's 3,285 acres of vineyards are planted on limestone soils on the left bank of the Moselle. High-yielding Elbling and Rivaner (Müller-Thurgau) vines dominate, but there are also significant acreages of Auxerrois, Pinot Blanc, Pinot Gris, Riesling and Gewürztraminer. These give light to medium-bodied (10.5–11.5°) dry, white wines in a French style. Of all Luxembourg's wines 70% are produced and marketed by the Vins Moselle cooperative. The Domaine et Tradition estates association founded in 1988 is working to promote fine quality Luxembourg wines from the noble grape varieties. The last five vintages in Luxembourg were all good, the 1990 vintage outstanding.

Best producers: M Bastian, Caves Gales, Clos des Rochers, Clos Mon Vieux Moulin, Aly Duhr et Fils, Château de Schengen, Sunnen-Hoffmann.

Central & Southeast Europe

LANGENLOIS — WEINVIERTEL

WACHAU — Vienna

Austria — MATRAAL

SOMLÓ — Budapest

SOPRON

BURGENLAND

Graz — BALATON — Hungary

STYRIA

LUTOMER — VILLANYI-PECS

Ljubljana

SLAVONIA

SLOVENIA — VOJVODIN

Trieste — Zagreb

CROATIA

BOSNIA-HERZEGOVINA

DALMATIA

Sarajevo

Split

Adriatic Sea

MONTENEG

Dubrovnik

CORFU

To say that parts of the region covered by this map are somewhat provisional these days is an understatement. But new regional autonomies and new statehoods are rapidly being followed by higher aspirations. So far Hungary and Czechoslovakia, as well as Bulgaria, have taken the lead in what has become an area to follow with fascination.

In this section references are arranged country by country, all referring back to the map on this page. Labelling in all the countries involved, except Greece and Cyprus, is broadly based on the international pattern of place name plus grape variety. Main grape varieties are therefore included alongside areas and other terms in the alphabetical listings. Quality ratings are given where experience justifies more than a single, everyday star.

Austria

Austria has re-emerged, after a difficult period in the 1980s, as a vigorous but well-regulated producer of hearty white wines, including aromatic ones in the German style (but more potent) and liquorous ones closer to Sauternes. Her red wines have yet to make an international reputation but this will come. New laws, passed in 1986 and revised for the 1991 vintage, include curbs on yields (Germany please copy) and impose higher levels of ripeness for each category than their German counterparts. Many regional names, introduced under the 1986 law, are still unfamiliar outside Austria.

Recent vintages

1991 Good to average quality along with a few vg wines from Burgenland.

1990 One of the best vintages of the last 50 yrs.

1989 Some weather problems reduced crop. Quality fair to good, best in Burgenland and Styria.

1988 Good quantity, some excellent wines.

1987 A third small harvest, but quality is reasonable.

1986 An outstanding vintage in most cases, though small.

1985 A small but excellent quality harvest.

Altsteirischer Mischsatz Styrian term for a GEMISCHTER SATZ.

Apetlon Burgenland w (r) s/sw sw ★→⋆⋆ Village of the SEEWINKEL making good whites and some reds on sandy soil, incl vg sweet wines, esp *Prädikat* wines from LENZ MOSER.

Ausbruch Term used for traditional, v sweet wines between *Beerenauslese* and *Trockenbeerenauslese* (*see* Germany) in richness but with the vinous quality and alcoholic strength of Sauternes.

Baden Vienna r w dr sw ★→⋆⋆⋆ Town and wine region S of VIENNA now incl in THERMENREGION.

Blauburger Middling-quality red grape. Best producer: W B S Retz.

Blauer Burgunder The Pinot N. Best from BURGENLAND, KAMPTAL-DONAULAND, THERMENREGION.

Blaufränkisch Reputedly the Gamay grape, though v different to taste. Gives powerful reds – often *barrique*-aged. 'Kékfrankos' in Hungary.

Blauer Portugieser With BLAUFRANKISCH, one of the two main red-wine grapes of Austria, giving dark but rather characterless wine. The best is from Haugsdorf, WEINVIERTEL. Best grower: Lust.

Bouvier Native Austrian grape giving soft, low-acid but aromatic wine, esp for *Beerenauslese* and *Trockenbeerenauslese.*

Bründlmayer Large (123-acre) estate in KAMPTAL-DONAULAND. Excellent wines in a variety of Austrian and international styles.

Burgenland r w dr sw ★→⋆⋆⋆ Region of 45,000 acres on the Hungarian border, with ideal conditions for sweet wines around the NEUSIEDLER SEE. Four wine regions: Neusiedlersee (E of the lake), Neusiedlersee-Hügelland (W shore and around EISENSTADT) and Mittel- and Südburgenland (RUST and the SEEWINKEL). 'Noble rot' occurs regularly on both sides of the Neusiedler See (but not in Mittel- or Südburgenland) and AUSBRUCHE, *Beerenauslesen*, etc are abundant. (*See also* Illmitz, Mörbisch, Rust, etc.)

Buschenschank Country cousin of Viennese HEURIGE.

Donauland-Carnuntum Unwieldy new name for the Danube (Donau) valley wine region incl KLOSTERNEUBURG.

Dürnstein w dr sw ⋆⋆→⋆⋆⋆ Wine centre of the WACHAU with a famous ruined castle and the important FREIE WEINGARTNER. Some of Austria's best whites, esp Rheinriesling and GRUNER VELTLINER.

Eisenstadt Burgenland w (r) dr sw ⋆⋆→⋆⋆⋆ Capital of BURGENLAND and historic seat of ESTERHAZY family. Best growers: Barmherzigen Brüder.

Esterházy Noble and historic family (patrons of Haydn) whose AUSBRUCH and other BURGENLAND wines are often of superlative quality.

Falkenstein *See* Weinviertel.

Freie Weingärtner Important coop in DURNSTEIN in the WACHAU. Large quantities of excellent GRUNER VELTLINER and RIES (**→***).

Gemischter Satz A blend of grapes. This is the wine of the HEURIGEN.

Gols Largest wine-producing commune in Austria, on the E side of the NEUSIEDLER SEE. Best producers: Heinrich, Nittnaus, Stiegelmar.

Grinzing Vienna w ** DYA   Suburb of VIENNA, once famous for quality wines, now principally for often delicious, lively HEURIGE wines.

Grüner Veltliner Austria's most characteristic white grape (36% of white v'yds): makes short-lived but at best spicy, flowery, racy, vital wine.

Gumpoldskirchen Vienna w (r) dr sw **→***   Pretty resort S of VIENNA with wines of great character from ROTGIPFLER and ZIERFANDLER grapes. *See* Thermenregion.

Heurige Means both 'new wine' and the tavern where it is drunk. Traditionally made from a mixture of grapes. *See* Gemischter Satz.

Hirtzberger, Franz Top WACHAU grower with 22 acres at Spitz. RIES (Hochrain, Singerriedl) and gutsy GRUNER VELTLINER.

Igler, Hans Coming name for reds (BLAUFRANKISCH, Cab) at Deutschkreuz in MITTELBURGENLAND.

Illmitz Sweet wine centre of the SEEWINKEL: *Beerenauslese*, *Trockenbeerenauslese* and 'Riedmandl' wines. Best producers: Kracher, Opitz.

Jamek, Josef The man who brought dry white wines to the WACHAU in the '50s. Controversial for his use of malolactic fermentation for RIES and GRUNER VELTLINER (**→***).

Kahlenberg Vienna w **→***   Village and v'yd hill N of VIENNA, formerly celebrated for quality, now more famous for HEURIGEN.

Kamptal-Donauland w (r) dr sw *→**   Wine region around KREMS and the Kamp valley, a tributary of the Danube (Donau). Pleasant GRUNER VELTLINER and RIES Best growers: BRUNDLMAYER, Dolle, Hiedler, Jurtschitsch, MALAT-BRUNDLMAYER, Mantler, Nigl, SALOMON, Topf.

Klöch Styria p w (r) *→***   The chief wine town of STYRIA, the SE province.

Klosterneuburg Donauland r w *→***   District just N of VIENNA, with a famous monastery, a wine college and a research station.

Kloster Und New wine college and tasting centre in restored Capuchin monastery at KREMS, run by Erich SALOMON.

Krems Donauland w *→***   Town and district just E of the WACHAU with good GRUNER VELTLINER and Rheinriesling, esp from Austria's biggest WINZERGENOSSENSCHAFT. Best growers: Aigner, Ditz, SALOMON.

Langenlois Langenlois r w *→**   Chief town of the KAMPTAL with many modest and some vg wines, esp peppery GRUNER VELTLINER and Rheinriesling from loess and volcanic soils around Zöbing. Reds less interesting, but NB Pinot N from BRUNDLMAYER.

Lenz Moser Major grower now in the 5th generation. Lenz Moser III invented a high vine system. His grandson, Lenz Moser V, makes good to excellent wine at Rohrendorf (nr KREMS), APETLON and elsewhere. Leases the Schlossweingut Malteser Ritterorden (formerly the estate of the Knights of Malta) at MAILBERG. Experiments with Cab S, Merlot and Pinot N. Took over SIEGENDORF in '88.

Mailberg Weinviertel r w **   Town of the WEINVIERTEL known for lively, light wine (red and white) and the Malteser Ritterorden Bordeaux blends.

Malat-Bründlmayer, Gerald Major (50-acre) grower at Furth-Palt in KAMPTAL-DONAULAND. Successful 'international' wines: Chard, Pinot N, Cab S.

Mayer, Franz *→***   VIENNA's biggest grower, with 90 acres. HEURIGE wines but also serious RIES and Chard.

Mittelburgenland The best region for BLAUFRANKISCH and now a little Cab S. Best growers: Gesellmann, Igler. *See* Burgenland.

Mörbisch Burgenland r w dr sw *→*** Leading wine village of BURGENLAND. Good sweet wines. Reds and dry whites not inspiring. But NB oak-aged BLAUFRANKISCH from Schindler, the Burgermeister.

Morillon Name given to Chard in STYRIA.

Müller-Thurgau Far less interesting than GRUNER VELTLINER; represents 10% of all Austria's vines.

Muskat-Ottonel The strain of Muscat grape grown in E Europe, incl Austria. Can be dry and pungent. Also interesting *Prädikat* wines.

Neuburger Popular white grape: pleasant wine in KREMS and LANGENLOIS, but soft and coarse in BURGENLAND. Excellent *Prädikat* wines.

Neusiedler See A shallow lake in flat, sandy country on the Hungarian border. Autumn mists encourage botrytis in the wines of BURGENLAND. Under the new law, it is the centre of 2 wine regions: *see* Burgenland.

Niederösterreich Lower Austria: ie all the NE corner of the country, with 5 wine regions: DONAULAND-CARNUNTUM, KAMPTAL-DONAULAND, THERMEN-REGION, WACHAU, WEINVIERTEL.

Nikolaihof Estate in Mautern in the WACHAU with top RIES and GRUNER VELTLINER wines. Owns a small chunk of Austria's most famous v'yd: RIED Steiner Hunt in KREMS-Stein.

Nüssdorf Vienna w ** Suburb of VIENNA with well-known HEURIGEN. RIED Nüssberg was a first-growth in Imperial times.

Oggau Burgenland w (r) sw **→*** One of the wine centres of BURGENLAND, famous for dry whites and big reds.

Pichler, Franz X Top WACHAU grower with 11 acres at Oberloiben nr DÜRNSTEIN. RIES, GRUNER VELTLINER and Sauv Bl.

Prager, Franz With JAMEK an innovator of dry white wine in the WACHAU.

Retz Weinviertel w (r) * Wine centre of the WEINVIERTEL, known for GRUNER VELTLINER, etc. Its particularly arid climate makes it good also for big reds. Best grower: W B S Retz.

Ried Single v'yd: when named on the label it is usually a good one.

Riesling When used alone it is German Riesling. Welschriesling, which is almost always inferior, is labelled as such.

Rotgipfler Good and high-flavoured grape peculiar to GUMPOLDSKIRCHEN. Used with ZIERFANDLER to make powerful but lively whites. V heavy or sweet on its own.

Rust Burgenland w (r) dr sw *→*** Most famous wine centre of BURGENLAND, justly famous since the 17th C for its AUSBRUCH, often made of mixed grapes. Increasing amounts of red wine now from anything from the BLAUFRANKISCH to Pinot N, Nebbiolo or even Syrah. Best producers: Schandl, Triebaumer (Paul *and* Ernst), Wenzel.

St-Laurent Traditional Austrian red grape, faintly Muscat-flavoured.

Salomon, Fritz **→*** Top grower of oak-aged RIES, WEISSBURGUNDER and Gewürz at Weinkelleri Undhof in the Danube valley nr KREMS. The estate is run by Erich S, a partner in the KLOSTER UND wine college.

Sattler, Willi Leading S STYRIAN grower at Gamlitz. Celebrated for Sauv Bl and MORILLON (alias Chard) innocent of oak.

Schilcher Pleasant sharp rosé, a speciality of W STYRIA. Best from Gundersdorf and Deutschlandsberg.

Schloss Grafenegg w dr sw **→*** Famous castle and estate of the Metternich family nr KREMS. Good standard whites; a few *Auslesen*; some dry (*trocken*).

Seewinkel 'Lake corner': the sandy district around the NEUSIEDLER SEE, famous for sweet wines.

Siegendorf, Klosterkeller First-class 60-acre BURGENLAND wine estate experimenting with Cab S and Merlot.

Sievering Vienna w ** Picturesque suburb of VIENNA with notable HEURIGEN.

Spätrot Another name for the ZIERFANDLER grape.

Spitzenwein Top wine – as opposed to TISCHWEIN (ordinary table wine).

Stift Monastery. These still are v important in Austria's winemaking, combining tradition and high standards with modern resources.

Styria (Steiermark) Province in the SE, not famous for quality wine until v recently. Three wine regions: Süd (south), Süd-Ost (southeast) and West-Steiermark. Sauv Bl, Chard (*see* Morillon) and Muskateller showing promise here. Top producers: Graf Stürgkh, Gross, Lackner-Tinnacher, Neumeister, Platzer, Polz, Sattler, Tement.

Südburgenland Wine region in S of BURGENLAND, away from the lake. Some steep slopes. Grapes include Welschriesling and BLAUFRANKISCH.

Thallern Vienna w (r) dr sw ***→**** Village near GUMPOLDSKIRCHEN and trade name of wines from Stift Heiligenkreuz.

Thermenregion New name for region S of VIENNA, incl BADEN and GUMPOLDSKIRCHEN. Some good, lively, high-flavoured wines; whites best from ROTGIPFLER and ZIERFANDLER grapes. Reds best from BLAUER PORTUGIESER, Cab S, Pinot N, esp from Tattendorf and Teesdorf. Top producers: (whites) Biegler, Kurz, Schafler, Schellmann, Stadlmann; (reds) Fischer, Gisperg, Reinisch. *See also* Gumpoldskirchen.

Tischwein Everyday wine, as opposed to SPITZENWEIN.

Traiskirchen Vienna w (r) ** Village nr GUMPOLDSKIRCHEN with similar wine.

Veltliner *See* Grüner Veltliner.

Vienna (Wien) The capital city, with 1,750 acres of v'yds in its suburbs to supply its cafés and HEURIGEN.

Vöslau Thermenregion r (w) * Spa town S of BADEN (and VIENNA) known for its reds. Best are Cab (NB Schlumberger), Pinot N, ZWEIGELT. Also light wines of BLAUER PORTUGIESER, etc.

Wachau Wine region on the bank S of the Danube round DURNSTEIN with cliff-like slopes giving some of Austria's best whites, esp RIES and GRUNER VELTLINER. Best growers: Alzinger, Hirtzberger, JAMEK, Knoll, NIKOLAIHOF, PICHLER, PRAGER, Schmidl.

Weinviertel 'Wine quarter': name given to the huge and productive district between VIENNA and the Czech border. Mainly light, acidic white wines. Formerly divided into Falkenstein-Matzen (E) and RETZ (W).

Weissburgunder Alias Pinot Bl. Increasingly used for solid, often dry wines, but also good in sweet *Prädikat* wines.

Winzergenossenschaft Growers' coop.

Zierfandler White grape of high flavour, peculiar to the BADEN area. Used in a blend with ROTGIPFLER.

Zweigelt Productive red variety. If heavily pruned, can make juicy, cherry-scented wine.

Hungary

Hungary is the unquestioned regional leader in terms of both tradition and quality. Magyar taste is for fiery, hearty, full-blooded wines, which their traditional grapes (mainly white) perfectly provide, but which are being superseded in many cases by 'safer' international varieties. Since the end of Communism several French, German and other concerns have bought land or entered into joint ventures, especially in Hungary's most famous region, Tokay. Expect to hear much more of this. Meanwhile visitors to the country will find plenty of excellent wines in the old style.

Alföld Hungary's Great Plain, producer of much everyday wine and some much better, esp at HAJOS, HELVECIA, KECSKEMET, KISKUNHALAS, Szeged.

Aszú Rotten: applied to v sweet wines esp TOKAY (Tokaji), where the *aszú* is late-picked and 'nobly rotten' as in Sauternes. (*See* page 47.)

Aszú Eszencia Tokaji br sw **** 57 63 The second highest quality of TOKAY commercially available: superb amber wine like a cross between Sauternes and sherry.

Badacsony Balaton w dr sw **→**** Famous 426-m hill on the N shore of L BALATON whose basalt soil can give rich, high-flavoured white wines, among Hungary's best.

Balaton Balaton r w dr sw *→**** Hungary's inland sea and Europe's largest freshwater lake. Many wines take its name and many are good. The ending 'i' (eg Balatoni, Egri) is the equivalent of -er in Johannisberger.

Balatonboglár Balaton r w p *→** Progressive cellars with sound, modern-style wines, esp whites.

Balatonfüred Balaton w (r) dr sw ** Town on the N shore of Lake BALATON, centre of the Balatonfüred-CSOPAK district. Good but softer, less fiery wines.

Bikavér Eger r * 'Bulls Blood': the historic name of the best-selling red wine of EGER: at best full-bodied and well balanced, but dismally variable in its export version today.

Csopák Village next to BALATONFURED, with similar wines but drier whites, incl good Chard, Sauv Bl, SZURKEBARAT, etc.

Debrö Mátraalya w sw ** Town of the MATRAALYA famous for its mellow, aromatic HARSLEVELU.

Eger Eger district r w dr sw *→** Best-known red wine centre of N Hungary; fine baroque city of cellars full of BIKAVER. Also delicate white LEANYKA (perhaps its best product today), OLASZRIZLING, Chard and Cab.

Eszencia The fabulous quintessence of TOKAY (Tokaji): intensely sweet wine from grapes wizened by botrytis. Formerly grape juice of v low, if any, alcoholic strength, reputed to have miraculous properties: this is now called NEKTAR. Today's Eszencia must attain 6% alcohol, which makes, in reality, a super ASZU Eszencia.

Ezerjó The grape grown at MOR to make one of Hungary's best dry white wines ; potentially distinguished, fragrant and fine.

Felsobabad Regional cellar, S of Budapest with authentic, fragrant Pinot N.

Furmint The classic grape of TOKAY (Tokaji), with great flavour and fire, also grown for table wine on Lake BALATON.

Gyongyos Mátraalya w (r) ** Northern district offering real promise in dry whites of SZURKEBARAT, Chard, MUSKOTALY, etc.

Hajós Alföld r * Village in S Hungary known for good, lively, Cab S reds of medium body and ageing potential. Also a good Pinot N.

Hárslevelü The 'lime-leaved' grape used at DEBRO and as the second main grape of TOKAY. Gentle, mellow wine.

Helvécia (Kecskemet) Historic ALFOLD cellars. V'yds ungrafted: phylloxera cannot negotiate sandy soil. Whites and rosés modernist; reds traditional.

Hungarovin Wine traders with huge cellars at Budafok near Budapest, selling mainly 'western varietals'.

Kadarka The commonest red grape of Hungary, grown in vast quantities for light, everyday wine on the plains in the S; capable of ample flavour and interesting maturity (eg at SZEKSZARD and VILLANY).

Kecskemet Major town of the ALFOLD. Much everyday wine, some better.

Kékfrankos Hungarian for Blaufränkisch; reputedly related to Gamay. Makes good, light and full-bodied reds in many areas, esp at SOPRON on the Austrian border, and is used in 'Bulls Blood' at EGER.

Kéknyelü High-flavoured white grape making the best and 'stiffest' wine of Mt BADACSONY. It should be fiery and spicy stuff.

Kiskunhalas Huge-scale plains winery, good esp for KADARKA.

Különleges Minöség Special quality: highest official quality grading.

Leányka Old Hungarian white grape also grown in Transylvania. Makes admirable aromatic, faintly Muscat dry wine in many areas. Kiral ('Royal') Leányka is supposedly superior.

Mátraalya Wine district in the foothills of the Mátra range in N Hungary, incl DEBRO, GYONGYOS and Nagyrede.

Mecsekalja District in S Hungary, known for the good whites of PECS.

Médoc Noir Grape, apparently similar to Merlot, used to make sweet red at VILLANY and in the blend of BIKAVER at EGER.

Minöségi Bor Quality wine. Hungary's *appellation contrôlée.*

Mór N Hungary w dr ★★→★★★ Town famous for its fresh dry EZERJO. Now also Ries, Sauv Bl.

Muskotály Makes light, though long-lived, Muscat wine at TOKAY (Tokaji) and EGER. Very occasionally makes ASZU at Tokay.

Nagyburgundi Literally 'great burgundy' – an indigenous grape and not Pinot N as sometimes thought. Makes sound, solid wine in S Hungary, esp around VILLANY and SZEKSZARD.

Nagyrede Mátraalya Foothill winery. Competent and modern.

Nektar Under new laws, this is the term for the unfermented juice that used to be called ESZENCIA.

Olaszrizling Hungarian name for the Italian Riesling or Welschriesling.

Oporto Red grape increasingly used for soft, jammy wines to drink young.

Pécs Mecsek w (r) dr ★→★★ Major wine city of S Hungary. Good source of OLASZRIZLING, Pinot Bl, etc.

Pezsgö Sparkling wine, mostly made by transfer method, but can often be v palatable.

Pinot Noir Normally means NAGYBURGUNDI. But *see* Felsobabad.

Puttonyos The measure of sweetness in TOKAY (Tokaji). A 7-gal container from which ASZU is added to SZAMORODNI. One 'putt' makes it sweetish; 6 v sweet indeed. Each putt is a 20–25 kilo hod of ASZU grapes added to 136 litres of base wine. The minimum now made is 3 putts, the maximum 6.

Siklos Southern district known for its white wines.

Somló N Hungary w dr ★★ Isolated small v'yd district N of BALATON, making white wines – formerly of high repute – from FURMINT.

Sopron W Hungary r ★★ Little enclave S of the Neusiedler See (*see* Austria). Light KEKFRANKOS reds and some Austrian-style sweet wines.

Szamorodni Word meaning 'as it comes'; used to describe TOKAJI without the addition of ASZU grapes. Can be dry or (fairly) sweet, depending upon proportion of *aszú* grapes naturally present. Sold as an aperitif.

Szürkebarát Literally means 'grey friar': Pinot G, which makes rich (not necessarily sweet) wine in the BADACSONY v'yds and elsewhere.

Szekszárd r ★★ District in south-central Hungary. KADARKA red wine which needs age (say 3–4 yrs). Also good organic wines.

Tokay (Tokaji) Tokaji w dr sw ★★→★★★★ The ASZU is Hungary's famous strong sweet wine, comparable to a maderized Sauternes, from hills in the NE close to the Soviet border. *See* Aszú, Eszencia, Furmint, Puttonyos, Szamorodni.

Villány Siklos r p (w) ★★ Southernmost town of Hungary and well-known centre of red wine production. Villányi Burgundi is largely KEKFRANKOS and can be good. Cabs S and F are v promising. *See also* Nagyburgundi.

Bulgaria

In little more than a decade Bulgaria has become one of the world's top four wine exporters, exporting 85% of production. Enormous new vineyards and industrial-sized wineries have overwhelmed an old, if embattled, wine tradition. The formerly state-run and state-subsidized wineries learnt almost everything from the New World and offer Cabernet, Chardonnay and other varieties at bargain prices. Controlled appellation ('Controliran') wines, introduced in 1985, have been joined by wood-aged 'Reserve' bottlings. A drop in sales to the USSR has led to renewed emphasis on quality wines, somewhat higher prices and a ban on planting outside the 27 Controliran regions. A tasting in London in 1989 demonstrated the ability of top red wines to improve for 15–20 years. In 1990 the organizing monopoly, Vinprom, was disbanded to give wineries autonomy. A brisk air of competition is now provoking even greater efforts towards quality.

Asenovgrad Main MAVRUD-producing cellar on the outskirts of PLOVDIV.

Bourgas Black Sea resort and source of easy whites, Aligoté and a MUSCAT-Ugni Bl blend.

Cabernet The Bordeaux grape is highly successful in N Bulgaria. Dark, vigorous, fruity and well-balanced wine drinks well young, but top qualities mature well for a surprisingly long time.

Chardonnay Rather less successful. V dry but full-flavoured wine, improves with a yr in bottle. Some recent oak-aged examples are promising.

Dimiat The common native white grape, grown in the E towards the coast. Agreeable dry white without memorable character.

Euxinograd (Château) Ageing cellar on the coast, part of the ex-King's palace. Wines reserved for State functions and top restaurants.

Fetiaska The same grape as Romania's Feteasca and Hungary's Leányka. Pleasant pale wine, best a trifle sweet, sold as Donau Perle.

Gamza Good red grape. Aged wines, esp from SUHINDOL, can be delicious.

Han Krum The most modern makers of white wine, esp oak-aged CHARD, nr VARNA in the east.

Haskovo Southern region, principal source of MERLOT for export.

Iskra Sparkling wine, normally sweet but fair quality. Red, white or rosé.

Kadarka Grape chiefly exported to Germany as sweet bulk red .

Karlovo Town famous for its 'Valley of Roses' and pleasant white MISKET.

Khan Krum *See* Han Krum.

Korten Subregion of SLIVEN. Korten CAB is firmer than most.

Mavrud Grape variety and darkly plummy red from S Bulgaria, esp ASENOVGRAD. Can mature 20 yrs. Considered the country's best.

Melnik City of the extreme southeast and its highly prized grape. Dense red wine that locals say can be carried in a handkerchief. Needs at least 5 yrs and lasts for 15. Also CAB, ripe and age-worthy.

Merlot Soft red grape variety grown mainly in HASKOVO in the south.

Misket RIES x DIMIAT cross; makes mildly aromatic wines, often used to fatten up white blends.

Muscat Ottonel Normal Muscat grape, grown in E Bulgaria for medium-sweet, fruity whites.

Novi Pazar Controlled appellation CHARD winery nr VARNA with finer wines.

Novo Selo Controlian good GAMZA from the north.

Oriachovitza Major southern area for Controlian CAB-MERLOT. Rich savoury red best at 4–5 yrs. Recent RESERVE Cab releases have been good, esp 84, 86.

Pamid The light, soft everyday red of the southwest and northwest.

Pavlikeni Northern wine town with a prestigious estate specializing in GAMZA and CAB of high quality. Also light 'Country wine' blend of MERLOT and Gamza.

Petrich Warm SW region for soft, fragrant MELNIK, also blended with CAB.

Pleven Northern cellar important for PAMID, GAMZA and CAB. Also Bulgaria's wine research station.

Plovdiv Southern wine town and region, source of good CAB.

Provadya Another centre for good white wines, esp dry CHARD.

Rkatziteli One of Russia's favourite white grapes for strong, sweet wine. Produces bulk dry or medium whites in NE Bulgaria.

Reserve Used on labels of selected and oak-aged wines.

Riesling (In Bulgaria) normally refers to Italian Riesling (Welschriesling). Some Rhine Riesling is grown: now made into Germanic-style white.

Russe Northeastern wine town on the Danube. Fresh whites, esp

Welschriesling-MISKET blend and straight medium-dry Welschriesling. Now also reds, esp Controliran Yantra Valley CAB S.

Sakar Southeastern region for quality MERLOT, some of Bulgaria's best.

Sauvignon Blanc Grown in E Bulgaria, recently released for export.

Schumen Bulgaria's largest white wine cellar, esp noted for SAUV BL. Also makes rather good brandy.

Sliven Southern region, esp for CAB. Also MERLOT and Pinot N. Merlot is blended with Pinot N in a 'Country Wine'.

Sonnenkuste Brand of medium-sweet white sold in Germany.

Suhindol PAVLIKENI's neighbour, site of Bulgaria's first coop (1909). Good cellar for GAMZA, CAB and PAMID.

Sungarlare E town giving its name to a dry Controliran MISKET; also CHARD.

Svishtov CAB-producing winery by the Danube in the north. A front-runner in Bulgaria's controlled appellation wines.

Sylvaner Some pleasant, dry Sylvaner is exported as 'Klosterkeller'.

Tamianka Sweet white wine based on aromatic grape also of this name; the same as Romania's Tamiioasa.

Targovichte Independent white wine cellar near SCHUMEN. Concentrates on medium and sweet wines.

Tirnovo Strong, sweet, dessert red wine.

Varna Major coastal appellation for CHARD, SAUV BL. Also Allgoté, Ugni Bl.

Czechoslovakia

While there is little or no tradition of exporting from this mainly white wine producing country, there are good wines to be had, especially from Moravia, the central province (capital Brno) and Slovakia (capital Bratislava). Moravian wines are the favourites in Prague. A short list of the best cellars includes the state wineries and cooperatives of Znojmo, Blatnice, Hustopece, Saldorf and Velké Pavlovice in Moravia and Pezinok and Nitra in Slovakia. Best wines are the young Rieslings, Sauvignons Blancs, Rülanders (Pinot Gris), Traminers, Muskotaly and Grüner Veltliner. All are worth trying for value.

The Former Yugoslav States

Before its disintegration in 1991 Yugoslavia was well-established as a supplier of wines of international calibre, if not generally of exciting quality. Current political disarray makes commercial contacts difficult. Slovenian 'Riesling' was the pioneer, since followed by Cabernet, Pinot Blanc and Traminer, as well as such worthwhile specialities as Zilavka, Plavac and Prokupac. All regions except the central Bosnian highlands make wine, almost entirely in giant cooperatives. Tourists on the Dalmatian coast and in Macedonia will find more original products, all worth trying, whose roots go deep into the ancient world.

Croatia

Babic Standard red of DALMATIA, ages better than ordinary PLAVAC.

Banat Partly in Romania: up-to-date wineries making adequate RIES.

Bogdanusa Local white grape of the DALMATIAN islands, esp Hvar and Brac. Pleasant, refreshing, faintly fragrant wine.

Burgundac Bijeli Chard, grown in SLAVONIA and VOJVODINA (N Serbia).

Dalmaciajavino Important coop based at Split and selling a full range of DALMATIAN coastal and island wines.

Dalmatia The coast of Croatia, from Rijeka to Dubrovnik. Has a remarkable variety of characterful wines, most of them potent.

Dingac Heavy, sweetish red from the local PLAVAC grape, speciality of the mid-DALMATIAN coast.

Faros Substantial, age-worthy PLAVAC red from the island of Hvar.

Grk White grape, speciality of the island of Korcula, giving strong, even sherry-like wine, and also a lighter pale one.

Istria Peninsula in the N Adriatic, Porec its centre, with a variety of pleasant wines, the MERLOT as good as any.

Marastina Strong dry white of the DALMATIAN islands, best from Cara Smokvica on Hvar.

Opol Pleasantly light, pale red made of PLAVAC grapes around Split and Sibenik in DALMATIA.

Plavac Mali Native red grape of DALMATIA; wine of body and strength, can age well. *See* Dingac, Opol, Postup, etc. Ordinary reds are often called Plavac. There is also a white, Plavac Beli.

Portugizac Austria's Blauer Portugieser: plain red wine.

Posip Pleasant white of the DALMATIAN islands, notably Korcula.

Postup Sweet and heavy DALMATIAN red from the Peljesac peninsula nr Korcula. Highly esteemed locally.

Slavonia N Croatia, on the Hungarian border between Slovenia and Serbia. A big producer of standard wines, mainly white, incl most 'Yugoslav Riesling'.

Teran Stout dark red of ISTRIA. *See* Refosco (Slovenia).

Vugava Rare white variety of Vis in DALMATIA. Linked (at least in legend) with the Viognier of the Rhône valley.

Slovenia

The northwest state, including Yugoslavia's most European-style vineyards and wines, eg Ljutomer. Slovenija-vino, the sales organization, is the Yugoslav regions' biggest. Some small producers with good Sauvignon, etc.

Beli Pinot The Pinot Bl, a popular grape variety.

Cvicek Traditional pale red or dark rosé of the Sava valley.

Grasevina Slovenian for Italian RIESLING (also called Welschriesling, LASKI RIZLING, etc.). The normal Riesling of the region.

Jerusalem Slovenia's most famous v'yd, at LJUTOMER. Its best wines are late-picked RAJNSKI RIZLING, LASKI RIZLING.

Kraski Means grown on the coastal limestone or 'karst'.

Laski Rizling Yet another name for Italian RIES.

Ljutomer (or Lutomer) -Ormoz Slovenia's best-known and probably best white wine district, in the northeast, famous for its LASKI RIZLING: at its best, rich and satisfying wine. Export qualities are variable.

Malvasia Ancient white grape giving luscious wine.

Maribor Important centre in the northeast. White wines, mainly from VINAG, incl LASKI RIZLING, RIES, Sauv Bl, Pinot Bl, Traminer.

Merlot Grown in Slovenia with reasonable results. Also in Croatia (ISTRIA), and Serbia.

Radgonska Ranina Ranina is Austria's Bouvier grape. Radgona is nr MARIBOR. The wine is sweet and carries the trade name Tigrovo Mljeko (Tiger's Milk).

Rajnski (or Renski) Rizling The Rhine RIESLING: rare in these regions, but grown a little in LJUTOMER-ORMOZ, and in FRUSKA GORA in VOJVODINA (Serbia).

Refosco Italian grape grown in the east and in ISTRIA (Croatia) as TERAN.

Riesling Used without qualification formerly meant Italian Riesling. Now legally limited to real Rhine Riesling.

Sipon Name for Furmint of Hungary.

Slamnak A late-harvest LJUTOMER estate RIES.

Tigrovo Mljeko *See* Radgonska Ranina.

Tocai The Pinot G, making rather heavy white wine.

Vinag Huge production cellars at MARIBOR.

Serbia, Bosnia-Herzegovina, Macedonia

Amselfelder German marketing name for the Red Burgundac (Pinot N or Spätburgunder) wine of KOSOVO. Disagreeably sweet.

Bijelo (Beli) White.

Blatina The red grape and wine of MOSTAR. White ZILAVKA is much better.

Bosnia-Herzegovina Mountainous western republic. Little wine produced apart from around MOSTAR.

Cabernet Now introduced in many places with usually pleasant, occasionally exciting results. *See* Kosovo.

Crno Black – ie red wine.

Fruska Gora Hills in VOJVODINA, on the Danube NW of Belgrade, with modern v'yds and a wide range of wines, incl Traminer and Sauv Bl.

Kadarka The major red grape of Hungary, widely grown in SERBIA.

Kosovo (or Kosmet) Region in the S between SERBIA and MACEDONIA, with modern v'yds. Source of AMSELFELDER and some lively CAB.

Leskovac Region in SERBIA producing good whites, eg Sauv Bl.

Macedonia Southern republic bordering Greece, Albania and Bulgaria, growing principally red wines.

Montenegro Small republic in southwest, known for its VRANAC red wines.

Mostar Islamic-looking little city inland from DALMATIA, making admirable dry white from the ZILAVKA grape. Also BLATINA.

Muskat-Ottonel The E European Muscat, grown in VOJVODINA.

Navip The big growers' coop of SERBIA, with its HQ at Belgrade.

Oplenac CAB-producing region in SERBIA.

Plovdina Native red grape of MACEDONIA in the south, giving mild wine. Generally blended with tastier PROKUPAC.

Prokupac Principal red grape of S SERBIA and MACEDONIA: 85% of production. Makes dark rosé (RUZICA) and full-bodied red of character, esp at ZUPA. PLOVDINA is often added for smoothness.

Ruzica Rosé, usually from PROKUPAC. Darker than most; and better.

Serbia The eastern state of Yugoslavia, with nearly half the country's v'yds, stretching from VOJVODINA to MACEDONIA.

Smederevka Major white grape of SERBIA and KOSOVO. Fresh dry wines.

Traminac The Traminer. Grown in VOJVODINA and Slovenia.

Velika Morava Area of SERBIA famous for LASKI RIZLING.

Vojvodina An autonomous province of N SERBIA developing substantial v'yds. Wide range of grapes, both European and Balkan.

Vranac Red grape making attractive vigorous wine in MONTENEGRO.

Vranje Region in S SERBIA producing good quality reds: CAB, Pinot, MERLOT.

Zilavka The white wine of MOSTAR in Herzegovina. Can be one of Yugoslavia's best: dry, pungent and memorably fruity, with a faint flavour of apricots. Exported samples are usually disappointing.

Zupa Central SERBIAN district giving its name to above average red and rosé (or dark and light red) of PROKUPAC and PLOVDINA: respectively Zupsko CRNO and Zupsko RUZICA.

Romania

Romania has a long winemaking tradition and good potential for quality, wasted during decades of supplying the Soviet Union with the sweet wine the Russians like. The present political situation sadly allows for little progress, although the potential is there to rival the success of Bulgarian wines.

Alba Iulia Town in the TIRNAVE area of Transylvania, known for off-dry whites from Italian RIES, FETEASCA and MUSKAT-OTTONEL.

Aligoté The junior white burgundy grape makes pleasantly fresh white wine in Romania.

Babeasca Traditional red grape of the FOCSANI area: agreeably sharp wine tasting slightly of cloves.

Banat The plain on the border with Serbia. Workaday Italian RIES and light red CADARCA.

Cabernet Increasingly grown, particularly at DEALUL MARE, to make dark intense wines, though often too sweet for Western palates.

Cadarca Romanian spelling of the Hungarian Kadarka.

Chardonnay Used at MURFATLAR to make sweet dessert wine.

Cotesti Part of the FOCSANI area making reds of PINOT N, Merlot, etc, and dry whites claimed to resemble Alsace wines.

Cotnari Romania's most famous historical wine but rarely seen: light dessert wine from MOLDAVIA. Rather like v delicate Tokay.

Dealul Mare Important up-to-date v'yd area in the SE Carpathian foothills. Red wines from CAB, Merlot, PINOT N, etc. Whites from TAMIIOASA, etc.

Dobruja Black Sea region round the port of Costanta. *See* Murfatlar.

Dragasani Region on the R Olt south of the Carpathian Mts. Both traditional and 'modern' grapes. Good MUSKAT-OTTONEL.

Feteasca Romanian white grape with spicy, faintly Muscat aroma, the same as Hungary's Leányka.

Focsani Important eastern region incl COTESTI, ODOBESTI and NICORESTI.

Grasa A form of the Hungarian Furmint grape grown in Romania and used in, among other wines, COTNARI.

Moldavia The northeast province.

Murfatlar Big modern v'yds nr the Black Sea, specializing in sweet wines, incl CHARD. Now also dry reds and whites.

Muskat-Ottonel The E European Muscat, a speciality of Romania.

Nicoresti Eastern area of FOCSANI, best known for its red BABEASCA.

Odobesti The central part of FOCSANI; white wines of FETEASCA, RIES, etc.

Oltenia Wine regions including DRAGASANI. Sometimes also a brand name.

Perla The speciality of TIRNAVE: a pleasant blended semi-sweet white of Italian RIES, FETEASCA and MUSKAT-OTTONEL.

Pinot Noir Grown in the south: can surprise with taste and character.

Pitesti Principal town of the Arges region south of the Carpathian Mts. Traditionally whites from FETEASCA, TAMIIOASA, RIES.

Premiat Reliable range of higher quality wines for export.

Riesling Italian Riesling. Very widely planted. No exceptional wines.

Sadova Town in the SEGARCEA area exporting a sweetish rosé.

Segarcea Southern wine area near the Danube. Rather sweet CAB.

Tamiioasa Traditional white grape known as 'frankincense' for its exotic scent and flavour. Pungent sweet wines.

Tîrnave Important Transylvanian wine region, known for its PERLA.

Trakia Export brand. Better judged for Western palates than most.

Valea Calugareasca 'The Valley of the Monks', part of the DEALUL MARE v'yd, with a well-known research station. CAB, Merlot and PINOT N are generally made into heavy, sweetish wines.

Greece

Since Greece's entry into the EC its antique wine industry has moved into a higher gear. Much Greek wine is still fairly primitive, but a new system of appellations is in place and the past five years have seen substantial investment in equipment and expertise. Modern, well-made but still authentic Greek wines are worth tasting.

Achaia-Clauss Well-known wine merchant with cellars at PATRAS, N PELOPONNESE. Makers of DEMESTICA, etc.

Agiorgitiko Widely planted red-wine grape, esp at NEMEA.

Agioritikos Mount Athos, the monastic peninsula in Chalkidiki. Source of Cab and other grapes for TSANTALI. Brand name of a good medium-dry white and rosé.

Attica Region round Athens, the chief source of RETSINA.

Autocratorikos New sparkling medium-dry white from TSANTALI.

Botrys Old-established Athenian wine and spirits company.

Boutari Merchants and makers with high standards in MACEDONIAN and other wines, esp NAOUSSA and SANTORINI. Grand Réserve is the best wine (84).

Cair Label of the RHODES coop. Makes Greece's only classic sparkling wine.

Calliga Modern winery with 800 acres on CEPHALONIA. ROBOLA white and Monte Nero reds from indigenous grapes are adequately made.

Cambas, Andrew Important wine-growers and merchants in ATTICA.

Carras, John Estate at Sithonia, Chalkidiki, N Greece, producing interesting red and white wines under the names Château Carras (75, 79, 81, 83, 84), Porto Carras and COTES DE MELITON. Ch Carras is a Bordeaux-style barrel-aged red, worth 2–6 yrs in bottle.

Castel Danielis One of the best brands of dry red wine, from ACHAIA-CLAUSS.

Cava Legal term for blended, aged red.

Cephalonia (Kephalonia) Ionian (western) island with good white ROBOLA and red Thymiatiko. Also MAVRODAPHNE. See Calliga, Gentilini.

Corfu Adriatic island with wines scarcely worthy of it. Ropa is the traditional red.

Côtes de Meliton Appellation of the CARRAS estate applying to red and white wines, incl Château Carras.

Courtakis, D Athenian merchant with mild RETSINA and good dark NEMEA.

Crete Island with the name for some of Greece's better red wine. Appellations are: Archanes, Daphnes, Peza and Sitia. But Cretan white can also be suprisingly good.

Demestica A reliable brand of dry red and white from ACHAIA-CLAUSS.

Emery Maker of good CAVA Emery red and vg Villare white on RHODES.

Gamalafka Speciality of Mykonos. Alarmingly like sherry vinegar.

Gentilini New ('84) up-market white from CEPHALONIA, a ROBOLA blend, soft and appealing. Now a v promising oak-aged version. To watch.

Goumenissa (Appellation) Good quality, oak-aged, mid-weight red from western MACEDONIA. Look for BOUTARI.

Ilios Very drinkable standard RHODES wine.

Kokkineli The rosé version of RETSINA: like the white. Drink cold.

Kouros Highly rated white from Kourtakis of ATTICA; also red.

Kretikos White wine made by BOUTARI from CRETAN varieties.

Lac des Roches Sound, blended white from BOUTARI.

Limnos (Appellation) N Aegean island with sweet golden Muscat wine.

Lindos Name for the higher quality of RHODES wine, whether from Lindos itself or not. Acceptable, no more.

Macedonia Quality wine region in the north, for NAOUSSA, etc.

Malvasia The famous grape is said to originate from Monemvasia in the S PELOPONNESE. See Rhodes.

Mantinia (Appellation) A fresh white from the PELOPONNESE, by CAMBAS.

Mavro Black – the word for dark (often sweet) red wine.

Mavrodaphne (Appellation)   Literally 'black laurel': dark, sweet, concentrated red, a speciality of the PATRAS region, N PELOPONNESE.

Mavroudi The red wine of Delphi and the northern shore of the Gulf of Corinth: dark and plummy.

Metsovo Town in Epirus (north) producing Cab blend called Katoi.

Minos Popular CRETAN brand; the Castello red is best.

Naoussa (Appellation) Above average strong dry red from MACEDONIA in the north, esp from BOUTARI and TSANTALI.

Nemea (Appellation) Town in the E PELOPONNESE famous for its lion (a victim of Hercules) and its fittingly forceful MAVRO.

Patras (Appellation) White wine and wine town on the Gulf of Corinth.

Pegasus, Château NAOUSSA estate for superior red (esp 81, 86, 88).

Peloponnese The southern landmass of mainland Greece, with half of the country's v'yds, incl NEMEA and PATRAS.

Retsina White wine with Aleppo pine resin added, tasting of turpentine and oddly appropriate with Greek food. The speciality of ATTICA. Much modern retsina is made disappointingly mild.

Rhodes Easternmost Greek island. Chevalier de Rhodes is a pleasant red. *See also* Cair, Emery, Ilios.

Robola or Rombola (Appellation) The fashionable dry white of CEPHALONIA, island off the Gulf of Corinth. Can be a pleasant soft wine of some character.

Samos (Appellation) Island off the Turkish coast with an ancient reputation for its sweet, pale golden Muscat. Best are (fortified) Anthemis and (natural) Nectar.

Santorini Dramatic volcanic island north of CRETE, making sweet Vinsanto from sun-dried grapes, and dry white Thira. Santino and Atlantis are dry reds. Unrealized potential here.

Semeli, Château Estate nr Athens making good white and red, incl Cab S.

Tsantali Producers at Agios Pavlos with a wide range of table wines, including MACEDONIAN Cab, wine from the monks of Mt Athos, NEMEA, NAOUSSA and Muscat from SAMOS and LIMNOS. CAVA is a blend.

Vaeni Promising red from NAOUSSA producers' coop.

Xynomavro The best of many indigenous Greek red grapes, basis for NAOUSSA and other northern wines.

Zitsa (Appellation) Region of 6 villages in mountainous N Epirius. Delicate Debina (grape) white, still or fizzy.

Cyprus

Cyprus exports 75% of its production, mostly strong wines of reasonable quality, especially low-price Cyprus 'sherry'; though old Commandaria, a treacly dessert wine, is the island's finest product. Until recently only traditional grape varieties of limited potential were available; now better kinds are beginning to improve standards, but regrettably slowly.

Afames Village at the foot of Mt Olympus, giving its name to dry, tangy red (MAVRO) wine from SODAP.

Aphrodite Consistent, full-bodied, medium-dry white from KEO, named after the Greek goddess of love.

Arsinöe Dry white wine from SODAP, named after an unfortunate female whom Aphrodite turned to stone.

Bellapais Fizzy, medium-sweet white from KEO, named after the famous abbey nr Kyrenia. Essential refreshment for holidaymakers.

Commandaria Good quality brown dessert wine made since ancient times in the hills north of LIMASSOL, named after a crusading order of knights. The best (sold as '100 yrs old') is superb, of incredible sweetness. Most is standard Communion wine.

Domaine d'Ahera Modern-style lighter red from KEO.

Emva Brand name of well-made fine, medium and cream SHERRIES.

Etko *See* Haggipavlu.

Haggipavlu Well-known wine merchant at LIMASSOL. Trades as Etko.

Keo The biggest and most go-ahead firm at LIMASSOL. Standard Keo Dry White and Dry Red are vg value. *See also* Othello.

Khalokhorio Principal COMMANDARIA village, growing only XYNISTERI.

Kokkineli Rosé: the name is related to 'cochineal'.

Kolossi Red and white table wines from SODAP.

Laona The largest independent winery, at Arsos. Good range of wines incl a *'nouveau'* and an oak-aged red.

Limassol 'The Bordeaux of Cyprus'. The wine port in the south.

Loel Major producer, with Amathus and Kykko brands, Command Cyprus SHERRY and good Negro red.

Mavro The black grape of Cyprus (and Greece) and its dark wine.

Monte Roya Modern winery at Chryssoroyiatissa Monastery. Dry white esp well made.

Mosaic KEO's brand of Cyprus SHERRIES. Includes a fine dry wine.

Muscat All major firms produce pleasant low-price 15° Muscats.

Othello A good standard dry red: solid, satisfying wine from KEO.

Palomino Soft dry white made of this (Sherry) grape by LOEL. V drinkable ice-cold.

Pitsilia Region south of Mt Olympus producing the best white and COMMANDARIA wines.

Rosella Brand of strong, medium-sweet rosé.

St Panteleimon Brand of strong, sweet white from KEO.

Semeli Good traditional red from HAGGIPAVLU.

Sherry Cyprus makes a full range of sherry-style wines, the best (particularly the dry) of vg quality.

SODAP Major wine coop at LIMASSOL.

Xynisteri The native white grape of Cyprus.

Zoopiyi Principal COMMANDARIA village, growing MAVRO grapes.

Asia & North Africa

Algeria

As a combined result of Islam and the EC the once massive vineyards of Algeria have dwindled in the last decade from 860,000 acres to under 200,000. Red, rosé and white wines of some quality are still made in the coastal hills of Tlemcen, Mascara, Haut-Dahra, Zaccar, Tessala, Médéa and Ain-Berrem. Sidi Brahim is a drinkable red brand. Most goes for blending.

China

Germans and Russians started making wine on the Shantung (now Shandong) peninsula in the early 1900s. Since 1980 a modern industry, initiated by Rémy Martin, has produced the adequate white Dynasty and Tsingtao wines; and new, more sophisticated plantings of better varieties in Shandong and Tianjin, further north, promise more interest in the future. Basic table wines are made of the local Dragon Eye and Muscat Hamburg grapes (especially in Tianjin). In Quingdao, Italian Riesling has been followed by Chardonnay, and the Hua Dong winery started experimental plantings of a number of different varieties in 1985. Events up to now have delayed further progress.

India

In 1985 a Franco-Indian firm launched a Chardonnay-based sparkling wine, Omar Khayyam, made at Narayangoan, near Poona, southeast of Bombay. Plans are to export up to 2 million bottles and to add still wines of Chardonnay and Cabernet. Omar Khayyam sets an astonishing standard.

Japan

Japan has a small wine industry in Yamanashi Prefecture, west of Tokyo. Most of the production here is blended with imports from South America, Eastern Europe, etc. Premium wines of Sémillon, Chardonnay, Cabernet and the local white grape, Koshu, are light but can be good, though expensive. The main producers are Mann's, Mercian and Suntory. Château Lumière and Château Mercian lead the way with high quality Chardonnay, Cabernet, etc. Perhaps the most interesting (and expensive) are Suntory's Sauternes-like Château Lion and Mercian's Kikyogahara Merlot. In 1985 tainted Austrian wine was discovered being sold as Japanese by a major company. Regrettably, Japanese labelling laws have been so lax that misrepresentation of imported wines as 'Japanese' has been the rule rather than the exception. A new law stipulates that if the percentage of imported bulk wine in the bottle is above 50% it must be indicated (the larger percentage should be written before the smaller).

Lebanon

The small Lebanese wine industry, based on Ksara in the Bekaa valley northeast of Beirut, continues against all odds to make red wine of real vigour and quality. Château Musar (★★★) produces splendid matured reds, largely of Cabernet Sauvignon; a full-blooded white, surprisingly capable of ageing 10–15 yrs; and recently a lighter red, 'Tradition', which is 75% Cinsaut, 25% Cabernet Sauvignon.

Morocco

Morocco today makes North Africa's best wine, from vineyards along the Atlantic coast and round Meknes. In 10 years the vineyards have declined from 190,000 to 35,000 acres. The main producers are Chaudsoleil, Meknes Vins and Sincomar. Tarik and Toulal are two drinkable reds. Vin Gris is the best bet for hot-day refreshment.

Tunisia

Tunisia now has 22,000 acres of vines (compared with 120,000 10 years ago). Her speciality is sweet Muscat, but reasonable reds and rosés come from Cap Bon, Carthage and Mornag.

Turkey

Most of Turkey's 1.5 million acres of vineyards produce table grapes. But her wines, from Thrace, Anatolia and the Aegean, are remarkably good. Indigenous varieties such as Narince (for white) and Bogazkere (for red) are used along with Riesling, Sémillon, Pinot Noir and Gamay. Trakya (Thrace) white and Buzbag (Anatolian) red are the well-known standards of Tekel, the State producer. Doluca, Karmen, Kavaklidere and Taskobirlik are private firms of good quality. Doluca's Villa Neva red from Thrace is very well made. Buzbag is a (sometimes rough and ready) bargain.

The Former Soviet Union

With over 3 million acres of vineyards the republics of the former USSR collectively form the world's fourth-biggest wine producer – almost entirely for home consumption. Ukraine (including the Crimea) is the biggest vineyard republic, followed by Moldova, the

Russian Federation and Georgia. The Soviet consumer has a sweet tooth, for both table and dessert wines. Of the latter best come from the Crimea. In 1990 Sotheby's auction house sold wines from the Tsar's private Crimean cellars at Massandra and revealed their splendid quality. Moldova and Ukraine use the same grapes as Romania, plus Cabernet, Riesling, Pinot Gris, etc. The 1963 Negru de Purkar released in 1992 gave a startling glimpse of Moldova's potential quality. The Russian Federation makes the best Riesling (Anapa, Arbau, Beshtau) and sweet sparkling Tsimlanskoye 'Champanski'. Georgia uses antique methods to make extremely tannic wines for local consumption, and (relatively) modern methods to make blended products for export (eg Mukuzani, Tsinandali). Kakhetià (East Georgia) is historically famous for both reds and whites of withering tannin content. Imeteria (West Georgia) makes milder, highly original wines. When the equipment (eg good bottles) becomes available Georgia will be a hit on the export market. Georgian sparkling is extremely cheap and drinkable. Clearly the potential of the unfolding republics will give some exciting wines in the future.

Israel

Israeli wine, since the industry was re-established by a Rothschild in the 1880s, has been primarily of kosher interest until recently, when Cabernet Sauvignon, Riesling, Sauvignon Blanc, Sémillon, Petite Sirah and Grenache of fair quality have been introduced. Three-quarters of Israel's annual 15-million-bottle production is white, most of it Riesling. The main producers follow.

Ashkelon Family-owned firm making red and white wines. Labels are Segal's and Ben-Ami.

Baron Small family grower best known for their Muscat. Also some Cab S.

Carmel Israel's largest coop, est 1882, with two newly modernized wineries. Top wines are Rothschild Cab S and Emerald Ries. Also good Sauv Bl and Chard.

Eliaz Medium-sized winery producing light-style red and white wines.

Gamla & Golan Mainly Cab S, produced by YARDEN.

Yarden Young ('83), modern, sophisticated winery in the Golan Heights, involving Californian oenologists and setting highest standards for Israel. Over 20 wines: top is full-bodied, oaky Galil Cab S (85); good Mount Hermon Chard; recently some sparkling.

MENDOCINO
RUSSIAN RIVER
SONOMA
NAPA
CARNEROS
Sacramento
LODI
SANTA CRUZ
SAN JOAQUIN VALLEY
SALINAS
SAN LUIS OBISPO
SANTA BARBARA
SOUTHERN CALIFORNIA

North Coast

Sacramento R.

Russian R.

San Joaquin R.

Central Coast

Sierra Nevada

San Francisco

Modesto

Monterey

Los Angeles

San Diego

Pacific Ocean

The wine boom that carried California to dizzy heights in the 1970s and '80s faltered at the end of the latter decade. The old puritan streak in America seems to have formed an unholy alliance with the country's not-so-latent hypochondria and the recession that followed inflated expectations. In such conditions retrenchment is inevitable – however good the product. Expansion has slowed, but progress continues; not to mention changes of ownership, management, style... This edition records some 260 of the nearly 600 wineries now operating. Brevity is not dismissive; it is intended to be practical. Vintage dates given (usually for Chardonnay and Cabernet) reflect the probable maturity of wines kept in, say, reasonable restaurant conditions. It is certain that some considerably older bottles kept in ideal cellars will still be excellent. Chardonnays can sometimes mature for 10 years with ease, Cabernets for 20.

Appellation areas (AVAs) are an important recent fact of life: they are being registered thick and fast; the current total is over 50, with five in the Napa Valley alone and four more proposed. It is still too soon to use them as a guide to style. Listed below are the broad regions usually referred to. But grape varieties combined with brand names are still the key to California wine.

Principal vineyard areas

Alexander Valley/Russian River (Sonoma) Top quality area from Alexander Valley (N of Napa Valley) towards the sea (Russian River). Incl Dry Creek Valley.

Amador County in the Sierra foothills E of Sacramento. Grows vg Zinfandel, esp in Shenandoah Valley.

Carneros, Los Important cool region N of San Francisco Bay, shared between Napa and Sonoma counties.

Central Coast A long sweep of coast with increasing though scattered wine activity, from San Francisco Bay S to Santa Barbara.

Hecker Pass (Central Coast) Pass through the Santa Cruz Mts S of San Francisco Bay with a cluster of small old-style wineries.

Livermore Valley E of San Francisco Bay long famous for white wines but now largely built over.

Lodi Town and district at the N end of the San Joaquin Valley, its hot climate modified by a westerly air-stream.

Mendocino Northernmost coastal wine country; a varied climate coolest in Anderson Valley nr the coast, warm around Ukiah inland.

Monterey *See* Salinas Valley.

Napa The Napa valley, N of San Francisco Bay, long established as a top quality wine area. Coolest at S end (Los Carneros).

Russian River *See* Alexander Valley.

Salinas Valley/Monterey (Central Coast) The Salinas Valley runs inland SE from Monterey. After frenzied expansion in the '70s, many vines were removed. What are left make wines of great character.

San Joaquin Valley The great central valley of California, fertile and hot, the source of most of the jug wines and dessert wines in the State.

San Luis Obispo (Central Coast) Edna Valley just S of San Luis Obispo (1,000 acres) and more scattered v'yds nr Paso Robles (5,000 acres).

Santa Barbara (Central Coast) Santa Maria valley is dominant, esp for vg Chardonnay and Pinot Noir. The smaller Santa Ynez valley also has cool foggy conditions for white wines.

Santa Cruz Mts (Central Coast) Wineries (though few v'yds) are scattered round the Santa Cruz Mts S of San Francisco Bay, from Saratoga down to the Hecker Pass.

Sonoma County N of San Francisco Bay, between Napa and the sea. Most v'yds are in the north (*see* below). A few, historically important, are in the Valley of the Moon in the south. Vineyards extend S into Los Carneros. (*See also* Napa.)

Temecula (Rancho California) New small area in S California, 25 miles inland, halfway between San Diego and Riverside.

California grape varieties

California has adopted the world's repertoire of 'classic' grapes: for notes on these *see* pages 6–9. Grapes specific to California include:

Carmine, Carnelian, Centurion, Ruby Cabernet University-bred hybrids of Cabernet, Carignan and Grenache intended to add Cabernet class to humble wines. Rarely, if ever, seen as 'varietals'.

Gamay Beaujolais Not true Gamay but a Pinot Noir clone.

Gray Riesling Not Riesling; makes full-bodied but standard white.

Johannisberg Riesling Real (also called White) Riesling.

Petite Sirah No relation to Syrah; a synonym for the obscure French Durif.

Symphony A recent Muscat-based hybrid from UC Davis for sweet and sparkling wines. Planted in Sonoma and San Joaquin.

Zinfandel [Zin] California's own red, open to many interpretations, from light-weight and fruity to galumphing. The current fad is for white or 'blush' Zinfandel. The red is capable of ageing to high quality.

NB Fumé Blanc: Sauvignon Blanc (usually in its oak-aged manifestation).

Recent vintages

The Californian climate is far from being as consistent as its reputation. Although, on the whole, grapes ripen regularly, they are subject to spring frosts in many areas, sometimes a wet harvest-time and too often drought.

Wines from the San Joaquin Valley tend to be most consistent year by year. The vintage date on these, where there is one, is more important for telling the age of the wine than its character.

Vineyards in the Central Coast region are widely scattered; there is little pattern. The Napa and Sonoma valleys are the areas where comment can usefully be made on the last dozen or more vintages of the top varietal wines: Cabernet Sauvignon and Chardonnay.

Chardonnay

NB These ageing assessments are based on well-balanced wines with fruit flavours dominant. Very rich and oaky examples tend to be v short-lived: 2 yrs at most. Marker wines for good ageing qualities incl eg Chappellet, Clos du Bois-Calcaire, Dehlinger, Freemark Abbey, Matanzas Creek, Shafer, Silverado, Simi, Sonoma-Cutrer, Trefethen.

1991 Abundant but delayed harvest may lack acid balance. Overall vg.
1990 Healthy and trouble-free. At least good; some outstanding.
1989 Mainly firmly balanced. A leanish vintage; not obvious but may age well.
1988 Big, soft, quick-developers. Many lack focus. Drink up soonish.
1987 Ideal weather; vg wines for this year.
1986 Many solid and worthy. Nothing to wait for.
1985 Big crop, good acidity, excellent and maturing well. Mostly ready.
1984 A dull vintage, mostly past it.
1983 Good once, but only the very best carry on.
1982 Cool harvest; the best wines were lean and tart and have aged well.
1981 Good if not too strong. Drink up.

Cabernet Sauvignon

NB As with Chardonnays, over-rich and over-oaky wines usually collapse quickly. The markers for the assessments below are not Reserves, but fine standard Cabernets from eg Beaulieu, Beringer-Knights Valley, Caymus, Chappellet, Clos du Val, Fetzer-Barrel Select, Freemark Abbey, Hafner, Jordan, Laurel Glen, Louis Martini-Monte Rosso, Parducci, Raymond, Shafer, Silverado-Alexander Valley Vineyards.

1991 Long cool summer, ideal autumn. Excellent.
1990 Clearly a good vintage; solid; wait and see.
1989 First tastes v promising. Dark, intense but not overripe wines.
1988 Most are more charming than solid. Can be drunk.
1987 Evolving as perhaps the best of the decade overall.
1986 Quickly approachable vintage. Baby fat is now fleshy.
1985 Lean, firm to hard, deep-flavoured. Slow-maturing but impressive.
1984 Showy early: ripe and fragrant. Possibly best now and 3 more years.
1983 Several awkward hard wines. The best have depth but need time to reveal it.
1982 Epitome of a charming vintage, good now and (for the best) a while longer.
1981 Promptly picked examples have substance and depth. Probably at peak.
1980 High reputation but merely good and solid. Ready to drink.
1979 Apparently lightish, but the best keep going sturdily.
1978 Excellent. Generally ready, and many fading.
1977 Attractive wines now mainly crumbling.
1976 Drought made v concentrated wines. Good ones are v ripe and potent now.
1975 Delicate, charming; mature.
1974 Very like '84; few have the balance to keep going.
1973 Big crop of good wines. Drink up.
1970 One of the best ever. Mature.

California wineries

Acacia Napa ★★★ (Chard) 85 86 87 88 89 90 (Pinot N) 81 82 83 84 85 86 87 88 89 Specialist in single-v'yd Carneros Chard (Marina) and Pinot N (Lund, St-Clair, Madonna) of depth and durability. Owned by CHALONE. 25,000 cases.

Adelaida Cellars San Luis Obispo ★★ Soft Chard and supple Cab from Paso Robles. 4,500 cases.

Alderbrook Sonoma ** (Chard) 87 88 89 90   Indelibly flavoured, age-worthy Dry Creek Sém, crisp Chard, Sauv Bl. 20,000 cases.

Alexander Valley Vineyards Sonoma **→*** (Chard) 87 88 90 (Cab S) 75 78 81 82 83 84 85 86 87 88   Long-lived, richly varietal Cab leads list; Chard has regained form after brief lapse. Also dark, sturdy Pinot N, mild Ries. 60,000 cases.

Almaden San Joaquin *   Famous pioneer name, now a Heublein-owned everyday brand, operated from Madera alongside Inglenook Navalle, Blossom Hill and others. 1+ million cases.

S Anderson Vineyard Napa **→*** (Chard) 87 88 89   Robust Chard and robuster classic sparkling. 15,000 cases.

Arrowood Sonoma **→*** (Chard) 87 88 89 (Cab S) 87 88   Long-time CHATEAU ST JEAN winemaker Dick A makes leaner wines on his own behalf. 8,000 cases going to 15,000.

Atlas Peak Napa   Huge international investment in E hills. Coming shortly.

Au Bon Climat Sta Barbara **→*** (Chard) 86 87 88 90   Ultra-toasty style for Chard; also well-wooded Pinot N. The same dynamic, experimental little winery produces QUPÉ and VITA NOVA wines in Sta Maria Valley. 5,000 cases.

Balverne Sonoma **   Hiccuppy record, but CHALK HILL v'yd promises well, esp for Chard.

Beaulieu Vineyard Napa *** (Cab S) 70 74 76 77 79 78 80 81 82 83 84 85 86 87   Long-time growers and makers of justly famous, age-worthy Georges Delatour Private Reserve Cab S. Also vg Rutherford Cab S, approachable Beautour Cab S and crackerjack dry, oak-free Sauv Bl. 400,000+ cases.

Bel Arbors Oddly spelt second label of FETZER.

Belvedere Sonoma **   Bold Grapemaker Chard, Cab S and Merlot from in-dividual v'yds are top of line; Discovery series is value. 250,000 cases.

Beringer Napa **→*** (Chard) 83 85 86 87 88 89 90 (Cab S) 78 79 80 81 82 83 84 85 86 87   Century-old winery restored to front rank. Reserve Chard and esp Reserve Cab S outstanding. Solid FUMÉ BL, ZIN, Knights Valley Cab S. 1.4 million cases. Everyday label: Napa Ridge.

Benziger *See* Glen Ellen.

Black Mountain Sonoma **   Chard, Sauv Bl, ZIN. 20,000 cases. Second label: J W Morris.

Boeger El Dorado **   Steady Cab S, Merlot, ZIN, Sauv Bl from Sierra Foothills. 12,000 cases.

Bonny Doon Sta Cruz Mts ** (Chard) 87 88   Rabid francophile led the charge towards Rhône varieties: esp red Cigare Volant (Grenache-Mourvèdre), white Cuvée des Philosophes (Marsanne-Roussanne). Now trying Italian. Never a dull moment. 8,000 cases.

Bouchaine Napa ** (Chard) 87 88 (Pinot N) 86 87 88 89   Specialist in well-wooded Carneros Chard, Pinot N. Also dips into bone-dry, so far impressive Gewürz (88, 89). 15,000 cases.

Brander Vineyard Sta Barbara **   Impressive, intense Sauv Bl (90) from Sta Ynez Valley. Good Cab F-S blend Bouchet (84, 85, 86, 87) and 87 Merlot. 8,000 cases.

David Bruce Sta Cruz Mts ** (Chard) 87 88 89 90   Long-time source of heavyweight Chard has moderated somewhat. Also Pinot N, Cab S. Red called Shandon is of interest. 32,000 cases.

Buehler Napa ** (Cab S) 85 86 87 88   Impressive 20,000 estate in E hills has turned sharp corner; recent Cabs, ZINS to watch. Vg Pinot Bl.

Buena Vista Sonoma ** (Chard) 87 88 89 90 (Cab S) 83 84 85 86 87 88   Pioneer name now German-owned and an utterly reliable source of taste-like-the-grapes Chard, Sauv Bl, Cab S, Merlot, Gewürz, Ries, mainly from own 1,100-acre v'yd in Carneros. 110,000 cases.

Burgess Cellars Napa ** (Chard) 87 88 89 (Cab S) 80 81 82 83 84 85 86 87 (Zin) 82 83 85 86 87   Emphasis on dark, weighty, well-oaked reds. 30,000 cases.

BV Abbreviation of BEAULIEU VINEYARD used on its labels.

Davis Bynum Sonoma ** (Chard) 87 88 89 (Cab S) 83 84 85 86 87 Reliable, sometimes stylish wines go beyond special selection Chard, Cab S to include correct Pinot N, enticing dry Gewürz. 28,000 cases.

Byron Vineyards Sta Barbara *** (Chard) 87 88 89 90 (Pinot N) 84 85 86 87 88 89 Robert MONDAVI-owned source of tasty, polished Pinot N and vg Chard from estate v'yds. Also small lots of Cab S, Sauv Bl from nearby.

Cain Cellars Napa ** (Cab S) 84 85 86 87 88 Emphasis is on Cain Five, blended from Cab family varieties grown in estate v'yd on Spring Mt. Also Cab S, Chard. 30,000 cases.

Cakebread Napa *** (Chard) 87 88 89 90 (Cab S) 81 82 83 84 85 86 87 88 Bold style rules in memorable Sauv Bl as well as excellent Chard and Cab. 40,000 cases.

Calera San Benito *** (Pinot N) 80 81 82 83 84 85 86 87 88 (Chard) 87 88 89 90 Dark, often tannic, sometimes heady estate Pinot Ns are much in fashion; each named after a section of the hilly, chalky v'yd (Jensen, Selleck, Reed). Also smoky, well-knit Chard. 10,000 cases.

Callaway S California ** (Chard) 87 88 89 90 Mild, easy whites incl lees-aged Chard, oak-aged FUMÉ. 150,000 cases.

Cambria Sta Barbara Affiliate of KENDALL-JACKSON produces extra-smoky Chard, well-oaked Pinot N from own grapes. 18,000 cases and growing fast.

Carey Cellars Sta Barbara ** (Chard) 87 88 89 90 (Cab S) 85 86 87 Since acquisition by FIRESTONE, an impressive little (mainly estate) winery. Vg Chard, Merlot, Sauv Bl.

Carmenet Sonoma **→*** (Cab S blend) 83 84 85 86 89 CHALONE-owned mountain v'yd and winery above Sonoma town produces classy, plummy, full, Cab-based blend. Also Edna Valley white based on Sauv Bl. 27,000 cases.

Carneros Creek Napa *** (Chard) 87 88 89 90 (Pinot N) 81 82 83 84 85 86 87 88 Resolute explorer of climates and clones in Carneros focuses on Pinot N. Well-oaked Reserve, lightheartedly fruity Fleur and reliable estate bottlings. Also deftly oaked Chard. 25,000 cases.

Caymus Napa *** (Cab S) 76 77 78 79 80 81 82 83 84 85 86 87 88 Dark, firm, herbaceous estate Cab S is the celebrated core; weightier, more oaky Reserve and slightly lighter Napa Cuvée cover the flanks. Also dark ZIN, ultra-ripe Pinot N. 35,000 cases. Good value second label: Liberty School.

Chalk Hill Sonoma ** In hills nr Windsor, revitalized winemaking is leading to more stylish Chard, Sauv Bl, Cab S from large estate v'yd. 65,000 cases.

Chalone Monterey **** (Chard) 81 83 84 85 86 87 88 89 90 (Pinot N) 80 81 82 83 84 85 86 87 88 Unique hilltop estate high in the Gavilan Mts; source of smoky, woody, flinty, slow-ageing Chard and (latterly) dark, tannic Pinot N, both meant to imitate burgundies. Also Pinot Bl and Chenin Bl styled after Chard. 25,000 cases. Company also owns ACACIA, CARMENET, EDNA VALLEY, Gavilan. Links with (Lafite) Rothschilds.

Chappellet Napa *** (Chard) 82 83 84 85 86 87 88 89 90 (Cab S) 74 75 76 77 78 79 80 81 82 83 84 85 86 87 Beautiful amphitheatrical hillside v'yd yields lean, racy Cab S, understated Chard and California's best dry Chenin Bl – all long-lived. 30,000 cases.

Chateau Montelena Napa *** (Chard) 85 86 87 88 89 (Cab S) 75 76 77 78 79 80 81 82 83 84 85 86 87 Understated, firm, age-worthy Chard and epically tannic Cab S. 28,000 cases.

Château Potelle Napa French-owned, newcomer producer of balanced, quietly impressive Napa Chard, Alexander Valley Cab S, Mt Veeder ZIN. 22,000 cases.

Chateau St Jean Sonoma *** (Chard) 85 86 87 88 89 90 Intensely flavoured, richly textured, individual-v'yd Chards (Robert Young,

Belle Terre, McCrea), FUMÉ BLS (Petite Étoile), and sweet botrytised Ries and Traminers (Robert Young, Belle Terre). Just starting with reds again. Idiosyncratic classic sparkling from separate winery. Owned by Suntory. 150,000 cases.

Château Souverain Sonoma ** (Chard) 87 88 89 90 (Cab S) 85 86 87 88   Reliable, accessible wines. Price-worthy Reserve Chard, Cab S and Dry Creek ZIN, all distinctive, not overdone. 150,000 cases.

Château Woltner Napa *** (Chard) 87 88 89   Ex-owners of Ch la Mission Haut Brion now encamped on Napa hillside making 4,000 cases extra-toasty, overpriced Chards from 3 separate blocks of their v'yd.

Chimney Rock Napa **   Chard and recently impressive Cab S from Stag's Leap district. 12,000 cases.

Christian Brothers Napa **   Since '89 acquisition by Heublein, settling in at the low end of Napa price scale. Sound wines. Volume in flux.

Cline Cellars Contra Costa   'Rhône Ranger' offers Mourvèdre etc. 5,000 cases.

Clos du Bois Sonoma **→*** (Chard) 87 88 89 90 (Cab S) 78 79 80 81 82 83 84 85 86 87 88   Sizeable Allied-Hiram Walker firm at Healdsburg has consistent Cab S, Chard, Gewürz. Single-v'yd Chard (Calcaire, Flintwood), Cab S (Briarcrest), Cab S blend (Marlstone), all from Alexander and Dry Creek Valleys, can be memorable. 320,000 cases.

Clos du Val Napa *** (Chard) 87 88 89 90 (Cab S) 75 78 79 80 81 82 83 84 85 86 87 88   French-run. Supple, polished Cab S, Merlot, bold ZIN from Stag's Leap district; improving Chard, Pinot N from Carneros. Joli Val is label for non-estate wines (Chard, Cab, Sém). 55,000 cases.

Clos Pegase Napa **→*** (Chard) 87 88 89 90 (Cab S) 86 87 88   Post-modernist winery-cum-museum (or vice versa) with ever-improving, deftly understated wines. 40,000 cases.

Concannon Livermore **   Deinhard of Germany now owns this historically famous source of Sauv Bl. Also Chard, Cab S. 85,000 cases.

Congress Springs Sta Cruz Mts **→*** (Chard) 87 88 89 90   Excellent reputation for esp ripe, well-rounded Chard, Pinot Bl. New owner and winemaker settling in. 30,000 cases.

Conn Creek Napa **→*** (Chard) 87 88 89 90 (Cab S) 80 81 82 83 84 85 86 87 88   Best known for supple, almost juicy Cab. Chard gaining reputation. Owned by Château Ste Michelle (Washington). 30,000 cases.

Cooks 'Cooks Champagne': *see* Guild.

Corbett Canyon San Luis Obispo ** (Chard) 87 88 89 (Pinot N Res) 84 85 86 87 88 89   Recently memorable Reserve Pinot N is best. Reserve lots small; good value Coastal Classics line abundant. 100,000+ cases.

Culbertson Temecula **   Sparkling wine specialist blends local and Sta Barbara grapes with medal-winning results. Recently some table wines too. 40,000 cases.

Cuvaison Napa *** (Chard) 87 88 89 90 (Cab S) 86 87 88   Lean, crisp Carneros Chard is steadily in the top rank. Dark, ripe Merlot and up-valley Cab S are following suit. 65,000 cases.

Dehlinger Sonoma **→*** (Chard) 87 88 89 90 (Pinot N) 80 81 82 83 84 85 86 87 88 89   Firm, fruit-filled Chard and dark, full, complex Pinot N from Russian River estate. Both long-lived. 9,000 cases.

DeLoach Vineyards Sonoma *** (Chard) 87 88 89 90 (Pinot N) 79 80 81 82 83 84 85 86 87 88 89   Unctuous, super-fruity Chard and dark, slow-ageing Pinot N are best known. Bold, often heady ZIN (and uncommonly fine white Zin) should be. Also solid Gewürz, Sauv Bl. 70,000 cases.

DeLorimier Sonoma **   Still settling into style, but estate Alexander Valley Chard, Sauv-Sém and Cab family blends show promise. 5,000 cases.

DeMoor Napa **   Chard, Cab S, Sauv Bl. 14,000 cases.

Diamond Creek Napa *** (Cab S) 75 76 77 78 79 80 81 82 83 84 85 86 87 89   Austere, long-ageing Cabs from hilly v'yd nr Calistoga go by names of v'yd blocks, eg Gravelly Meadow, Volcanic Hill. 3,000 cases.

Domaine Carneros Napa (★★★) Showy US outpost of Taittinger in Carneros exaggerates the austere style of its parent in Champagne. Some 14,000 cases.

Domaine Chandon Napa ★★→★★★ Californian outpost of Moët & Chandon is most broadly known for reliable Brut and Blanc de Noirs; most praised for Reserve and locally available Club Cuvée. Shadow Creek is second (non-Napa) label. 500,000 cases.

Domaine Napa Napa ★★→★★★ (Chard) 87 88 89 (Cab S) 85 86 87 French owner/grower and NZ winemaker collaborate on consistently supple, well-balanced Chard, Cab S, Sauv Bl. 10,000 cases.

Dominus Napa (★★★★) 83 84 85 86 87 88 89 Partnership of Christian Moueix of Pomerol and inheritors of INGLENOOK to make increasingly intense, massively tannic Cab-based blend. None of it is even nearly mature. 89 looks magnificent.

Dry Creek Vineyard Sonoma ★★ Unimpeachable source of dry, tasty whites, esp Chard and FUMÉ BL but also Chenin Bl. Cab S, ZIN rather underrated. David Stare label for somewhat weighty reserve Cab blend, Sauv blend, and Chard. 80,000 cases.

Duckhorn Vineyards Napa (Merlot) 82 83 84 85 86 87 89 (Cab S) 81 82 83 84 85 86 87 88 Best known for dark, tannic, almost plummy-ripe reds, esp single-v'yd Merlot (Three Palms, Vine Hill). Also Sauv Bl. 18,000 cases.

Dunn Vineyards Napa (★★★) (Cab S) 81 82 83 84 85 86 87 88 On his own, ex-CAYMUS winemaker Randall Dunn makes dark, tannic, austere Cabs from Howell Mountain, slightly milder ones from the valley floor. 4,000 cases.

Durney Vineyard Monterey ★★ (Cab S) 79 80 81 82 83 84 85 86 87 Estate in Carmel Valley. Dark robust Cab. Chard joining list. 15,000 cases.

Eberle Winery San Luis Obispo ★★ Well-oaked, fat Chard and supple Cab from Paso Robles. 12,000 cases.

Edna Valley Vineyard San Luis Obispo ★★→★★★ (Chard) 89 90 (Pinot N) 84 85 86 87 88 Characterful Chard from a joint venture of local grower and CHALONE. Pinot N starts well but fades quickly in most vintages. 48,000 cases.

Estancia *See* Franciscan.

Etude Napa ★★→★★★ Winemaker-owned label of Tony Soter (long-time CHAPPELLET, now respected consultant). Front-rank Carneros Pinot N (85, 86, 87, 88, 89), excellent Cab; both burnished and supple. 4,000 cases.

Far Niente Napa ★★ (Chard) 87 88 89 (Cab S) 84 85 86 87 88 V oaky Chard, more restrained Cab at high prices. 36,000 cases.

Ferrari-Carano Sonoma ★★★ (Chard) 88 89 90 (Cab S) 86 87 Stylish Chard (Reserve seriously over-oaky), FUMÉ BL and, more recently, Merlot and Cab S from 1,000 still-developing acres in Alexander, Dry Creek and Knights Valleys. 50,000 cases.

Fetzer Mendocino ★★→★★★ (Chard) 87 88 89 90 (Cab S) 84 85 86 87 88 Rapidly expanding winery with always reliable (Sun Dial Chard, Valley Oaks FUMÉ), sometimes memorable (Barrel Select Chard, Cab S and Reserve ZIN) range. Bel Arbors is good value second label. 1.5 million cases.

Ficklin San Joaquin ★★★ First in California to use Douro grapes. Still California's best 'port', Tinta. Sometimes vintages. 10,000 cases.

Field Stone Sonoma ★★ Sturdy, increasingly steady; esp for PETITE SIRAH. 12,000 cases.

Firestone Sta Barbara ★★★ (Chard) 87 88 89 90 (Merlot) 84 85 86 87 88 89 Increasingly fine Chard overshadows but does not outshine delicious Ries. Merlot is intriguing; Cab one of Sta Barbara's best; Sauv Bl and Gewürz also vg. 75,000 cases. Also owns nearby CAREY.

Fisher Sonoma ★★ Mountain estate for often fine Chard; Napa grapes dominate steady Cab. 10,000 cases.

Flora Springs Wine Co Napa *** (Chard) 87 88 89 90 (Cab S) 84 85 86 87 88   Old stone cellar. Fine Sauv Bl became Soliloquy, to parallel flavoury Cab and luxury Cab blend, Trilogy. Now both are just top-line Flora Springs. Regular bottlings now called Floréal. Good Chard, too. 18,000 cases.

Folie à Deux Napa ** Impeccable Chards; unexpectedly fine Chenin Bl. Cab a recent addition. 8,000 cases.

Foppiano Sonoma ** Long-established wine family annually turns out fine reds, esp transcendent PETITE SIRAH. Reserve label for Chard, Cab (fine 85, 87) is Fox Mountain; good value second label is Riverside Farms. About 50,000 cases.

Forman Napa *** The winemaker who brought STERLING its first fame in the '60s now makes excellent Cab, Chard on his own. 15,000 cases.

Franciscan Vineyard Napa ** (Chard) 87 88 89 (Cab S) 85 86 87 Substantial v'yd at Oakville produces increasingly stylish Chard, Cab and Cab blend MERITAGE. Sister label Estancia goes on good value Sauv Bl and Monterey Chard. 100,000+ cases.

Franzia San Joaquin * Penny-saver everyday wines under Franzia and other labels; varietals under William Bates brand. All say 'Made and bottled in Ripon'. 5 million cases.

Freemark Abbey Napa ***→**** (Chard) 85 86 87 88 89 (Cab S) 74 75 76 78 79 80 81 82 83 84 85 86 87 88 Inexhaustible Cabs (esp single-v'yd Bosché, Sycamore) of great depth and style. Almost-bold Chards, including single-v'yd Carpy. Late harvest Ries Edelwein always among the finest. 33,000 cases.

Frog's Leap Napa ** Small winery as charming as its name (and T-shirts). Good for richly flavourful ZIN (85, 87), solid Cab (82, 85, 87). Chard, Sauv Bl are worth second looks too. 16,000 cases.

Gainey Vineyard, The Sta Barbara ** Chard, Sauv Bl, Cab. 12,000 cases.

Gallo, E & J San Joaquin *→** (Cab S) 80 81 82 (Zin) 81 84 The world's biggest winery, pioneer in both quantity and quality. Family-owned. Hearty 'Burgundy' and 'Chablis Blanc' set national standards. Vintage-dated Cab has won wide approval. Varietals for a determined assault up-market come from the company's huge Sonoma v'yds. Also André fizz and many lines. 40 million+ cases.

Gan Eden Sonoma (**) Kosher producer of serious Chard and Cab won wide critical acclaim for early vintages; wobbling in recent seasons. 25,000 cases.

Gary Farrell Sonoma (**→***) Winemaker's label for well-oaked, full-flavoured Pinot Ns (Howard Allen Ranch, Russian River Valley). Also vg Chards and Sauv Bl.

Gauer Estate Sonoma Young estate, ambitious with well-oaked Chard and CAB from large Alexander Valley v'yd. 10,000 cases.

Geyser Peak Sonoma *→** Following brief marriage with Penfolds of Australia, extensive v'yds of Henry Trione in Alexander and Russian River Valleys (lovely grapes) produce oaky Aussie-style wines. 500,000 cases.

Giumarra San Joaquin * Penny-saver everyday wines. 500,000+ cases.

Glen Ellen Sonoma **→*** Fast-growing family winery puts its best efforts into excellent Benziger of Glen Ellen Chard, Cab, Sauv Bl, etc from Sonoma grapes; works hard on value-for-money but misnamed Proprietor's Reserve line of easy quaffers. Also M G Vallejo, priced one step up from Prop Reserve. 3.5 million cases.

Gloria Ferrer Sonoma ** Substantial classic sparkling winery of Spain's Freixenet has scored well, esp for Cuvée Royale and Cuvée Carneros. 65,000 cases.

Grand Cru Sonoma ** (Chard) 87 88 89 (Cab S) 84 85 86 87 88 Has ended a long, stubborn resistance to Chard and Cab with notable success; keeps on with good Sauv Bl, off-dry Gewürz and Chenin Bl. 60,000 cases.

Green and Red Napa ★★ Tiny winery. Vigorous Italianate ZIN. 2,000 cases.

Greenwood Ridge Mendocino ★★ Established specialist in Anderson Valley Ries now offers attention-getting Cab (83, 84), Sauv Bl (88), ZIN. 3,000 cases.

Grgich Hills Cellars Napa ★★★ (Chard) 85 86 87 88 89 (Cab S) 84 86 87 Winemaker Grgich and grower Hills join forces on a stern Chard, impressively rich Cab, Sauv Bl, and – too little noticed – *Spätlese*-sweet Ries. Also plummy, thick Sonoma ZIN. 40,000 cases.

Groth Vineyards Napa ★★★ (Chard) 87 88 89 (Cab S) 85 86 87 88 89 Estate at Oakville challenges the leaders with, esp, a polished, refined Cab (and weightier, woodier Reserve). Also vg Chard. 30,000 cases.

Guenoc Vineyards Lake County ❋ Ambitious winery/v'yard venture just N of Napa county line. NB for ZIN (81, 84, 85, 88), PETITE SIRAH, other reds. Chard coming nicely. Property once belonged to Lillie Langtry, hence Reserve Langtry label for MERITAGES and Domaine Breton for second label varietals. 75,000 cases.

Guild San Joaquin ★ Ex-coop owned by Canandaigua of New York. B Cribari is the main table wine label, Cooks American Champagne a runaway success among tank-fermented sparklers. Also owns Mendocino V'yds (ex-Cresta Blanca) in Mendocino and Dunnewood. 3 million cases?

Gundlach-Bundschu Sonoma ★★ (Chard) 87 88 89 90 (Cab S) 78 79 80 81 82 83 84 85 86 87 88 Pioneer name solidly revived by newest generation. Rhinefarm Vineyard on label signals worthy Gewürz, Cab, Chard. 50,000 cases.

Hacienda Sonoma (Chard) 87 88 89 90 (Cab S) 85 86 87 88 Good quality Chard, Gewürz, Sauv Bl, Cab, and Cab blend called Antares. Ultra-ripe, curiously Rhône-like Pinot N. 25,000 cases.

Hagafen Napa ★★ First and perhaps still finest of the serious kosher producers. Cab, Chard, JOHANNISBERG RIES. 6,000 cases.

Handley Cellars Mendocino ❋ (Chard) 87 88 89 90 Winemaker-owned small producer of refined Chard and Gewürz (90), classic sparkling and refreshing Brightlighter (Gewürz-based). 12,000 cases.

Hanzell Sonoma (Chard) 87 88 89 (Pinot N) 83 84 85 86 87 88 The late founder revolutionized California Chards, Pinot Ns in late '60s. Two owners later Hanzell remains a throwback source of its original ripe, full-flavoured style. 2,000 cases.

Haywood Vineyard Sonoma ★★ Bought in '91 by BUENA VISTA to continue as an independent estate source of intense ZIN and conventional Chard. 34,000 cases before sale.

Heitz Napa ★★★★ (Cab S) 76 77 78 79 80 81 82 83 84 85 86 87 An individualist winemaker has set lofty standards for his peers with his dark, deep, emphatic Cabs, esp Martha's Vineyard but also Bella Oaks and Napa Valley. Other wines eccentric or worse. 40,000 cases.

Hess Collection, The Napa ❋→★★★★ (Chard) 89 90 (Cab S) 89 A Swiss art collector's winery-cum-museum in former Mont La Salle winery of CHRISTIAN BROTHERS. Steadily improving Cab, Chard. Hess Selection label is vg value. 15,000 cases, aiming for 50.

Hill Winery, William Napa ★★★ (Chard) 87 88 89 90 (Cab S) 80 81 82 83 84 85 86 87 88 V'yds high in Mayacamas Mts yield steady Chard; ever more stylish (and restrained) Cabs. 12,000 cases.

Hop Kiln Sonoma ★★ Good source of bold-as-brass PETITE SIRAH and ZIN. Even Gewürz is full-flavoured and large-scale. 10,000 cases.

Husch Vineyards Mendocino ❋ Reliable Chard, Sauv Bl, Cab; sometimes outstanding Pinot N and Gewürz from Anderson Valley. 15,000 cases.

Inglenook Napa ★★→★★★ (Chard) 87 88 89 90 (Cab S) 80 83 84 85 86 87 88 Great old Napa winery, now owned by Grand Met, has regained much of its earlier footing, esp with supple Cab, heartier Cask (Reserve) Cab and thoroughly tannic Reunion Cab. Merlot, Gravion (Sauv Bl-Sém) and Reserve Chard also to watch. 110,000 cases.

Iron Horse Vineyards Sonoma ✶✶✶ (Chard) 87 88 89 (Cab S) 80 81 82 83 84 85 86 87 88 Substantial Russian River property concentrates increasingly on v successful classic sparkling with real finesse, but continues with Chard and Pinot N from same estate v'yd. Cab, Sauv Bl from affiliated Alexander Valley v'yd can be memorable. Joint venture coming up with Laurent-Perrier. 40,000 cases.

Jekel Vineyards Monterey ✶✶ (Chard) 87 88 89 90 (Cab S) 80 81 82 83 84 85 86 87 88 Jekel's ripe, juicy Ries is the most successful wine from Salinas v'yds. Also good Chard, intensely regional (fruit-flavoured) Cab. Financial complications here. 60,000 cases.

Jepson Vineyards Mendocino ✶✶ Chard, Sauv Bl, classic sparkling, and pot-still brandy from estate in Ukiah area. 30,000 cases.

Johnson-Turnbull Napa ✶✶ (Cab S) 80 81 82 83 84 85 86 87 Rich, full, minty Cabs from estate facing the Robert MONDAVI winery; Chard from Sonoma grapes. 10,000 cases.

Jordan Sonoma ✶✶✶ (Chard) 87 88 89 (Cab S) 78 79 80 81 82 83 84 85 86 87 Extravagant Alexander Valley estate models its Cab on supplest Bordeaux. But it lasts. Chard is oaky, smoky and smooth. New classic sparkling called simply 'J' is deft, fresh, luxurious. 75,000 cases.

Karly Amador ✶✶ Among the more ambitious sources of Sierra Foothills ZIN. 12,000 cases.

Keenan Winery, Robert Napa ✶✶ (Chard) 87 88 89 90 (Cab S) 82 83 84 85 86 87 Winery on Spring Mountain has veered away from overweight, heavily oaked to more restrained Cab, Merlot, Chard. 12,000 cases.

Kendall-Jackson Lake County ✶✶ (Chard) 87 88 89 90 (Cab S) 85 86 87 88 89 Dynamic maker of popular, slightly sweet Chards and Sauv Bls; v oaky Cab. Hard-to-get single-v'yd ZINS (labelled Ciapusci, DePratt, Mariah) can be memorable, as can Syrah (Durrell). 500,000 cases. *See also* Cambria.

Kenwood Vineyards Sonoma ✶✶→✶✶✶ (Chard) 87 88 89 90 (Cab S) 78 79 80 83 84 85 86 87 88 Substantial producer of winning Sauv Bl and ZIN, solid Chard (incl single-v'yd Beltane) and Cab S (single-v'yd Jack London can challenge the best). 150,000 cases.

Kistler Vineyards Sonoma (Chard) 87 88 89 90 Chards much in the smoky, buttery style. Pinot N and Cab more recent. 9,000 cases.

Konocti Cellars Lake County ✶✶ Excellent value Sauv Bl, Chard, Cab from a small growers' coop. Recent MERITAGES (red and white) show promise. 40,000 cases.

Korbel Sonoma ✶✶ Long-established classic sparkling specialists who place extra emphasis on fruit flavours, lots of fizz. Natural, Brut and Blanc de Blancs are best. 1.5 million cases.

Kornell, Hanns Napa ✶✶ Family-owned producers of classic sparkling, incl Germanic Sehr Trocken. Merger under discussion. 25,000 cases.

Krug, Charles Napa ✶✶ (Chard) 87 88 89 90 (Cab S) 78 79 80 83 84 85 86 87 Historically important winery with generally sound wines. Cabs at head of the list. CK-Mondavi is jug brand. 200,000 cases.

La Crema Sonoma (Chard) 87 88 89 (Pinot N) 80 81 82 83 84 85 86 87 Russian River grapes dominate in deftly oaked Chard and often deep-flavoured Pinot N. 80,000 cases.

Lakespring Napa ✶✶ Merlot, Cab, Chard, Sauv Bl. 18,000 cases.

Lambert Bridge Sonoma ✶✶ (Chard) 87 88 89 (Cab S) 80 81 82 83 84 85 86 87 Distinctive Chard and solid Cab usually need age. 25,000 cases.

Landmark Sonoma (Chard) 87 88 89 90 Ever steadier Chard-only producer offers 3 (Sonoma County, Sonoma Valley, DeMaris Reserve). 15,000 cases.

Laurel Glen Sonoma ✶✶✶ (Cab S) 81 82 83 84 85 86 87 88 Fine, distinctly regional Cab from steep v'yd in Sonoma Mountain AVA. 5,000 cases.

Laurier Sonoma ✶✶✶ (Chard) 87 (Cab S) 78 79 80 81 82 83 84 85 86 Lovely wines formerly; but now only a label owned by FRANZIA. Await developments.

Lazy Creek Mendocino ★★   'Retirement hobby' of a long-time restaurant waiter is yielding serious Anderson Valley Gewürz and Chard. Also Pinot N. 2,000 cases.

Leeward Winery Ventura (Chard) 87 88 89   Ultra-toasty Central Coast Chards are the mainstay. 18,000 cases.

Lohr, J Central Coast ★★   A wide range of steady varietals from wineries in Sta Clara and San Luis Obispo. V'yds there, in Napa and Clarksburg on the Sacramento River. 200,000 cases.

Long Vineyards Napa ★★ (Chard) 87 88 89 (Cab S) 79 80 81 82 83 84 85 86 87   Tiny hillside neighbour of CHAPPELLET produces lush Chard and flavoury Cab S. 3,000 cases.

Lyeth Vineyard Sonoma ★★   Former winery, now a brand owned by J C Boisset (Burgundy). Christophe is more modest label for bought wines.

Lytton Springs Sonoma ★★   Now owned by RIDGE: ink-dark, hard, heady ZINS. 15,000 cases.

Madrona El Dorado ★★   Loftiest v'yds in Sierra Foothills good for steady Chard (among others). 10,000 cases.

Maison Deutz San Luis Obispo ★★★   Californian arm of Champagne Wm Deutz shows a firm sense of style, using grapes from v'yds nr Sta Barbara county line. 25,000 cases.

Mark West Vineyards Sonoma ★★ (Chard) 87 88 89 (Pinot N) 80 81 82 83 84 85 86 87 88   V satisfactory Gewürz from v'yd in coolest part of Russian River valley. Also sturdy to rustic Chard, Pinot N and, at times, classic Blanc de Noirs sparkling. 22,000 cases.

Markham Napa ★★ (Chard) 87 88 89 90 (Cab S) 80 81 82 83 84 85 86 87 88   Japanese-owned. Sound, steady. 20,000 cases.

Martin Bros San Luis Obispo ★★ (Chard) 87 88   Fine dry Chenin Bl, good oaked Chard. Family winery aims to establish Paso Robles as California's Piedmont with Nebbiolo.

Martini, Louis M Napa ★★→★★★ (Chard) 87 88 89 90 (Cab S) 51 55 59 60 64 65 69 74 75 77 78 79 80 81 82 83 84 85 86 87 88   Family-owned winery with high standards at every level, esp v'yd Cab (Monte Rosso), Merlot (Los Vinedos del Rio), Pinot N (La Loma). Emerging source of crisp Russian River/Carneros Chard and delicate Sauv Bl. Second label Glen Oaks. 235,000 cases.

Masson Vineyards Monterey ★→★★★   Chard, Ries, Cab, Pinot N on a big scale.

Matanzas Creek Sonoma ★★★ (Chard) 85 86 87 88 89 90 (Merlot) 85 86 87   Fine ripely fruity Chard, Sauv Bl; well-regarded Merlot. 27,000 cases.

Mayacamas Napa ★★★ (Chard) 85 86 87 88 (Cab S) 70 73 74 75 78 79 80 81 82 83 84 85 86   First-rate small v'yd offering rich Chard and firm (but no longer steel-hard) Cab. Sometimes Sauv Bl, ZIN. 5,000 cases.

McDowell Valley Vineyards Mendocino ★★   Obligatory Chard, Cab, but owners' hearts are with Rhône varieties, esp Syrah from ancient vines and Grenache (labelled Les Vieux Cépages). 100,000 cases.

Meridian San Luis Obispo ★★→★★★   Nestlé-owned latecomer property. Impressive Sta Barbara Chard (88, 89, 90), Pinot N (88) and Paso Robles Syrah (88), Cab. 30,000 cases.

Meritage Trademarked name for reds or whites using Bordeaux grape varieties. Little followed; may soon expire.

Merry Vintners Sonoma (★★)   Winemaker-owned producer of well-oaked regular and reserve Chards. Branching into Pinot N.

Milano Mendocino ★★   Chard. 10,000 cases.

Mill Creek Sonoma ★★   Cab, Merlot, Chard, Sauv Bl. 15,000 cases.

Mirassou Central Coast ★★   Fifth generation grower in Sta Clara, pioneer in Monterey (Salinas Valley). Cab, Chard, Sauv Bl, Gewürz, Pinot N and v pleasant classic sparkling. 350,000 cases.

Mondavi, Robert Napa ★★→★★★★ (Chard) 87 88 89 90 (Cab S) 74 75 76 77 78 79 80 81 82 83 84 85 86 87 88   Winery with a brilliant quarter-century record of innovation in styles, equipment and technique. Famous successes incl Cab, Sauv Bl (sold as FUMÉ BL), Chard, even

Pinot N. 'Reserves' are marvels, regularly among Napa's best wines. 500,000 cases. Mondavi-Woodbridge label for less expensive California appellation varietals. *See also* Opus One.

Monterey Peninsula Monterey ** Small winery in Monterey town makes chunky, long-living reds, esp ZIN and Cab, from Salinas and other grapes. 12,000 cases.

Monterey Vineyard, The Monterey ** Seagram-owned label for Chard, Pinot N and Cab in Classic and more costly Limited Release lines. 550,000 cases.

Monteviña Amador ** (Cab S) 80 81 82 83 84 85 86 87 88 89 (Zin) 80 81 82 83 84 85 86 87 88 Major force in revitalizing hearty-style Sierra Foothill ZINS. Now, under ownership of SUTTER HOME, turning also to a major exploration of Italian varieties. 50,000 cases.

Monticello Cellars Napa **→*** (Chard) 87 88 89 (Cab S) 81 82 83 84 85 86 87 Ultra-modern winery nr Napa City. Outstanding Gewürz (now v limited) first caught the eye. Refined Jefferson Ranch, darkly tannic Corley Reserve Cabs and sternly oaky Chards now the major effort. Domaine Montreaux is classic sparkling. 25,000 cases.

Mont St John Napa ** Old Napa wine family makes good value Pinot N, Chard from own Carneros v'yd; buys in for solid Cab. 20,000 cases.

Morgan Monterey ** →*** (Chard) 87 88 89 90 Winemaker-owned producer of steady local Chard and fine Alexander Valley Sauv Bl. 20,000 cases.

Mount Eden Vineyards Sta Cruz Mts ** (Chard) 87 88 89 Expensive, big-scale Chard from old Martin Ray v'yds and gentler one from Monterey. Also Pinot N, Cab. 4,000 cases.

Mount Veeder Napa ** (Cab S) 74 75 76 77 78 79 80 81 82 83 84 85 86 87 Once oaky Chards and austere Cabs are gentler and better balanced since acquired by FRANCISCAN. Now MERITAGE (88). About 8,000 cases.

Mumm Napa Valley *** G H Mumm-Seagram joint venture out of the box fast with fine vintage (85, 86) and NV Brut. Also distinctive single-v'yd Winery Lake 'cuvée'. 125,000 cases.

Navarro Vineyards Mendocino **→*** (Chard) 87 88 89 Firm, fine Chard, outstanding dry Gewürz and Ries from cool Anderson Valley. Pinot N begins to find a footing. 12,000 cases.

Nalle Sonoma **→*** (Zin) 84 85 86 87 88 89 Winemaker-owned cellar in Dry Creek Valley gets to the very heart of ZIN. Wonderfully berryish young; that and more with age. Now also a trickle of Cab. 2,500 cases.

Newton Vineyards Napa *** (Chard) 87 88 89 (Cab S) 84 85 86 87 Luxurious estate growing more so; formerly ponderous style now reined back to the merely opulent for Chard, Cab, Merlot. 15,000 cases.

Niebaum Collection Napa **→*** Heublein-owned label: small lots from some of highest quality v'yds they acquired with BEAULIEU and INGLENOOK. V superior Chards (Reference, Laird, Bayview), Sém (Chevrier), good Cabs from winemaker Judy Matulich-Weitz. 20,000 cases.

Opus One Napa **** (Cab S) 78 79 80 81 82 83 84 85 86 87 88 Joint venture of R MONDAVI, Baronne Philippine de Rothschild. Spectacular new winery opened in '92. Wines are showpieces, too. 10,000 cases.

Parducci Mendocino ** (Chard) 87 88 89 (Cab S) 78 80 81 82 83 84 85 86 87 88 Long-established v'yds and winery ever reliable for Cab, Cab-Merlot, ZIN, Barbera. No-oak Chard, off-dry Sauv Bl. 350,000 cases.

Pecota, Robert Napa ** Cab, Sauv Bl, Chard, Gamay. 18,000 cases.

Pedroncelli Sonoma ** (Chard) 87 88 89 90 (Cab S) 81 82 83 84 85 86 87 88 Old family firm with above-average, sturdy, vinous Cab, ZIN (esp Reserves). Chard, Sauv Bl are growing stylish. 125,000 cases.

Pepi, Robert Napa **→*** (Chard) 87 88 89 90 (Cab S) 82 83 84 85 86 87 88 Founded as Sauv Bl specialist; now thoughtfully restrained Chard, Cab, winning Sangiovese Grosso (Colline di Sasso, 89). 20,000 cases.

Phelps, Joseph Napa *** (Chard) 85 86 87 88 89 90 (Cab S) 74 75 76 77 78 79 80 81 82 83 84 85 86 87 88 Deluxe winery and beautiful v'yd with impeccable standards. Vg Chard, Cabs (esp Backus Vineyard), pioneer Syrah and splendid late-harvest Ries, Gewürz. Reserve red Insignia can be over-tannic at times. 60,000 cases.

Philippine Baronne P de Rothschild's new brand. (*See also* Opus One.)

Pine Ridge Napa **→*** (Chard) 87 88 89 90 (Cab S) 79 80 81 82 83 84 85 86 87 88   Winery nr Stag's Leap makes consistently well-oaked Chard, Cab (several) and Merlot. 50,000 cases.

Piper Sonoma Sonoma ***   A venture of Piper-Heidsieck using mostly Russian River valley grapes for vg classic sparklers. They benefit from age in bottle. 125,000 cases.

Preston Sonoma *** (Cab S) 83 84 85 86 87 88   Small winery with excellent Dry Creek Valley v'yd esp for ZIN, Cab, SIRAH-Syrah blend. Also Sauv Bl. 25,000 cases.

Quady Winery San Joaquin **   Imaginative dessert wines from Madera incl port-like Starboard, celebrated orangey Muscat Essencia, dark Muscat Elysium and, latest, Moscato d'Asti-like Electra. 15,000 cases.

Quail Ridge Napa ** (Chard) 85 86 87 88 89   Specialist in barrel-fermented Chard. Also Cab. Recently added vg Sauv Bl and Merlot. Owned by Heublein. 15,000 cases.

Quivira Sonoma **   Melony Sauv Bl and intensely berryish ZIN lead the list. Regnum is Zin-Syrah blend of considerable promise. 12,000 cases.

Qupé Sta Barbara **→***   Never-a-dull-moment cellar-mate of AU BON CLIMAT. Marsanne, Pinot Bl, Syrah are worth trying.

Rafanelli, A Sonoma ** (Zin) 84 85 86 87 88   Hearty, somewhat rustic Dry Creek ZIN; Cab of striking intensity. 6,000 cases.

Rancho Sisquoc Sta Barbara **   Highly personal little winery shows vivid quality of Sta Maria valley grapes, incl Ries, Chard, even Sylvaner.

Ravenswood Sonoma **   Best known for dark, sturdy ZINS. 15,000 cases.

Raymond Vineyards and Cellar Napa *** (Chard) 85 86 87 88 89 90 (Cab S) 74 75 77 78 79 80 81 82 83 84 85 86 87 88   Old Napa wine family now with Japanese partners. Emphatically fruity Chard and Sauv Bl; dark, sturdy keeper Cabs. 110,000 cases.

Ridge Sta Cruz Mts **** (Cab S) 78 80 81 82 83 84 85 86 87   Winery of highest repute among connoisseurs draws from Napa, Sonoma, San Luis Obispo and its own mountain v'yd for concentrated Cabs and ZINS, needing long maturing in bottle. Most notable efforts from single v'yds, esp Monte Bello, York Creek (Spring Mt) Cabs, Geyserville, Dusi Zins. Now also fine smoky Chard. 40,000 cases.

Roederer Estate Mendocino ⬛⬛⬛   Anderson Valley branch of Reims Champagne house, since '88. The resonant Roederer style is apparent. Built to make 90,000 cases.

Rombauer Vineyards Napa ** (Chard) 87 88 89 90 (Cab S) 84 85 86 87   Well-oaked Chard, dark Cab (esp reserve-style 'Meilleur du Chai'). 15,000 cases.

Roudon-Smith Sta Cruz Mts **   Chard, Cab. 10,000 cases.

Round Hill Napa **   Formerly wide range now narrowed to Cab, Chard, Merlot, Sauv Bl, but in 3 price ranges: bargain House, regular Round Hill, separate top-of-the-line Rutherford Ranch label. 350,000 cases.

Rutherford Hill Napa **→*** (Chard) 87 88 89 (Cab S) 80 81 82 83 84 85 86 87 88   Larger stable-mate of FREEMARK ABBEY. Good and still improving with several flavoury Chards (Jaeger, XVS), sturdy Cabs (XVS) and Merlots. Also worth watching for good dry Gewürz. 100,000 cases.

Rutherford Ranch *See* Round Hill.

Rutherford Vintners Napa ⬛⬛ (Cab S) 78 79 80 81 82 83 84 85 86 87 88   Subtle but eminently age-worthy Cabs are the main event; Château Rutherford is Reserve lot. 12,000 cases.

St Andrews Napa ** (Chard) 85 86 87 88 89 90 (Cab S) 83 84 85 86 87 88   Steadily excellent Chard estate on Silverado Trail nr Napa City. Is abandoning Cab S. Recently acquired by CLOS DU VAL. 15,000 cases.

St Clement Napa **→**** (Chard) 87 88 89 90 (Cab S) 78 80 81 82 83 84 85 86 87 88   Distinctive Sauv Bl worth ageing. Austere Chard, sturdy Cab and Merlot. Japanese-owned. 15,000 cases.

St Francis Sonoma ** (Chard) 85 86 87 88 89 90   Gaining speed after slow start. Firm, v tasty Sonoma Valley estate Chard (esp 90). Steady Merlot. Also Gewürz, Cab. 34,000 cases.

St Supery Napa **   French-owned, supplied by 500-acre estate v'yd in Pope Valley. Good Sauv Bl, accessible Cab. Also Chard – and now Merlot. 25,000 cases, able to expand tenfold.

Saintsbury Napa *** (Chard) 85 86 87 88 89 90 (Pinot N) 84 85 86 87 88 89   Carneros producer of finest (and slowest-ageing) Pinot N of region. Lighter Pinot N Garnet and oaky Chard also vg. 35,000 cases.

Sanford Sta Barbara *** (Chard) 86 87 88 89 90 (Pinot N) 82 83 84 85 86 87 88 89   Specialist in clean-fruity, intense, age-worthy Pinot N (esp Barrel Select). Almost outrageously bold Chard; firmly regional Sauv Bl and a little Pinot N 'Gris'. 30,000 cases.

Santa Barbara Winery Sta Barbara ** (Chard) 87 88 89 (Pinot N) 85 86 87 88 89   Former jug-wine producer, now among regional leaders, esp for Reserve Chard. Also Pinot N, ZIN, Cab. 28,000 cases.

Santa Cruz Mountain V'yd Sta Cruz Mts **   Huge, tannic, heady Pinot N and Cab dominate. 2,500 cases.

Santa Ynez Valley Winery Sta Barbara **   Sauv Bl, Chard, Merlot. 20,000 cases.

Santino Amador **   Stylish Sierra Foothills ZINS (Fiddletown, Grand Père); also crackerjack white Zin. Italian varieties too. 30,000 cases.

Scharffenberger Mendocino **   First to try Mendocino for serious classic sparkling. Now Pommery-owned and doing well. 25,000 cases.

Schramsberg Napa ****   Dedicated specialist makes California's best 'champagne' in historic caves. Reserve splendid; Bl de Noir outstanding, deserves 2–10 yrs' age. Luxury 'cuvée' from '92. 50,000 cases.

Schug Cellars Sonoma (Chard) 85 86 87 88 89   German-born and trained owner-winemaker developing refined Chard and Pinot N from Carneros. Relocated from Napa to Carneros in '91. 10,000 cases.

Sebastiani Sonoma **   Substantial old family firm works in several different market levels. Single-v'yd Sonoma Cab (Bell Ranch, Cherryblock) at top; Sonoma and North Coast appellation varietals in middle; August Sebastiani Country wines in jugs. 4 million cases.

Seghesio Sonoma ** (Chard) 87 88 89 90 (Pinot N) 81 83 86 87 89   Long-time jug-wine producer recently turned to bottling its own wines with striking results. Vg Chard, Pinot N; often exceptional ZINS (esp Dry Creek, Alexander Valley Reserves). 85,000 cases.

Sequoia Grove Napa **→**** (Chard) 87 88 89 90 (Cab S) 83 84 85 86 87 88   Vg Chards age well. Alexander Valley, Napa Cabs dark, firm. 16,000 cases.

Shadow Creek *See* Domaine Chandon.

Shafer Vineyards Napa **→**** (Chard) 87 88 89 90 (Cab S) 78 79 80 81 82 83 84 85 86 87 88   Polished Chard, stylish Cab (esp Hillside Select) and Merlot from v'yd and 16,000-case cellar in Stag's Leap district.

Shaw Vineyards and Winery, Charles F Napa ** (Chard) 87 88 89 90   Founded as Gamay specialist; has added fine Sauv Bl and increasingly stylish Chard. But future uncertain. 40,000 cases.

Sierra Vista El Dorado **   Steady Chard, Cab S, ZIN, Syrah from Sierra Foothills grapes. 6,000 cases.

Silver Oak Napa **→**** (Cab S) 78 79 80 81 82 83 84 85 86 87   Cabs, thoroughly American-oaked, incl pricey Bonny's V'yd. 24,000 cases.

Silverado Vineyards Napa *** (Chard) 87 88 89 90 (Cab S) 83 84 85 86 87 88 89   Showy hilltop winery in Stag's Leap district. Cab, Chard, Sauv Bl all consistently refined; Cabs from '81 on ageing well. 75,000 cases.

Simi Alexander Valley *** (Chard) 83 85 86 87 88 89 90 (Cab S) 79 81 84 85 86 87 88   Restored historic winery has flowered under expert direction of Zelma Long. Wonderfully long-lived Chard, Sauv Bl. Vg Cab. Fruity Chenin Bl and Cab rosé for summer fests. 130,000 cases.

Smith & Hook Monterey ** (Cab S) 80 81 82 83 84 85 86 87 Specialist in dark, intensely regional Cabs – so herbaceous you can taste dill. Also Merlots. Lone Oak is second label for Cab, Chard. 10,000 cases.

Smith-Madrone Napa ** Soft, round but durable Spring Mt Ries. Also Cab, Chard. 6,000 cases.

Sonoma-Cutrer Vineyards Sonoma ***→**** (Chard) 82 83 84 85 86 87 88 89 90 Ultimate specialist in Chard. Advanced techniques display characters of individual v'yds, as in Burgundy. So far Les Pierres is No 1 ager; Russian River Ranches is quickly accessible. 75,000 cases.

Spotteswoode Napa ***→**** (Cab S) 84 85 86 87 88 Seductive, resonant Cab from tiny estate v'yd right in St Helena town. Also supple, polished Sauv Bl. 3,500 cases.

Spring Mountain Vineyards Napa ** Renovated 19th C property, setting for 'Falcon Crest'. Coasting with Cab, Chard, Sauv Bl. 25,000 cases.

Stag's Leap Wine Cellars Napa ***→**** (Chard) 87 88 89 90 (Cab S) 78 79 80 81 82 83 84 85 86 87 88 Celebrated v'yd and cellar for Cabs (Napa, Stag's Leap V'yd, and recently controversial top-of-line Cask 23). Also vg Chard, Ries and improving Sauv Bl. 40,000 cases.

Sterling Napa *** (Chard) 87 88 89 90 (Cab S) 82 83 84 85 86 87 88 Proficient (also scenic) winery owned by Seagram. Strong, tart Sauv Bl and Chards. Burly Cab, Three Palms (Merlot-based) and Reserve (Cab-based). Winery Lake V'yd Pinot N still promises more than it performs. 150,000 cases.

Stonegate Napa ** Estate Chard, Sauv Bl, Cab, Merlot. 15,000 cases.

Stony Hill Napa *** (Chard) 83 84 85 86 87 88 89 Hilly v'yd/winery for many of California's v best whites over past 30 yrs. Founder Fred McCrea died in '77, widow Eleanor in '91; son Peter carries on powerful tradition. Chard less steely, more fleshy than before. Oak-tinged Ries and Gewürz understated but age-worthy. 4,000 cases.

Stratford Napa ** Merchant label for reliable Cab, Merlot, Chard. 20,000 cases.

Strong Vineyard, Rodnay Sonoma ** (Chard) 85 86 87 88 89 90 (Cab S) 77 79 81 83 84 85 86 87 88 Formerly Sonoma V'yds, draws mostly on Russian River Valley for steady Chards (esp Chalk Hill V'yd) and Pinot N; Alexander Valley for Cabs (esp single-v'yd Alexander's Crown) and Sauv Bl. 375,000 cases.

Sutter Home Napa ** (Zin) 78 80 81 82 83 84 85 86 87 88 89 Best known for sweet white ZIN; most admired for sometimes heady Amador Zin. Starting with bargain-priced Cab, Chard. 3 million cases.

Swan, Joseph Sonoma ** (Pinot N) 85 86 (Zin) 74 76 77 78 79 80 81 82 83 84 85 86 Ultra-bold style for ZINs and Pinot Ns of late Joe Swan continues under direction of his son-in-law. 2,000 cases.

Taft Street Sonoma ** After muddling along, has hit an impressive stride with good value Russian River Chards, good Sauv Bl. 18,000 cases.

Trefethen Napa **→*** (Chard) 83 84 85 86 87 88 90 (Cab S) 74 75 76 77 78 79 80 81 82 83 84 85 86 87 88 Respected family-owned winery in Napa's finest old wooden building. Vg dry Ries, tense Chard for ageing (late-released Library wines show how well). Cab shows increasing depths. Value in low-priced blends: Eshcol Red, White. 70,000 cases.

Tudal Napa ** (Cab S) 79 80 81 82 83 84 85 86 87 88 Tiny estate winery N of St Helena; steady source of dark, firm, ageable Cabs. 2,500 cases.

Tulocay Napa ** (Chard) 87 88 89 (Pinot N) 84 85 86 87 88 89 Tiny winery at Napa City. Chard and esp Pinot N can be really accomplished. Cab S is also worth attention. 2,400 cases.

Ventana Monterey ** (Chard) 87 88 89 90 '78 winery on large v'yd keeps shuffling its range, but Chards (fruity Gold Stripe, oakier Cristal) remain on top. 42,000 cases.

Viansa Sonoma ** (Chard) 87 88 89 (Cab S) 84 85 86 87 Reliable source of

Napa-Sonoma Chard, Sauv Bl and Cab is turning attention to Sangiovese. No 91 wine made.

Vichon Winery Napa ★★→★★★ (Chard) 87 88 89 90 (Cab S) 81 82 83 84 85 86 87 88 MONDAVI-owned. Subtle, agreeable Chevrignon (Sauv Bl-Sém) pairs with equally worthy Cab. Stern oaky Chard. 50,000 cases.

Villa Mt Eden Napa ★★ (Chard) 87 88 89 90 (Cab S) 80 83 84 85 86 87 88 Rich, nearly plummy Cab made the name of this small Oakville estate. Bought by Château Ste Michelle group (*see* Washington) and improving strongly. 24,000 cases and expanding.

Vita Nova Sta Barbara Label from stable of AU BON CLIMAT. To watch.

Weibel Alameda and Mendocino ★→★★ Mainly tank-made sparklers; also range of accessible table wines for current drinking. 7,500 cases.

Wente Bros Livermore and Monterey ★→★★ Historic specialists in whites, esp Livermore Sauv, Sém. Monterey sweet Ries can be exceptional. Of growing importance for classic sparkling. 300,000 cases.

Whitehall Lane Napa ★★ Recent Japanese purchase. Obligatory Chard, Cab and weighty Merlot, but to follow for fresh, lively Pinot N (81, 82, 83, 84, 85, 86, 87, 88, 89). 20,000 cases.

White Oak Sonoma ★★ (Chard) 87 88 89 90 Source of underrated, vibrantly fruity Alexander Valley Chards and Sauv Bls. 11,000 cases.

Wild Horse Winery San Luis Obispo ★★→★★★ (Pinot N) 85 86 87 88 Reaches into Sta Barbara for impressive Pinot N. Also Chard, Cab. 15,000 cases.

William Wheeler Sonoma ★★ (Chard) 87 88 89 90 (Cab S) 82 83 84 85 86 87 88 Historic emphasis on emphatically dark, tannic Cab and lively Sauv Bl from Dry Creek Valley. Since French acquisition, also for affable Rhône-type RS Reserve. 19,000 cases.

Zaca Mesa Sta Barbara ★★ (Chard) 87 88 89 90 (Pinot N) 84 85 86 87 88 89 Deliberately down-sized from 80 to 35,000 cases and refocused on buttery Chard and well-wooded Pinot N. Also Cab, Syrah.

ZD Napa ★★→★★★ (Chard) 87 88 89 90 (Pinot N) 84 85 86 87 88 89 Lusty Chard well marked by American oak is the ZD signature wine. Pinot N is often finer. 18,000 cases.

The Pacific Northwest

This region occupies the same latitudes on the Pacific Coast as France does on the Atlantic. As in California, the modern wine industry dates back to the early '60s. Each of the northwestern States (Oregon, Washington, Idaho) is developing a distinct identity, with wine of similar quality to that of north California.

Oregon's vines (about 5,000 acres) lie mainly in the cool-temperate Willamette and warmer Umpqua valleys between the Coast and Cascade Ranges, in climates not unlike those of France, leading to delicate flavours.

Washington's vineyards (about 11,000 acres) lie mainly east of the Cascades in a drier, more severe climate tempered by the Yakima and Columbia Rivers, and Idaho's east of Oregon along the Snake River. Both are regions with warm days and cold nights which preserve acidity and intensify flavours.

In Oregon most of the 70-odd wineries are small and highly individual; and vintages are as uneven as in Burgundy, whose Pinot Noir is this state's most celebrated grape. A rare succession of good vintages for Pinot Noir, '88, '89 and '90, have also yielded notable Chardonnay and Pinot Gris.

The Washington industry, with about 90 wineries, is remarkably consistent over a wide range. Cabernet and Merlot grow excellently, as well as all the classic white varieties. A run of fine vintages, '88, '89, '90, '91, has coincided with maturing winemaking talent. Despite small harvests in 1990 and 1991, most wines remain excellent bargains.

Oregon

Adelsheim Vineyard Willamette Valley   Nicely oaked Pinot N, Chard often best early. Pinot G fresher.

Alpine Vineyards Willamette Valley   Small estate winery with high spots, incl Pinot N, Ries.

Argyle Willamette Valley   Since '87, Australia's NW outpost, led by Brian Croser. Dry Ries, Chard and vg sparkling.

Amity Willamette Valley   Distinctive Pinot N, several styles, good Gewürz.

Bethel Heights Willamette Valley   Deftly made, thoughtfully styled Chard and Pinot N from estate nr Salem have won consistent praise.

Cameron Willamette Valley   Neighbour of KNUDSEN-ERATH attracting attention for Pinot N.

Château Benoit Willamette Valley   Most consistent successes have been Müller-T and Ries. A recent entrant into sparkling wines.

Drouhin Willamette Valley   Bold enterprise of one of Beaune's great names. Fine 89 Pinot N.

Elk Cove Vineyards Willamette Valley   Pinot N from small estate is somewhat erratic but can rival the best. Also fresh Ries, well-oaked Chard and Pinot G.

The Eyrie Vineyards Willamette Valley   Pioneer ('65) winery with burgundian convictions. Oregon's most famous and consistently good Pinot N and v oaky Chard. Also Pinots G (irreplaceable with salmon) and Meunier, and dry Muscat.

Knudsen-Erath Willamette Valley   Oregon's second-largest winery, established itself with good value Pinot N and Chard, less consistent in recent vintages.

Montinore Willamette Valley   Ambitious winery with, for Oregon, huge 465-acre v'yd nr Forest Grove.

Oak Knoll Willamette Valley   Started with fruit wines but has turned into one of Oregon's larger and more skilful Pinot N producers.

Ponzi Willamette Valley   Small winery almost in Portland, well known for Ries. Also Pinot G, Chard and delicate Pinot N.

Rex Hill Willamette Valley   Well-financed assault on top levels of Pinot N (quality, price): some success, esp from single v'yds. Also Chard, Ries.

Shafer Vineyard Cellars Willamette Valley   Meticulous small producer of frequently good Pinot N, sometimes excellent, delicate Chard.

Sokol Blosser Willamette Valley   One of the larger Oregon wineries; aims at popular taste with easy, accessible Chard, Ries and Pinot N. Also Sauv Bl, Merlot (seldom grown in Oregon).

Tulatin Vineyards Willamette Valley   Substantial estate winery: Chard, Pinot N (and white from Pinot N), Gewürz of ever more personal style.

Tyee Willamette Valley   Recent arrival. Early vintages of Gewürz, Chard, Pinot N are well made.

Yamhill Valley Willamette Valley   Young estate near college town of McMinnville focuses on Chard and Pinot N.

Washington/Idaho

Arbor Crest Spokane (Washington)   Expanding winery has had ups and downs. Ups are Chard and Sauv Bl.

Barnard Griffin Prosser (Washington)   Small producer of well-made Merlot, Chard and Sauv Bl.

Château Ste Chapelle Caldwell (Idaho, nr Boise)   Top-drawer wine-making keeps intensely flavoured, impeccably balanced Chard, Ries from Washington and local v'yds nr forefront in NW. Reds on the rise.

Château Ste Michelle Ubiquitous in Washington The regional giant grows ever larger. The owning corporation had Château Ste M and COLUMBIA CREST at 750,000 cases before their '91 acquisition of SNOQUALMIE, the state's second-largest producer. Major v'yd holdings, first-rate equipment, and skilful winemakers keep Chard, Sém, Sauv Bl, Ries, Cab and Merlot in the front ranks. First serious efforts at sparkling are attractive.

Columbia Crest Columbia Valley (Washington) CHATEAU STE MICHELLE label for well-made, accessible wines priced one cut lower, most of them from big River Run v'yd.

Columbia Winery Woodinville (Washington) A pioneer ('62, as Associated Vintners): still a leader. Balanced, stylishly understated single-v'yd wines, esp Merlot (Milestone), Cabs (Otis, Red Willow) and Syrah (Red Willow). Oak-fermented Chard, elegant Pinot N, fruity Sém impressive.

Covey Run Yakima Valley (Washington) Mostly estate wines. Intriguing Aligoté and Caille de FUMÉ; intense, often heady Merlot and Cab.

Gordon Brothers Columbia Valley (Washington) Tiny but promising cellar for Chard, Merlot and Cab.

Hogue Cellars Yakima Valley (Washington) Leader in the region, best known at start for off-dry whites (esp Ries, Chenin Bl, Sauv Bl), but more recently memorable for stylish, balanced Chard, Merlot, Cab.

Kiona Vineyards Yakima Valley (Washington) Good v'yd producing substantial Cabs and Lembergers (from Austria); fruity Chard, Ries.

Latah Creek Spokane (Washington) Small cellar, mainly for off-dry Chenin Bl, Ries. Erratic, esp with drier, oak-aged types.

Leonetti Walla Walla (Washington) Harmonious though individualistic Cab and fine, big-scale Merlot.

Neuharth W Washington Olympic Peninsula winery uses Yakima Valley grapes for supple, balanced Cab (Chard fair, though not equal to reds).

Preston Wine Cellars Columbia Valley (Washington) Early winery with wide range of wines. Some eccentric, some sound and conventional.

Salishan Vancouver (Washington) Promising Pinot N producer across river from Willamette Valley.

Silver Lake nr Seattle (Washington) Fine regular and reserve Chard and Sauv Bl; promising Cab, Merlot.

Snoqualmie Columbia Valley (Washington) One-time top label of a group that also included F W Langguth, Saddle Mountain; in '91 purchased by owners of CHATEAU STE MICHELLE.

Staton Hills Yakima Valley (Washington) Reliable, occasionally excellent source of Cab in recent yrs; still good for off-dry whites, esp Ries, Chenin Bl, Gewürz. Also sparkling.

Stewart Vineyards Yakima Valley (Washington) Estate v'yds well suited to whites, esp Chard and Ries. Latterly some promising Cabs.

Paul Thomas Bellevue (Washington) What started as (and still is in part) a fruit winery, now makes full-flavoured Chard, Sauv, Chenin Bl. Reds show promise.

Waterbrook Walla Walla (Washington) Young winery gaining ground on leaders with esp Cab, Merlot, Sauv Bl.

Woodward Canyon Walla Walla (Washington) Small cellar with well-oaked, ultra-bold Cab and buttery Chard.

The North & East

Producers in New York and other eastern states, as well as Ohio and Ontario, Canada, traditionally made their wine from hardy native North American grapes, varieties of *Vitis labrusca*. These grapes yield a wine flavour known (nobody really knows why) as 'foxy' – a taste that many easterners consider as comfortably American as apple pie. To escape the one-dimensionalism of *labrusca*, growers then turned to more nuanced French-American hybrids; today fashion has largely bypassed the hybrids, although Seyval Blanc keeps its fans. Eastern growers are turning, ever more successfully, to European varietals. They have little choice, if they want their products to survive in the competition against those from other states and countries.

Aurora (Aurore) One of the best white French-American hybrids, the most widely planted in New York. Good for sparkling.

Baco Noir One of the better red French-American hybrids. High acidity but clean dark wine that usually needs ageing.

Banfi V'yd at Old Brookville, LONG ISLAND, with steadily improving Chards.

Bedell LONG ISLAND winery that has become synonymous with world-class Merlot, the varietal that is the region's strongest suit.

Brights Canada's biggest producer, in Ontario. Wine from Canadian and foreign grapes. 11 blends under the Sawmill Creek label incl worthy Chard, FUMÉ BL, dry Ries. VIDAL ICE WINE and regular and late-harvest BACO NOIR are nifty. Also in British Columbia.

Canandaigua Wine Co Major producer (the third largest in the US, behind Gallo and Heublein), of *labrusca*, dessert and sparkling wines. Bought WIDMERS in '86. Also in California.

Catawba Old native American grape, perhaps the second most widely grown. Pale red and 'foxy' flavoured. Appears in crowd-pleasing, dry, off-dry and sweet styles.

Cayuga White hybrid created at Cornell Univ. Delicate, fruity, off-dry wine.

Chaddsford Pennsylvania producer since '82; reputation rests on burgundy-style Chard.

Chambourcin Red grape of French origin; under-appreciated Bordeaux-like reds and agreeable rosé.

Château des Charmes Small Ontario winery with good Chard, Pinot N.

Chautauqua The biggest grape-growing district in the east, along the S shore of LAKE ERIE from New York to Ohio. 20,000 acres.

Chelois Popular red hybrid. Dry, medium-bodied, burgundy-style wine.

Clinton Vineyards Hudson River winery known for clean dry Seyval Bl and spirited Seyval sparkling.

Concord *Labrusca* variety, by far the most widely planted grape in New York (94,342 acres). Heavy, 'foxy', sweet red wines, but mostly grape juice and jelly. Long a staple of kosher wines.

Debonné Vineyards Popular Ohio estate: hybrids, eg CHAMBOURCIN and VIDAL; and *vinifera*, eg Chard, Ries.

De Chaunac French-American hybrid found in New York and Canada. Too often the usually full, dark wine can be disagreeable.

Delaware Old pink American grape. Makes charming, floral, slightly 'foxy' dry and off-dry white still wines. Also used in 'champagne'.

Finger Lakes Beautiful, historic upstate NY cool-climate region, source of most of the state's best wines, and the seat of its *'vinifera* revolution'.

Firelands Ohio estate, on Isle St George in LAKE ERIE, growing Chard and Cab. Owned by Meier's Wine Cellars, Ohio's biggest producer.

Frank, Dr Konstantin (Vinifera Wine Cellars) Small but influential winery. The late Dr F was a pioneer in growing European vines in the FINGER LAKES. Wines good, if uneven. Vg new Chateau Frank sparkling.

Glenora Wine Cellars Established FINGER LAKES producer of outstanding sparkling wine and good Chard.

Great Western Brand name of a 'champagne', one of New York's oldest and best, owned by Vintner's International.

Gristina Promising young winery on LONG ISLAND's North Fork.

Hargrave Vineyard Pioneering, well-established winery on North Fork of LONG ISLAND. Good Pinot N and Cab.

Heron Hill Vineyards Small FINGER LAKES estate specializing in Ries (also under Otter Spring label).

Hillebrand Estate Winery Ontario winery attracting attention for Chard, VIDAL ICE WINE and dry Ries.

Hunt Country Vineyards FINGER LAKES winery; makes friendly white blends and Vignoles (*see* Ravat).

Ice wine Wine made from frozen grapes. *See* Eiswein, page 107.

Inniskillin Top Ontario winery at Niagara-on-the-Lake. Skilful burgundy-style Chard, Pinot N; Ries, notable VIDAL ICE WINE. Good MARÉCHAL FOCH.

Johnson Estate Solid old down-home property in LAKE ERIE-CHAUTAUQUA region. Reds and whites from American and hybrid grapes.

Knapp Versatile FINGER LAKES winery. Tasty Cab, Ries and Blanc de Blancs sparkling.

Lake Erie The biggest grape-growing district in the east; 25,000 acres along the shore of Lake Erie, incl portions of New York, Pennsylvania and Ohio. 90% is CONCORD, most heavily in CHAUTAUQUA County.

Lenz Classy winery on N Fork of LONG ISLAND. Good Chard, Gewürz, Merlot.

Long Island The most talked about new wine region E of the Rockies. Still defining itself. Most of its 15 wineries are on the North Fork. Best varieties: Chard, Cab, Merlot. A long growing season.

Maréchal Foch Workmanlike red French hybrid. Depending on vinification, yields boldly flavoured or *nouveau*-style wines.

Millbrook The No 1 Hudson River region winery. Money-no-object viticulture has lifted Millbrook into New York's firmament. Chards are splendid, Cab F can be delicious.

Niagara Quintessential *labrusca* greenish-white grape, sometimes called 'white Concord'. Makes lovely aromatic sweet wine and wants to be gobbled right off the vine.

Palmer Serious LONG ISLAND producer becoming a byword in the rough-and-tumble metropolitan market. Good Chard and Merlot.

Pindar Vineyards Huge 245-acre mini-Gallo winery on North Fork, LONG ISLAND. Wide range of popular varietals, incl Chard, Merlot, and an esp good Bordeaux-type red blend, Mythology.

Ravat (Vignoles) French-American white hybrid of intense flavour and high acidity, often made in yummy 'late harvest' style.

Rivendell Since '87 this Hudson River producer has drawn increasing applause for Chard, Seyval Bl and proprietary blends.

Sakonnet Largest New England winery, based in Little Compton, Rhode Island. Its regional reputation, resting on Chard, VIDAL and dry Gewürz, has blossomed since '85.

Seibel Celebrated French grape hybridist. Many successful French-American hybrids, originally known by numbers, since christened as AURORA, DE CHAUNAC, CHELOIS.

Seyve-Villard Another well-known French hybridist. His best-known cross, no 5276 (Seyval Bl), is the most successful of its kind: clean, aromatic wine with good acidity. Well suited to Hudson River region.

Treleaven Promising FINGER LAKES winery. Good Ries and Chard.

Vidal White grape: crossing of Ugni Bl and SEIBEL 4986.

Vinland Estate Winery Good Ontario producer whose VIDAL ICE WINE, dry Ries and Ries Ice Wine are admired.

Wagner Vineyards Jewel of a winery in the FINGER LAKES – arguably New York's best – for succulent barrel-fermented Chard, dry and sweet Ries, RAVAT ICE WINE, NIAGARA and good Pinot N.

Widmer's Big FINGER LAKES winery specializing in native American wines, esp a fine sparkling NIAGARA. Good Cab and Chard. Also makes Manischewitz kosher wines.

Wiemer, Hermann J Creative, daring German-born FINGER LAKES winemaker. Outstanding Ries incl vg sparkling and 'late harvest' versions.

Woodbury Vineyards The top LAKE ERIE-CHAUTAUQUA winery. Good Chard, Ries and sparkling.

Virginia

Virginia's significant modern wine-growing, which began in 1972, is coming into its own. Whites, especially Chardonnay, lead the way. With 42 wineries producing good Chardonnay, Riesling, Cabernet Sauvignon, Cabernet Franc and Merlot from 1,400 acres of grapes, Virginia is one of the more promising new wine states. The most important producers include Prince Michel Vineyards (the largest), as well as Ingleside Plantation Vineyards, Linden Vineyards, Naked Mountain Vineyard, Meredyth Vineyards, Montdomaine Cellars, Oasis Vineyard (for its 'champagne') and the Williamsburg Winery.

Missouri

An interesting wine industry, with 29 producers, some of whom make good dessert Vignoles and Vidals. The best estate is Stone Hill, in Hermann, founded in 1847, which makes a chunky, savoury red from an American grape known as Norton (or Cynthiana). Hermannhof, in the same town, is drawing notice for the same varietals. Mount Pleasant Vineyards, in Augusta since 1966, makes an agreeable 'port' partly from the Cynthiana grape; also good Vidal ice wine and dry Seyval which can take bottle-age.

Maryland

Catoctin, a boutique winery with mountain vineyards, is building a reputation for solid, modestly priced Cabernet Sauvignons and Chardonnays. The state's best-known producer is Boordy Vineyards, which gets good marks for Seyval, Vidal and Cabernet Sauvignon.

The Southwest: Texas

In the past few years a brand-new Texan wine industry has sprung noisily to life. It already seems past the experimental stage, with 450 growers and 25 wineries now active. Texan wines have begun to show some form. Principal wineries are:

Bell Mountain Vineyards Hill-county winery at Fredericksberg. 52 acres. Erratic but known for Cab S.

Cordier Estates (Ste-Genevieve Vineyards) Much the largest producer, leasing 1,000 acres for Sauv Bl. Links with Cordier of Bordeaux.

Fall Creek Vineyards Hill-county estate with 65 acres, making fine Sauv Bl and Chard. Also Cab S.

Llano Estacado Pioneer nr Lubbock with 220 acres (210 leased). Known for Chard and Cab S.

Leftwich Small production of good Chard from v'yds at Lubbock; winery nr Austin.

South America
Argentina

Argentina has the world's fifth-largest wine production, most of it gratefully and uncritically consumed within S America. But things are stirring. The country's crop of gold medals at Vinexpo Bordeaux '89 surprised everyone. The quality vineyards (all irrigated) are concentrated in Mendoza province in the Andean foothills at about 2,000 feet. San Rafael, 140 miles south of Mendoza city, is the centre of a slightly cooler area. Salta, to the north, and Rio Negro, south, also produce interesting wines. Exports are increasing and a move towards quality is in the air.

Bianchi, Bodegas Well-known premium wine producer at San Rafael owned by Seagram. Don Valentin Cab and Bianchi Borgoña are bestsellers. 'Particular' is their top Cab.

Canale, Bodegas The Premier Rio Negro winery: Cab and Sém both won Bordeaux gold medals.

Crillon, Bodegas Owned by Seagram, only for tank-method sparkling.

Esmeralda Producers of a good Cab and Chard, St Felician, at Mendoza.

Etchart Salta winery making typical, aromatic but dry Torrontes white (gold medal at Bordeaux, '87) and sound range of reds in Salta and Mendoza.

Flichman, Bodegas Old Mendoza firm now owned by a bank. Top Caballero de la Cepa white and red, plus Syrah, Merlot and sparkling.

Goyenechea, Bodegas Basque family firm in San Rafael making old-style wines, including Aberdeen Angus red.

La Rural, Bodegas ('San Filipe') Family-run winery at Coquimbito (Mendoza) making some of Argentina's best Ries and Gewürz whites and some good reds. Also a charming wine museum.

Lopez, Bodegas Family firm best known for their Château Montchenot red and white and Château Vieux Cab.

Luigi Bosca, Bodegas Small Mendoza winery with excellent Malbec, Cab S and Syrah .

Martins Recent notable Malbec from Mendoza.

Nacari, Bodegas Small La Rioja cooperative. Its Torrontes white won a gold medal and Oscar at Vinexpo, Bordeaux '87.

Norton, Bodegas Old firm, originally English, now Austrian-owned. Reds (esp Malbec) are best. Perdriel is their premium brand. Also good sparkling wines.

Orfila, José Long-established *bodega* at St Martin, Mendoza. Top wines: Cautivo Cab and white Extra Dry (Pinot Bl).

Peñaflor Argentina's biggest wine company, reputedly the world's third largest. Bulk wines, but also some of Argentina's finest premium wines, incl TRAPICHE (esp Medalla), Andean Vineyards and Fond de Cave Chard and Cab. A 'sherry', Tio Quinto, is exported.

Perez Cuesta Small new winery with outstanding reds, esp Syrah (Gold Medal at Vinexpo '91).

H Piper Sparkling wine made under licence from Piper-Heidsieck.

Proviar, Bodega Producers of Baron B and M Chandon sparkling wine under Moët & Chandon supervision. Also still reds and whites including vg Castel Chandon, less exciting Kleinburg, Wunderwein (whites), smooth Comte de Valmont, Beltour and Clos du Moulin reds.

Robleviña Winery in S Mendoza. Cab took '89 Vinexpo Bordeaux Oscar.

Santa Ana, Bodegas Small, old-established family firm at Guaymallen, Mendoza. Wide range includes good Syrah Val Semina and sparkling.

San Telmo Modern winery with a Californian air and outstanding fresh, full-flavoured Chard, Merlot, Cab and esp Malbec.

Suter, Bodegas Swiss-founded firm owned by Seagram making best-selling Etiquetta Marron white and good Etiquetta Blanca red.

Toso, Pascual Old Mendoza winery at San José, making one of Argentina's best reds, Cabernet Toso. Also Ries and sparkling wines.

Trapiche Premium label of PEÑAFLOR and a spearhead of technical advance.

Weinert, Bodegas Small winery. Tough old-fashioned reds led by good Cab-Merlot-Malbec Cavas de Weinert and promising Sauv Bl.

Chile

Natural conditions are ideal for wine-growing in central Chile, the Maipo valley near Santiago, the Capital, and for 150 miles south. But the country's full potential has only really started to be explored in the past six years. Chilean Cabernets have led the way with original flavours that are rapidly gaining in quality. Other varieties, especially Sauvignon Blanc and Chardonnay, now show equal promise. Stainless steel tanks and new oak barrels have started to revolutionize standards. A new region (Casablanca), developing between Santiago and Valparaiso on on the coast, is proving especially good for Chardonnay.

Caliterra Former venture of ERRAZURIZ and Franciscan of California. Now solely owned by Errazuriz. Good value Chard, Cab (86).

Canepa, José Chile's most modern big *bodega*, of Italian origin, handling wine from several areas. Very good frank and fruity Cab from Lontué, Curico, 100 miles south; recently particularly good Chard (some oak-aged), RIES and Sauv Bl. Top wines from Domaine Caperana.

Concha y Toro The biggest and most outward-looking wine firm, with several *bodegas*, 2,500 acres in the Maipo valley, and growing. Remarkable dark and deep Cab, Merlot, Petit Verdot. Brands are Santa Cruz, Marqués de Casa Concha, Casillero del Diablo. Chard and Sauv Bl are now well established. The new top wine is Don Melchor Cab. Banfi of USA are minority shareholders.

Cousiño Macul Distinguished and beautiful old estate near Santiago. Very dry Sém and Chard. Don Luis light red, Don Matias dark and tannic are good Cabs. Antiguas Reservas (86) is top export Cab.

Domaine Oriental French-owned modern winery in Maule Valley, Talca. 300 acres.

Errazuriz Historic firm in Aconcagua valley, N of Santiago, modernized and making v rich full-bodied wines, esp Cab Don Maximiano (84).

Montes 250-acre estate at Curico emerging as a leader with good fresh Sauv Bl; Chard and Fumé Bl aged in American oak; light Merlot, good Montes Cab S and excellent Montes Alpha (87) from French oak.

Robles, Los Label of coop of Curico. Wines incl Cab (82) and Merlot (85).

Saint Morillon Lontué *bodega* with Sauv Bl, Chard, Cab, and Cab Reserva (85), co-owned with Bodegas Valdivieso.

San Pedro Long established at Lontué, Curico, and now under Spanish control. One of the biggest exporters, with a range of good to vg wines. Gato Negro and Gato Blanco are biggest sellers. Castillo de Molina is top. Santa Helena is associated.

Santa Emiliana A second *bodega* of CONCHA Y TORO.

Tarapaca Ex Zavala Producer rated in Chile for red wines.

Torres, Miguel Enterprise of Catalan family firm (*see* Spain) at Lontué sets a modern pace. Good Sauv Bl (Bellaterra is oak-aged) and Chard, vg Ries. Cab is made more 'elegantly' than other Chileans.

Undurraga Famous family business; one of the first to export to the USA. Wines in both old and modern styles: good clean Sauv Bl and oaky yellow Viejo Roble.

Vascos, Los Family estate in Colchagua Province. 400 acres making some of Chile's best Cab influenced by Bordeaux and California. Also stylish Sauv-Sém. Made headlines in '88 by link with Lafite-Rothschild (50% owners). Wines from '87 have been excellent.

Viña Carmen A second *bodega* of SANTA RITA.

Viña Linderos Small family winery in the Maipo valley exports good, full-bodied Cab which gains from bottle-age.

Viña Portal del Alto Small new *bodega* with excellent Cab-Merlot blend.

Viña Santa Carolina Architecturally splendid old Santiago *bodega* with old-style 'Reserva de Familia'.

Viña Santa Rita Long-established *bodega* in the Maipo valley S of Santiago. Medalla Real Cab and Reserva are best-sellers abroad.

Vinicola Montealegre A second *bodega* of CANEPA. Labels are Rowan Brook and Peteroa.

Brazil

International investments, especially in the Rio Grande do Sul, are starting much talk. Exports are beginning.

Mexico

The oldest American wine industry has upgraded quality. Good wines are made in Baja California (especially Cab S from L A Cetto in Valle de Guadaloupe) and at Aguascalientes.

Peru

Viña Tacama near Ica exports some very promising wines, especially the Gran Vino Blanco white.

Uruguay

Great efforts are being made, with French advice, to improve the wine from the 30,000 acres of warm and humid vineyards. At present it is of local and tourist interest only. 50% is planted with hybrids.

CLARE/
WATERVALE   MURRAY VALLEY
                                    MUDGEE
BAROSSA   RIVERINA
    ● Adelaide   Canberra
SOUTHERN LANGHORNE
VALES   CREEK   RUTHERGLEN
    PADTHAWAY   CENTRAL   NORTH EAST
    KEPPOCH   VICTORIA   VICTORIA
COONAWARRA   GREAT
    WESTERN   YARRA VALLEY
                        ✕ Melbourne
            GEELONG

Australia's wine industry is now the most dynamic, creative and
self-critical in the world. Not only are all importing countries
aware of the quality and value for money of its wines, but other
producing countries, even France, are reflecting its influence.
Yet it is little more than 20 years since new technology made top
quality Australian table wines possible. Old-style wines were
burly Shiraz reds, or Sémillon or Riesling whites, grown in
warm regions. A progressive shift to cooler areas, to new wood
fermentation and ageing, with Cabernet, Pinot Noir,
Chardonnay and Sauvignon Blanc at the forefront, has seen a
radical change in style which still seems to gather pace.
Nonetheless flavour and strength continue to be Australian
hallmarks and the best wines still have great character and the
ability to age splendidly.

Exports have been the great success story over the last seven
years, increasing from eight million to 70 million litres. But it is
not easy to keep tabs on individual wines. There are now almost
600 wineries in commercial production. Labels are becoming
less garrulous (but less informative) as Australian consumers
become more sophisticated. Such information as they give can
be relied on, while prizes in shows (which are highly
competitive) mean a great deal. In a country lacking any formal
grades of quality the buyer needs all the help he or she can get.

Wine areas

The vintages here are those rated as good or excellent for the reds of the
areas in question. Excellent recent vintages are marked by an accent.

Adelaide Hills (S Aus) 84' 85 86' 88 90 91'   Spearheaded by PETALUMA:
    numerous new v'yds at v cool, 450-metre sites in the Mt Lofty ranges.
Adelaide Plains (S Aus) 82 84' 86' 87 88' 90 91   Small area immediately N
    of Adelaide, formerly known as Angle Vale. Wineries incl Lauriston,
    Minton Grove, PRIMO ESTATE.
Barossa (S Aus) 66 76 80 82 84' 86' 87 88 90' 91   Australia's most

important winery (though not v'yd) area, processing grapes from diverse sources (local, to MURRAY VALLEY; high quality cool regions: from adjacent hills, to COONAWARRA far to the south) to make correspondingly diverse wines.

Bendigo/Ballarat (Vic) 73 75 80' 82' 84 87 88 89 91' Widespread small v'yds, some of extreme quality, recreating the glories of the last century. 17 wineries incl BALGOWNIE, CHATEAU LE AMON, HEATHCOTE and Passing Clouds.

Canberra District (ACT) 18 wineries now sell 'cellar door' to local and tourist trade. Quality is variable, as is style.

Clare Watervale (S Aus) 71' 75' 80' 82 84' 85 86' 89 90 91 Small, high quality area 90 miles N of Adelaide, best known for Ries; also planted with Shiraz and Cab. 23 wineries spill over into new adjacent subdistrict of Polish Hill River.

Coonawarra (S Aus) 66 71 76' 79 80' 82' 84' 86' 87 88 90' 91 Southernmost and finest v'yd of state, making most of Australia's best Cab S. Successful with Chard and (esp botrytised) Ries. New arrivals incl Balnaves, PARKER ESTATE and Penley Estate.

Geelong (Vic) 80' 82' 84 85 86 88 90 91 Once famous area destroyed by phylloxera, re-established mid-'60s. V cool, dry climate produces firm table wines from premium varieties. Names incl BANNOCKBURN, IDYLL, Scotchman's Hill.

Goulburn Valley (Vic) 68 71' 76 80' 82 85 86 88 90 91' A mixture of v old (eg CHATEAU TAHBILK) and relatively new (eg MITCHELTON) wineries in a temperate region; full-flavoured table wines.

Granite Belt (Qld) 85 87' 88 90 Rapidly developing, high altitude and (relatively) cool region just N of NSW border, with 15 wineries: spicy Shiraz and rich Sém-Chard are district specialities.

Great Western (Vic) 78 80' 82' 84' 85 86 88 90 91 Temperate region in central W of state. High quality table and sparkling wines. Now 9 wineries, 7 of recent origin.

Hunter Valley (NSW) 66' 67 73 75' 79' 82 83 85 86' 87 91 The great name in NSW. Broad, soft, earthy Shiraz reds and Sém whites that live for 30 yrs. Cab not important; Chard increasingly so.

Margaret River (W Aus) 73' 76 79' 81 82' 85' 86' 87 90 91 New cool, coastal area producing superbly elegant wines 174 miles S of Perth. 30 operating wineries; others planned.

Mornington Peninsula (Vic) 84' 86' 87 88 90 91 28 commercial wineries on dolls-house scale, making exciting wines in new, cool, coastal area 25 miles S of Melbourne. Total plantings of 400 acres. Wineries incl DROMANA, ELGEE PARK, Merricks.

Mount Barker/Frankland River (W Aus) 80 81' 83 85 86 87 89 90 Promising, new, far-flung, cool area in extreme S of state; GOUNDREY and PLANTAGENET are the two biggest and best wineries.

Mudgee (NSW) 74 75 78 79 83 84' 86 87 90 91 Small, isolated area 168 miles NW of Sydney. Big reds of colour and flavour and full Chards, from 23 wineries.

Murray Valley (S Aus, Vic & NSW) vintages not normally important Important irrigated v'yds nr Mildara, Swan Hill (Vic and NSW), Berri, Loxton, Morgan, Renmark and Waikerie (S Aus). Principally 'cask' table wines. 40% of total Australian wine production.

NE Victoria 66' 70' 71' 75' 80' 82' 86' 87 88 90 Historic area incl Corowa, Rutherglen, Wangaratta. Generally heavy reds and magnificent sweet dessert wines. 25 wineries.

Padthaway (S Aus) 80 82' 84 85 86' 87 88 90 Large v'yd area (no wineries) developed by big companies as anoverspill of COONAWARRA. Cool climate; some good Pinot N reds, excellent Chard (esp LINDEMANS and HARDY'S), also Chard-Pinot N sparkling wines.

Perth Hills (W Aus) Fledgling area 19 miles E of Perth with 10 wineries and a larger number of growers on mild hillside sites.

Pyrenees (Vic) 82 84 85 86 87 88 90 91'   Central Vic region with 8 wineries, producing rich, minty reds and one or two interesting whites, esp Fumé Blanc.

Riverina (NSW) NV   Large-volume producer centred around Griffith; good quality 'cask' wines (esp white), great, sweet, botrytised Sém.

Southern Vales (S Aus) 71' 77 80' 82' 84 85 86' 87 88 90   Covers energetic McLaren Vale/REYNELLA regions on S outskirts of Adelaide. Big reds now being rapidly improved; promising Chard.

Swan Valley (W Aus) 75' 78' 81' 82' 84' 85' 86 88 89' 90   The birthplace of wine in the west, on the N outskirts of Perth. Hot climate makes strong, low-acid table wines, but good dessert wines. Declining in importance viticulturally.

Tasmania 82' 84' 86 87 88' 90 91'   31 v'yds now offer wine for commercial sale, producing over 300,000 litres. Great potential for Chard, Pinot N and Ries in cool climate.

Upper Hunter (NSW) 75' 79' 80' 81' 83' 85' 86' 87 90   Est early '60s; irrigated vines producing mainly white wines, lighter and quicker-developing than Lower Hunter whites. Often good value.

Yarra Valley ('Lilydale') 76' 78' 80' 81 82' 84' 85 86' 88' 90' 91   Historic wine area nr Melbourne, now being rapidly redeveloped by enthusiasts, with 33 small wineries. Growing emphasis on v successful Pinot N. A superb viticultural area with noble varieties only and almost 2,000 acres.

Wineries

Allandale (Hunter Valley) *→**   Small winery without v'yds, buying selected local grapes. Quality variable; can be good – esp Chard.

Allanmere (Hunter Valley) **→***   Small winery run by expatriate English doctor, making excellent Sém, Chard and smooth reds.

All Saints (NE Vic) *→**   Once famous old family winery bought in '92 by BROWN BROTHERS.

Angove's (Riverland, S Aus) *→**   Long-established family business in Adelaide and Renmark in the MURRAY VALLEY. Notable value in Cab and whites, esp Chard.

Arrowfield (Upper Hunter) **   Substantial v'yd on irrigated land. Light Cab, succulent 'Reserve' Chard; also 'wooded' Sém. Majority owned by a Japanese company.

Bailey's (NE Vic) **→*****   Rich, old-fashioned reds of great character, esp Bundarra Hermitage, and magnificent dessert Muscat and 'Tokay'.

Balgownie (Bendigo/Ballarat) ***   Specialist in fine reds, particularly straight Cab. Also occasional exceptional Chard. Now owned by MILDARA.

Bannockburn (Geelong) ***   Intense, complex Chard and Pinot N using Burgundian techniques.

Basedow (Barossa Valley) **→***   Small to medium winery buying grapes for reliably good range of red and white; Sém 'White Burgundy' esp good.

Berri-Renmano Coop (Riverland, S Aus) *→**   Australia's largest cooperative winery, now developing own brands on local and export markets. (*See* Renmano.)

Best's (Great Western) **→***   Conservative old family winery in GREAT WESTERN with good mid-weight reds, and Chard not half bad.

Blass, Wolf (Bilyara) (Barossa) ***   The ebullient German winemaker merged his business with MILDARA in late '91. Dazzling labels, extraordinary wine-show successes, mastery of blending varieties and areas, and lashings of new oak all continue, though the signs are that less extreme sensations are on the way.

Botobolar (Mudgee) **   Marvellously eccentric little organic winery. Gill Wahlquist exports successfully to the UK.

Bowen Estate (Coonawarra) ★★★ Small winery; intense but not heavy Cab and spicy Shiraz.

Brand (Coonawarra) ★★→★★★ Family estate now half owned by MCWILLIAMS. Fine, bold and stylish Cab and Shiraz under the Laira label. A few quality blemishes in late '70s/early '80s now rectified.

Brokenwood (Hunter Valley) ★★★ Exciting quality of Cab and Shiraz since '73 – Graveyard Shiraz is outstanding. New winery in '83 added high quality Chard and Sém.

Brown Brothers (Milawa, Vic) ★→★★★ Old family firm with new ideas, wide and reliable range of rather delicate varietal wines, many from cool mountain districts. Chard and dry, white Muscat continually outstanding. *See also* All Saints.

Buring, Leo (Barossa) ★★→★★★ 'Chateau Leonay', old white-wine specialists, now owned by LINDEMANS. Steady Reserve Bin Ries becomes great with age.

Campbells of Rutherglen (NE Vic)★★ Impressive, lively whites, smooth reds and good dessert wines.

Cape Clairault (Margaret River) ★★ Progressive producer of Sém, Sauv Bl and Cab, in reasonable quantities, with good progress in quality.

Cape Mentelle (Margaret River) ★★→★★★★ Idiosyncratic, robust Cab departs from district style and can be magnificent; also Zinfandel and v popular Sém. David Hohnen also founded Cloudy Bay, NZ. Both were bought in '90 by Veuve Clicquot.

Capel Vale (SW W Aus) ★★★ Outstanding range of whites, incl Ries and Gewürz. Vg Cab.

Cassegrain (Hastings Valley, NSW) ★★→★★★ New winery on NSW coast, taking grapes both from local plantings and from HUNTER VALLEY. Chard can be outstanding.

Chambers' Rosewood (NE Vic) ★★→★★★ Good, cheap table and great dessert wines, esp 'Tokay'.

Chateau Le Amon (Bendigo) ★★★ Very stylish minty Cab and peppery Shiraz.

Chateau Francois (Hunter Valley) ★★ Idiosyncratic operation of former Fisheries Director: clean reds, soft whites and great olives.

Chateau Hornsby (Alice Springs, N Territory) ★→★★ A charming aberration. Full-flavoured, clean reds from the Bush.

Chateau Rémy (Great Western/Avoca) ★★ Owned by Rémy Martin. Sparkling based on Chard and Pinot N is much improved. Also good Blue Pyrenees Cab S.

Chateau Tahbilk (Goulburn Valley) ★★→★★★ Beautiful and historic family estate making long-lived Cab, Shiraz, Ries and Marsanne. Private Bins are outstanding; value for money ditto. Sadly, Eric Purbrick died in '91. His grandson presses on.

Coldstream Hills (Yarra Valley) ★★★→★★★★ YARRA's second-largest winery, built in '87 by wine critic James Halliday. International acclaim for prize-winning Pinot N, vg Chard (esp Reserve wines), delicate Cab.

Conti, Paul (Swan Valley) ★★ Elegant 'Hermitage', also fine Chard and other whites.

Craigmoor (Mudgee) ★★ Oldest district winery, now part of ORLANDO group. Good Chard and Sém (the two are also blended), and Cab-Shiraz.

Croser (Adelaide Hills) ★★★→★★★★ Now Australia's top sparkling Chard-Pinot N blend. Offshoot of PETALUMA with Bollinger as partner. Lean, fine, with splendid backbone from Pinot N.

Cullens Willyabrup (Margaret River) ★★★ Mother-daughter team pioneered the region with butch but kindly Cab-Merlot, substantial but subtle Sauv Bl and bold Chard: all real characters. Also intense Botrytis Sém.

d'Arenberg (S Vales) ★→★★ Old-style family outfit making strapping, rustic reds and Ries.

De Bortoli (Griffith, NSW) ★→★★★ Irrigation-area winery. Standard reds and whites but magnificent sweet, botrytised, Sauternes-style Sém. *See also* next entry.

De Bortoli (Yarra Valley) ✸✸ Formerly Ch Yarrinya: bought by De Bortoli and now YARRA's largest producer. Main label good to adequate, Second label, Windy Peak, vg value.

Delatite (Central Vic) ✸✸✸ Rosalind Ritchie makes appropriately willowy and feminine Ries, Gewürz, Pinot N and Cab from this v cool, mountainside v'yd.

Diamond Valley (Yarra Valley) ✸✸→✸✸✸ Producer of outstanding Pinot N in significant quantities; other wines good rather than great.

Domaine Chandon (Yarra Valley) ✸✸✸ The showpiece of the YARRA VALLEY. Substantial production from grapes grown in all the cooler parts of Australia, with strong direction from owner Moët & Chandon. Quality of early *cuvées* has even amazed the owners.

Drayton's Bellevue (Hunter Valley) ✸✸ Traditional 'Hermitage' and Sém, occasionally good Chard; there have been recent quality improvements after a lapse.

Dromana Estate (Mornington Peninsular) ✸✸✸ Largest and best producer in district. Great skill in making glorious Cab, Pinot N and Chard. Second label: Schinus Molle.

Eaglehawk (Clare) ✸→✸✸✸ Formerly Quelltaler. Old winery once known for Granfiesta 'Sherry'. Recently good Ries and Sém. Owned by MILDARA BLASS.

Elgee Park (Mornington Peninsular) ✸✸ Region's longest-established v'yd producing good Cab-Merlot, Chard, Ries and a hatful of Viognier.

Enterprise Wines (Clare) ✸✸✸ Tim Knappstein, an exceptionally gifted winemaker, produces Ries, Fumé Blanc, Gewürz and Cab. Now part of MILDARA BLASS.

Evans and Tate (Swan Valley) ✸✸→✸✸✸ Fine, elegant reds from MARGARET RIVER, Redbrook and SWAN VALLEY Gnangara v'yds. Good Sém too.

Evans Family (Hunter Valley) ✸✸✸ Excellent Chard from small v'yd owned by family of Len Evans and made at ROTHBURY ESTATE. Fermented in new oak. Repays cellaring.

Forest Hills (Mount Barker) ✸✸→✸✸✸ Pioneer v'yd in region, now in common ownership with VASSE FELIX. Ries and Chard can be and usually are excellent.

Giaconda (Central Vic) ✸✸✸ Very small but ultra-fashionable winery nr Beechworth, producing eagerly sought Chard and Pinot N.

Goundrey Wines (Great Southern, W Aust) ✸✸✸ Recent expansion and quality upgrade. Now in first rank with esp good Cab and wooded whites.

Grant Burge Wines (Barossa) ✸✸→✸✸✸ Formerly Krondorf at Jacob's Creek. Rapidly-expanding output of silky-smooth reds and whites.

Hardy's (S Vales, Barossa, Keppoch, etc) ✸→✸✸✸ Historic family-run company using and blending wines from several areas. Top wines are 'Collection' series and (Australia's greatest) 'Vintage Ports'. Hardy's bought HOUGHTON and REYNELLA and, most recently, STANLEY. Reynella's beautifully-restored buildings are now group headquarters. Also investments in France and Italy – but in '92 financial problems loomed.

Heathcote (Bendigo) ✸✸→✸✸✸ Stylish producer of eclectic range of white and red varietals, showing abundant flavour and technical skill. But tends to syrupy Chard.

Heemskerk (Tasmania) ✸✸✸ Most successful commercial operation in TASMANIA: herby Cab, promising Chard, also Pinot N and Ries. Recent partnership with Louis Roederer produced Jansz sparkling wine.

Henschke (Barossa) ✸✸✸→✸✸✸✸ Family business known for delectable Shiraz, vg Cab and red blends. New high-country v'yds on ADELAIDE HILLS add excitement.

Hollick (Coonawarra) ✸✸✸ Ian and Wendy Hollick won instant stardom with trophy-winning 84 Cab; also vg Chard and Ries from small winery.

Houghton (Swan Valley) ***——****** The most famous old winery of WA. Soft, ripe 'White Burgundy' is their top wine; a national classic. Also excellent Cab, Verdelho etc. *See* Hardy's.

Huntington Estate (Mudgee) ****——***** Small winery; the best in MUDGEE. Fine Cabs, clean Sém and Chard. Invariably under-priced.

Idyll (Geelong) ******* Small winery making Gewürz and vg Cab in v individual style. Also 'Blush' rosé. A pioneer exporter.

Jeffrey Grosset (Clare) ****——***** Exceedingly elegant Ries, Chard and Cab made in consistent style by fastidious young winemaker.

Jim Barry Wines (Clare) ****——***** Hard-working family firm now doing esp well with Ries from ex-LINDEMANS Florita V'yd.

Kaiser Stuhl (Barossa) ***——***** Now part of PENFOLDS; a huge winery taking fruit from diverse sources. 'Green Label' Ries can be excellent. So can Red Ribbon reds.

Katnook Estate (Coonawarra) ******* Excellent, pricey Cab and Chard; also Sauv Bl, Pinot N, Ries.

Krondorf Wines (Barossa) ****——***** Part of MILDARA BLASS group with niche market brands: 'Chablis' Show Reserve wines are best.

Lake's Folly (Hunter Valley) ******** The work of an inspired surgeon from Sydney. Cab and new barrels make fine, complex reds. Also exciting, age-worthy Chard.

Lark Hill (Canberra District) ****——***** Best and most consistent CANBERRA producer making esp attractive Ries.

Leasingham (Clare) ***——***** Important, medium-sized, quality winery purchased by HARDY'S in '87. Good Ries, Sém, Chard and Cab-Malbec blends under Domaine label.

Leconfield (Coonawarra) ****——***** COONAWARRA Cab of great style. Ries improving.

Leeuwin Estate (Margaret River) ****——****** Leading W Australia estate, lavishly equipped, producing superb (and v expensive) Chard; developing fine Pinot N, vg Ries, Sauv Bl and Cab.

Lehmann Wines, Peter (Barossa) ****——***** Defender of the BAROSSA faith, Lehmann makes vast quantities of wine (some sold in bulk), with vg 'special cuvées' under his own label.

Lindemans (orig Hunter, now everywhere) ***——***** One of the oldest firms, now a giant owned by PENFOLDS. Owns BURING in BAROSSA, Rouge Homme in COONAWARRA, and important v'yds at PADTHAWAY: outstanding Chard and Coonawarra reds. Pioneer of new styles, yet still make fat, old-style 'Hunters'. Bin-number 'classics' can be v good. The dominant performer at wine shows.

Little's (Hunter Valley) ****** Popular little winery with wide range of wines; energetic exporters.

McWilliams (Hunter Valley & Riverina) ***——***** Famous family of HUNTER winemakers at Mount Pleasant: 'Hermitage' and Sém – 'Elizabeth' is the only bottle-aged Sém (6 yrs) sold and is vg value. Also pioneers in RIVERINA with noble varieties, incl Cab, and sweet, white Lexia. Quality showing marked improvement.

Marsh Estate (Hunter Valley) ****——***** Substantial producer of good Sém, Shiraz and Cab of growing quality.

Mildara (Coonawarra & Murray Valley) ***——***** 'Sherry' and brandy specialists at Mildara on the Murray River, also making fine Cab and Ries at COONAWARRA. Now also own BALGOWNIE, BLASS, KRONDORF and YELLOWGLEN.

Miramar (Mudgee) ****——***** Some of MUDGEE's best whites, esp Chard.

Mitchells (Clare) ******* Small family winery, excellent Ries and Cab.

Mitchelton (Goulbourn Valley) ****——***** Big, modern winery. A wide range incl a vg wood-matured Marsanne, Cab and classic Ries (both tingling-dry and botrytis-sweet) from COONAWARRA. Second label,

Thomas Mitchell, is esp good value.

Montrose (Mudgee) ****→****** Dynamic winemaking and marketing of vg Chard, and Cab blends. Now part of the ORLANDO group.

Moorilla Estate (Tasmania) ******* Senior winery on outskirts of Hobart on Derwent River, producing vg Pinot N and Chard; also Botrytis Ries in tiny quantities.

Morris (NE Vic) ****→******* Old winery at Rutherglen making Australia's greatest dessert Muscats and 'Tokays'; also recently vg low-price table wines.

Moss Wood (Margaret River) ******** To many the best MARGARET RIVER winery (with only 29 acres). Cab, Pinot N, Chard, all with rich fruit flavours, not unlike top-class Californian wines.

Mountadam (Barossa) ******* Winery of David and Adam Wynn at High Eden. Chard is rich, voluptuous and long.

Mount Langi Ghiran (Great Western) ****→***** Producer of superb rich, peppery, Rhône-like Shiraz, vg Cab and less exhilarating Ries.

Mount Mary (Yarra Valley) ******* Dr John Middleton is a perfectionist making tiny amounts of suave Chard, vivid Pinot N, and (best of all) Cab S-Cab F-Merlot. All age well.

Murray Robson Wines (Hunter Valley) ****** The reincarnation of Murray Robson in a winery nr ROTHBURY.

Oakridge (Yarra Valley) ****→****** Cab specialist, albeit in small quantities. 87, 88 disappointing, 90 Reserve terrific.

Orlando (Gramp's) (Barossa) ****→***** Great pioneering company, bought by management in '88 but now owned by Pernod Ricard of France. Full range from good, standard Jacob's Creek 'Claret' to excellent Jacaranda Ridge Cab from COONAWARRA. *See also* Wyndham Estate.

Parker Estate (Coonawarra) ******* New estate making exceptional Cab, esp Terra Rossa First Growth.

Penfolds (orig Adelaide, now everywhere) ***→****** Ubiquitous and excellent company in BAROSSA, COONAWARRA, CLARE, RIVERINA, etc. Bought LINDEMANS in '90. Grange Hermitage (78, 80, 82') is ********. Bin 707 Cab is not far behind. Other bin-numbered wines (eg Cab-Shiraz 389) can be outstanding. Consistently the best red-wine company in Australia. Grandfather 'Port' can be excellent. In late '90 the Penfolds/Lindemans group was taken over by the South Australian Brewing Co, already owner of SEPPELT.

Petaluma (Adelaide Hills) ******** A rocket-like success in the '80s with Cab from COONAWARRA, Chard from the ADELAIDE HILLS and Ries from CLARE; all processed at winery in the Adelaide Hills. Reds have become richer from 84 on, 88 and 90 are outstanding. Also: Bridgewater Mill label. *See also* Croser.

Petersons (Hunter Valley) ****→****** For a time the most accomplished small HUNTER winery, with exceptional Chard and vg Sém; recently a little wobbly.

Piper's Brook (Tasmania) ******* Cool-area pioneer with vg Ries and Pinot N, superb Chard from the Tamar Valley nr Launceston. Lovely labels.

Pirramimma (S Vales) ***→***** Big supply of good standard; reds best.

Plantaganet (Mount Barker) ****→***** The region's largest producer: wide range of varieties, esp rich Chard, Shiraz and vibrant, potent Cab.

Primo Estate (Adelaide Plains) ****** Successes incl vg botrytised Ries.

Quelltaler *See* Eaglehawk.

Redman (Coonawarra) ***→***** The most famous old name in COONAWARRA; makes two wines: 'Claret' and Cab. Recent quality disappointing.

Renmano (Murray Valley) ***→**** Huge coop (*see* Berri-Renmano). 'Chairman's Selections' vg value. Exceedingly voluptuous Chard.

Reynella (S Vales) ****→****** Historic red wine specialists S of Adelaide. Rich Cab (partly COONAWARRA), 'Claret' and excellent 'Port'. *See* Hardy's.

Reynold's Yarraman Estate (Upper Hunter Valley) ****** Former stone prison building promises well as winery of former HOUGHTON and WYNDHAM winemaker John Reynold.

Rockford (Barossa) **→*** Small producer, but a wide range of thoroughly individual wines, often made from grapes grown on v old, low-yielding v'yds.

Rosemount (Upper Hunter & Coonawarra) *→*** Rich, unctuous HUNTER 'Show' Chard is an international smash. This and COONAWARRA Cab lead the wide range.

Rothbury Estate (Hunter Valley) ***→**** A true estate with over 500 acres of v'yd. Wide share-holding (Len Evans and Chen families hold the majority). Traditional HUNTER Shiraz and Séms to keep for ever. Rich, buttery Cowra Chard is vg and good value too. HUNTER Chard now barrel-fermented. New: Chard and Sauv Bl v'yds in Marlborough, NZ.

St Huberts (Yarra Valley) **→*** Erratic but much sought-after Cab; recent change in winemaking has improved consistency for this large YARRA winery.

St Leonards (NE Vic) ** Excellent varieties sold only 'cellar door' and by mailing list, incl exotics, eg Orange Muscat.

St Matthias (Tamar Valley, Tas) ** Joined the 'big three' TASMANIA wineries almost overnight; superbly situated v'yd and cellar-door shop on banks of Tamar estuary. Wines made under contract at HEEMSKERK.

Saltram (Barossa) *→*** Seagram-owned winery making wines of variable quality. Pinnacle Selection are best; also Mamre Brook.

Sandalford (Swan Valley) *→** Fine old winery with contrasting styles of red and white varietals from SWAN and MARGARET RIVER areas. Wonderful old Verdelho.

Saxonvale (Hunter Valley) ** Medium-sized operation making good, early-maturing Sém and Chard. Also good, soft Cab and Shiraz. Owned by WYNDHAM.

Schinus Molle *See* Dromana Estate.

Seaview (S Vales) ** Brand name owned by PENFOLDS; used for good value Cab, Chard and sparkling wine.

Seppelt (Barossa, Great Western, Keppoch, etc) *→*** Far-flung producers of Australia's most popular sparkling wine (Great Western Brut); also good dessert wines and some vg private bin wines, incl Chard from GREAT WESTERN AND Drumborg (Vic), PADTHAWAY and BAROSSA (S Aus). Top sparkling wine is highly regarded 'Salinger'. Now joined with PENFOLDS/LINDEMANS/BURING, etc, to form Australia's biggest wine company.

Seville Estate (Yarra Valley) **→*** Tiny winery with Chard, v late-picked Ries, Shiraz, Pinot N and vg Cab.

S Smith & Sons (alias Yalumba) (Barossa) *→*** Big, old family firm with considerable verve, using computers, juice evaluation, etc, to produce full spectrum of high-quality wines, incl Hill-Smith Estate. Heggies V'yd is best. Angas Brut, a good value sparkling wine, is now a world brand.

Stanley *See* Leasingham.

Stanton & Killeen (NE Vic) ** Small old family firm. Rich Muscats, also strong Moodemere reds.

Taltarni (Great Western/Avoca) *** Dominique Portet, brother of Bernard (Clos du Val, Napa), son of André (ex-Ch Lafite), produces huge but balanced reds for long ageing, good Sauv Bl and adequate sparkling wine.

Tarrawarra (Yarra Valley) *** Multi-million dollar investment making limited quantities of idio-syncratic and expensive Chard (86 outstanding). Also Pinot N.

Taylors Wines (Clare) *→** Large wine-producing unit making range of inexpensive table wines.

Terrace Vale (Hunter Valley) ★★   Small, syndicate-owned winery with French winemaker. Good Sém and Chard.

Tisdall Wines (Goulburn Valley) ★★→★★★★   Large winery in the Echuca area, making local (Rosbercon) wines and finer ones from central ranges (Mt Helen Cab, Chard, and Ries).

Tollana (Barossa) ★★→★★★   Old company once famous for 'Brandy', has latterly made some fine Cab and Ries. Acquired by PENFOLDS in '87.

Tulloch (Hunter Valley) ★→★★★   An old name at Pokolbin, with dry reds, Chard and Verdelho, now part of PENFOLDS group but a shadow of its former self.

Tyrrell (Hunter Valley) ★★→★★★★   Some of the best traditional HUNTER wines, 'Hermitage' and Sém. Also big, rich Vat 47 Chard and delicate Pinot .

Vasse Felix (Margaret River) ★★→★★★★   With CULLENS, pioneer of the MARGARET RIVER. Elegant Cabs, notable for mid-weight balance, bought by the late Robert Holmes à Court in '87.

Virgin Hills (Bendigo/Ballarat) ★★★★   Tiny supplies of one blended red (Cab-Shiraz-Malbec) of legendary style and balance.

Westfield (Swan Valley) ★→★★   John Kosovich's Cab, Chard and Verdelho show particular finesse for a hot climate. Also good 'Port'.

Wirra Wirra (S Vales) ★★→★★★★   Under PETALUMA influence: high quality, beautifully-packaged whites and reds have made a big impact.

Woodleys (Barossa) ★★   Well known for low-price Queen Adelaide label. Acquired by SEPPELT in '85.

Wyndham Estate (Branxton, NSW) ★→★★   Aggressive large HUNTER and MUDGEE group with brands: CRAIGMOOR, Hollydene, Hunter Estate, MONTROSE, Richmond Grove and SAXONVALE. Acquired by ORLANDO in '90.

Wynns (Coonawarra) ★★→★★★★   Since its acquisition by PENFOLDS in '85 has produced even better wines: Ries, Chard, Shiraz and Cab – all very good, esp John Riddoch Cab.

Yalumba *See* S Smith & Sons.

Yarra Ridge (Yarra Valley) ★★→★★★★   Expanding young winery, v successful with Chard, Cab, Sauv Bl and Pinot N, all with flavour and finesse at modest prices.

Yarra Yering (Yarra Valley) ★★★→★★★★★   The best-known Lilydale boutique winery. Esp racy, powerful Pinot N, deep Cab (Dry Red No 1) and Shiraz (Dry Red No 2), but doubtful bottles mar a high reputation.

Yarrinya Estate *See* De Bortoli (Yarra Valley).

Yellowglen (Bendigo/Ballarat) ★→★★   High-flying sparkling winemaker owned by MILDARA. Sales are more impressive than quality.

Yeringberg (Yarra Valley) ★★★   Dreamlike historic estate still in the hands of the founding family, now again producing v high quality Chard, Cab, Pinot N, in minute quantities.

New Zealand

Over the last decade New Zealand has made an international impact with white table wines of startling quality, well able to compete with those of Australia or California. In 1982 it exported 12,000 cases; in 1991 some 160,000. It is now regarded as the foremost cool-climate region among the world's newer wine countries.

In recent years new vineyard areas have opened up in Martinborough (North Island, north of the capital city Wellington), Canterbury and Central Otago (South Island).

White grapes predominate. Formerly dominant Müller-Thurgau is being rapidly overtaken by varieties in demand overseas: Sauvignon Blanc, Chardonnay and Riesling for whites, Cabernet Sauvignon and Merlot for reds. Booming exports at first led to acute shortage of fruit but now, apart from new plantings of Pinot Noir and Malbec, supplies meet the demands.

Intensity of fruit, varietal character and crisp acidity are the hallmarks of New Zealand's wines. No region on earth can match the pungency of its best Sauvignon Blanc. Barrel fermentation and/or ageing are adding to the complexity and interest of the wines. And recently there has been much interest in botrytised Riesling, especially from Marlborough. 1989 was perhaps the first vintage to produce really worthy reds. The principal areas and producers follow.

Auckland Largest city in NZ. Location of head offices of major wineries, with a largest number of medium and small wineries in outskirts.

Babich (Henderson, nr Auckland) Old Dalmatian family firm of some size, highly respected in NZ for consistent quality and value. Also using GISBORNE and HAWKES BAY grapes. Good Chards (esp Irongate), Sauv Bl, Sém-Chard, Gewürz, Cab S and Cab-Merlot. Pinot N still not so good.

Brajkovich *See* Kumeu River.

Cellier Le Brun (Renwick, nr Blenheim) Small winery est by son of Champagne family: *méthode champenoise* – vg Bl de Blancs.

Cloudy Bay (Blenheim) Offshoot of W Australia's Cape Mentelle, both bought in '90 by Veuve Clicquot. Top name for Sauv Bl, Chard. Richly subtle, excellent Cab-Merlot blend 89 shows high promise for reds.

Collard (Henderson, nr Auckland) Small family winery using grapes from several areas; Chard, Sauv Bl, dry Chenin Bl and Cab-Merlot.

Cooks (Te Kauwhata, S of Auckland and Hawkes Bay) Large company now merged with CORBANS and McWilliams, using grapes from GISBORNE and HAWKES BAY. Steadily good record with Chard (esp Longridge), Gewürz, Chenin Bl and Cab S (esp Fernhill); now making fresh, nettly Sauv Bl, also late-picked Müller-T.

Coopers Creek (Huapai Valley, NW of Auckland) Small winery augmenting own grapes with GISBORNE, HAWKES BAY and MARLBOROUGH fruit. Exporting good Chard, Sauv Bl, Ries, Gewürz and popular blends: Coopers Dry (white) and Coopers Red.

Corbans (Henderson, nr Auckland) Old-established firm with wineries at GISBORNE and HAWKES BAY. Now incorporates COOKS and McWilliams. V'yds in MARLBOROUGH producing vg Sauv Bl, Chard, Ries and Cab S. Wide range of sound wines under Corbans label. New premium brand: Stoneleigh. Additional premium wines under Robard & Butler label.

De Redcliffe (Mangatawhiri, SE of Auckland) Small progressive winery with associated resort 'Hotel du Vin'; good Chard, Sém, Cab-Merlot.

Delegat's (Henderson, nr Auckland) Medium-sized family winery, using grapes from GISBORNE and HAWKES BAY; good Chard, Sauv Bl, Cab S, and impressive 'Auslese' Ries. Proprietor's Reserve Cabs, Merlots (87, 89) are good. Oyster Bay is successful export brand for Chard, Sauv Bl.

Deutz (Auckland) The Champagne firm in a pioneer joint venture with MONTANA. Sparkling results.

Esk Valley (Bayview, Hawkes Bay) Former large family concern, now merged with VILLA MARIA/VIDAL group. Concentrating on small range of premium whites and reds, incl vg dry Chenin Bl and some of NZ's best Cab-Merlot blends (esp '89).

Giesen Estate (Burnham, S of Christchurch, and Canterbury, S Island) German family winery using own v'yd and some MARLBOROUGH grapes. Good Chard, Sauv Bl, botrytised Ries and reds.

Gisborne Site of 3 large wineries, CORBANS, MONTANA and PENFOLDS, and centre of large viticultural area incl MATAWHERO and Tolaga Bay. Good area for Müller-T, Chard, Sém and Gewürz.

Goldwater (Waiheke Island in Hauraki Gulf, nr Auckland) Small v'yd at sea edge, known best for Cab-Merlot and Sauv Bl.

Hawkes Bay Large viticultural region on E coast of North Island, S of GISBORNE, known for high quality grapes, esp Chard and Cab S.

Hunters (Marlborough) Small, progressive winery using only MARLBOROUGH grapes. Highly reputed for outstanding Sauv Bl (oaky 'Fumé' style), and Chard. Ries since '89. Also Cab.

Jackson Estate (Blenheim) Large private v'yd. First vintage 91: Sauv Bl v impressive. Also Chard, Ries and Pinot N. One to watch.

Kumeu River (Kumeu, NW of Auckland) Premium label of small San Marino family winery, establishing reputation for Fumé-style Sauv, Chard, Cab-Merlot and light, fruity Cab F under Brajkovich family crest label.

Lincoln Vineyards (Henderson, nr Auckland) Medium-sized family winery now producing varietals, esp Chard, Chenin Bl and Cab. 88 shows real promise.

Marlborough Leading export wine region at N end of South Island, on stony plain formed by Wairau River. Well suited to white varieties Chard, Sauv Bl and Ries, but also good Cab S and promising Pinot N. Potential here for vg sparkling.

Martinborough New smallish appellation in S Wairarapa (N of Wellington, North Island). Stony soils, similar to MARLBOROUGH.

Martinborough Vineyards (Martinborough) Largest of the small operations in the area. Awards already for Chard, 'Fumé' Sauv Bl and Pinot N. 89 very good.

Matawhero (nr Gisborne) Small winery with established name for Gewürz, Chard and Sauv Bl.

Matua Valley (NW of Auckland) Medium-sized family winery, pioneer with new varieties. Own grapes supplemented by fruit from HAWKES BAY and GISBORNE. Well known for Judd Chard (Gisborne), intense, unwooded Sauv Bl and oaky Reserve, unique Pinot N-Bl, good Cab S, Merlot, Ries, Gewürz and late-harvest Muscat.

McDonald (Hawkes Bay) MONTANA's new venture. Philosophy: premium wine from new v'yds. Great potential.

Merlen (Marlborough) Small dynamic winery producing Sauv Bl, botrytised Ries, Chard and Sauv 'Fumé'.

Mills Reef (Bay of Plenty) Small-scale producer of v attractive Chard, Sauv Bl, Ries and Gewürz.

Millton (nr Gisborne) Small new producer using organic cultivation. Good Sauv Bl-Sém blend, Chard and Ries (both dry and late harvest). Splendid barrel-fermented Chenin Bl 87, 89, like a v fine Anjou.

Mission (Greenmeadows, Hawkes Bay) Oldest continuing winemaking establishment in NZ, founded by French missionaries and still operated by Society of Mary. Good Sém-Sauv Bl and Cab-Merlot.

Montana (Auckland) Largest winemaking enterprise in NZ, with wineries in GISBORNE and MARLBOROUGH; incorporating Penfolds label (in NZ only). Pioneered viticulture in Marlborough, but also draws grapes from Gisborne and HAWKES BAY. Marlborough labels incl Sauv Bl, Chard, Ries, Cab S, Pinot N. Gisborne Chard also sound wine and a big seller. Original Lindauer sparkling joined by excellent *cuvée* DEUTZ.

Morton Estate (Katikati, nr Tauranga, E coast, North Island)   Expanding new winery with high reputation for Chard from HAWKES BAY (esp Premium Black Label), full-bodied Sauv Bl and impressive (89) Cab-Merlot blend. Released first (vg) *méthode champenoise* in '87.

Nautilus (nr Auckland)   Young winery: Chard from MARLBOROUGH and Sauv Bl from HAWKES BAY.

Neudorf (Nelson)   Charming, small-scale winery: rich Chard, Ries, Sauv Bl and reds.

Ngatarawa (nr Hastings, Hawkes Bay)   Boutique winery in old stables of established HAWKES BAY family. Good Chard, Sauv Bl and Cab-Merlot under Glazebrook family label.

Nobilo (Huapai Valley, NW of Auckland)   NZ's largest family-owned winery: own grapes plus fruit from GISBORNE, HAWKES BAY, MARLBOROUGH and MARTINBOROUGH. Good Chard (esp from Gisborne), pungent Sauv Bl, Sém, and old reputation for age-worthy reds: Cab S and Pinot N. Associate label Classic Hills. Concept One is Huapai Cab-Pinotage.

Pask, C J (Hawkes Bay)   Up-and-coming producer: vg Cab S; also Chard, Pinot N, Sauv Bl.

Penfolds *See* Montana.

Riverview Vineyard (Hawkes Bay)   Promising new winery for Sauv Bl, Chard and Cab.

Robard & Butler *See* Corbans.

Rongapai (Waikato, S of Auckland)   German-influenced winery renowned for botrytised wines.

Savidge Estate (Gisborne)   Past grape suppliers, now successfully marketing own Chard, Chenin Bl, Sauv Bl and red.

St Nesbit (Karaka, nr Papakura, S of Auckland)   Expanding boutique winery: single red wine blended from Cab S, Cab F and Merlot, well made and matured in *barriques*.

Selak's (Kumeu, NW of Auckland)   Small family firm with good export reputation for fresh, sharpish Sauv Bl, Sauv Bl-Sém blend (in 'Fumé' style), Chard, Cab S. (Founders is label for top Chard and Cab wines.)

Stoneleigh *See* Corbans.

Stonyridge (Waiheke Island, nr Auckland)   Boutique winery concentrating on two reds in Bordeaux style: Larose exceptional, Airfield very good.

Te Kairanga (Martinborough)   Largest winery in region, with underground facilities.

Te Mata (Havelock North, Hawkes Bay)   Restored winery producing good Chard (esp Elston) and Sauv Bl from nearby v'yds, plus excellent 'Coleraine' Cab-Merlot from proprietor's home v'yd.

Vavasour (Awatere Valley, nr Blenheim)   Recent venture into uncharted region. Top quality reds: Cab S and F.

Vidal (Hastings, Hawkes Bay)   Atmospheric old winery, now merged with VILLA MARIA. Good HAWKES BAY Chard, Sauv Bl, Cab S and Pinot N.

Villa Maria (Mangere, S Auckland)   Large company, incorporating VIDAL and ESK VALLEY. Grapes from Ihumatao (nr Auckland airport), GISBORNE and HAWKES BAY. Full range, esp barrel-fermented Chard, Sauv Bl (and wooded 'Fumé' variation), Gewürz, Cab S and Cab-Merlot.

Waipara Springs (N Canterbury)   Recent producer of model Sauv Bl, Chard and Pinot N. To follow.

Wairau River (Marlborough)   New small winery producing full-flavoured Sauv Bl and Chard.

Weingut Seifried (Upper Moutere, nr Nelson, S Island)   Small winery started by Austrian immigrant. Good Chard, Sauv Bl, Ries (in dry and late-harvest styles) and Pinot N.

South Africa

Quality in South Africa's table wines began around 1975 when vineyard owners began to add to their plantings of Cabernet Sauvignon, already successful, the greater challenges of Chardonnay, Sauvignon Blanc and even Pinot Noir. New laws in 1973 defining Wines of Origin encouraged new small estates. The success of small new wineries in the 1980s has encouraged others to buy oak barrels from France. Cellarmasters are now showing more care in harvesting and cellar treatment and standards are rising steadily. In addition to estates listed, several cooperatives bottle quality wine.

Recommended vintages refer to the wine preceding them in brackets.

Allesverloren r *→*** (Cab S) 86 87 89   Old 395-acre family estate, best known for 'Port'. Also hefty, well-oaked but not always long-lived CAB and Shiraz from hot wheatlands district of Malmesbury.

Alphen ★   Gilbey's brand name for wines from STELLENBOSCH area.

Alto r **→**** (Cab S) 86 87 89   High 247-acre mountain v'yds S of STELLENBOSCH, facing the Atlantic. Solid CAB; and blended Cab with Merlot and Shiraz. Best since mid-'80s (with new French oak).

Altydgedacht r w ★→** (Cab S) 85 86 87 88 89   Durbanville estate, best for CAB; also good, gutsy Tintoretto blend of Barbera and Shiraz.

Avontuur r w ** (red) 87 89 90   A 200-acre STELLENBOSCH v'yd, bottling since '87. Soft, Bordeaux-style blend, Avon Rouge; respectable CAB S, Merlot, promising CHARD.

Backsberg r w **→*** (red) 84 88 87 (Chard) 86 88 89 90   Frequently prize-winning 395-acre estate at PAARL. Pioneered oak-fermented CHARD in mid-'80s with US advice. Delicious Bordeaux blend Klein Babylonstoren is best; also vg oaked SAUV BL, John Martin. Proprietor Sydney Back is going strong after 55 vintages.

Bellingham r w ★   Big-selling brand name of DGB (Douglas Green, Bellingham). Sound reds, popular whites, esp sweet, soft CAPE RIES-based Johannisberger (exported as Cape Gold).

Bergkelder Big wine concern at STELLENBOSCH, member of Oude Meester group, making and distributing many brands (FLEUR DU CAP, GRUN-BERGER) and 19 estate wines. First to use French oak commercially; now has 10,000 barrels, outstripping all for finely oaked reds.

Bertrams r **→*** 84 88 87 89   Gilbeys brand of good to vg varietals, esp Shiraz, PINOTAGE. Also Robert Fuller Reserve Bordeaux-style blend.

Beyerskloof r ***   (Cab S) 89 90 91   New small STELLENBOSCH property, devoted to vg, tannic, deep-flavoured CAB S.

Blaauwklippen r w **→*** (red) 84 86 87 88 90   STELLENBOSCH winery making among the Cape's finest, bold, lasting reds, esp CAB Reserve. Also S Africa's best Zin; patchy but improving CHARD; good off-dry RIES.

Bloemendal r w ★→** (Cab S) 88 89 (Chard) 90 91   Young sea-cooled estate at Durbanville. Fragrant, light CAB; soft, elegant CHARD.

Boberg Controlled region of origin for fortified wines consisting of the districts of PAARL and TULBAGH.

Bon Courage w sw ★→** ROBERTSON estate; vg dessert whites, incl GEWURZ, botrytis RIES, respectable CHARD.

Boplaas r w ★*   V'yds at Calitzdorp in the dry, hot, Karoo area. Earthy, deep 'Vintage Reserve Port' best since '87, and fortified Muscadels. Links with Grahams in Portugal.

Boschendal w sp **→*** (Chard) 89 91   617-acre estate nr Franschhoek in PAARL area. Good CHARD and *méthode champenoise;* also Cape's first 'blush' off-dry Blanc de Noirs. Owned by Anglo-American Corp.

Bouchard-Finlayson r w (★★★) New and first French-Cape partnership, between Paul Bouchard of Bouchard Ainé in Burgundy and Peter Finlayson, at Hermanus, Walker Bay. Maiden release 91 v promising, esp PINOT N.

Breede River Valley Fortified and white wine region E of Drakenstein Mts.

Buitenverwachting r w sp ★★★ (Chard) 89 90 91 Exceptional, German-financed, recently replanted v'yds at CONSTANTIA. Outstanding SAUV BL, both plain and oaked (Blanc Fumé), and CHARD. Vg Bordeaux blend (88, 89) and Merlot. Lively, clean *méthode champenoise* from Pinot G and Pinot Bl. Restaurant worthy of a Michelin star.

Cabernet Sauvignon The great Bordeaux grape, most successful in COASTAL REGION. Range of styles from sturdy, long-lived to elegant, fruity. More use of new French oak since '82 is making great improvements. Best vintages of past decade: 82, 84, 86, 87, 89, 91.

Cape Independent Winemakers Guild Young group of winemakers in the vanguard of quality and without direct links to the major wholesalers. Holds an annual auction of progressive-style wines.

Cape Riesling *See* Riesling.

Cathedral Cellars *See* KWV.

Cavendish Cape ★★ Range of remarkably good 'Sherries' from the KWV.

Chardonnay Classic white variety, fairly new in S Africa due to official restrictions. Recent release of good vines resulted in leap in quality in number. Great expectations. There are now over 100 Chard labels; a decade ago, 3. Best vintage so far is 89; 91 also very good.

Chateau Libertas ★ Big-selling CAB S brand made by SFW.

Chenin Blanc Work-horse grape of the Cape; one vine in three. Adaptable, sometimes vg. KWV makes good value example. *See also* Steen.

Cinsaut The principal bulk-producing French red grape in S Africa; formerly known as Hermitage. V seldom seen with varietal label.

Coastal Region Demarcated wine region, incl CONSTANTIA, Durbanville, PAARL, STELLENBOSCH, SWARTLAND, TULBAGH.

Colombard French white grape, as popular in the Cape as in California. Crisp, lively, flowery but usually short-lived wines; often used for blending, also for brandy.

Constantia Once the world's most famous sweet, Muscat-based wine (both red and white), from the Cape.

Delaire Vineyards r w ★★ (Chard) 89 91 (red) **90 91** Full-flavoured CHARD, Bordeaux blend named Barrique, and elegant off-dry RHINE RIES, from young winery at Helshoogte Pass above STELLENBOSCH.

Delheim r w dr sw ★★→★★★ (red) 86 87 88 89 Big winery with high mountain v'yds at Driesprong nr STELLENBOSCH. Elegant, barrel-aged CAB S, Merlot, Cab F blend, Grand Reserve. Good value Cab, PINOTAGE, Shiraz; variable PINOT N; improving CHARD and SAUV BL. Outstanding sweet wines incl GEWURZ and botrytis STEEN.

De Wetshof w sw ★★→★★★ (Chard) 87 88 89 Pioneering ROBERTSON estate, with powerful CHARD and fresh, dry RHINE RIES. Also dessert GEWURZ, Rhine Ries under Danie de Wet label.

Douglas Green ★→★★ Cape Town merchants, marketing range of sound wines, incl 'Sherries' and 'Ports' mostly from KWV. Recently merged with Union Wine, owners of BELLINGHAM.

Drostdy ★ Good range of 'Sherries' from BERGKELDER.

Drostyhof r w ★ Well-priced range incl CHARD made at TULBAGH cellars.

Edelkeur ★★★★ Excellent, intensely sweet white made with nobly rotten grapes (*see* page 47) by NEDERBURG.

Eikendal Vineyards r w ★★→★★ (red) 87 88 90 (Chard) 91 Swiss-owned STELLENBOSCH 100-acre v'yds and winery. Vg CHARD; CAB S-Merlot blend Classique. Fresh whites incl semi-sweet CHENIN BL.

Estate wine Official term applying only to wines from registered estates that grow and make their own wines, which may be bottled elsewhere. Estate v'yds need not be contiguous or even nearby provided they enjoy similar 'ecological conditions'. In Afrikaans 'estate' is LANDGOED.

Fairview Estate r w dr sw **→*** (red) 88 90 (Chard) 90 91   Enterprising PAARL estate with wide range. Best are Reserve Merlot, PINOTAGE, Bordeaux blend Charles Gerard Reserve. Also lively Gamay, good CHARD, plus sweet CHENIN BL.

Fleur du Cap r w sw **→*** (red) 86 87 **88 90**   Underrated, good value range from BERGKELDER at STELLENBOSCH, particularly excellent CAB S in good yrs since '86. Also Merlot, improving CHARD, fine GEWURZ and botrytis CHENIN BL.

Gewürztraminer The famous spicy grape of Alsace, best at NEDERBURG, SIMONSIG and (for drier style) STELLENRYCK. Naturally low acidity makes this variety difficult to handle at the Cape.

Glen Carlou r w **→*** (red) 89 **90 91** (Chard) 90 91   New PAARL property: excellent Bordeaux blend, Classique, and Merlot; also fine CHARD.

Graça *   Huge-selling, slightly fizzy white blend in Portuguese-style bottle.

Grand Cru (or Premier Grand Cru) Term for a totally dry white, with no quality implications. Generally to be avoided.

Groot Constantia r w **→***   Historic estate, now government owned, nr Cape Town. Source of superlative Muscat wine in the early 19th C. Renaissance in progress; so far fine CAB (esp blended Gouverneur's Reserve), Shiraz and whites. Dessert Muscat will come later.

Grünberger *   BERGKELDER brand using STEEN to make range of dry and semi-sweet white wines.

Hamilton Russell Vineyards r w ***→**** (Pinot N) 85 86 87 89 **90 91** (Chard) 86 87 89 90 91   The Cape's top 'Burgundy' v'yds and cellar. Small yields, French-inspired vinification in cool, most southerly region of Walker Bay. Many awards. Priciest wines in S Africa.

Hanepoot Local name for the sweet Muscat of Alexandria grape.

Hartenberg r w **   STELLENBOSCH estate, recently modernized; rich, well-aged Shiraz.

Kanonkop r ***→**** (red) 84 86 **89 90 91**   Outstanding estate in N STELLENBOSCH. Individual, powerful CAB S and Bordeaux-style blend Paul Sauer. Benchmark PINOTAGE, barrel-finished since '89 with dramatic improvement.

Klein Constantia r w sw ***→****   A new Cape star: old subdivision of famous Groot Constantia neighbour. Emphatic CHARD, SAUV BL, and fine, powerful CAB S, Bordeaux-style blend, Shiraz. A Muscat Frontignan 86, Vin de Constance, revives an 18th-C Constantia legend. Revamped since early '80s. Frequent national champions.

KWV The Kooperatieve Wijnbouwers Vereniging, S Africa's national wine cooperative created in 1917 to absorb surpluses. Vast premises in PAARL making a range of good wines, esp Cathedral Cellars reds, RIES and 'Sherries' and sweet dessert wines.

La Bri **   Whites made in Franschhoek coop cellar from SAUV BL and RHINE RIES and Sém. Sauvage de la Bri is best.

Laborie r w *→**   KWV-owned showpiece estate in PAARL district. Blended white and red.

La Motte r w *** (red) 86 87 88 **89 91**   Lavish new Rupert family estate nr Franschhoek. Lean but stylish, intensely flavoured reds: CAB S, Shiraz, Merlot, Bordeaux-style blend Millennium. Racy SAUV BL.

Landgoed Afrikaans for 'estate': a word that appears on official seals and frequently on ESTATE-WINE labels.

Landskroon r w *→**   Family estate owned by Paul and Hugo de Villiers. Good dry reds, esp Shiraz, CAB S, CAB F.

Late Harvest Term for a mildly sweet wine. 'Special Late Harvest' must be naturally sweet (no added concentrate). 'Noble Late Harvest' is the highest dessert wine quality level.

Le Bonheur r w *** (red) 84 86 87   STELLENBOSCH estate often producing classic, tannic, minerally CAB, big-bodied SAUV BL. CHARD improving.

Lemberg w ** Tiny estate in TULBAGH, making full-bodied, wood-aged Hárslevelü and SAUV BL labelled Aimée.

JC Leroux ** Old brand revived as BERGKELDER's sparkling wine house. SAUV BL (*charmat*) and PINOT N (*méthode champenoise*). Also CHARD.

Lievland r w **→*** (red) 87 89 90 STELLENBOSCH estate making top Cape Shiraz and vg CAB S, Merlot. Also range of whites incl intense RIES, off-dry and promising Sauternes-style dessert wine.

L'Ormarins r w sw *** (red) 84 86 87 89 (Chard) 89 90 One of two Rupert family estates nr Franschhoek. CAB S and vg claret-style Optima. Fresh, lemony CHARD, forward, oak-aged SAUV BL, and outstanding GEWURZ-Bukkettraube botrytis dessert wine.

Louisvale w ** (Chard) 90 91 New STELLENBOSCH winery making only attractive CHARD.

Meerendal r ** Estate nr Durbanville producing traditional robust reds (esp Shiraz and PINOTAGE) marketed by BERGKELDER.

Meerlust r w *** Old family estate S of STELLENBOSCH: outstanding Rubicon (Médoc-style blend), Merlot and PINOT N. CHARD in the pipeline.

Middelvlei ** STELLENBOSCH estate making good PINOTAGE and CAB. Marketed by BERGKELDER.

Monis *→*** Well-known wine concern of PAARL, with fine 'Vintage Port'.

Morgenhof r w dr s/sw * Recently refurbished cellars and v'yd, making range of improving reds; dry and semi-sweet whites; 'Port'.

Muratie Ancient estate in STELLENBOSCH, best known for its 'Port'. Recently sold; bright future expected.

Nederburg r w p d dr sw s/sw sp **→**** (red) 82 84 86 87 89 91 (Chard) 89 90 91 Probably the best-known label in S Africa, with large, modern winery at PAARL (700,000 cases pa, of some 50 wines). Celebrated its bicentenary in '92. Grapes from scattered suppliers and own v'yds. Sound CAB S, Shiraz, CHARD, RIES and blends in regular range. Limited Vintages and Private Bins often outstanding. '80s pioneer of botrytis dessert wines from eg CHENIN BL, GEWURZ, SAUV BL, Muscat, even Chard. Stages Cape's biggest annual wine event, the Nederburg Auction.

Neethlingshof r w sw **→*** (red) 87 89 90 91 (Chard) 91 Rising estate, replanted with classic varieties, cellar revamped at huge cost since '85 by German investor. Vg CAB S, Merlot, CHARD coming on stream to join fresh, crisp SAUV BL, excellent GEWURZ and blush Blanc de Noir. National Champion dessert botrytis from RIES, Sauv Bl.

Neil Ellis Wines r w *** (red) 86 87 89 91 (Chard) 89 91 Good wines made in Devon Valley nr STELLENBOSCH, from 16 widely spread coastal v'yds. Spicy, structured CAB S; excellent Whitehall SAUV BL; full, bold CHARD.

Nuy Cooperative Winery r w dr sw sp ** Small Worcester Coop, frequent local-award winner. Outstanding dessert wines, traditional fortified Muscadels, regularly excellent Cape COLOMBARD. Good S African RIES.

Oak Valley Wines * New export brand, blend of good coop cellar wines from STELLENBOSCH, incl CAB-Shiraz, SAUV BL-CHENIN BL blends.

Overgaauw r w ** (red) 84 86 87 89 90 91 Old family estate W of STELLENBOSCH; CHARD, CAB S, and Bordeaux-style blend Tria Corda. Also 'Port' from 5 Portuguese varieties.

Paarl Town 30 miles NE of Cape Town, and the surrounding demarcated district, among the best in the country, particularly for 'Sherry'.

Pierre Jourdan sp *** Fine NV *méthode champenoise* made at Clos Cabriere estate, Franschhoek. Most notable: Brut Sauvage and Cuve Belle Rose (pure PINOT N).

Pinot Noir Like counterparts in California and Australia, Cape producers struggle for fine, burgundy-like complexity. They are getting closer. Best are BLAAUWKLIPPEN, HAMILTON RUSSELL, MEERLUST, RUSTENBERG.

Pinotage S African red grape, a cross between PINOT N and CINSAUT, useful for high yields and hardiness. The results can be delicious but, more often, overstated flamboyant esters dominate. Recent experiments and barrel-ageing show potential for finesse.

Premier Grand Cru *See* Grand Cru.

Rhebokskloof r ★→★★ (red) 90   New 200-acre estate behind PAARL mountain, with a sound, small range. Most promising is CAB. Has the Cape's first American winemaker.

Rhine Riesling Produces full-flavoured dry and off-dry wines, but reaches perfection when lusciously sweet as 'Noble LATE HARVEST'. Generally needs 2 yrs or more of bottle-age. Also called Weisser Ries.

Riesling S African Ries (actually Crouchen Bl) is v different from RHINE RIES, providing neutral, easy-drinking wines. Known locally as Cape Ries.

Rietvallei w sw ★★   ROBERTSON estate producing excellent fortified Muscadel. Also CHARD.

Robertson Demarcated district E of and inland from the Cape. Mainly dessert wines (notably Muscat), with white table wines on the increase. Few reds. Incl Bonnievale. Irrigated v'yds.

Roodeberg ★   Sound red from the KWV: blend of PINOTAGE, Shiraz, Tinta Barocca, CAB S in about equal parts.

Rozendel r ★★★ (red) 83 84 86 87 89   Small STELLENBOSCH v'yd cellar, making excellent CAB-Merlot blend.

Rustenberg r w ★★★→★★★★ (red/not Pinot N) 80 82 84 86 87 88 89 91 (Chard) 86 87 89 90   The most beautiful old STELLENBOSCH estate, founded 300 yrs ago, making wine uninterruptedly for the last 100. Grand, fine reds, esp Rustenberg Gold CAB and Médoc-style blend. Also lighter Cab-CINSAUT-Merlot blend. Variable PINOT N, sometimes v attractive, best recent 88. Individual and charming CHARD. Formerly marketed whites under sister estate's name, Schoongezicht.

Rust en Vrede r ★★→★★★ (Cab S) 86 87 89   Well-known estate just E of STELLENBOSCH: red only. Good CAB S, Shiraz, vg Bordeaux-style blend.

Sauvignon Blanc Adapting well to warm conditions. Widely grown and marketed in both 'wooded' and 'unwooded' styles. Also v sweet.

Schoongezicht *See* Rustenberg.

Simonsig r w sp sw ★★→★★★ (Cab S) 84 86 87 89 91 (Chard) 88 89 90 91   Malan family STELLENBOSCH estate with a wide range, starring vg CAB, CHARD, PINOTAGE, GEWURZ (dessert-style). Also popular wood-matured dry white Vin Fumé and first Cape *méthode champenoise*.

Simonsvlei r w p sw sp ★   One of S Africa's best-known coop cellars, just outside PAARL. A prize-winner with PINOTAGE.

Spier r w ★   Estate of 5 farms W of STELLENBOSCH producing reds and whites. PINOTAGE is probably best.

Steen S Africa's commonest white grape, said to be a clone of CHENIN BL. It gives strong, tasty, lively wine, sweet or dry, normally better than S African RIES. Short-lived if dry; lasts better when off-dry or sweet.

Stein Name often used for commercial blends of semi-sweet white wine. Not necessarily to be despised.

Stellenbosch Town and demarcated district 30 miles E of Cape Town (oldest town in S Africa), extending to the ocean at False Bay. The heart of the wine industry, with all 3 of the largest companies. Most of the best estates, esp for red wine, are in the mountain foothills.

Stellenbosch Farmers' Winery (SFW) S Africa's biggest winery (after the KWV) with several ranges of wines, incl NEDERBURG and ZONNEBLOEM. Wide range of mid- and low-priced wines.

Stellenryck Collection r w ★★★   Top quality BERGKELDER range. RHINE RIES, Fumé Blanc, CAB among S Africa's best.

Swartland Cooperative r w dr s/sw sw sp ★   Vast range of big-selling, low-priced wines, chiefly white CHENIN BL and off-dry or sweet, but (recently) penetrating, dry SAUV BL, and big, no-nonsense PINOTAGE. From dry wheatland area, among Cape's hottest.

Talana Hill r w ★★ (red) 88 89 (Chard) 89 90 91   New STELLENBOSCH winery: good CHARD and Bordeaux-style blend Royale.

Tassenberg ★   Popular PINOTAGE-based blend by SFW, known fondly as 'Tassies'. Traditional student party and *braalvleis* (barbecue) wine.

Oom Tas, a dry Muscat, is white equivalent.

Thelema r w ******* (Cab S) 89 **90 91** (Chard) 88 89 90 91 Outstanding new v'yds and winery at Helshoogte, above STELLENBOSCH. Impressive, minty CAB, excellent CHARD, and both oaked and unoaked SAUV BL.

Theuniskraal w * TULBAGH estate: whites incl S Afrian RIES, GEWURZ.

Tulbagh Demarcated district N of PAARL best known for the white wines of THEUNISKRAAL and TWEE JONGEGEZELLEN, and the dessert wines from DROSTDY. *See also* Boberg.

Twee Jongegezellen w sp ****** Old TULBAGH estate, helped pioneer cold fermentation in '60s, night harvesting in '80s; still in family of 18th-C founder. Esp whites: best known are v popular, dry TJ89 (*mélange* of a dozen varieties), and Schanderl off-dry Muscat-GEWURZ-based blend. Recently added *méthode champenoise* Cuvée Krone Borealis Brut from CHARD, PINOT N.

Uiterwyk r w * Old estate W of STELLENBOSCH. CAB, Merlot, pleasant whites.

Uitkyk r w ****** (red) 86 87 89 Old estate (400 acres) W of STELLENBOSCH famous for Carlonet (big gutsy CAB) and Carlsheim (SAUV BL) white. Recently added Pinot G, CHARD.

Union Wine Wine-growers and wholesalers at Wellington with BELLINGHAM v'yds at Franschhoek, recently merged with DOUGLAS GREEN.

Van Loveren r w sw sp ****** Go-ahead ROBERTSON estate: big range of whites incl muscular CHARD and scarcer varieties eg Fernao Pires, Hárslevlü.

Verglegen One of Cape's oldest wine farms, long neglected, now undergoing spectacular revival, incl French-designed, sunken, hilltop cellar. Replanted v'yds too young still, but kicked off 92 vintage with purchased grapes.

Vergenoegd r w sw * Old family estate in S STELLENBOSCH, supplying high-quality 'Sherry' to KWV and bottling CAB S, Shiraz.

Villiera r w ******* PAARL estate with popular NV *méthode champenoise*, Tradition. First-rate SAUV BL, good RHINE RIES; fine Bordeaux-style blend CAB-Merlot, Cru Monro. Recently exceptional Merlot.

Vriesenhof r w ****→***** (Cab S) 82 84 86 **88 89** (Chard) 88 89 91 Highly rated, slow-developing CAB S and Bordeaux blend, Kalista. Since '88, excellent CHARD. Also Pinot Bl.

Warwick r w ****→***** (red) 86 87 **89 91** New STELLENBOSCH estate, run by one of Cape's few woman winemakers. CAB and vg Médoc-style blend, Trilogy.

Weisser Riesling *See* Rhine Riesling.

Welgemeend r ****→***** (red) 86 87 89 Boutique PAARL estate producing Médoc-style blends, delicate CAB and Amadé, a Grenache-Shiraz-PINOTAGE blend.

Weltevrede w dr sw ***→**** (Chard) 89 90 Progressive ROBERTSON estate. Blended, white and fortified wines; vg CHARD.

Wine of Origin The S African equivalent of *appellation contrôlée*. Demarcated regions are described on these pages.

Woolworths Wines Best S African supermarket wines, many specially blended for the chainstore. Tops are young reds, incl Merlot, Bordeaux-style blends and CHARD.

Worcester Demarcated wine district round the BREEDE and Hex river valleys, E of PAARL. Many coop cellars make mainly dessert wines, brandy and dry whites.

Zandvliet r ***→**** (Shiraz) 86 87 Estate in the ROBERTSON area making a fine light Shiraz and more recently a CAB S and PINOT N.

Zandwijk r w New estate in PAARL district producing quality kosher wine.

Zevenwacht r w ****→***** (Cab S) 84 86 87 89 Large STELLENBOSCH estate with wines only available through shareholders and restaurants. CAB S is impressive.

Zonnebloem r w ****** (Cab S) 82 84 86 87 89 (Chard) 90 Good quality range from SFW incl CAB S, Merlot, Bordeaux-style blend, Shiraz, PINOTAGE, SAUV BL, CHARD.

A few words about words

In the shorthand essential for this little book (and sometimes in bigger books as well) wines are often described by adjectives that can seem irrelevant, inane – or just silly. What do 'fat', 'round', 'full', 'lean' and so on mean when used about wine? Some of the more irritatingly vague are expanded in this list:

Attack
The first impression of the wine in your mouth. It should 'strike' positively, if not necessarily with force. Without attack it is feeble or too bland.

Attractive
Means 'I like it, anyway'. A slight put-down for expensive wines; encouragement for juniors. At least refreshing.

Big
Concerns the whole flavour, including the alcohol content. Sometimes implies clumsiness, the opposite of elegance. Generally positive, but big is easy in California and less usual in, say, Bordeaux. So the context matters.

Charming
Rather patronizing when said of wines that should have more impressive qualities. Implies lightness and possibly slight sweetness. A standard comment regarding Loire wines.

Crisp
With pronounced but pleasing acidity; fresh and eager.

Deep/depth
This wine is worth tasting with attention. There is more to it than the first impression; it fills your mouth with developing flavours as though it had an extra dimension. (Deep colour simply means hard to see through.) All really fine wines have depth.

Easy
Used in the sense of 'easy come, easy go'. An easy wine makes no demand on your palate (or intellect). The implication is that it drinks smoothly, doesn't need maturing, and all you remember is a pleasant drink.

Elegant
A professional taster's favourite term when he or she is stuck to describe a wine whose proportions (of strength, flavour, aroma), whose attack, middle and finish, whose texture and all whose overall qualities call for comparison with other forms of natural beauty.

Fat
With flavour and texture that fills your mouth, but without aggression. Obviously inappropriate in eg a light Moselle, but what you pay your money for in Sauternes.

Finish
See Length.

Firm
Flavour that strikes the palate fairly hard, with fairly high acidity or tannic astringency giving the impression that the wine is in youthful vigour and will age to gentler things. An excellent quality with high-flavoured foods, and almost always positive.

Flesh
Refers to both substance and texture. A fleshy wine is fatter than a 'meaty' wine, more unctuous if less vigorous. The term is often used of good Pomerols, whose texture is notably smooth.

Flowery
Often used as though synonymous with fruity, but really means floral, like the fragrance of flowers. Roses, violets, etc are sometimes specified.

Fresh
Implies a good degree of fruity acidity, even a little nip of sharpness, as well as the zip and zing of youth. All young whites should be fresh: the alternative is flatness, staleness... ugh.

Fruity
Used for almost any quality, but really refers to the body and richness of wine made from good ripe grapes. A fruity aroma is not the same as a flavoury one. Fruitiness usually implies at least a slight degree of sweetness.

	Attempts at specifying *which* fruit the wine resembles can be helpful. Eg grapefruit, lemon, plum, lychee.
Full	Interchangeable with full-bodied. Lots of 'vinosity' or wineyness: the mouth-filling flavours of alcohol and 'extract' (all the flavouring components) combined.
Hollow	Lacking a satisfying middle flavour. Something seems to be missing between first flavour and last. A characteristic of wines from greedy proprietors who let their vines produce too many grapes. A very hollow wine is 'empty'.
Lean	More flesh would be an improvement. Lack of mouth-filling flavours; often astringent as well. Occasionally a term of appreciation of a distinct and enjoyable style.
Length	The flavours and aromas that linger after swallowing. In principle the greater the length the better the wine. One second of flavour after swallowing = one 'caudalie'. Ten caudalies is good; 20 terrific.
Light	With relatively little alcohol and body, as in most German wines. A very desirable quality in the right wines.
Meaty	Savoury in effect with enough substance to chew. The inference is lean meat; leaner than in 'fleshy'.
Oaky	Smelling or tasting of fresh-sawn oak, eg a new barrel.
Plump	The diminutive of fat, implying a degree of charm as well.
Rich	Not necessarily sweet, but giving an opulent impression.
Robust	In good heart, vigorous, and on a fairly big scale.
Rough	Flavour and texture give no pleasure. Acidity and/or tannin are dominant and coarse.
Round	Almost the same as fat, but with more approval.
Structure	The 'plan' of the flavour, as it were. Without structure wine is bland, dull, and won't last.
Stylish	Style is bold and definite; wears its cap on its ear.
Supple	Often used of young red wines which might be expected to be more aggressive. More lively than an 'easy' wine, with implications of good quality.
Well balanced	Contains all the desirable elements (acid, alcohol, flavours, etc) in appropriate and pleasing proportions.

A few words about smells

As the number of interested and discriminating wine-drinkers increases, wine commentary and criticism is becoming increasingly professionalized. In the past ten years it has developed rapidly in two directions. One is scoring by numbers. The other is describing wines by association with other aromatic and otherwise sensually specific substances.

The name-a-fruit technique by which a Chardonnay, for example, is characterized as 'peachy' or 'melony', and its name-a-chemical variant, by which an aroma is labelled as ethyl acetate or mercaptan, were given academic clout by the University of California (UC Davis) with its development of an Aroma Wheel, analogous to the well-established colour wheel.

The Aroma Wheel breaks down the whole spectrum of aromas first into such broad compartments as fruity, floral, vegetative, chemical, woody or earthy. It subdivides eg fruity into berries, tree fruits, citrus, tropical and dried fruits. These spokes of the wheel then lead to, at the rim, specific fruits. Berries are either straw-, rasp-, black- or blackcurrant; citrus either orange, grapefruit or lemon; tree fruit either cherry, peach, pear, apple or apricot.

There is no question that this deliberate approach to description by analysis can be extremely effective and surprisingly accurate. On the other hand it encourages writers looking for effect to fling basketfuls of fruit and flowers at wines that could well be more modestly described.

The University's object was in part to limit the use of such 'vague, ambiguous terms' as 'graceful', 'elegant', 'full', 'supple' – indeed, the whole traditional vocabulary of wine. To replace it with precise references is a natural scientific goal. In truth, the two approaches are complementary.

There is no virtue in restricting one's use of the full resources of language to describe something as elusive as wine. Such words as 'tough', 'masculine', 'adolescent', 'coarse', 'breed' or 'silky' express aspects of wine's complexity that are not describable in terms of mere aromas. Good wines have personalities that need a poet as much as a scientist to describe them.

A few words about judgement

'No one has ever attempted to stick a report card on Mozart's "Requiem". The art world would be appalled if the Metropolitan Museum of Art began rating the works it houses on a "pleasure scale". Imagine the scenario: two ardent and knowledgeable art lovers stride purposefully through the Egyptian Rooms, which recently received a paltry 80 ("good to very good, art with special qualities") in their haste to reach the Futurists exhibit, proud owner of a 94 ("outstanding, art of superior character and style"). Yet wine is subjected to such treatment every day.

'Evaluating a wine's virtues using numbered scales, whether 1 to 20, 1 to 100, or 1 to 1,000, is a dicey proposition. The true message of ranking systems is not that Wine A, which got a 95, is better than Wine B, which received a 89. It is that at one moment in time, one or sometimes two bottles of Wine A appealed more to one person's palate than did Wine B. In the case of a tasting panel, the impressions are averaged.

'The tasting of wine is complicated by many factors. When we're thirsty, the first sip will often taste better. The food consumed even hours before tasting wine can affect a wine's flavor, just as any food consumed alongside the wine will alter our perception of it. The body's biorhythms play a part too; even the most accomplished tasters can have "off" days. Add the natural bias of tasters for or against a particular wine, and individual variations in taste courtesy of genetic inheritance, and the intriguingly subjective nature of wine tasting becomes apparent.'

Extracted from the Bulletin of the Society of Medical Friends of Wine, March 1992.

What to drink in an ideal world

Wines at their peak in 1993

Red Bordeaux
Top growths of '87, '84, '83, '81, '79, '78, '76, '75, '70, '66, '62, '61
Other *crus classés* of '87, '86 (St-Emilion/Pomerol), '85, '83, '82
    (St-Emilion/Pomerol), '81, '79, '78, '70, '66, '61
Petits châteaux of '89, '88, '86, '85, '83, '82, '81, '79

Red Burgundy
Top growths of '86, '85, '82, '80, '79, '78, '76, '72, '71, '69, '66, '64
Premiers Crus of '87, '86, '85, '83, '78, '76
Village wines of '90, '89, '88, '87, '86, '85

White Burgundy
Top growths of '87, '86, '85, '83, '82, '79, '78...
Premiers Crus of '88, '86, '85, '83, '78...
Village wines of '90, '89, '88, '86, '85

Champagne
Top wines of '85, '83, '82, '81, '79, '78, '76, '75,...

Sauternes
Top growths of '85, '84, '83, '82, '81, '80, '79, '78, '76, '75, '71, '70, '67...
Other wines of '89, '88, '86, '85, '83, '82, '81, '79, '78, '76, '75...

Sweet Loire wines
Top growths (Anjou/Vouvray) of '86, '85, '82, '81, '79, '78, '76, '75, '73,
    71, '69, '64...

Alsace
Grands Crus and late-harvest wines of '88, '87, '86, '85, '83, '81, '79,
    '78, '76...
Standard wines of '91, '90, '89, '88, '86...

Rhône reds
Hermitage/top northern Rhône reds of '87, '86, '85, '83, '82, '80, '79, '78,
    '71, '70
Châteauneuf-du-Pape of '88, '86, '85, '84, '83, '81

German wines
Great sweet wines of '85, '83, '76, '75, '71...
Auslesen of '85, '83, '79, '76...
Spätlesen of '89, '88, '86, '85, '83, '79, '76...
Kabinett and QbA wines of '89, '88, '85, '83...

California wines
Top Cabernets/Zinfandels of '86, '85, '84, '82, '81, '80, '78, '76, '75, '74
Most Cabernets etc of '89, '88, '87, '86, '85, '84...
Top Chardonnays of '89, '88, '87, '86, '85, '84...
Most Chardonnays of '90, '89, '88, '87...

Australian wines
Top Cabernets and Shiraz of '86, '84, '82, '80, '79, '75, '71...
Most Cabernets etc of '90, '89, '88, '87, '86...
Top Chardonnays of '91, '90, '88, '86
Most Chardonnays of '91, '90
Top Sémillons and Rieslings of '91, '90, '88, '86, '82, '79...

Vintage Port
'82, '80, '75, '70, '66, '63, '60...

Quick reference vintage charts for France and Germany

These charts give a picture of the range of qualities made in the principal areas (every year has its relative successes and failures) and a guide to whether the wine is ready to drink or should be kept.

I	drink now	— needs keeping
✓	can be drunk with pleasure now, but the better wines will continue to improve	⊼ avoid
		0 no good 10 the best

FRANCE

	RED BORDEAUX		WHITE BORDEAUX	
	MEDOC/GRAVES	POM/ ST-EM	SAUTERNES & SW	GRAVES & DRY
91	3-7 —	2-5 ∠	4-7 —	6-8 ⊾
90	7-10 —	8-10 —	7-9 ⊾	7-8 ✓
89	7-9 ∠	7-9 ∠	7-9 —	6-8 ⊾
88	7-9 ∠	7-10 ∠	6-10 ⊾	7-9 ✓
87	3-6 ✓	3-6 ✓	2-5 ⊼	7-10 ✓
86	6-9 ⊾	5-7 ⊾	7-10 ✓	7-9 ✓
85	6-8 ⊾	7-9 ⊾	6-8 ⊾	5-8 ✓
84	4-7 ✓	2-5 ✓	4-7 ✓	5-7 ⊼
83	6-9 ⊾	6-9 ⊾	6-10 ⊾	7-9 I
82	8-10 ⊾	7-9 ⊾	3-7 ✓	7-8 I
81	5-8 ✓	6-9 ✓	5-8 ✓	7-8 I
80	4-7 I	3-5 I	5-9 I	5-7 I
79	5-8 I	5-7 I	6-8 I	4-6 ⊼
78	6-9 ✓	6-8 I	4-6 I	7-9 I
77	3-5 ⊼	2-5 ⊼	2-4 ⊼	6-7 ⊼
76	6-8 ✓	7-8 ✓	7-9 ✓	4-8 ⊼
75	4-8 I	5-9 I	8-10 ✓	8-10 I
74	4-6 ⊼	3-5 ⊼	0 ⊼	4-6 ⊼

FRANCE — BURGUNDY

	COTE D'OR RED	COTE D'OR WHITE	CHABLIS	ALSACE
91	5-7 ∠	4-7 ⊾	4-6 ✓	5-8 ⊾
90	7-10 —	7-9 ⊾	6-9 ⊾	7-10 ⊾
89	6-9 ⊾	6-9 ⊾	7-10 ⊾	8-10 ⊾
88	7-10 ⊾	7-9 ⊾	7-9 ⊾	6-9 ✓
87	6-8 ✓	4-7 ✓	5-7 I	7-8 I
86	5-8 ✓	7-10 ✓	7-9 ✓	7-8 I
85	7-10 ⊾	5-8 ✓	6-9 I	7-10 ✓
84	3-6 ⊼	4-7 ⊼	4-7 ⊼	4-6 I
83	5-9 ✓	6-9 I	7-9 I	8-10 I
82	4-7 I	6-8 I	6-7 I	6-8 I
81	3-6 ⊼	4-8 I	6-9 I	7-8 I
80	4-7 I	4-6 ⊼	5-7 I	3-5 ⊼
79	5-6 I	6-8 I	6-8 ⊼	7-8 I

Beaujolais: 91 was excellent, the fourth very good vintage in a row. Mâcon-Villages (white) 91, 90 and 89 are good now. **Loire:** Sweet Anjou and Touraine. Best recent vintages: 90, 89, 88, 85, 84, 83, 82, 79, 78, 76. **Upper Loire:** Sancerre and Pouilly Fumé 90, 89, 88 are good now. **Muscadet:** DYA.

FRANCE	RHONE		GERMANY	RHINE		MOSELLE	
91	4-7 ⊾		91	5-7 ⊾		5-7 ⊾	
90	5-9 ⊾		90	8-10 ⊾		8-10 ∠	
89	6-9 ⊾		89	7-10 ⊾		8-10 ⊾	
88	7-9 ⊾		88	6-8 ⊾		7-9 ⊾	
87	3-6 ✓		87	4-7 ✓		5-7 ✓	
86	5-8 ⊾		86	4-8 I		5-8 ✓	
85	5-8 ✓		85	6-8 ✓		6-9 ✓	
84	5-7 I		84	4-6 ⊼		4-6 ⊼	
83	6-9 ✓		83	6-9 ✓		7-10 ✓	
82	5-8 I		82	4-6 ⊼		4-7 ⊼	
81	5-7 I		81	5-8 I		4-8 ⊼	
80	6-8 I		80	4-7 ⊼		3-7 ⊼	
79	6-7 I		79	6-8 I		6-8 I	